Library of
Davidson College

IMPERILED HERITAGE: TRADITION, HISTORY, AND UTOPIA IN EARLY MODERN GERMAN LITERATURE

For Gerhart Hoffmeister

Imperiled Heritage: Tradition, History, and Utopia in Early Modern German Literature

Selected essays by Klaus Garber
edited and with an introduction by
Max Reinhart

Studies in European Cultural Transition

Volume Five

General Editors: Martin Stannard and Greg Walker

Ashgate

Aldershot • Burlington USA• Singapore• Sydney

© Max Reinhart, 2000

All rights reserved. No part of this publication may be reproduced, stored in a retrieval system, or transmitted in any form or by any means, electronic, mechanical, photocopying, recording or otherwise without the prior permission of the publisher.

The editor has asserted his right under the Copyright, Designs and Patents Act, 1988, to be identified as the editor of this work.

Published by
Ashgate Publishing Limited
Gower House
Croft Road
Aldershot
Hants GU11 3HR
England

Ashgate Publishing Company
131 Main Street
Burlington, VT 05401–5600 USA

Ashgate website: http://www.ashgate.com

British Library Cataloguing-in-Publication data

Imperiled heritage: tradition, history, and utopia in early modern German literature. – (Studies in European cultural transition; v. 5)
1.German literature – Early modern, 1500–1700 – History and criticism
2.Utopias in literature. 3.History in literature
I. Reinhart, Max
830.9'003

Library of Congress Cataloging-in-Publication Data

Imperiled heritage: tradition, history, and utopia in early modern German literature / edited with an introduction by Max Reinhart ; [translated by Joe G. Delap ... et al.]. p. cm (Studies in European cultural transition; v. 5)
Includes bibliographical references and index.
1.German literature – Early modern, 1500–1700 – History and criticism
2. History in literature 3.Utopias in literature. I. Reinhart, Max II. Garber, Klaus. III. Series

PT238 .I55 2000
830.9–dc21   00-0025730

ISBN 0 7546 0059 9

Typeset by Pat FitzGerald and printed on acid-free paper and bound in Great Britain by MPG Books Ltd, Bodmin, Cornwall

Man kann überhaupt nur auf das in der Vergangenheit fruchtbar zurückgreifen, das selber im gleichen Akt auf uns voraufgreift . . . Diese lebendig gewordene Geschichte wäre nun die Tradition, in der das Leben nicht erstorben ist und eine große Breite entsteht; vergleichbar dem, was in der Astronomie die Parallaxe ist, die breite Erdbahn, wo am 21. März und 21. September ein ganz verschiedener Blick auf näher gelegene Fixsterne möglich zu sein scheint wegen der größeren Breite des Gesichtskreises darin. So daß Vergangenheit durchaus belehrt, auffordert und durchaus das Unsere herausgibt. Es gibt also, mit einem keineswegs paradoxen Ausdruck, eine Unmenge *Zukunft in der Vergangenheit*, die nicht getan worden ist und die als Forderung unabgegolten weitergeht . . . Das ist eine andere Tradition als die übliche, die mit Recht abgelehnt wird . . . [D]er gesellschaftliche Rahmen und die Substanz der Sache haben sich gewandelt; und trotzdem ist etwas darin, das bewegt und aufgreift und in großen Werken uns immer wieder entgegenkommt mit Nachreife.

It is useful to reach back into the past only for something that reaches forward to us at the same time . . . This living history is the kind of tradition in which life has not expired; one in which a great breadth appears that we may liken to what astronomers call the parallax: that wide orbit of the earth where on 21 March and 21 September an entirely different perspective on the nearer fixed stars becomes possible as a result of the greater horizon of visibility. So it is that the past instructs, challenges, and reveals who and what we are. It is thus no paradox to say that there exists an immense *future in the past* that has not been completed and that continues undiminished as a challenge to us . . . That kind of tradition is different from the usual one, which we may properly reject . . . The social framework and general substance have changed. Still, something in it remains that arouses and stimulates and speaks to us in great works again and again as it continues to mature.

Ernst Bloch,
'Die neue Linke und die Tradition'

General Editors' Preface

The European dimension of research in the humanities has come into sharp focus over recent years, producing scholarship which ranges across disciplines and national boundaries. Until now there has been no major channel for such work. This series aims to provide one, and to unite the fields of cultural studies and traditional scholarship. It will publish the most exciting new writing in areas such as European history and literature, art history, archaeology, language and translation studies, political, cultural and gay studies, music, psychology, sociology and philosophy. The emphasis will be explicitly European and interdisciplinary, concentrating attention on the relativity of cultural perspectives, with a particular interest in issues of cultural transition.

Martin Stannard
Greg Walker

University of Leicester

Contents

List of Plates	viii
Preface by Klaus Garber	ix
Editor's Introduction	xvi
1 Prophecy, Love, and Law: Visions of Peace from Isaiah to Kant (and beyond)	1
2 'Your arts shall be: to impose the ways of peace' – Tolerance, Liberty, and the Nation in the Literature and Deeds of Humanism	19
3 The Republic of Letters and the Absolutist State: Nine Theses	41
4 Paris, Capital of European Late Humanism: Jacques Auguste de Thou and the Cabinet Dupuy	54
5 Utopia and the Green World: Critique and Anticipation in Pastoral Poetry	73
6 Nuremberg, Arcadia on the Pegnitz: The Self-Stylization of an Urban Sodality	117
7 Begin with Goethe? Forgotten Traditions at the Threshold of the Modern Age	209
Bibliographical Note on the Essays	252
About the Translators	254
Index	256

List of Plates

1 Martin Opitz (1597–1639). Engraved portrait by J. v. d. Heyden.   55
  Frontispiece to *Umständliche Nachricht von des weltberühmten Schlesiers, Martin Opitz von Boberfeld, Leben, Tode und Schriften, nebst einigen alten und neuen Lobgedichten auf Ihn*. Part I. Edited by Kaspar Gottlieb Lindner. Hirschberg: Immanuel Krahn, 1740. (Bibliothek des Interdisziplinären Instituts für Kulturgeschichte der Frühen Neuzeit, Universität Osnabrück. Used by permission.)

2 Jacques Auguste de Thou (1553–1617). Frontispiece to JACOBI   58
  AVGVSTI THVANI, *Historische Beschreibung deren Namhaffigsten/ Geistlichen vnd Weltlichen Geschichten/ so sich beydes in- vnd ausser dem Römischen Reich/ [...] nun vber die 100. Jahr [...] zugetragen*. Frankfurt a.M.: Egenolff Emmel (printer), Peter Kopff (publisher), 1671. (Bibliothek des Interdisziplinären Instituts für Kulturgeschichte der Frühen Neuzeit, Universität Osnabrück. Used by permission.)

3 Sigmund von Birken (1626–81). Engraved portrait by J. von Sandrart.   99
  Frontispiece from *Festschrift zur 250jährigen Jubelfeier des Pegnesischen Blumenordens gegründet in Nürnberg am 16. Oktober 1644*. Edited by Theodor Bischoff and August Schmidt. Nürnberg: Johann Leonhard Schrag, 1894. (Bibliothek des Interdisziplinären Instituts für Kulturgeschichte der Frühen Neuzeit, Universität Osnabrück. Used by permission.)

4 *PEGNESISCHES SCHAEFERGEDICHT/ in den BERINORGISCHEN*   127
  GEFILDEN/ angestimmet von STREFON und CLAIUS.
  Nürnberg: Wolfgang Endter, 1644. Title-page engraving. From *Pegnesisches Schäfergedicht 1644–1645*. Edited by Klaus Garber. Deutsche Neudrucke, Reihe: Barock, 8. Tübingen: Niemeyer, 1966.

5 *Die Nymphe NORIS IN Zweyen Tagzeiten vorgestellet [...] DURCH*   166
  einen Mitgenossen der PegnitzSchäfer etc. By Johann Hellwig. Nürnberg: Jeremia Dümler, 1650. Frontispiece. (Bibliothek des Interdisziplinären Instituts für Kulturgeschichte der Frühen Neuzeit, Universität Osnabrück. Used by permission.)

6 'Peace Banquet' of 25 September 1649 in the Nuremberg *Rathaus*.   200
  Copper engraving by G.D. Heumann after a portrait by J. von Sandrart (right front). From ACTA PACIS WESTPHALICAE PUBLICA. *Oder Westphälische Friedens-Handlungen und Geschichte*. Part I (following p. 364), by Johann Gottfried von Meiern. Hannover: Joh. Chr. Ludolph Schultz, 1734. (Universitätsbibliothek Osnabrück. Used by permission.)

Preface by Klaus Garber

Since about the mid-1980s European literary history has witnessed the rise of a new epochal category: the early modern period, also called early modernity, after the German term *Frühe Neuzeit*. As a period designation 'early modern' has the advantage of being unencumbered by the tiresome debates over such evaluative concepts as mannerism and baroque. Its chronological markers are intuitively grasped and command general consensus: the five centuries between the early Italian Renaissance (Trecento) and the northern civil revolutions of the late eighteenth century. Over this half-millennium the structures of the Middle Ages – political, social, and constitutional, intellectual, religious, and mental – were transformed into those of modern Europe. Mutability is perhaps the central reality of the age, its only constant; early modern historical events and artistic creations present a dynamic and often ambivalent face to the observer. Visible in equal measure in the features of early modernity are the early light of dawn and the glow of departing day.

A wealth of new discourses arose in the early modern period, each encased, to be sure, in multiple layers of tradition and carried forward by university-trained, mainly secular professionals. Within this learned elite, or *nobilitas literaria*, a corporate mentality evolved that was predicated on the values of knowledge, competence, and professional experience; these were applied in such a way as to challenge intellectual norms and social hierarchies of the Middle Ages, not the least of which was the church's control of the classical literary heritage. Early modern discourses modified and adapted the content of ancestral discourses, influenced the process of their reception, and generated new anatomies; their secrets can be uncovered only by arduously following the branching paths of their formal and functional history from start to finish. Methodologically speaking, two complementary procedures are necessary for this task: one involves taking both pro- and retrospective views of the broad evolutionary stages of ideas; the other requires descending into the micrological structures of individual texts, exploring their particular forms, and isolating their heterogeneous elements. The widening of philology's scope to include a large European perspective, encouraged by medievalists after World War II, has become *de rigueur* for early modern studies as well. The aim, however, is not so much to create an ideal cultural unity and historical continuity, but rather precisely to reveal the differences that arose through the ubiquitous crises of the age. As modern scholars and readers, we frequently experience these differences as shocks or other forms of resistance to our assumptions.

It is, of course, difficult to fix in precise terms the temporal parameters of the early modern period, especially its *terminus a quo*. Many developments typically considered to be early modern in fact owe their existence to reformist initiatives or other political, social, religious, and economic changes already underway in the later Middle Ages. If, however, we look to literature itself for clues, one moment very much stands out: Dante's thunderous proclamation of the dignity of a national-vernacular language and literature. Over the centuries that follow, intellects from Nicolas Boileau-Despréaux to Dr Johnson to Johann Christoph Gottsched continued to wrestle with the same problem, and with no less intensity or greater finality than Dante; because of Dante, every literary discourse became firmly embedded within the cultural discourse of its particular nation's identity and self-expression. The infinite variability of national symbols, myths, and etiologies in the early modern period can be brought into clear relief in each case only through comparative synchronic and diachronic analysis.

Early modern cultural history must seek to decipher and interpret these richly layered codes and structures of the various geographical areas as they evolved over their long term (*longue durée*). Thought, writing, and order continued throughout the early modern period to rest heavily on the authority of tradition. Indeed, neither of the two great intellectual and philosophical revolutions of the early modern period, the Renaissance and the Reformation, was truly original; each appropriated the past in fundamental ways. Viewed with a wide lens from Dante to Goethe, the Renaissance may fairly be described as a long-term process of refashioning the philosophical and literary cosmos of antiquity; insofar as the Reformation laid new religious and communal foundations, it did so only by wresting Scripture free of well-established, if obfuscatory, scholastic reasoning. Early modern intellectual creations were modeled on previous images, concepts, and topoi, and can be retraced usually to either Judeo-Christian or ancient pagan origins. With the rarest of exceptions, early modern texts marshaled the reserves of tradition as the groundwork for their own acts of creative *imitatio* and *variatio*. To appreciate what is unique about early modern European literature depends on knowledge of these traditions. The art of doing cultural history consists largely in explaining transitions within permanence, distinguishing individuality from inheritance, discovering the island within the stream of time. This is achieved by forcing a confrontation between the political-intellectual macrosystem and the microform of the individual work.

Failure to recognize this complexity and to deal with it through a sufficiently rigorous methodology is often glaring in the literary criticism of later periods, especially for the eighteenth century. One often hears the assertion, for example, that Sentimentalism encouraged a classless nobility of soul and virtue. That is true; but it is simplistically put and historically naive. Lacking in this assertion is an acknowledgment of the classical arguments of self-ennoblement, revived by Dante and Albertino Mussato, and operative in subsequent literary practice deep into the Enlightenment. Similarly, studies related to eighteenth-century intellectual societies often exhibit little if any grasp of the earlier movement of humanist intellectual societies from Dante to Ficino to Celtis to Ronsard to Leibniz. This is to say nothing of the parallel movement of religious confraternities emanating from Joachim of Fiore and the Franciscan Spiritualists. If the spiritualist instinct for selectivity and isolation is disregarded, with its characteristic separation from orthodoxy, the ideal of the 'noble few' is inadequately expressed by headings such as 'the sentimental transformation of life and art after 1750'. Or again, while the assertion is true that the Renaissance return to the sources reintroduced the western world to the natural philosophy and science of antiquity, the related attempt to explain the impact of deism or Spinozism or monadology on the eighteenth century usually lacks a clear exposition of the re-inscription of neo-Platonism in the Florentine Renaissance and its continued philosophical invigoration down through the Enlightenment. Or, as a final example, with respect to the emancipation of women in the 1700s, this development too was nourished by a centuries-old discourse concerning male–female equality based on virtue and piety, knowledge and innate gifts. It is upon the awareness of this and related early modern discourses, which were practiced fully matured long before the eighteenth century, that modern gender studies must establish its historical footing. To begin the study of modern literature with Lessing or Diderot or Pope, expecting from that vantage point to gain a valid grasp of its origins, is to ignore five centuries of vigorous pre-Enlightenment culture and thus to forfeit the historical basis for competent scholarship.

In the 1960s theoretical interest turned markedly toward the study of early modern European society in the hope of discovering the principles behind the rise of the modern bourgeois social world.[1] There are remarkable affinities, even in terminology, between the scholarship of the 1960s and that done shortly before and after the Nazi regime by German and Austrian émigrés, among them Bernhard Groethuysen, Norbert Elias, Arnold Hirsch, Leo Kofler, Max Horkheimer, and Eric Fromm. Conceived on a progressive teleological model, the foremost aim of the earlier project was to trace the constitutive elements of modernity from their medieval sources to their hypothetical culmination in the Enlightenment. This program was revived in the 1960s. Curiously, however, most of the younger 'early modern' scholars of the 1960s migrated to the relatively late field of comparativist Enlightenment studies. The self-imposed challenge to produce monographs of the complete history of the formation of bourgeois society and culture and to analyze its literary representations over the entire period remained unfulfilled. The Rankean dream of a 'grand narrative' has been decisively repudiated. The enthusiasm in the 1970s and early 1980s for *Literatursoziologie* waned with embarrassing suddenness when it became clear that the

---

[1] [Editor's note: German *bürgerlich* does not have the problematical socioeconomic overtones of its French cognate *bourgeois*, also possible in English. In some cases, we may translate it as *middle-class*, though this term obviously does not accurately reflect the social complexities of early modern society, divided as it was into estates, groupings, and *Schichten* 'levels'. Other times it implies the concept of 'civic', as found in the work of Hans Baron. But Garber frequently applies *bürgerlich* in keeping with his view of how the middle class developed out of the northern Italian city-states and in early capitalism and came to maturity in the later eighteenth century. In those instances, it may properly be rendered as *bourgeois*.]

necessary empirical research was lacking.² Projects of this nature have all but ceased in the meantime.³ New Historicist studies (or 'cultural poetics') have uncovered gaps and leaps within general progressions, dark recesses in brightly lit zones, complexity and ambivalence in what appears clear and seamless only to naive eyes.

No philosopher of culture grasped these historical discontinuities and the correlative abandonment of the myths of totality and linear progress more insightfully than Walter Benjamin. His theory of *Doxadurchsetztheit* 'doxa-permeation', which concerns the divided origins of every object – permeated by δόξα 'error' or 'ideology'⁴ – has found repeated validation in the anti-historicism of Foucault, Althusser, and the cultural anthropologists, among others, and continues to affect our awareness of how power strategies and difference affect the representation of history. Unlike most post-structuralists, however, Benjamin renounces with equal decisiveness any reduction of intellectual content to strategies or constructions of power, institutions, or politics – any surrender, that is, of the *work of interpretation* to the fancies of individual interests or to mere representation.⁵ Because for Benjamin history first manifests itself in the

---

² [Editor's note: Not surprisingly, in the decade inspired by Habermas's theory of the modern public sphere, most of these social histories of literature centered on the Age of Enlightenment: e.g., Viktor Zmegac (ed.), *Geschichte der deutschen Literatur vom 18. Jahrhundert bis zur Gegenwart* (1978), 2nd edition (Königstein, Czech.: Athenäum, 1984); the collectively written volume 6 of *Geschichte der deutschen Literatur von den Anfängen bis zur Gegenwart* (Berlin: Verlag Volk und Wissen, 1979); Rolf Grimminger (ed.), *Deutsche Aufklärung bis zur Französischen Revolution 1660–1789*, Hansers Sozialgeschichte der deutschen Literatur vom 16. Jahrhundert bis zur Gegenwart, 3 (Munich: Hanser, 1979); Ralph-Rainer Wuthenow (ed.), *Zwischen Absolutismus und Aufklärung: Rationalismus, Empfindsamkeit, Sturm und Drang 1740–1786*, Deutsche Literatur: Eine Sozialgeschichte, 4 (Reinbek b.H.: Rowohlt, 1980). Slightly later, for the early modern period, Harald Steinhagen (ed.), *Zwischen Gegenreformation und Frühaufklärung: Späthumanismus, Barock 1572–1740*, Deutsche Literatur: Eine Sozialgeschichte, 3 (Reinbek b.H.: Rowohlt, 1985).]

³ [Editor's note: Vol. 2 (literature of the seventeenth century) of the ill-fated Hanser series was postponed for nearly twenty years until a suitable theoretical framework could be worked out. It has just appeared: *Die Literatur des 17. Jahrhunderts*, ed. Albert Meier, Hansers Sozialgeschichte der deutschen Literatur, 2 (Munich: Hanser, 1999). Meier explains, 'Meanwhile it has become clear that the original intention of establishing a common "heuristic goal" (vol. 3, p. 9) that, notwithstanding certain broad ranges of independence, would be essentially applicable to all volumes across the entire historical spectrum from the sixteenth century to the immediate present, was not realistic' (9).]

⁴ [Editor's note: Garber is referring to remarks intended by Benjamin for his introduction to *Das Paris des Second Empire bei Baudelaire*; the compound *Doxadurchsetztheit* is Garber's own. For a more complete discussion by Garber, see his *Rezeption und Rettung: Drei Studien zu Walter Benjamin*, Studien und Texte zur Sozialgeschichte der Literatur, 22 (Tübingen: Niemeyer, 1987). 'Doxa-permeation' is also considered in the Editor's Introduction below.]

⁵ [Editor's note: The concept of 'representation' as used in new historicist scholarship does not imply 'reflection' or 'mediation' of concrete historical objects or events or causalities; it articulates rather the process of text formation that occurs when diverse

phenomenal world as natural history, the category of progress per se is invalid. Even as he goes resolutely about the process of deconstruction, Benjamin practices constructive reading: reading in 'constellations' determined by experiences of reality in the form of shocks that reveal buried semantic potential. The connection, revealed by these shocks, between human knowledge and action is limited, of course, and must be newly determined generation by generation. What counts in this reworking is not primarily the discovery of some permanent content in tradition but rather especially the exposure, identification, and appropriation of whatever is applicable and usable. The lesson in Benjamin for early modern literary studies is that, as cultural historians, we must engage in the critical labor of sifting through the past in order to rediscover useful images for the present and future.

It is thus that affinities may appear (memories 'flash up', Benjamin says) between early modernity and our own present. Looking back on the early modern period, we no longer see the solid harmony pictured by liberal bourgeois historiography, but an abyss – drastically depicted by Benjamin in *The Origin of German Tragic Drama* (1925) – that is as violent as it is fascinating. What a horrifying image of society at the threshold of early modernity with which Dante opens his *Divine Comedy*! The universal centers of power, the papacy and the empire, have collapsed, and in cities and territories a wild battle rages among the great families and seigneuries. Dante's vision of the renewal of Roman power on Italian soil springs from the exile's personal experience but is veiled in the spiritual contemplation of God. So much the more sublime, then, was the reappearance in the second half of the sixteenth century, in the very heart of this darkness, of a pure and transcendent faith as it found expression in spiritualist and mystical writings. The idea of an unsullied faith above and beyond religions and nations was at work as much as two centuries in advance of the Enlightenment, in parts of Spain and Poland, where it manifested itself in opposition to the violence of the witch hunts, pogroms, and suppression of heterodoxy, the disease that represented the deepest fears and obsessions of a society shaken to the core by confessional and political wars. Similarly, the conflicts within and among the new nation-states were accompanied by the first regulations of international law. Against the mutually destructive parties in civil war, humanistically educated jurists formulated the first inviolable principles of state's sovereignty on behalf of the protection of all citizens.

Focuses: Europe, the Nation, and the Region

Early modern literary studies can be conducted only from the perspective of Europe at large. Chauvinist nineteenth- and earlier twentieth-century versions of

cultural relationships come together in textlike patterns, stimulated by 'social energy' (Greenblatt) having little to do with literary texts as such. Garber's different understanding of the text will be the subject of further discussion in the Editor's Introduction below.]

the nation and nationalism obscured or made taboo relevant areas of investigation. It is also true, however, that literary and cultural processes were regionally governed to a degree scarcely imaginable today. Although the forces generated by this triad of perspectives, Europe, the nation, and the region, were often contradictory and demand microhistorical analysis, cultural history should not fail to consider them in the combination in which they in fact occurred in both synchronic and diachronic terms.

It is customary to think of the nation, or territorial state, as constituting the political precondition for regional scholarship. Notwithstanding the common-sense value of this assumption, it excludes too many factors. Let us take the area of confessionalism, for example. Confessional boundaries were typically more narrowly drawn than territorial or national boundaries. This fact requires us to focus greater attention on regional or even local (city and village) specifics. At the same time, confessional communities, often bundled together in small spaces, were also connected over wide geopolitical distances. Questions even about personal networks and interaction often can be solved by applying the confessional key, as demonstrated in the studies of Herbert Schöffler, the noted German scholar of English language and literature.[6] An array of institutions, especially educational ones, had their particular confessional ties and contributed to the development of unique social forms, knowledge of which is essential to a proper understanding of how individual lives were conducted. When Bohemians, Silesians, or Poles wandered far from home around 1600 to visit universities in Heidelberg and Strasbourg, Basel and Padua, Orléans and Leiden, they did so in search of noted teachers who were sympathetic to the Reformed faith. Eventually they returned home equipped with worldly and religious experience sufficient to combat the threat of post-Tridentine Catholicism. From Danzig to Thorn, Beuthen, Zamosc, and Weissenburg in Transylvania, certain secondary schools offered strongholds of religious tolerance in the face of prevailing fanaticism. It is significant that the more liberal and open, usually republican, political systems, both in cities as well as territories and states, typically exhibited greater religious generosity and tolerance than did monarchical nation-states like France and Spain, which commonly excluded heterodox practice. From the fall of Granada in 1492 to that of La Rochelle in 1628/29 – justified in 1685 by the retraction of the Edict of Nantes – state violence moved in yoke with the dominant church, a fateful early omen of modern totalitarianism. On the other hand, we recognize in early modern Europe an equal number of splendid counter-examples, from Amsterdam to Venice, in which diverse peoples, faiths, and world views achieved impressive forms of cooperation.

The national icons, primordial myths, and models of legitimation in early modern humanist discourse have nothing in common with the malignant

---

[6] See, e.g., *Deutsches Geistesleben zwischen Reformation und Aufklärung von Martin Opitz zu Christian Wolff*, 2nd edition (Frankfurt a.M.: Klostermann, 1956).

imperialist or fascist nationalism promoted in later centuries. In humanist nationalism one's own state's sovereignty was staunchly affirmed, but not at the expense of neighboring states. Here again the national monarchies constituted a threat to this liberalism, first in Spain, then in France. In the 1490s humanists were horrified by France's invasion of Italy, which effectively truncated early civic humanism and the hope for *una societas christiana*. With high absolutism under Louis XIV the hegemonic power-state emerged fully; in Alsace and Strasbourg deep-seated animosities exploded into wars that destroyed old Europe. Yet even in the eighteenth century a steady flow of young German intellectuals continued to matriculate at the venerable University of Strasbourg, where so many of Europe's great scholars were to be found – scholars for whom the European option was self-evident.

Early modern intellectuals were accustomed to wandering between and beyond political and ideological, spatial and mental, borders. Later bourgeois ideologues judged them harshly for their European mentality. Perhaps today we are more willing to appreciate their cultural openness and insistence on free intellectual inquiry. Martin Opitz is one prominent example. A native Silesian, Opitz became a respected middle-European diplomat in the 1620s and 1630s. In his service to the Polish king, he happily remarked that peaceful toleration was the order of the day in multicultural, multireligious Danzig. Opitz's life and work in fact are illustrative of the highest aspirations of the European intellectual elite. As responsible as these late humanists were for the transmission of the classical heritage, they also worked – without any particular anxieties over nationalist trends – towards a peaceful, liberal Europe and did not hesitate to condemn fanaticism wherever they recognized it. For our part, to bring Old Europe to life in all the variety of its cultural landscapes; to hear across space and time the voices that praised this multiplicity as a valuable possession; to be inspired by the past to respond to our own needs – these tasks constitute the noblest goal of early modern literary studies today.*

---

* Translated by Michael T. Jones and Max Reinhart.

Editor's Introduction

Although he may be the most prolific historian of early modern German literature in the twentieth century, Klaus Garber has remained largely unknown to English-language scholars. This is curious, to be sure, but understandable in at least three ways that reflect on the organization of the professional field: First, its structuring in discrete historico-aesthetic periods (Renaissance, Reformation, Baroque, Early Enlightenment) allows for little appreciation of Garber's integrated view of the *Frühe Neuzeit* between approximately 1350 and 1750. Second, Garber's view embraces far more than the German or even transalpine literary experience and thus breaks with the traditionalist canonization of culture into national categories and the related premise of a German *Sonderweg* 'special path'. And third, literary history for Garber is, in addition to being intellectual history, political and social history. Garber's research demands are extraordinary and harken back to an earlier time when literary historians routinely worked within larger frames of reference. Nowhere, for example, in the past half-century in English-language research has there been a voice that dared to express the ambition 'to reintegrate the original connections between Renaissance, Baroque, and Enlightenment into the early modern European national literary movement, together with its cultural and institutional manifestations' (53). Garber's penchant for thinking in these large categories makes his work provocative.

The deeper reasons for this provocation are political in part. Garber was a pioneer in the 1970s in the movement to write a social history of German literature. The fact that most of these efforts were deemed unsuccessful or remained incomplete[1] led to an undifferentiated dismissal of research in the vein of literary sociology, and this with particular vehemence after 1989 in the conservative backlash that formed in the wake of German reunification. Even the initial American interest in Garber's work on reception history, which crested in the early 1980s with lectures sponsored in part by the MLA affiliate Society for German Renaissance and Baroque Literature, did not sustain itself. Since then, German Renaissance and Baroque studies in the US have mainly continued in the work-immanent mode of the New Criticism and have, with only pockets of exception, stayed aloof from developments in New Historicist and New Cultural Studies as well as interdisciplinary approaches. This owes in part to an allergy for theory, especially social theory, among most scholars of German Renaissance and Baroque literature, but even for history itself when critically applied to literature.

There is a related difficulty. To come to terms with Garber's method means cultivating a familiarity not only with the classical twentieth-century German aesthetic and cultural philosophers, among them Adorno, Bloch, Elias, and

---

[1] Garber himself in 1976 announced a monograph on pastoral and society to be called *Arkadien und Gesellschaft*. It was never completed; but his reflections on the project over many years are now available in English translation in Chapter 6 of this book, 'Nuremberg, Arcadia on the Pegnitz: The Self-Stylization of an Urban Sodality.'

Benjamin, but also with the universalist cultural historians Burdach, Harnack, Troeltsch, Heer, and others. All of these names have determining influence on how Garber apprehends the dynamics of literature and culture between early Italian humanism and the French Revolution. Furthermore, Garber possesses a daunting grasp of early modern discourses, from theology to poetics to political theory, and draws on many kinds of 'marginal' sources as well, including occasional poetry, public ordinances, administrative codes, and the programs, agendas, and libraries of European intellectual societies. One also needs to have at hand a substantial amount of sociological data on the individuals, both great and small, connected with the sodalities, confessions, and other institutions of the republic of letters. Garber organizes all of this information under three major rubrics: Europe, Nation (including the court and territorial state), and Region (including cities and villages). One of the implications of Garber's example that has made itself felt is that early modern literary scholars are now expected, because there is no excuse not to be, given the data-collecting, filing, and analysis advantages that come with computer technology, to account for a much broader informational and statistical base than was thought feasible for many years.[2]

The moment in Garber's methodology that informs all of this basis material with meaning is 'integration', the operation that most distinguishes his work from other social history in German literature of the early modern period. Even the 1999 volume in the Hanser series, while careful to avoid the most egregious of earlier errors, continues to seek, if apologetically, to uncover the 'system' of the 'Baroque epoch', dutifully once more separating seventeenth-century writing into the lock-step categories of 'courtly', 'spiritual', and 'bourgeois'.[3] Historical integration is the missing link in most system-based studies, leaving readers with the impression that these spheres existed independently of each other. Garber insists rather that in every investigation 'it is necessary, in ever broader analytical steps, to integrate everything historically' (250). He does not so much disagree with the pragmatics of categorization as insist that we see that the historical authors constructed these distinctions for strategic effect, and that we are therefore better instructed by looking for the 'overlapping social and production conditions' of the texts.[4] These overlappings owed above all to the commonality of social position and education of the authors. Garber demonstrates this at length in terms of the content and contours of traditions, discourses, and institutional

---

[2] The computer databanks at the Interdisziplinäres Institut für Kulturgeschichte der Frühen Neuzeit in Osnabrück, where Garber is director, are full of just this kind of information.

[3] *Die Literatur des 17. Jahrhunderts*, ed. Albert Meier, Hansers Sozialgeschichte der deutschen Literatur vom 16. Jahrhundert bis zur Gegenwart, 2 (Munich: Hanser, 1999). 'The literary genres are disposed according to the three major functional areas "courtly," "spiritual," and "bourgeois" in order thus to build a sufficiently comprehensive total-system (*Gesamtsystem*)' (13).

[4] 'Vorwort', in *Europäische Bukolik und Georgik*, Wege der Forschung, 355 (Darmstadt: Wissenschaftliche Buchgesellschaft, 1976), xv.

regulations and behavior in which the overwhelming majority of seventeenth-century German writers actively participated. He does not hesitate to identify this commonality as 'learned bourgeois'. We will return to this controversial part of Garber's method at the end of this introduction.

The second, and simultaneous, operation whereby Garber integrates the multiplicity of information and phenomena is that of reception history. On this ground he is an acknowledged master; his two major reception monographs, on Opitz and on Benjamin, are unsurpassed in knowledge and skill.[5] Reception history, so Garber echoing Benjamin, must encompass

> the entire spectrum of meaning laid open by the works, including how their authors and epochs were viewed in each case, gathering in the process the totality of the reception-determining energies and collecting them into a single focus. It is imperative that literary scholarship reconstruct the historical movement between the works and their various appropriations, the latter defined as a narrowed perspective on the post-history of the given objects of investigation.[6]

Put differently, every reception study must describe a diachronic arc that stretches from the origins of the traditions to its synchronic treatments of the given work, where the traditions intersect, all the way down to the present. Obviously, if Garber's practice is consistent with his intent, the essays that follow will address a good deal more than early modern German literature proper; and that is indeed so. The respective subject, whether Sannazaro's pastoral novel, Erasmus on peace, or Leibniz's concept of a German scientific academy, lies in the palm of a great historical hand. The poles of this arc, in Garber's Benjaminian reception theory, constitute the pre- and post-history parameters of the work – the grasp of its being, influence, and appropriation – within which the social and other environmental conflicts that shape it become manifest, and out of the friction of which the work, like a pearl, is stimulated into existence. In a word, one must 'account simultaneously for totalizing structures and individual forms' (249).

Garber's style, which has been modulated somewhat, perhaps instinctually, by the American translators of this volume, tends in the original German to rush and often to crest in highly complex sentences. The point of this observation is not to criticize his style but to suggest that it is in part symptomatic of an impatience with the drift of literary scholarship away from its historical responsibilities. In his reception history of Opitz, Garber established the watershed in this

---

[5] *Martin Opitz – 'der Vater der deutschen Dichtung:' Eine kritische Studie zur Wissenschaftsgeschichte der Germanistik* (Stuttgart: Metzler, 1976); see review by Marian Szyrocki in *Daphnis* 10, nos 2–3 (1981): 548–53. *Rezeption und Rettung: Drei Studien zu Walter Benjamin*, Studien und Texte zur Sozialgeschichte der Literatur, 22 (Tübingen: Niemeyer, 1987) [hereafter in notes: *RR*]; see John McCole, *Walter Benjamin and the Antinomies of Tradition* (Ithaca: Cornell University Press, 1993), 13 n. 9.

[6] *Martin Opitz* 7–8.

relationship rather precisely with the mid-nineteenth-century aestheticization of literature, which he argues led to the 'empathy fallacy' in historicism.[7] Garber by no means holds this opinion alone. It received its first serious explication with Benjamin, who decried the false ontologization of works of art and placed empathy, along with a number of other 'deadly sins', on his 1935 index for elimination; it continues to be deconstructed today. What most disturbs Garber – differently to be sure, but not unlike Curtius in his day – is modern literary scholars' forgetfulness of history and its aesthetic products. The frustration articulated in his preface, beginning with the lament 'Failure to recognize this complexity . . .' (x), concerns trends that practice their discourses without discernible appreciation for historical precedents or groundwork. This litany should not be mistaken for conservative sour grapes over political correctness. Quite to the contrary. Garber, much like Bloch, is fully in sympathy with potentially utopian trends arising from modern discontent. His objection is that their words are falling on barren ground and will not bear fruit if the scholarship does not find a historical foundation. To begin only with the Enlightenment, as is common, 'is to ignore five centuries of vigorous pre-Enlightenment culture and thus to forfeit the historical basis for competent scholarship' (xi).

As will be clear in these essays, Garber does not devote a great deal of attention to theory as such. He is a historian first and a theorist only second. For example, while his categories are often reminiscent of Marxian social thought, he does not derive them directly, nor even primarily, from that source. As the wide spectrum of examples will attest, to whatever degree Garber relies on theory to make his case, his approach to theory is distinctly text-based. Nevertheless, his debt to theoretical thinkers, Benjamin more than any other – Bloch and others only less explicitly – is striking and deserves to be brought to the surface. One way to approach this task is in terms of the three concepts that constitute the subtitle of the book: tradition, history, and utopia. Central to this set of concepts is history, to which Garber refers constantly. What does he understand by history? Specifically, how does he see the relationship between history and literature?

History is for Garber the glue that binds everything else; in that respect, at least, literature is a contingent phenomenon. But this is misleading, for history too is ever-changing: 'Mutability is perhaps the central reality of the age, its only constant' (ix). Benjamin's remarks on the ideology-permeated origins of works of art are seminal to understanding how Garber views history in general and reception history in particular. In a draft of observations reflecting on how to structure a reception study of Baudelaire, Benjamin explains:

> In the materialistic method, the division of the true from the false is not the point of departure but the goal. That is, it begins with the object (*Gegenstand*), which is permeated with error, δόξα. The divisions from

---

[7] *Martin Opitz* 113–17.

which it starts (the method is after all essentially a dividing one) are divisions within the object, which is greatly split; indeed it is impossible to overstate the degree to which this object is divided . . . [8]

The split nature of the 'original' work of art and the related purpose of method to distinguish the true from the false in the later history of the work describe a state of affairs that is the very opposite of the organic nature of great literary works presumed in standard literary history. But if literary history begins from this false position, then everything that follows will perpetuate that error. That is what is 'wrong' with literary studies on the early modern period. Thus the incalculable importance of those historians who 'step forward', to borrow one of Garber's admiring phrases, to correct false traditions. Such a critic was the pietist Gottfried Arnold, whose cleansing *Wiederkehr* 'return' to the primitive sources of religion revealed a church that had built upon a false base and thereby turned saints into heretics. 'The further proliferation of legends, so Arnold, must be stopped, once and for all' (223). This corrective operation of return is the 'aqua fortis' that liberates from enslavement to false traditions; for Arnold, the true saints, the official heretics, are properly identified in this way. And such critics, Garber implies, are especially needed today.

In his rejection of the ontology of origins and therefore also of Literature, and in other remarks that emphasize the multi-discursive nature of texts, Garber sounds like a new historicist. In fact, however, this resemblance is more a reflection of shared opposition to traditional historicist practice; beyond that the appearance of commonality fades rapidly. The place-oriented and mainly micrological perspectives usual in the method of the new historicists and cultural anthropologists give way to Garber's instinctual preference for the *longue durée* with its totalizing implications. Like Benjamin, Garber works *from* texts both backwards and forwards in order to describe the larger 'ferment' that contains the work, and from there he ultimately seeks the *Werkgehalt* 'work content' that reveals the lasting truth of the work in its traditions and reception. Garber does insist that the elements of the work first be isolated in order to determine there the 'conflicts' giving rise to the work and its reception.[9] There may be a homology

---

[8] Benjamin, introductory fragment to *Das Paris des Second Empire bei Baudelaire*, quoted in *Gesammelte Schriften*, ed. Rolf Tiedemann and Hermann Schweppenhäuser (Frankfurt a.M.: Suhrkamp, 1974), I-3, 1160 [hereafter in notes: *GS*].

[9] 'This task can be accomplished only in tracing the evolution of the historical content back to the making (*Faktur*) of the works and thereby demonstrating the conflicts into which the works and their reception enter' (*RR* 43). Garber often applies the metaphor of descent in articulating this return to the earliest stages of the work; e.g., in the preface he speaks of the complementary procedure to the broad-based view of a work as 'descending into the micrological structures of individual texts, exploring their particular forms, and isolating their heterogeneous elements' (ix). Descent has both a temporal and a geographical dimension: it means both returning in time ad fontes as well as exploring the deep environment of the genre. In Garber's dialectical method these two operations are separated only for the sake of analysis.

between these conflicts and Greenblatt's 'social energy',[10] the fortuitous field in which multiple discourses intersect to form the 'representation' that is the 'text'. But the likeness is superficial, for Garber understands texts as having greater stability than do mere energy fields; this despite his image of the surrounding 'ferment'.[11] This ferment is grounded in truth (or at least the traces of truth), which is carried by the traditions and discourses bound up in texts – and here we get a glimpse of how texts relate to utopia. This truth element he verifies by recourse to Benjamin's early philosophical work, the importance of which Garber stresses repeatedly; he uses it for instance as the basis of his criticism of the weak historical element in the reception theory of Jauss and others.[12] There is no 'work' without history.

With this formulation of 'work' a second and equally important connotation comes into play in Garber's method. It relates both to the object of reception history and to the historical act of carrying out the discipline, which is also 'work'. This action of work has an ethical component. The discipline required of the historian is labor-intensive: the 'secrets' of early modern discourses, Garber states, 'can be uncovered only by arduously following the branching paths of their formal and functional history from start to finish' (ix); or, the humanists 'worked . . . towards a peaceful, liberal Europe' (xv); in another place he speaks of 'the historical work of human hands' (133). I do not think it far-fetched to discern a mystical element in Garber's thinking about work and the work ethic of historians, particularly given the influence on him of Benjamin's early writing on the philosophy of language, with its magical and creation-theological overtones. In his essay 'On Language in General and the Language of Man' Benjamin attributes to man's fall from grace the splitting of language into 'multiplicity' (*Vielheit*) and the condition of 'being made indirect' (*Mittel-barmachung*). In the post-lapsarian condition – in history, that is – man must toil to approximate the original fullness of expression.[13] Garber strikes this chord early on in the first essay by asserting that, in sounding out answers to today's crises, 'real satisfaction may be found only through a laborious return into the depths of

---

[10] Stephen Greenblatt, *Shakespearean Negotiations: The Circulation of Social Energy in Renaissance England*, New Historicism: Studies in Cultural Poetics, series no. 4 (Berkeley: University of California Press, 1988).

[11] Greenblatt's positive view of the text as the representation of multiple discourses, which restores to the concept of texts an 'active participation in history' that has been lacking in past decades (Peter Uwe Hohendahl, 'Nach der Ideologiekritik: Überlegungen zu geschichtlicher Darstellung', in *Geschichte als Literatur: Formen und Grenzen der Repräsentation von Vergangenheit*, ed. Hartmut Eggert et al. [Stuttgart: Metzler, 1990], 88), is shared by Garber, broadly speaking. However, where Greenblatt sees representation as a largely fortuitous play of social energy, Garber parts company.

[12] 'Benjamin's reception theory is unique and great in that it always conceives of the acts of reception critically and thus, under changed conditions, keeps the faith with the truth-based criticism of his early work' (*RR* 43).

[13] 'Über die Sprache überhaupt und über die Sprache des Menschen', in *Angelus Novus: Ausgewählte Schriften 2* (Frankfurt a.M.: Suhrkamp, 1988), 23–4.

time' (1). The role of the historian in this return will be further elaborated below. For now it is important to see that the first destination of the return in Garber's historical method is the text.

The text is the site of mediation between tradition, history, and utopia. Unlike new historicist thinking, Garber invests at least seminal texts – however split they may be into multiple discourses[14] and ultimately explicable only inclusive of their reception – with a definite authority and power both relative to and independent of their time and place. These great works, whose only 'loyalty' is to 'their own laws' (142), possess a negative capacity to critique their own time and place (Garber extends this power to the critique of their own reception), a view that evinces affinity for Adorno's understanding of genuine works of art as having a unique structure of aesthetic totality that resists, or negates, social reification.[15] For the early modern period Garber finds this 'negative principle' (112) most actively applied in pastoral, whose formal givens place it at a critical distance from society; pastoral is therefore the quintessential carrier of utopian traces.[16] However, Garber is undeterred by the 'desultory preoccupation' of Adorno that 'blocks the potential for a genuinely *liberating* negative dialectic';[17] nor does he appear to be convinced by Benjamin's transitory registration of utopian images that 'flash up' (*aufblitzen*) and disappear.[18] His theory of the text is largely

---

[14] Garber uses the term 'discourse' rather liberally, sometimes more or less synonymously with 'tradition' (e.g., in speaking of 'affinities with multiple traditions and discourses' [123]), though usually distinguished as a secondary 'carrier' of tradition (e.g., 'A wealth of new discourses arose in the early modern period, each encased, to be sure, in multiple layers of tradition' [ix]). Other times it is more to style or the expressive mode of a given genre (e.g., 'Pastoral discourse is indirect discourse' [76]); or nearly synonymous with allegory or allegorical narration (e.g., 'allegorical discourse' [84]); or as the narrative movens of a topos (e.g., 'the classical discourse of true nobility' [101]). It is generally in consonance with Greenblatt's understanding of discourse as an expressive ductus of one of the many energies of the historical time, including but not limited to literature; but Garber also uses it, if less precisely than Greenblatt, with greater versatility as a vehicle of traditional semantics.

[15] Elucidated well in Fredric Jameson, 'Reification and Utopia in Mass Culture', *Social Text* 1 (1979): 130–48.

[16] Especially developed in Chapters 5 and 6 below: 'Utopia and the Green World' and 'Nuremberg, Arcadia on the Pegnitz'.

[17] John Pizer's comment on Jameson's response to Adorno, in 'Jameson's Adorno, or, the Persistence of the Utopian', *New German Critique* 58 (1993), 132–3, could apply equally well to Garber.

[18] 'Über den Begriff der Geschichte', Thesis 6. A degree of productive misunderstanding may be detectable here, given the rather forced way in which Garber, in context of his criticism of how texts are often dealt with today, explicates Benjamin's 'work of interpretation': 'Unlike most post-structuralists, however, Benjamin renounces with equal decisiveness any reduction of intellectual content to strategies or constructions of power, institutions, or politics – any surrender, that is, of the *work of interpretation* to the fancies of individual interests or to mere representation . . . Even as he goes resolutely about the process of deconstruction, Benjamin *practices constructive reading* . . .' (xii–xiii; my emphasis in second instance).

congruent with that of Bloch, for whom 'great works' (*grosse Werke*) 'speak' to us 'again and again' through the instrument of 'tradition'.[19] Garber is, of course, highly selective. Not all literary texts are great; certainly not all texts in the standard canon are great; whereas some unassuming and overlooked texts are great when taken in their totality (aesthetics, function, reception). With respect to the early modern period, the primary criterion for greatness in Garber's pantheon is that the text be deeply allegorical. Here too Garber and Bloch are in consonance. Allegory, which is *extended* metaphor, is for both thinkers the trope that bears the utopian strain through time, through the linear narration of the text, maturing as it goes, allowing an image of the utopian to form and be held, archived, so that it may be accessed repeatedly, always in the confidence that it will be there. In Bloch's formulation, 'the Arcadian holds at the ready' utopian elements of friendliness, peacefulness, and humanity.[20] 'The images may be utopian', Garber observes in apparent allusion to Bloch's doctrine of concrete utopia, 'but they derive from concrete texts and therefore share the reality of which the texts themselves are a part' (1).

It is an ostensible inconsistency in Garber's theory of the text, which he claims to derive in large part from Benjamin (but also from Gervinus, whose achievement was to isolate the historical from the aesthetic text for greater objectivity), that, despite his acknowledgment of the constructed and contingent nature of the text, and despite the admonition against approaching the text with empathy, 'staunend staat scheidend' (lit. 'being amazed instead of dividing'), there are nevertheless certain authors and texts that clearly awaken awe in him. They seem to originate beyond any functional context or production. Dante's 'thunderous proclamation' (x), for example, is said all on its own to have established the tradition of national-vernacular language. Such work-events resemble nothing in their sublimity if not a Big Bang independent of history. While Garber surely would not agree on these terms, the recurrence of similarly reverent descriptions is too frequent in his writing to dismiss as anything but meaningful. In Chapter 1 he establishes a quasi-canon of peace visionaries including, besides Dante, Vergil, Jesus, Augustine, Erasmus, Kant, and Benjamin. Garber finds that the work of each of these individuals revolutionized the static forces of control and revealed new and timely truths – a view that recalls the messianic consciousness in Benjamin's fifteenth thesis on the concept of history, in which the 'continuum of history' is to be 'exploded' (*aufzusprengen*). On the other hand – and here Garber can sound almost Curtian in his respect for traditions – putative great works or even intellectual revolutions may be soberly reevaluated simply as high moments in long processes of discourses and traditions: 'Indeed, neither of the two great intellectual and philosophical

---

[19] 'Die neue Linke und die Tradition' (1969), in *Abschied von der Utopie? Vorträge*, ed. Hanna Gekle (Frankfurt a.M.: Suhrkamp, 1980), 165 (quoted in the epigraph above).

[20] 'Arkadien und Utopien', in Garber, *Europäische Bukolik* 6.

revolutions of the early modern period, the Renaissance and the Reformation, was truly original; each appropriated the past in fundamental ways' (x). If there is a conservative element in Garber (though an answer to this question is of little significance here), then its genealogy too may probably be traced through Benjamin, whose criticism Habermas faulted as 'redemptive' (*rettend*).[21] To continue the parallel, which seems legitimate, this feature of Garber's method may be more properly called 'preservative' (*bewahrend*) criticism, as Peter Bürger countered Habermas.[22] That is, Garber 'preserves' the text by locating it in a vital tradition, so as to be able to have points of comparison with later appropriations and to make the utopian content in the text manifest.

There is no work without history. By the same token, as the legal historian Michael Stolleis observes, 'history essentially relies on texts', and these texts become organized in historiography into semantic forms of communication.[23] To suggest a metaphor appropriate to Garber: the book of history is organized into chapters of traditions. Tradition, which is one of the guiding themes of his work, is the tissue of texts even as it is formed from texts and the interpreters (understood in the broadest sense and extending to the institutional mentality that determines the interpretive field) of texts.[24] Tradition and institution, like tradition and discourse, are inseparable entities, for each determines the other. This argument runs throughout the present book and is developed at length in the explication of pastoral texts within their specific institutional program in the chapter on Nuremberg's poetic sodality. The reciprocity that existed there between text, author, tradition, and institution becomes particularly clear in the section 'Orphic Song and Institutional Identity'. Garber's observation that the poet shepherds acted 'directly from the center of a specific form of life' (163) is distinctly reminiscent of the concept of 'sociogenesis' in the work of the historian of civilization Norbert Elias, whose influence, like that of Bloch, on Garber is not often explicitly acknowledged but nonetheless apparent. In an essay on Thomas More, Elias defines the interrelationship between (social) institution and speaker as situationally specific:

---

[21] This 1972 essay by Habermas was translated as 'Consciousness-Raising or Redemptive Criticism: The Contemporaneity of Walter Benjamin', *New German Critique* 17 (1979): 30–59.

[22] 'Benjamins 'rettende Kritik': Vorüberlegungen zum Entwurf einer kritischen Hermeneutik', in *Vermittlung – Rezeption – Funktion: Ästhetische Theorie und Methodologie der Literaturwissenschaft*, 160–72 (Frankfurt a.M.: Suhrkamp, 1979).

[23] 'Einleitung', in *Staat und Staatsräson in der frühen Neuzeit: Studien zur Geschichte des öffentlichen Rechts*, suhrkamp taschenbuch wissenschaft, 878 (Frankfurt a.M.: Suhrkamp, 1990), 9.

[24] The concept of the 'field' of interpretation suggests a valence to Pierre Bourdieu, 'Intellectual Field and Creative Project', *Social Science Information* 8 (1969): 89–119. But, as in the case of Greenblatt, Garber would have to be forced into either camp. In this regard his understanding of the (mental-institutional) boundaries of interpretation more closely relates rather to Norbert Elias's concept of early modern 'sociogenesis'.

The originators (Urheber) speak out of a social situation, or a social situation that they have experienced; they speak into a social situation, or one based on experience, which is characteristic of a very specific . . . society . . . and for a specific public, a specific grouping of people.[25]

These specifics are the shared experiences and knowledge both of their present situations as well as of their heritage, made known through traditions. As Bloch says, traditions are 'living' when they provide the participants (Elias: originators), through the perspective of 'great breadth', with self-understanding: tradition 'instructs, challenges, and reveals who and what we are'. When, therefore, Garber makes the occasional claim that history has 'standards' (29) or 'workable answers' (30) to present crises, it is not mere rhetorical color but is anchored in a theory of how institutional and textual and biographical specifics in the here and now interrelate with and mutually determine the instructive perspectives of history and tradition.

Given this 'living' concept of tradition, it is also understandable that Garber often speaks of tradition in a personal way, as though it acted by its own volition. The voluntary aspect of tradition, however, is driven by the narrative motor of the text. In this sense we may perhaps define the thrust behind Garber's entire work as the trope of allegory.

But the trope, like the text, is not self-generating; it depends on a controlling, or at least guiding, presence: that is the critical historian, the main protagonist in Garber's conceptualization of the evolution of early modern German literature. Historians curate and mediate texts and traditions. Their job is to 'refashion' and 'retrace' texts, which sounds vaguely like a figure for Schleiermachian hermeneutics, recalling his aggressive metaphor of 'splitting the shell' of the book.[26] Again, however, this image is only one pole of a dialectic that is always turning. 'Method is detour', Garber recalls in his Benjamin monograph, quoting from the epistemological preface to *The Origin of German Tragic Drama*, reminding that the work of interpretation must take the circuitous route of reception history.[27] Still, it is impossible not to be impressed by the centrality and power of the historian in Garber's method.[28] The tide of history pushes with

---

[25] 'Thomas Morus' Staatskritik: Mit Überlegungen zur Bestimmung des Begriffs Utopie', in *Utopieforschung* (1982), ed. Wilhelm Voßkamp, suhrkamp taschenbuch, 1159 (Frankfurt a.M.: Surkamp, 1985), 2:101.

[26] 'diese Schale zu spalten'; in 'Über das Wesen der Religion', in *Über die Religion: Reden an die Gebildeten unter ihren Verächtern*, ed. Carl Heinz Ratschow, Universal-Bibliothek, 8313 (Stuttgart: Reclam, 1997), 34.

[27] *RR* 42.

[28] Benjamin has many names for the historian. Among those operative in Garber's method is the less exalted one of the rag-picker (*chiffonnier*), who goes about, doubtful yet ever hopeful, gathering what shreds of history he can. Garber concludes his meditation on images of peace in Chapter 1 with a borrowing of Benjamin's comment on Marx's theory of pauperization, which he took to be the precondition for revolution: 'As long as there is one beggar left, there will still be myth.' (18)

discouraging force against any hope of determining meaning in the multiplicity of phenomena and information attaching to the *Gegenstand* of research, that is, 'the thing in itself' (*die Sache an sich*). For Benjamin, in trying to grasp the unwieldy reception history of his *Gegenstand*, namely, Baudelaire's work – which is to say, the entire oeuvre in all its manifestations, including the author himself – it ultimately must come down to a question of propriety: 'Whose mills are being driven by this flood?' and 'Who is operating the controls?'[29] The historian as mill keeper has both the right and the obligation to control the flow of data. Failure to accept the task makes us victims of the undifferentiated flood of information and opinion and turns us into little more than bureaucrats or petty academicians, registering the appearance of documents, not discriminating between good and bad, useful and worthless.

The mechanism with which the historian controls the flow of data is fraught with ethical responsibility, deriving as it does again from Benjamin's early essay on prelapsarian and postlapsarian language. Critical historians, because they are learned and open to the voice of tradition – both essential prerequisites in Garber – have the Adamic duty to 'call things by name', that is, to interpret. For Garber, historians are qualified only if they have adequate 'diagnostic powers' and the 'capacity for criticism'.[30] Armed with these qualifications, the historian becomes an equal partner among the influences that affect the historical fate of literary works. In an extraordinary gesture in his deliberations on the reception of Baudelaire, Benjamin grants the historian the ability, not just to 'alter the image of the landscape' (i.e., the reflected image of the work), but indeed 'the landscape itself' (i.e., the work itself).[31] What does it mean in reality that the historian can alter the work itself? Viewed within the Garber-Benjamin method of reception history, in which the 'work itself' is split and contingent and dependent on supplemental appropriations, the historian corrects the false trammels and 'deviant paths' of tradition (29). This procedure affects the historical shape of the original work itself and makes possible a richer appreciation of the *Werkgehalt*, which is the fullest possible realization of the work at any given time.

The deep seriousness with which Garber accepts the ethical responsibility of doing literary history lies at the heart of his theory and practice. It explains, for instance, his insistence on retaining the controversial category of 'bourgeois' in early modernity. Modern literary history corresponds to the bourgeois phase of history, and insofar as bourgeois scholars have mostly failed since the Enlightenment to account for the complex dynamic between history and literature, electing instead to organize the map of literary history mechanically into familiar periods and to valorize certain individuals and their works as morally and aesthetically transcendent, we recognize an arc of bourgeois literary

---

[29] *RR* 39, with reference to Benjamin's introductory fragment to *Das Paris des Second Empire* (*GS* I-3, 1160–61).
[30] *RR* 48.
[31] *GS* I-3, 1164; discussed in *RR* 40–41.

criticism whose trajectory began in reformation and ended in ideology.[32] What started off in early humanism as a critical form of 'bourgeois thinking' that 'contributed to the undermining of the social and intellectual base of feudalism' (246) was at length transformed, by no less a form of bourgeois thinking, into 'chauvinistic distortions' (52). In this passage, Garber is thinking particularly of the exploitation of nationalism in the nineteenth and earlier twentieth century; but other abuses are also distortions, if less severe in their consequences, and include the trend in recent years away from a historical basis for literary studies.

Some readers will doubtless be scandalized by Garber's term 'bourgeois humanism', perceiving in it either superfluity or a reflex of failed socialist theory.[33] I think that taking sides on it after a quarter century of use – its staying power, if nothing else, lends it a certain authority – is of as little importance as arguing the question of Garber's possible conservatism. His perspective is unique and must be taken on its own terms; to do otherwise it to risk missing the richness of his insight into the evolution of humanist literature between Dante and Goethe. Besides, for all the differentiation in humanist thought that has been emphasized in recent scholarship, it is hardly passé to be reminded in newly challenging ways, as Garber does, that humanists were demonstrably motivated by social, economic, educational, and institutional factors that they shared broadly. Precisely in identifying this collective character ('Within this learned elite, or *nobilitas literaria*, a corporate mentality evolved' [ix]), Garber is able to investigate humanism as a social institution and, ultimately, to explain the utopian impulse running through the various traditions and media of the European republic of letters. This manner of conjuring utopia is directly opposite that of Adorno and others who claim that the negative space necessary for the emergence of utopia is precluded by identity. Against the charge of identitarianism, Garber would argue that the humanists themselves went to work resolutely 'forging an

---

[32] Cf. Victor Zmegac (ed.), *Geschichte der deutschen Literatur vom 18. Jahrhundert bis zur Gegenwart*, 2nd edition (Königstein, Czech.: Athenäum, 1984), xxi: 'The literary histories of the bourgeois tradition make it easy on themselves by simply turning away from these questions and instead lining up poet after poet. Explanations are borrowed from the realm of other, equally unconvincing, forms of production. This anti-intellectual attitude arises from ideology . . .'

[33] It has been criticized in Germany as well, beginning with the comment by Conrad Wiedemann, 'I consider it of little use to investigate Baroque formal culture in terms of the genesis of a bourgeois mentality, in hopes, thereby, of polishing up an old chestnut', in 'Barocksprache, Systemdenken, Staatsmentalität: Perspektiven der Forschung nach Barners *Barockrhetorik*', in *Internationaler Arbeitskreis für deutsche Barockliteratur*, ed. Paul Raabe (Hamburg; Hauswedell, 1976), 41. A few years later it erupted in a polemical exchange, published in the journal edited by Wiedemann, between Dieter Breuer, 'Gibt es eine bürgerliche Literatur im Deutschland des 17. Jahrhunderts? Über die Grenzen eines sozialgeschichtlichen Interpretationsschemas', *Germanisch-romanische Monatsschrift* 30 (1980): 211–26, and Garber, 'Gibt es eine bürgerliche Literatur im Deutschland des 17. Jahrhunderts? Eine Stellungnahme zu D. Breuers gleichnamigem Aufsatz', *Germanisch-romanische Monatsschrift* 31 (1981): 462–70.

identity' (42) through the cultivation of certain traditions and genres – hence the generous attention Garber gives especially to the tradition of Vergilian eclogue.

Garber's sensitivity, like that of Greenblatt, to the presence of traditions and discourses at the site of the text, is highly developed. And not only at the site of the text, but at that of society and its institutions as well, which allows him to discern 'a correspondence between the formal richness of bucolic and georgic types of poetry and the multiplicity of their social functions'.[34] This insight leads far beyond the view of orthodox *Geistesgeschichte* (which Garber, at the beginning of Chapter 4, puts in the mouth of the renowned Baroque literary historian Paul Hankamer), that the writings, especially of the late humanists, had degenerated into empty exercises in self-affirmation. Garber finds, rather, especially in Chapters 3 and 4, the humanist societies to have been loci of fervent and even revolutionary change; and as he reads early modern pastoral, it functioned as the institution-critical genre par excellence. What Garber writes about 'the inner workings of the radical transformation of political thought around 1600' (50) clearly owes to Benjamin's theory of 'immanent critique', that is, of how an institution is critiqued from within.[35] Garber understands the origins of 'bourgeois humanism' precisely as internal revolution, and one abetted in particular by the strategic use of pastoral forms, as he explains in an encyclopedia article on learned societies:

> In schools and universities, courts and churches, [humanists] encountered social institutions that they had had no hand in forming but to which they were obligated to conform. In their academies, language and literature societies, and sodalities, however, they could act according to rules that they themselves had devised . . . Most importantly, societal thinking puts its stamp on their aesthetic creations much more emphatically than has been appreciated so far, and none more deeply than the Arcadian Utopia, which can be interpreted as the very aesthetic and fictional codification of the societies.[36]

This revolutionary activity took place in the early modern phase of humanism, and insofar as its practitioners may be identified as bourgeois, Garber is satisfied

---

[34] *Europäische Bukolik* xiii.

[35] On institutional critique as a correction to naive reception aesthetics, see Peter Uwe Hohendahl, 'Trends in Literary Criticism', *German Quarterly* (Spring 1988), 280: Reception aesthetics, so Hohendahl, tends to 'neglect the institutional questions, not merely of literary communication, but the basic, primary concepts like text, reader, etc.' McCole, *Walter Benjamin and the Antinomies of Tradition* 27, explains: 'A critique may be especially powerful if undertaken by someone whose original intellectual commitments are heavily saturated by the orthodoxies of a field. [It] may take the special form of an *immanent* critique – a critique "from within" that intervenes in the dynamics of a tradition by playing off certain of its moments against others'.

[36] 'Sozietäten, Akademien, Sprachgesellschaften', in *Europäische Enzyklopädie zu Philosophie und Wissenschaften*, ed. H.J. Sandkühler (Hamburg: Meiner, 1990), 366–7.

to refer to this period of activity as 'bourgeois humanism'. As he demonstrates in Chapter 5, the loss of the negative-utopian, or 'anticipatory', element in pastoral can be pinpointed at the same time that the political vitality of humanism began to fade, namely, in the later eighteenth century. This marks the beginning of the late-bourgeois anti-classical, anti-historical watershed. The cultural knowledge and wisdom threatened in our own day with extinction is a final, dreadful consequence of this historical forgetfulness, and is ultimately what Garber means by the 'imperiled heritage'.[37]

A Word on the Edition

The essays gathered in this book were, of course, written at different times (from the mid-1980s to the present) and for different occasions and audiences. The selection of essays and their disposition here were guided by my sense of what constitutes the 'essence' of Garber's oeuvre, which I have tried to suggest in the book's title. This sense is based on some twenty-five years of following his work with great interest – since the appearance of his groundbreaking *Der locus amoenus und der locus terribilis: Bild und Funktion der Natur in der deutschen Schäfer- und Landlebendichtung des 17. Jahrhunderts* (1974; Locus amoenus and locus terribilis: Image and Function of Nature in German Bucolic and Georgic Literature of the Seventeenth Century), but especially since the appearance of his magisterial *Martin Opitz, 'der Vater der deutschen Dichtung': eine kritische Studie zur Wissenschaftsgeschichte der Germanistik* (1976; Martin Opitz, 'the Father of German Poetry': A Study in Critical Reception History in the Field of Germanistics). Other essays might have done as well, but I believe that the ones chosen here have natural coherence. In order to assist the reader somewhat in recognizing the logic behind their sequencing, I have provided minimal transitions, either at the end or at the beginning of each essay. My intention was to keep this enhancement unobtrusive and completely within the key and style of the respective essay. The principle of coherence and clarity was also behind the occasional decisions to redispose certain passages or small sections – always mindful, however, of not violating content. Two additional editorial interventions were exercised regularly. As mentioned above, the translators agreed that it often seemed judicious to modulate the 'tone' of Garber's prose for English readers. This largely meant applying some control on the length and syntactical complexity of sentences. The second intervention concerned the length and style of footnoted documentation. It is typical of Garber's method that he constantly registers the tendencies in the scholarly reception of his subject, and this can lead to extremely detailed notes. In the

---

[37] The term, borrowed for the title of this book, comes from the original German title of Chapter 7: 'Gefährdete Tradition'.

interest of economy, these notes were somewhat abbreviated, though, again, with an eye to maintaining the integrity of Garber's method. Unless otherwise attributed, all translations from German, Spanish, French and Latin are those of the translators or editor. For their untiring efforts on behalf of seeing the work of Klaus Garber reach an English-language readership, the translators are due my heartfelt thanks. Short biographies of the translators can be found at the end of the book. Finally, my hope is that readers will be stimulated by what they find in the following pages to explore Garber's further work on their own.

Max Reinhart
Athens, Georgia

Chapter 1

Prophecy, Love, and Law: Visions of Peace from Isaiah to Kant (and beyond)*

In this essay I wish to revisit a number of images from the distant and recent past that in some ways seem to have acquired greater relevance for today's troubled Europe than ever before. They belong to some of the great calls for peace that have been sounded down through the centuries. In contrast to the insatiable hunger of our leisure society for faraway Shangri La, these images show us that real satisfaction may be found only through a laborious return into the depths of time. Surely time is sometimes preferable to space; for distance has meaning insofar as its deep dimension becomes visible in time. The images may be utopian, but they derive from concrete texts and therefore share the reality of which the texts themselves are a part.

---

* [Editor's note. This essay, as much a personal meditation as a scholarly study, was written in the early 1990s as the fuller consequences of reunification were becoming obvious and beginning to provoke conflicting political responses in Germany and abroad. In its original form the essay was prefaced with the following reflection. 'The images of history that we carry within ourselves change constantly. This of course does not mean that history changes according to our wishes, as we are too instinct-bound to be able to generate new images ourselves. Rather, the forces of historical change imprint themselves upon our sight, our emotions, and our perception of time. Recent history has subjected us to yet another change. This one manifests itself as a general mistrust of anyone who continues to harbor optimism about the ability of human beings to live together in peace. The age belongs to the skeptics, the pessimists, the advocates of extreme caution. Less than half a century was all it took for hopes to wither in eastern Europe. It had long been clear that a crisis would strike; yet who could have predicted that the departure of socialism would be succeeded as quickly as it has by racial and religious fanaticism; by fragmentation into ever smaller boundaries; by the resurrection of *Blut und Boden*; by the exclusion and persecution of outsiders? Once more our darkest fantasies threaten to be outstripped by reality itself. The Europe that we cherish as the home of unbounded democracy and inexhaustible culture is fading before our very eyes. Historians: the interpreters of Europe, the curators of its past, the backward-looking prophets, are needed today as never before. A three-thousand-year-old storehouse of tradition is bursting with possible answers to Europe's crises. Though we may not be optimistic about how well these answers apply to current problems, as historians we must do our work lest these answers simply disappear into a subjective black hole beyond history. If historians ever enjoyed the leisure of complacency or self-satisfaction, that time is no more. Concerns that lose their relevance under the hot light of today's crises do not really matter.']

Isaiah: the Prophetic Voice

It is Judea at the turn of the seventh century BC, about one hundred years before the chosen people are to set out on their bitter journey into exile. Jerusalem has not yet fallen, though the destruction of the Holy City looms on the horizon. The prophet Isaiah rises to speak, and he strips the coming destruction of its mystery and surprise: The destruction is to be, he says, God's judgment on his chosen people's unbelief. The children of Israel now must drain the bitter cup of sorrow to the dregs. And yet, they are not left without the promise of final salvation:

> A shoot shall come out from the stump of Jesse,
>   and a branch shall grow out of his roots.
> The spirit of the Lord shall rest on him,
>   the spirit of wisdom and understanding,
>   the spirit of counsel and might,
>   the spirit of knowledge and the fear of the Lord.
> His delight shall be in the fear of the Lord.
> He shall not judge by what his eyes see,
>   or decide by what his ears hear;
> but with righteousness he shall judge the poor,
>   and decide with equity for the meek of the earth;
> he shall strike the earth with the rod of his mouth,
>   and with the breath of his lips he shall kill the wicked.
> Righteousness shall be the belt around his waist,
>   and faithfulness the belt around his loins.
> The wolf shall live with the lamb,
>   the leopard shall lie down with the kid,
> the calf and the lion and the fatling together,
>   and a little child shall lead them.
> The cow and the bear shall graze,
>   their young shall lie down together;
> and the lion shall eat straw like the ox.[1]

In this utopian vision political justice and peace in nature are drawn from the same cloth. The Prince of Peace cares not for the high and mighty, but for the poor, the meek, the lowly. For peace to come the hostile forces of nature and society must be reconciled; evil must be transformed into good. The wolf, the leopard, and the lion must lose their instinct to prey on weaker creatures; the cycle of consuming and being consumed must be broken. This reversal of natural reality amounts to nothing less than a return to Edenic origins, where no justification exists for the killing of the poor, the weak, and the needy. As Isaiah

---

[1] Isa. 11:1–7. Biblical citations are taken from the New Revised Standard Version.

envisions the future, even God's original appointment of Adam as lord of creation will be terminated, since all creatures will live together in peace. As in nature, a return to beginnings is fundamental to Isaiah's conception of future government. Justice, goodness, and peace are possible in the here and now. Fallen mankind may avail itself instantly of the gifts of its origins and not simply place all problems in the hands of the Lord Jehovah. Isaiah's messianic kingdom lies somewhere along the border between history and eternity, between the worldly and the heavenly kingdoms. The image partakes both of the beginning and the end of history; it is at once the well-spring and the goal of all human action: the coming-about of a repentant, converted, and devout people. The prophecy speaks of an earthly future, but it intersects with the messianic kingdom of Paradise.

Vergil's Emperor of Peace

Europe's intellectual face is stamped as deeply with the Judeo-Christian as with the Greco-Roman tradition; the two are so thoroughly intertwined as to be nearly indistinguishable. Three-quarters of a millennium after Isaiah a similar message of peace is articulated in Rome, *imperium mundi*. Like Isaiah, Vergil foretells the arrival of an Emperor of Peace, but this time in the person of a divine child:

> For you, little child, spontaneously, as first gifts,
> the earth will lavish creeping ivy and foxglove,
> everywhere, and Egyptian lilies with smiling acanthus.
> Goats will come home by themselves with udders full
> of milk, nor will the oxen fear the lion's might.
> Your very cradle will flower with buds to caress you.
> The serpent will die as well as poison's treacherous plant,
> and everywhere Assyrian balsam will come to bloom.[2]

As Isaiah before him, Vergil envisions a political peace accompanied by peace in the natural kingdom, but with a fine distinction: the threatening serpent, seductress in Eden, playmate in Isaiah, is absent. Vergil diminishes the necessity

---

[2] *Ecl.* 4.18–25. Translation: Barbara Hughes Fowler, *Vergil's Eclogues* (Chapel Hill: University of North Carolina Press, 1997).
> At tibi prima, puer, nullo munuscula cultu
> errantis hederas passim cum baccare tellus
> mixtaque ridenti colocasia fundet acantho.
> ipsae lacte domum referent distenta capellae
> ubera, nec magnos metuent armenta leones;
> ipsa tibi blandos fundent cunabula flores.
> occidet et serpens, et fallax herba veneni
> occidet; Assyrium volgo nascetur amomum.

of enemies being transformed, since, in keeping with Roman political practice, those who fail to adapt to imperial peace are excluded. Caught in the bloody struggles between the triumvirs and their rivals, Rome is being torn apart by civil wars and revolts along her borders. Property ownership can no longer be protected. Generals ruthlessly exploit the real estate, expropriating and reallocating it to purchase the loyalty of soldiers and sympathizers. The land shakes, literally and figuratively. Isaiah foresaw the destruction of Israel; Vergil's vision coalesces amidst the whirl of present-day Rome.

Out of the Republic's horrifying disintegration the poet steps forth to voice a promise. Vergil is no Isaiah, no religious prophet, but a *vates*, a messenger of a future unknown yet certain. In the eyes of the seer, the future is dawning even now: the child is growing; signs of the coming salvation are already discernible in his features and character. Soon he will have entered into his manhood, and peace will be made universal, embracing the entire reach of Rome's jurisdiction. He who comes is none other than the triumvir Octavian. First he will subdue Pompey; then Marc Antony; later, as Augustus, he will lay claim to Roman sovereignty. It is in this unstable moment of transition from civil war to principate that Vergil drafts the political mission of the Roman Empire, devoting his entire oeuvre – the *Eclogues*, the *Georgics*, the *Aeneid* – to this cause. The Hebrew prophet adapted and applied the revealed word historically; the Roman poet composes a national epic of his empire's origin, rise, and destiny, concluding with the ultimate pacification of the world under Octavian. Isaiah's promised kingdom existed apart from the present, separated by a great gulf. Vergil's peacemaker matures within the poet's own time; his scepter still bears the stain of the civil wars that he has brought to an end.

With this image Vergil bequeathed to western literature its most powerful application of the topos of *laus regentis* 'praise of ruler'. Its dialectical face is striking: the ruler is extolled as the *fundator pacis* 'author of peace' even as he is obligated to act on it, to establish and preserve the peace. The images of pacified nature symbolize a pacified human world. But by what political means can Octavian reconcile his simultaneous commitments to domestic harmony and peace with his conquest of foreign peoples?

Pax Romana, the singular creation of the Augustan poets, rested upon the premise that the destiny of world domination served equally the interest of peace. In the Christian world, prior to the outbreak of revolutions in the sixteenth, seventeenth, and eighteenth centuries, the Roman idea of an Emperor of Peace had no less transformative an influence on the conceptions of ruler and peace than did the Old Testament prophetic idea. This idea was made possible, however, only by engaging a complementary one: the idea of radical Christian love.

Jesus: the Gospel of Earthly Peace and the Commandment of Love

Jesus's preaching was adapted in the early Christian community through the kerygma of the crucified and risen Christ,[3] as a paradoxical message of radical peace and discord. This kerygmatic message emphasized the coming of the kingdom of God. What Jesus himself had heralded as a coming event became for his believers the present time as embodied in his person, the very Son of God, foretold by the prophets.

In the New Testament view, especially that of Paul, the world is divided along the line of faith in or rejection of Jesus Christ. For the early church all of Jesus's preaching is encapsulated in the Sermon on the Mount and held up as the ideal of Christian behavior. At its core is the principle of love as mercy, love as hunger for justice, love as humility. The privilege of Sonship is given to the peacemaker:

> Blessed are the merciful,
>   for they will receive mercy.
> Blessed are the pure in heart,
>   for they will see God.
> Blessed are the peacemakers,
>   for they will be called children of God.
> Blessed are those who are persecuted for righteousness' sake,
>   for theirs is the kingdom of heaven.[4]

In this respect peacemaking goes directly to the heart of the gospel. Just as Jesus Christ effects reconciliation between God and man, so the fellowship of the faithful is based upon knowledge of this reconciliation and is to be practiced by individual believers to their fullest ability. At the same time, however, Jesus Christ brings the sword of enmity: 'Do not think that I have come to bring peace to the earth; I have not come to bring peace, but a sword.'[5] Jesus divides husband and wife, parents and children, brothers and sisters – the people, that is, who are naturally closest to one another; by the same token he joins those who are farthest apart. His provocative words mean simply one thing: the world is divided with respect to the question of Jesus Christ into believers and non-believers.

Paradoxically, wherever the unbeliever – unloving, unpeaceful – is lifted up to a life of faith through acts of forgiveness and love, it is precisely there that the deepest chasm forms between individuals. Carl Friedrich von Weizsäcker, the noted philosopher of twentieth-century science and culture, grapples with this paradox in his *History of Nature*:

---

[3] The *kerygma* is the Christian (esp. early-Christian) preaching of salvation through Jesus Christ.
[4] Mt. 5:7–10.
[5] Mt. 10:34.

> Christian love . . . is a turning toward man such as had not been known before. It intends to be just that. But it creates at the same time a distance between man and his instinct-bound fellow such as had also not been known before. This distance is something Christianity does not intend but cannot avoid. Instinctive love and instinctive hate are bound to their partner with equal blindness. Christian love sees the other human being, and only because of this it is free toward him. But nearly every one of us has a spot where he would much rather be hated blindly than understood clearly. By its mere presence, the love that sees forces a choice upon him whom it sees. This is why it meets with resistance where it cannot arouse love in return.[6]

The Christian Messiah will bring about the Empire of Peace. But it will be an empire that is free of politics and that transcends nations and societies, an empire created wherever two people come together and are nourished by a force beyond this world. Hence, the ancient sociopolitical concentration on the *polis* or the *res publica* or Augustus – both are used as alternating figures in the perfecting of human existence – is countered by the radical proclamation of Christian life predicated solely on faith. Over the centuries this message has provoked an array of responses, ranging from the sober acceptance of reality to the utopian construct of an earthly kingdom of men and women who live by faith alone, completely in the spirit of Christ.

Augustine: *civitas terrena, civitas coelestis*

Some four centuries after Jesus, at the threshold of the Middle Ages, another utopian voice is heard: Augustine of Hippo, articulating a vision of peace in a heavenly city. *On the City of God* was for centuries considered to be Augustine's greatest book; its fame has been eclipsed only in the past two centuries by his *Confessions*. It comprises twenty-two books, a number that signifies the combination of the ten books of the Platonic state (*politeia*) and the twelve books of the Platonic laws (*nomoi*).[7] Was Augustine's idea of a heavenly city meant to supersede the ancient statist philosophy, which reached its high points in the Greece of Plato and Aristotle and in the Rome of Cicero and Horace? That seems likely, given the irreconcilable differences in the ancient and Augustinian conceptions of the state. The life of the ancient citizen found fulfillment in the polis, the res publica; participation in public life was his foremost obligation. The

---

[6] Weizsäcker, *The History of* Nature, trans. Fred D. Wieck (Chicago: University of Chicago Press, 1949), 189.
[7] As Edgar Salin, an adherent of the George Circle and one of twentieth-century Europe's great cultural morphologists, shows in his own book entitled *Civitas Dei*, ch. 3: 'Civitas Dei und Civitas Terrena', 166–85 (Tübingen: Mohr, 1926).

free citizen stood ready to sacrifice everything for the welfare of his city, his state; life itself ceased to be the greatest good when the freedom or survival of the state came under threat. Peace was held to be the necessary precondition for prosperity, security against foreign domination the indisputable, absolute good. Augustine's integration of the ancient statist ethos into his idea of a heavenly *civitas* was a brilliant move. Peace for Augustine is at once the highest mundane good and the highest heavenly good. In the secular city, the *civitas terrena*, peace may be desired, but it is never complete and always in peril. Perfect, unassailable peace, will reign only in the City of God:

> There we shall enjoy the gifts of nature, that is to say, all that God the Creator of all natures has bestowed upon ours – gifts not only good, but eternal – not only of the spirit, healed now by wisdom, but also of the body renewed by the resurrection. There the virtues shall no longer be struggling against vice or evil, but shall enjoy the reward of victory, the eternal peace which no adversary shall disturb. This is the final blessedness, this is the ultimate consummation, the unending end.[8]

To imagine that the two cities exist in a relationship of simple temporal succession would of course be to misunderstand Augustine. The City of God accompanies the secular city continuously until the end of time. *Civitas terrena* and *civitas coelestis* are inextricably connected on this earth; only at the Last Judgment will they part company. It is present here and now in every believer and every community of believers. The secular city is home not only to believers but to unbelievers as well. But just as believers do not always remain steadfast in the faith, unbelievers can also occasionally exercise faith. Everlasting peace in the heavenly city is prepared for believers only; the secular city will sink, according to God's inscrutable but perfect will, into eternal damnation. The ancient state, though it still echoes in Augustine's title, is bereft of all worldly, social, and political reality. The polis, formerly conceived of as a real place, is transformed into an invisible, incorporeal Kingdom of Belief, dualistically opposed to the earthbound Kingdom of Unbelief. Augustine attempts neither to work out a concept of secular empire in objective political terms nor to elaborate the specifically institutional character of the community of believers. While he

---

[8] *De civ. D.* 19.10. Translation: Marcus Dods, *The City of God*, ed. Philip Schaff (1948; reprint in vol. 2 of *A Select Library of the Nicene and Post-Nicene Fathers of the Christian Church*, Grand Rapids: Eerdmans, 1956). 'Ibi enim erunt naturae munera, hoc est, quae naturae nostrae ab omnium naturarum Creatore donantur, non solum bona, verum etiam et sempiterna; non solum in animo, qui sanatur per sapientiam, verum etiam in corpore, quod resurrectione renovabitur. Ibi virtutes, non contra ulla vitia vel mala quaecumque certantes, sed habentes victoriae praemium aeternam pacem, quam nullus adversarius inquietet. Ipsa est enim beatitudo finalis, ipse perfectionis finis, qui consumentem non habet finem.'

speaks of this community as the church on earth, in existence since the first coming of Jesus Christ, he makes no effort to outfit it with regulations, hierarchy, or legal power. Far from constituting a legal entity, this church is a spiritual metaphor for the band of believers who make up the body of Christ on earth.

The complexities of Augustine's dual-city conception represented a daunting task for medieval political philosophers. In a digression in Book 5, Chapter 12, which is dedicated to the cosmopolitan city of Rome, Augustine essays a profile of the ideal Christian ruler – a profile that would continue to be reworked, starting with the Carolingians, for the next thousand years. Charlemagne, in reflecting on the distinct functions of secular and spiritual authorities, carefully distinguishes his own role as emperor from that of the pope:

> Our duty is first, strengthened by godly devotion, to defend the Church externally with weapons against the heathen onslaught and the ravages of unbelievers, and second, to support the Church internally by sanctioning the Catholic faith. Your duty, Most Holy Father, is, like Moses with hands raised to heaven, to support us in this service.[9]

Augustine's two cities materialize in Charlemagne's explication as empire and papacy. As the chief representative of the *civitas terrena*, the emperor sees himself as both the protector of Christendom, in face of the ever-present danger of heresy and the invasion of ungodly forces from outside the empire, and as the guarantor of *una societas christiana* within. The pope's responsibility, on the other hand, is to administer the spiritual means of grace and to bless the political actions of the emperor, the purpose of which is the enforcement of divine commandments. Both powers, mundane and celestial, operate as co-potentiary agents of God on earth; peacekeeping is their foremost task.

The actual course of history, to be sure, turned out quite differently from this idealization. The Middle Ages were in time consumed by the struggles between the two rivals for supremacy; and the grandiose medieval aspiration of achieving universal Christendom – one great Christian Empire whereby a political *corpus mysticum* would be born on earth – disintegrated internally. In their protracted war of attrition, pope and emperor incited forces that led not only to the reform of church and empire, but in the long run to their very supersession.

One inspired answer to this crisis came from the revolutionary Calabrian abbot Joachim of Fiore in the form of a spiritualization of the Pauline doctrine of the three historical ages, a proposition that incited a massive disruption of

---

[9] Charlemagne, *Epistola VIII ad Leonem III Papam*, in *PL* 98:908: 'Nostrum est, secundum auxilium divinae pietatis, sanctam ubique Christi Ecclesiam ab incursu paganorum et ab infidelium devastatione armis defendere, foris et intus catholicae fidei agnitione munire. Vestrum est, sanctissime Pater, elevatis ad Deum cum Moyse manibus, nostram adjuvare militiam.'

fundamental medieval assumptions.[10] The aftershocks of this radical transformation are discernible as late as Romanticism in the poetry of Friedrich Hölderlin and the philosophical writings of the young Hegel. In Joachim's scheme the Old Testament Age of the Father and the Law, followed by the New Testament Age of the Son and Love, are to be succeeded by a third, the Age of the Spirit. By the advent of this third age the respective authorities of state and church will have become obsolete, and people will live by the power of the Holy Spirit alone, unhindered by all worldly or spiritual orders. Indeed, Joachim avows, the Age of the Spirit is imminent; it will come to pass not in the next but in the present world and will bring peace to mankind.[11] Among the self-proclaimed heirs and executors of the Joachimian prophecy, the Franciscan Spiritualists, this vision of total renewal came to full maturity. With his profound connectedness to all nature, Francis of Assisi offered one of the most stirring messages of peace ever known to the world.[12]

Meanwhile, emperor and pope continued to sink into the bottomless whirlpool of defamatory rhetoric, each recognizing in the other the Antichrist; not even the greatest of the Hohenstaufen, Frederick Barbarossa, could rise above this culture of denunciation.[13] The defenders of medieval *ordo* were rapidly passing from the scene, and the path stood open to the spiritual heresies that would flourish throughout the early modern period. In face of this yawning leadership vacuum bold solutions were called for.

Dante's New World Emperor

> And since what holds true for the part is true for the whole, and an individual human being 'grows perfect in judgment and wisdom when he sits at rest', it is apparent that mankind most freely and readily attends to this activity – an activity which is almost divine, as we read in the psalm: 'Thou hast made him a little lower than the angels' – in the calm or tranquillity of peace. Hence it is clear that universal peace is the best of those things which are ordained for our human happiness. That is why the

---

[10] See esp. Ernst Benz, *Ecclesia Spiritualis: Kirchenidee und Geschichtstheologie der franziskanischen Reformation* (1934; reprint, Stuttgart: Kohlhammer, 1964), and Marjorie Reeves, *The Influence of Prophecy in the Later Middle Ages: A Study in Joachimism* (1969; reprint, Notre Dame: University of Notre Dame, 1993). As a general survey, see Morton Bloomfield, 'Joachim of Fiora: A Critical Survey of his Canon, Teachings, Sources, Biography, and Influence,' *Traditio* 13 (1957): 249–311.

[11] For an expansion on this connection, see Steven Ozment, *The Age of Reform 1250–1550: An Intellectual and Religious History of Late Medieval and Reformation Europe* (New Haven: Yale University Press, 1980), 107–9.

[12] See *The Little Flowers of St. Francis of Assisi*, trans. and ed. Cardinal Manning (London: Foulis, 1915).

[13] After his lengthy conflict with Pope Alexander III, Frederick at last had to admit the essential role of the papacy in the legitimation of the emperor.

> message which rang out from on high to the shepherds was not wealth, nor pleasures, nor honors, not long life, nor health, nor strength, nor beauty, but peace; for the heavenly host said: 'Glory to God on high, and on earth peace to men of good will.' And that is why the Savior of men used the greeting 'Peace be with you', for it was fitting that the supreme Savior should utter the supreme salutation.[14]

Once again, peace is the greatest good. Now, however, the winds of modernity are blowing unchecked by Christian spirituality. The mission of the political philosopher setting out upon his solitary path into the future is not to offer a blueprint for heavenly peace. Only the Joachimian-Franciscan model of faith will endure, for it leads away from the church's iniquities: the sinful reliance on property, power, and political influence, and back to Jesus, to the apostles, to the early Christian community.[15] Where Dante's *Monarchy* differs is in its concern with secular ideas and their consequences. Heavenly salvation is one thing, earthly happiness another, though no less important; only when these two realms are harmonized does humanity's purpose become clear. After more than a thousand years the ancient discipline of politics – that noble path to the best earthly constitution – thus regains its seat within the cosmos of the sciences,[16] a dignity that it will retain throughout the early modern age until the historical sciences emerge around 1800.

---

[14] *De Monarchia* 1.4, in *Dante Alighieri: Tutte le Opere*, ed. Luigi Blasucci (Florence: Sansoni Editore, 1989). Translation: *Dante: Monarchy*, trans. and ed. Prue Shaw (Cambridge: Cambridge University Press, 1996); orthography slightly adapted. 'Et quia quemadmodum est in parte sic est in toto, et in homine particulari contingit quod sedendo et quiescendo prudentia et sapientia ipse perficitur, patet quod genus humanum in quiete sive tranquillitate pacis ad proprium suum opus, quod fere divinum est iuxta illud "Minuisti eum paulominus ab angelis", liberrime atque facillime se habet. Unde manifestum est quod pax universalis est optimum eorum que ad nostram beatitudinem ordinantur. Hinc est quod pastoribus de sursum sonuit non divitie, non voluptates, non honores, non longitudo vite, non sanitas, non robur, non pulcritudo, sed pax; inquit enim celestis militia: "Gloria in altissimis Deo, et in terra pax hominibus bone voluntatis". Hinc etiam "Pax vobis" Salus hominum salutabat.' The dating of the *Monarchia* is uncertain, but likely 1302–5, during Dante's exile from Florence. The book was burned in public in 1329 on the orders of Cardinal Bertrando del Poggetto.

[15] Konrad Burdach, the great but now mostly forgotten cultural historian of the Italian and German Renaissance, never tired of explaining the wholesale changes brought about in thirteenth- and fourteenth-century Italy by this religious reawakening. See esp. *Vom Mittelalter zur Reformation: Forschung zur Geschichte der deutschen Bildung* (Halle: Niemeyer, 1893–1939).

[16] A development prepared by Marsilius of Padua in his search for 'tranquillity', which he saw as the 'highest temporal good'. See Marsilius, *The Defender of Peace: The 'Defensor Pacis' (1324)*, trans. Alan Gewirth, vol. 1 (1951–56; reprint, New York: Arno Press, 1979).

The repatriation of Aristotle, 'the Philosopher', with whom Dante is absorbed on nearly every page, was one of the results of this elevation of politics. Ancient pagan authorities, not ecclesiastics, are the first to speak. Politics is not a matter of faith but of thought; all propositions must undergo the scrutiny of reason. Reason, in the form of the Aristotelian syllogism, is the rake that clears away the rubble of unquestioned traditions. The best constitution, the one that serves the interests of peace most effectively, is monarchical. While this conclusion may elicit a yawn from readers at the outset of the twenty-first century, do we truly grasp the significance it held for Dante? For him the best constitution was nothing less than the embodiment of the political world-reason; enlightened thinkers as late as Kant continue to strive toward this ideal. Earthly political authority is charged with the high responsibility of guaranteeing access to and abetting the fulfillment of human potentiality through freedom. This charge no longer caters to particular interests but is committed to the well-being of all mankind.

Of what does this well-being consist? Precisely of that which enables the optimal application of reason as an instrument of knowledge; the free disposal of the will as the source of free action; the exercise of faith restricted by neither secular nor religious censure. 'World emperor' is Dante's name for the postulate of pure political reason that advocates the total realization of thought, action, and belief. That is why the political philosophy of Dante is relevant even today. His was a herculean achievement. Even that of the arch-humanist Petrarch, with his ingenious reappropriation of ancient culture for modern education, pales by comparison. Dante discards both major powers of the Middle Ages, papacy and empire, and replaces them with something so new, so forward-thinking, that political philosophy has yet adequately to appreciate it. His vision definitively separates faith and thought, religion and politics, church and state. To this is added the implicit demand for a radical commitment to a task formerly entrusted only to papacy and empire: the unconditional return to the original Christian message.

The titles 'Pope' and 'Emperor', steeped in tradition but loaded now with sweeping new content, are still the mainstays of the promise of this vision. They are a priori principles, as it were – Kant would say 'ideals' – whose objective is the fulfillment of life in its practical as well as metaphysical spheres. Whatever concessions are allowed to time in Dante's political philosophy, they do not signal a return to sterile constructs from the past, as many have argued, but singularly anticipate the future.

What nation deserves the honorable title 'world emperor'? Certainly not France, in Dante's view; but also not Germany. It belongs instead to Rome. The coincidental appearance of Christ and Octavian was not merely fortuitous but was symbolic of the supreme earthly destiny of Rome. This message is taken up by the post-Dantean generation of Petrarch and Cola di Rienzi. In Trecento humanism the rebirth of the world emperor signifies the rebirth of ancient Rome's political and cultural mission. Thus the enormous challenge posed by Italian humanism for the developing nations of northern Europe. The regulatory principle of all peoples unified in peace, personified by Dante in his new world emperor, continues all the way down to our own day to represent the sublime ideal of political philosophy.

Thus began the struggle between the forces that would expand the powers of modern nations and those that would limit them. The humanists, for their part, encouraged the rise of the modern nation until well into the Enlightenment – this despite the fact of religious divisions being heaped upon existing national divisions in the sixteenth century, an enormous complication that would ultimately lead to deep political and confessional ruptures. It surely bespeaks the measure of the intellectual and moral qualities of the late humanists that they dedicated their finest efforts to the search for solutions to these challenges. They helped themselves in doing so by regular attention to one guiding ethical light in particular: Erasmus.

Erasmus: the Return to the Original Christian Message

In 1494 the Spanish invaded southern Italy and the French northern Italy. Already divided and dominated by Venice, Florence, Milan, Rome, and Naples, Italy now found itself engulfed in the struggle for hegemony between Europe's two most advanced monarchies. The classical Quattrocento, during which civic and princely forms of humanism existed side by side,[17] experienced an abrupt end. The so-called High Renaissance of poetry, painting, and architecture would take place in a politically repressive land, which together with Spain would assume leadership of the Counter-Reformation. Some twenty-three years later Luther made his public appearance with the legendary posting of ninety-five Theses at the castle chapel in Wittenberg. The religious war that began subsequently on German soil and soon spread abroad would keep Europe in turmoil for more than a century. The Christian community of faith was now permanently split, Europe forever confessionally divided. The sacking of Rome by Imperial troops in 1527; the German Schmalkaldic War between Protestants and Catholics in 1546–47; the bloody suppression of French Calvinists in the St Bartholomew's Day Massacre in 1572; the defeat of Spain and the preservation of Calvinism in the Dutch War of Independence late in the century – these are a few of the pivotal moments in the turbulent sixteenth century that provide the context for the work from Erasmus through late humanism, a period of time that is still woefully underestimated and inadequately researched.

Erasmus's *Querela Pacis* (Complaint of Peace) was one of the first and most important literary responses to this emerging turmoil. First printed in 1516,

---

[17] See Chapter 3 below, 'The Republic of Letters and the Absolutist State', for a succinct presentation of civic and bourgeois humanism.

shortly before Luther's Theses, *Querela Pacis* was reprinted and translated almost annually for years thereafter. Once again within the reformist tradition, argumentation and criticism become acts of remembrance and renewal of the original Christian message:

> Survey the life of Christ from start to finish, and what else is it but a lesson in concord and mutual love? What do all his commandments and parables teach if not peace and love for one another? Think of the mighty prophet Isaiah: when he was inspired by the divine spirit and prophesied that Christ would come to unite the world, did he promise a tyrant, a sacker of cities, a warrior, a conqueror? He did not. What then did he promise? A prince of peace . . . He is the Prince of peace, he loves peace and is offended by discord . . . Whoever brings tidings of Christ brings tidings of peace. Whoever preaches war preaches one who is the very opposite of Christ . . . Every Christian word, whether you read the Old Testament or the New, reiterates one thing: peace with unanimity; while every Christian life is occupied with one thing: war . . . Men so minded should surely either cease to pride themselves on the name of Christian or put into practice the teaching of Christ through concord.[18]

Whereas Dante entrusted his revolutionary thought to Philosophy, Erasmus makes his rousing call for peace upon the ground of the Old and New Testaments. This is a shrewd rhetorical tactic, anticipating as it does the presuppositions of his readers. Erasmus speaks not as an individual but as the mouthpiece of Peace herself. Peace, in turn, plays the role of interpreter of the Christian proclamation. Through a complex filtration of words and tone, Erasmus manages to avoid the agitated tremolo that he always found so odious; this technique enables him to withdraw, as author, behind the words of his earthly and heavenly messengers. But far from sacrificing its authority, his voice, in assuming the dignity of tradition, waxes in authority.

---

[18] *Querela Pacis* [henceforth in notes: *QP*], in *Opera Omnia: Desiderii Erasmi Roterodami* (Amsterdam: North Holland Publishing Co., 1977), IV-2:68–76. Translation: Betty Radice, *A Complaint of Peace*, in *Collected Works of Erasmus* (Toronto: University of Toronto Press, 1986), 5:299–303. 'Vniuersam eius vitam contemplare: quid aliud est, quam concordiae mutuique amoris doctrina? Quid aliud inculcant eius praecepta, quid parabolae, nisi pacem, nisi charitatem mutuam? Egregius ille vates Esaias, cum caelesti afflatus spiritu Christum illum rerum omnium conciliatorem venturum annunciaret, num satrapam pollicetur, num vrbium euersorem, num bellatorem, num triumphatorem? Nequaquam. Quid igitur? Principem pacis . . . [P]rinceps est pacis, pacem amat, offenditur dissidio . . . Quisquis Christum annunciat, pacem annunciat. Quisquis bellum praedicat, illum praedicat, qui Christi dissimillimus est. . . Omnes Christianorum literae, siue vetus legas testamentum, siue nouum, nihil aliud quam pacem et vnanimitatem crepant, et omnis Christianorum vita nihil aliud quam bella tractat . . . Quin potius aut Christianorum titulo gloriari desinant aut Christi doctrinam exprimant concordia.'

Two themes need to be underscored here: the humanist *recurs ad fontes* 'return to the sources' and the early Christian community of peace. For Erasmus the *fontes* are almost exclusively biblical, drawn especially from the New Testament (ancient pagan sources are adduced only incidentally). This decision ignites a purifying firestorm that fits unharmoniously with the stock image of a peaceable humanist-prince who shuttles, with ironic wit, between opposing factions in the interest of compromise. But Erasmus's words are unambiguous: Christian Europe has failed all up and down the line; secular and religious powers and estates alike have repeatedly sinned against the One in whose name they pretend to act and under whose cross they construe their official self-image. As in the Enlightenment, in the philosopher-critic Pierre Bayle, for example, Erasmus's return to the sources is not synonymous with compliance with orthodoxy but represents rather a surgical operation by which even basic assumptions are questioned. The distant original Christian message, once taken at its word, explodes now in a blaze of religious, political, and social criticism; Luther at his most inflammatory was hardly more provocative. The present age, from the pope and the princes downward, must either reverse direction or else cease to drape its evil deeds in Christ's name. Christian Europe, heir to the purest gift of love, peace, and harmony known to the world, consistently perverts this legacy into its opposite, risking thereby the forfeiture of its own birthright. Time and again even the heathen put Christian Europe to shame; the Christian banner still waves in the shadow of that of the Augustan Empire of Peace. And yet, for Erasmus, the host of Old and New Testament voices calling for peace are reminder enough that Europe will at last be unified under the name of Christ.

The second theme, inseparable from the first, has received very little attention: the early Christian community of peace. Erasmus redirects the entire biblical tradition back to this simple core belief. In his view, religious schism is not only unnecessary but a violation of the true Christian message. All differences separating the faithful vanish in the light of the One, Jesus, in whom words and deeds were perfectly wedded. Unshakeable and incorruptible realist that he is, Erasmus identifies the problem to be not Christianity itself but its falsification, secularization, trivialization, and distortion by centuries of selfish pride. Every effort must be directed toward the elimination of these abuses and away from the dogmatic hairsplitting that distracts from the essence of faith and leads to discord, alienation, and, in the end, war. The evils of war are presented in *Querela Pacis* in such absolute terms as to silence all objections. Although the human race has always been well instructed by its moral teachers, it continues, undeterred, along the road to perdition. Peace warns against the failure to weigh the consequences:

> Are you longing for war? First take a look at what peace and war really are, the gains brought by one and the losses by the other; this will enable you to calculate whether there is anything to be achieved by exchanging peace for war. If it is something for admiration when a kingdom is

> prosperous throughout, with its cities soundly established, lands well cultivated, excellent laws, the best teaching, and the highest moral standards, consider how you will necessarily destroy all this happiness if you go to war.[19]

This is a bold proscription of war. Europe continued to burn, of course, for more than a century in the name of the One whom Erasmus apostrophized as the Prince of Peace. Can there have been a more blatant repudiation of his vision than that? And yet, how revealing to follow the echo of his voice into the Enlightenment!

If they were to have any retarding influence over the spread of confessional rage, the humanists were obliged to work within the new absolutist state. For a time, in the period of confessionalism,[20] the state abetted such efforts. Two centuries later, however, the Enlightenment would arise out of a welter of opinion that the absolutist state had become obsolete and a drag on progress; the Enlightenment cannot be properly understood apart from its anti-absolutist base. The revocation in 1685 of the Edict of Nantes[21] and subsequent expulsion of the Huguenots from the monarchy of the Sun King, is proof enough. In the later eighteenth century as well, images of utopian origins again became vehicles of political criticism. At this point, however, the images were drawn from peaceful, harmonious nature, and were adduced, not only in literature and art, but in legal philosophy as well.

Kant's Idea of a World Republic: Peace and the Law

> Then it may be said, 'Seek ye first the kingdom of pure practical reason and its righteousness, and your end (the blessing of perpetual peace) will necessarily follow . . .' If it is a duty to make real (even if only through approximation in endless progress) the state of public law, and if there is well-grounded hope that this can actually be done, then perpetual peace, as the condition that will follow what has erroneously been called 'treaties of peace' (but which in reality are only armistices), is not an empty idea. As

---

[19] *QP* 92–3; *Complaint* 316. 'Ad bellum gestis? Primum inspice, cuiusmodi res sit pax, cuiusmodi bellum, quid illa bonorum, quid hoc malorum secum vehat atque ita rationem ineas, num expediat pacem bello permutare. Si res quaedam admirabilis est regnum vndique rebus optimis florens bene conditis vrbibus, bene cultis agris, optimis legibus, honestissimis disciplinis, sanctissimis moribus, cogita tecum: haec felicitas mihi perturbanda est, si bello.'

[20] German: 'das konfessionelle Zeitalter'. The period covers more or less the second half of the sixteenth century following the signing of the Augsburg religious peace (1555).

[21] The accord was reached between Henry IV and the Huguenots in April 1598 and reflected Henry's politics of appeasement. It allowed for at least a temporary toleration of the Huguenots following years of persecution.

the times required for equal steps of progress become, we hope, shorter and shorter, perpetual peace is a problem which, gradually working out its own solution, steadily approaches its goal.[22]

Despite harboring deep pessimism with respect to human nature and the notion of a pre-historical, lawless, original state of nature, Immanuel Kant nevertheless continued into his old age – like Friedrich Schiller and the early Romantics – to speculate on the ultimate state of mankind. Indeed, he was obliged to do so. For his entire system of philosophy depends on the maintenance of regulative ideas that determine the boundaries of all theories of knowledge, action, and human social life. Whereas his critique of practical reason ultimately issues in the renewed figure of the saint as the representation of harmony between inclination and duty, will and obligation, sensuousness and categorical imperative, the final stage of his philosophy of law and history presents the ideal of a world republic as the guarantor of perpetual peace.

For Kant, only a republican constitution is worthy of mankind, for it alone is based on freedom, equality, and the exercise of the inalienable rights of all members of the *societas civilis*, or national citizenry.[23] Only when mankind has arrived at the point where a republican constitution has been installed everywhere on earth will universal peace be secure; for it is only civil society, the universal community of law, that guarantees all citizens their rights, including due process. Kant's idea of peace has greatness in that it refuses to fall back on moral or religious grounds.

At the same time, however, it is indicative of Kant's sublime obliviousness that his idea of a peaceful world republic ultimately proved incapable of restraining the private acquisition of property, an important feature in his original 'civil rights of liberty'. This explains the complications in which he would become entangled in his legal justification of original ownership (*acquisitio originaria*).[24] This problem runs like a nightmare throughout the philosophy of

---

[22] *Zum ewigen Frieden*, in *Kant's Werke*, ed. Königlich Preußische Akademie der Wissenschaften, 8:343–86 (Berlin: Walter de Gruyter, 1923), here 378, 386. Translation: Lewis W. Beck, *Perpetual Peace*, in *Immanuel Kant: Philosophical Writings*, ed. Ernst Behler, 270–311 (New York: Continuum, 1986), 303, 311. 'Da heißt es denn: "Trachtet allererst nach dem Reiche der reinen praktischen Vernunft und nach seiner *Gerechtigkeit*, so wird euch euer Zweck (die Wohltat des ewigen Friedens) von selbst zufallen..." Wenn es Pflicht, wenn zugleich gegründete Hoffnung da ist, den Zustand eines öffentlichen Rechts, obgleich nur in einer ins Unendliche fortschreitenden Annäherung wirklich zu machen, so ist der *ewige Friede*, der auf die bisher fälschlich sogenannte Friedensschlüsse (eigentlich Waffenstillstände) folgt, keine leere Idee, sondern eine Aufgabe, die, nach und nach aufgelöst, ihrem Ziele (weil die Zeiten, in denen gleiche Fortschritte geschehen, hoffentlich immer kürzer werden) beständig näher kommt.'

[23] The first 'definitive article' reads: 'The bourgeois constitution of any state must be republican' [Die bürgerliche Verfassung in jedem Staate soll republikanisch sein].

[24] For Kant, property (which belongs under the question of the universal law of rational right) is based upon the a priori, or ideal, republican principles of freedom,

law between Kant and Hegel. Very early in his career, in the Jena lectures, Hegel set about addressing its consequences for human social institutions – those 'figures of objective morality', as he called them – with an alarm that is exceeded neither by Friedrich Engels' *The Condition of the Working Class in England* (1845) nor by Karl Marx's 'The Secret of Primitive Accumulation' in his *Capital* (1867–94). The desperation of Hegel's 'philosophy of right' to escape the furies of private property helps to explain why there has rarely been a wittier or more ironic commentary on civil society in modern political-economic terms than Marx's *Critique of Hegel's 'Philosophy of Right'* (1843). It was in socialist thought – transmitted by Romanticism's summation of the great European tradition of the philosophy of nature – that the modern idea of peace between humans and nature reached its maturity as a political theory.

Epilogue: the Theological Heritage in Utopian Socialism – Death or Consummation of the Idea of Peace?

Walter Benjamin's meditation on the concept of history reminds us of the theological element in utopian socialism. He describes there the French philosopher Charles Fourier's social vision in a manner redolent of Isaiah's prophecy:

> According to Fourier, well-planned labor in society would cause four moons to light up the earthly night, the ice to withdraw from the poles, sea water no longer to taste salty, and beasts of prey to enter the service of mankind. All of this is illustrative of the kind of labor that, far from exploiting nature, is able to deliver nature of the creations slumbering in her womb.[25]

In reality, as we are well aware, mankind's problems have grown to nightmarish proportions over the course of the industrial age. Kant's cosmopolitanism, in which peace should be perpetual, was ultimately blind to the dangers posed by the concentrated acquisition of property and the mechanisms of competition.

---

equality, and contract. In his *Metaphysische Anfangsgründe der Rechtslehre: Metaphysik der Sitten* (pt. 1) Kant argues that, in principle, each citizen has property rights to anything that exists in the 'external world', including the correlative rights of exclusion and defense.

[25] Benjamin, *Über den Begriff der Geschichte*, in *Gesammelte Schriften*, ed. Rolf Tiedemann and Hermann Schweppenhauser, I-2: pt. 11, p. 699 (Frankfurt a.M.: Suhrkamp). 'Nach Fourier sollte die wohlbeschaffene gesellschaftliche Arbeit zur Folge haben, daß vier Monde die irdische Nacht erleuchteten, daß das Eis sich von den Polen zurückziehen, daß das Meerwasser nicht mehr salzig schmecke und die Raubtiere in den Dienst des Menschen träten. Das alles illustriert eine Arbeit, die, weit entfernt die Natur auszubeuten, von den Schöpfungen sie zu entbinden imstande ist, die als mögliche in ihrem Schoße schlummern.'

These dangers continue at the end of the twentieth century to threaten peace and prosperity throughout the world. The present trend toward a global society is, of course, irrevocable – and, as Benjamin once said, as long as there is one beggar left, there will still be myth.[26] Peace is imaginable now in fact only in global terms. Yet we remain infinitely distant from this peace. But if the last word falls to despair rather than to the promise of peace, our condemnation will be to live in silence.

The fear that besets us today of losing peace is not so different from what it was at certain times in the past, as this series of images has shown. Let us return now to the age of humanism, the historical center of this book, to examine several key texts and actions, whose influence on the evolution of humanist irenicism in the sixteenth century was no less than profound. We will begin by taking a closer look at the *Querela Pacis* of Erasmus, one of the world's great texts on peace. If it continues to speak to us even at the threshold of the twenty-first century, so much the better.*

---

[26] *Gesammelte Schriften* V, 505.
* Translated by Peter Rosenbaum.

Chapter 2

'Your arts shall be: to impose the ways of peace' – Tolerance, Liberty, and the Nation in the Literature and Deeds of Humanism*

I The Erasmian Legacy of Conciliation

Erasmus's *Querela Pacis* was occasioned by an international peace conference of territorial princes, scheduled to take place at Cambrai in 1517.[1] The invitation came from the Burgundian chancellor Jean Le Sauvage, probably at the behest of the young duke of Burgundy (later, Charles V). Although the Cambrai conference failed to materialize, Erasmus's *Querela Pacis* was written and has endured.[2]

---

* This essay was written for the occasion of the celebration in Münster and Osnabrück of the 350th anniversary of the Peace of Westphalia. It provided the text accompaniment of an art exhibit called *1648 – Krieg und Frieden in Europa* (*1648 – War and Peace in Europe*), mounted in the Westfälisches Landesmuseum für Kunst und Kulturgeschichte in Münster. The scholarship on the theme of this essay is massive and only a core of selected references can be provided in the footnotes that follow. For fuller context and documentation, see Garber, 'Die Friedens-Utopie im europäischen Humanismus: Versuch einer geschichtlichen Rekonstruktion', *Modern Language Notes* 101 (1986): 516–52; also Kurt von Raumer, *Ewiger Friede: Friedensrufe und Friedenspläne seit der Renaissance* (Munich: Francke, 1953), and Siegfried Wollgast (ed.), *Zur Friedensidee in der Reformationszeit: Texte von Erasmus, Paracelsus, Franck* (Berlin: Akademie, 1968).

[1] For a description of events and attitudes leading up to Cambrai and the influence of Erasmian ideas on the organizers, see the afterword by Alois M. Haas and Urs Herzog (eds), *Erasmus von Rotterdam: 'Ein Klag des Frydens': Leo Juds Übersetzung der Querela Pacis von 1521*, 49–80, esp. 52–5 (Zurich: Füssli, 1969). For context and ideas, besides Raumer, *Ewiger Friede*, see Siegfried Wollgast, *Zur Friedensidee*, and esp. Roland Bainton, 'The Querela Pacis of Erasmus: Classical and Christian Sources', *Archiv für Reformationsgeschichte* 42 (1951): 32–48.

[2] Although it appeared in Basel in 1516, its first major printing was by Froben in the following year. In 1518 it was printed in Louvain, Krakow, Leipzig, and Venice; 1519 in Florence and Strasbourg; 1525 in Paris; 1529 in Leiden; thereafter repeatedly until the turn of the seventeenth century. Translations soon followed the original: e.g., German in 1517 and 1521; Spanish in 1529; Dutch in 1567.

Generation after generation has drawn on its arguments against the madness of war. Why has *Querela Pacis* remained relevant all the way down to the present day?

First of all, surely, because of its form and style. Erasmus was not only a scholar, he was also a publicist, concerned with creating an impact and accordingly mindful of which style best suited a given topic. *Querela Pacis* has the form of a speech, and from the very start it is clear that the purpose is more than academic. Erasmus's aim is to convince, to influence, to change the minds of his readers, indeed, to establish human action upon a new basis. This arousing, summoning function of the genre of the speech was exploited from its very beginnings by the Sophists. In *Querela Pacis*, however, it is not Erasmus himself who speaks but a personification, the goddess Peace. Peace, the blossoming Eirene, along with Order (Eunomia) and Justice (Dice), appeared in Hesiod's *Theogony* some seven centuries before Christ. Together, these Horae – suggestive of the seasons, the ever-repeating sequence of nature, of order and regularity – tended the works of mortal men. In subsequent visions of peace, the natural and human worlds are parallel entities. Peace can only be comprehensive. With his words in the mouth of Peace, Erasmus's authority increases in reliability, dignity, and certainty. But why is Peace's speech a lamentation? Quite simply, because the vision of eternal blessedness cannot be separated from the horror evoked by the atrocities of war. Always a realist, Erasmus refused to avert his gaze from what was taking place in the heart of Europe, in the midst of a world that called itself Christian.

Erasmus the ironist, master of the subtly changing tone, eschews in general the playful and learned conventions of humanist wit. Combining piercing simplicity with deep knowledge, profound sorrow with unflagging hope, the voice has a divine quality, yet is entirely human, in unmistakable imitation of the One it cites repeatedly, Christ. The ancient goddess of Peace and the Christian Shepherd of Peace join in harmonious collaboration. Can this not be one of the secrets to the power and longevity of the *Querela Pacis*?

Querela Pacis was written in the midst of enormous political and intellectual developments that involved the entire Holy Roman Empire. The second half of the Quattrocento had seen the formation of the five leading powers in Italy – Venice, Milan, Florence, Rome, and Naples – all of which were enjoying a quiet interlude in the wake of the Peace of Lodi (1454).[3] It was the time when Florentine culture reached its maturity under the Médici; when Ficino and the Florentine academy undertook their great renewal of Platonic thought, fusing Greek, Byzantine, Arabic, and Christian elements into a great synthesis of the modern mind; the time of the first great printers, such as Manutius of Venice;

---

[3] Denys Hay, *The Italian Renaissance in its Historical Background* (Cambridge: Cambridge University Press, 1962); and Werner Goez, *Grundzüge der Geschichte Italiens in Mittelalter und Renaissance* (Darmstadt: Wissenschaftliche Buchgesellschaft, 1975).

when intellectual societies sprouted from the ground like mushrooms, providing a forum for the new learning; when cities and principalities discovered how to adapt the new learning to representative and profitable ends. This relative peace ended abruptly with France's assertion of old Anjou claims in the south of Italy.[4] One of the consequences of Charles VIII's invasion (1494) was the temporary banishment from Florence of the Médici, a family that, like the Neapolitan house of Aragon, was a distinguished patron of the new arts. But would France's competitors be content to sit back and watch Charles gain power? Within a year the 'Holy League' under the leadership of Spain had forced Charles to retreat. Now, interrupted by phases of 'holy alliances', a tug-of-war ensued for influence on the Apennine Peninsula, cradle of the Renaissance and humanism. Spain and the Holy Roman Empire of the German Nation (joined in personal union under Charles V in 1519) and the pope were steady contenders; the once proud Italian republics and principalities raced from one coalition to the next, more the sport than the sportsmen in an uncertain game. It was the heyday of Fortuna. In 1516, after Francis I of France and Charles V had divided between themselves Italy's spheres of influence into north and south, hopes of peace were temporarily aroused. But they were just as quick to evaporate when, in 1527, Rome was overrun (*sacco di Roma*) by rabid German mercenaries under Georg von Frundsberg. Churches, art treasures, libraries – much of Rome's cultural fluorescence perished in this violent iconoclasm. Another thirty years would elapse before the bloody struggle between Spain and France was finally ended by the Peace of Cateau-Cambrésis (1559). Erasmus was long dead. But he and the others of his generation had experienced the beginnings of the religious schism on German soil, which would soon grow into the Schmalkaldic War, just as they had witnessed the awakening of national expansionist politics. These developments would continue to dominate the Continent, finally reducing it to a heap of ruins in two world wars of the twentieth century.

Such was the background to *Querela Pacis*. Erasmus was very much aware of having two simultaneous tasks: integrating the themes of classical philosophy into the Christian conception of the world, and determining the essentials of God's Word to which all Christians were bound and could agree. *Querela Pacis* responds to these tasks by weaving diverse and often contradictory elements of the intellectual tradition into a single dense fabric.[5] He first scrutinizes the

---

[4] These well-known events provided the background for profound observations by Ludwig Dehio, *Gleichgewicht oder Hegemonie: Betrachtungen über ein Grundproblem der neueren Staatengeschichte* (Krefeld: Scherpe, 1948), on the affinities between history and the present, in this case the German disaster of WWII, as part of a general discussion of hegemonic European politics. Winfried Schulze, *Deutsche Geschichtswissenschaft nach 1945* (Munich: Oldenbourg, 1989), returns to this problem in light of previously unpublished reflections by Delhio.

[5] Details in Jean Claude Margolin (ed.), *Guerre et paix dans la pensée d'Erasme* (Paris: Aubier-Montaigne, 1973).

arguments for peace from nature, already largely formulated in classical philosophy and revived in the Renaissance; he then consults Christ, the person as well as the doctrine; in conclusion, he finds that all of these testimonies speak in favor of peace, and all, he avows, are open and understandable to people of all races and creeds.

The first argument of *Querela Pacis* is based on the sublime Renaissance doctrine of harmony, which holds that order and regularity prevail in both the macrocosm and the microcosm:

> Even between the many celestial bodies, different as they are in motion and power, throughout so many centuries treaties have been established and maintained. The conflicting forces of the elements are evenly balanced so as to preserve unbroken peace, and despite their fundamental opposition they maintain concord by mutual consent and communication.[6]

Whether in the largest or smallest of systems, nature confirms the basic law of all being, which is to unite divergence and opposition with harmony and equilibrium in a third, higher dimension, peace. Thus nature is man's instructor; man must only rise to the intuition of nature in order to discover there the *elementaria* of nature itself. Having gathered repeated examples of this truth, Erasmus concludes, 'So Nature provided all these arguments for peace and concord, so many lures and inducements to draw us towards peace, so many means of coercion' (296).

Erasmus does nothing to augment the revelation in the words of Christ; they speak for themselves, requiring no assistance, and are verified by the deeds of the One who proclaimed them. That is important. For while Erasmus does not state it in so many words, his implication is that Christ's voice is one of many that impart religion to the human race, all of which converge on a common point, love and conciliation – an idea later advanced in the Enlightenment. What matters in the end is not doctrine but behavior, which alone is the test of true, life-transforming faith. If the gospel message delivered by Peace is valid for all people, how much more then must it apply specifically to those who call themselves Christians? Dogmatic and confessional differences, while perhaps meaningful in some narrower sense, are never justifiable grounds for Christian people to violate peace, to hate and persecute one another, to refuse to be reconciled. Erasmus stresses only the most fundamental Christian principle of peace, which is unequivocally that war, terror, and persecution may not be carried out for any reason. Christ's teaching in its few essentials is unambiguous, clear,

---

[6] *A Complaint of Peace*, trans. Betty Radice, in *Collected Works of Erasmus* (Toronto: University of Toronto Press, 1986), 5:294, *QP* IV-2: 'Jam tot orbium coelestium, licet nec motus sit idem, nec vis eadem, tamen iis tot jam seculis constant vigentque foedera. Elementorum pugnantes inter se vires, aequabili libramine pacem aeternam tuentur, et in tanta discordia, consensu commercioque mutuo concordiam alunt.'

and binding in its insistence on peace. The supreme good of Christian doctrine is summed up in the triad of love – harmony – peace.

Many ornament themselves with Christ's name. But their actions belie their words. Let us listen again to the voice of Peace as she searches, desperately, for evidence of her blessings among the community of man:

> When I hear the word 'man' I run to him at once, as if to an animal specially created for me, confident that with him I shall be permitted to rest; when I hear the name 'Christian' I hurry all the faster, full of hope that I shall certainly come into my kingdom. But here too, I am ashamed and reluctant to say, assemblies, lawcourts, secretariats, and churches everywhere resound with strife, more so than among the heathen.[7]

The spiritual behavior of non-believers is no worse than that of Christians. Indeed, the heathen often put Christians to shame. Although their religions are less demanding, still they exercise greater authority over their believers. What right then do Christians have to set out on crusades, missionary journeys, or expeditions of spiritual conquest and subjugation, as long as the state of things at home remains as it is? Everywhere is discord, despite the fact that our leaders and princes are enjoined, in emulation of the foremost 'Teacher and Prince of concord' (297), Jesus Christ, to be the 'mind of their subjects and eye of their people' (296). Everywhere are rancorous disputes among the leading philosophers and theologians, priests and bishops, religious orders and communities, monasteries and cloisters, husbands and wives, yes, even within the very soul of the individual. Wherever Peace looks she discovers behavior unworthy of the title 'Christian', an entirely unacceptable condition, given that the life of Christ was nothing less than 'a lesson in concord and mutual love'. Christ was and is 'the Prince of peace, he loves peace and is offended by discord' (299).

But is it not true that in the Old Testament God is called the 'Lord of hosts and of vengeance'? Peace replies, first, that differences obtain between the images of God in the Old and the New Testaments. What is more to the point is that we seek the hidden meaning of God's Word, as did the early church fathers. For Christians are called above all to take up the fight against vice and sin and to [remove] 'these passions completely from [their] hearts' (302). Furthermore, the Old and New Testaments agree overwhelmingly that the message of consummate happiness is peace:

---

[7] *Complaint* 296 (ibid.). 'Cum hominis vocabulum audio, mox accurro velut ad animal mihi proprie natum, confidens fore ut illic liceat acquiescere: cum Christianorum audio titulum, magis etiam advolo, apud hos certe regnaturam etiam me sperans. Sed hic quoque pudet ac piget dicere: Fora, basilicae, curiae, templa sic undique litibus perstrepunt, ut nusquam apud Ethnicos aeque.'

> Whenever the Old Testament indicates perfect happiness it does so with reference to peace. Isaiah, for example, says that 'my people shall sit in the beauty of peace,' and another prophet says, 'Peace be over Israel'. Again, Isaiah marvels at the beauty of the feet of those who bring tidings of peace and prosperity. Whoever brings tidings of Christ brings tidings of peace. Whoever preaches war preaches one who is the very opposite of Christ . . . And it was because the name of Solomon means 'peace-making' or 'man of peace' that he was chosen to prefigure him; for though David was a great king, since he was a warrior and defiled with blood he was not permitted to build the house of the Lord – in this respect he was unworthy to prefigure a peace-making Christ.[8]

In good humanist fashion this return to the biblical sources discloses a truth that is as simple as it is radical, specific yet all-encompassing, appealing equally to reason and emotions. Ultimately, the true gospel belongs not to any one religion; rather, *humanitas* addresses all people of all faiths. Humanity calls for complete commitment and is an unerring test of true faith. Measured against the core values of Christianity as expressed in the Sermon on the Mount, the Christian lands of Europe fall far short and are accordingly obliged to listen to the bitterest of truths from the mouthpiece of the prince of humanists.

The Spanish and Italian translations of *Querela Pacis* were immediately placed on the Index. Thus, ironically, the church evinced the work the honor it deserves yet today for its unsparing exposure of the foul hypocrisy between word and deed, pretense and reality, in the lives of people and in the policies of their churches and governments. Bad, abstract, hopelessly overdrawn moralism? Farfetched utopia? Over the centuries *Querela Pacis* has been accused of all of this. Nothing could be further from the truth. *Querela Pacis* consistently articulates something new and unspoiled that exists at the border between the old age and the new, courageously declaring war on fraudulent authorities and institutions, boldly clearing the way for a purer life.

II   Peace and the Nation: The Experiment of Cola di Rienzi

Querela Pacis looked back over an eminent tradition that embraced Hesiod and Isaiah; Vergil's Emperor of Peace, Augustus; and Augustine's Empire of Peace,

---

[8] *Complaint* 300 (ibid.). 'quoties absolutam felicitatem significant arcanae litterae, pacis nomine id declarant. Velut Esaias: Sedebit, inquit, populus meus in pulcritudine pacis. Et alius: Pax, inquit, super Israel. Rursum, Esaias admiratur pedes annunciantium pacem, annunciantium bona. Quisquis Christum annunciat, pacem annunciat . . . Atque ob id Solomonem sui typum ferre voluit, qui nobis εἰρηνοποιός, id est, pacificus, dicitur. Quantumvis magnus erat David, tamen, quia bellator erat, quia sanguine fuerat inquinatus, non sinitur exstruere domum Domini, non meretur hac parte gerere typum Christi pacifici.'

the City of God.[9] The modern history of peace may be said to have begun at the juncture at which the two medieval powers, both of which promised universal peace, had exhausted themselves in battle with each other. In theory, pope and emperor were to cooperate, the one taking responsibility for the spiritual life of humans before God, the other for their welfare on earth.[10] The political history of the Middle Ages is the history of the struggle for supremacy between these two powers. The competition between Frederick II and Gregory IX marks the notorious moment of high crisis: to Frederick, Gregory was the 'monster of calumny'; Gregory in turn demonized Frederick as the Antichrist, provoking Frederick's invasion of the papal states. A half-century later the monarchy brought the pope under its sway and exiled him to Avignon; yet another good half-century and two men, one in Rome and one in Avignon, claimed the papal keys. Just as there had been emperor and counter-emperor, now there were both pope and counter-pope, and the dignity of both powers all but evaporated. The apostles of poverty, the Franciscans, Joachimites, Lullians, Hussites, and the Bohemian Brothers, among others, were symptomatic of the spiritual reaction to the secularized papacy and a church wallowing in corruption and power-mongering. In the mundane realm, however, the national state began to arise, at first theoretically, in Italy, then constitutionally, in France.

In the opening chapter we considered Dante's response to this crisis. His invention of a political utopian figure, the world emperor, would guarantee peace in the empire and the right of every individual to self-fulfillment. Dante was no mere dreamer. Notwithstanding his utopian tendency, he aimed at the kind of political power that could put a government of peace into practice for the benefit of all people. The German emperor no longer provided this hope. Nor did the pope, whose calling remained strictly and indubitably limited to the administration of the means of grace. It was rather in the past, in Octavian Augustus, whom Vergil had charged with the noblest of duties in his national epic, where Dante recognized a political model capable of guaranteeing universal freedom. Dante did not shy away from reminding his contemporaries of their national duty:

---

[9] The literature on the history of the idea of peace is too vast to survey here. Of particular relevance for the present discussion, however, is Gerhard Binder and Bernd Effe (eds), *Krieg und Frieden im Altertum* (Trier: Wissenschaftlicher Verlag, 1989); Jürgen Ebach, 'Ende des Feindes oder Ende der Feindschaft? Der Tierfrieden bei Jesaja und Vergil', in *Ursprung und Ziel: Erinnerte Zukunft und erhoffte Vergangenheit*, ed. Ebach, 75–89 (Neukirch-Vluyn: Neukirchener Verlag, 1986); and Walter Homolka and Albert H. Friedlander, *The Gate to Perfection: The Idea of Peace in Jewish Thought*, trans. of *Von der Sintflut ins Paradies: Der Frieden als Schlüsselbegriff jüdischer Theologie* (Providence: Berghahn Books, 1994).

[10] This understanding of the relationship between spiritual and worldly authority was expressed in a succinct and exalted formula, springing from the purest spirit of the Middle Ages, by Charlemagne, *Epistola VIII ad Leonem III Papam*, in *PL* 98:908. For quote, see Chapter 1 above, sect. 'Augustine: civitas terrena, civitas coelestis'.

> Roman, remember to rule over nations.
> Your arts shall be: to impose the ways of peace,
> Spare subject peoples, and subdue the proud.[11]

Dante deduces that it is the destiny of Roman politics to establish laws as the means to promoting the common weal:

> That the Roman people in conquering the world did have the good of which we have spoken as their goal is shown by their deeds, for, having repressed all greed (which is always harmful to the community) and cherishing universal peace and freedom, that holy, dutiful and glorious people can be seen to have disregarded personal advantage in order to promote the public interest for the benefit of mankind.[12]

It was by virtue of their devotion to law, therefore, that the old Romans' expansionist politics was justified. Now that the Holy Roman Empire (of the German Nation) has forfeited this noble title, it is up to the Italian nation to revive the work and complete it. Dante's fervent desire is to see restored what had formerly existed, the mission of his people fulfilled. As a citizen of the leading polis of his time, in which, in spite of everything, the spirit of antiquity was at least still alive, Dante recasts the republican morality of Florence into the utopian idea of rebirth of the Roman Empire as guarantor of the longed-for world peace.[13] It is in this sense that Dante stands at the beginning of modern national thinking.

Such an enthusiastic goal existed in reality in Italy. We may regard one dramatic episode in particular – it belongs to humanistic irenicism in its early phase – as a practical demonstration of Dante's theory. The day after Ash Wednesday 1347, the Roman notary Cola di Rienzi – the hero of Wagner's opera (1842) – announced, in a notice affixed to the church door of St Giorgio, an impending revolt. 'In a short time,' it read, 'Romans will return to their good old constitution (*buono stato*).' On the Friday before the following Pentecost one hundred citizens met in the Church of St Sabina on the Aventine to discuss the final details of the uprising.[14] It was to take place under the protection of the Holy

---

[11] *Aen.* 6.851–3; quoted in *De Mon.* 2.6; Shaw, *Monarchy* 47.

[12] *De Mon.* 2.5; Shaw 40. 'Quod autem romanus populus bonum prefatum intenderit subiciendo sibi orbem terrarum, gesta sua declarant, in quibus, omni cupiditate summota que rei publice semper adversa est, et universali pace cum libertate dilecta, populus ille sanctus pius et gloriosus propria commoda neglexisse videtur, ut publica pro salute humani generis procuraret.'

[13] Horst Heintze, *Dante Alighieri: Bürger und Dichter*, 2nd edition (Berlin, 1981).

[14] Paul Piur, *Cola di Rienzo: Darstellung seines Lebens und seines Geistes* (Vienna: Seidel, 1931), 43, describes the event as follows: 'On Whitsun Saturday the conspirators gathered at the Capitol Square. Supported by a hundred armed men, whom Rienzi had recruited with his own money – 150 gold florins – they drove out the Senate guards, the scribes, and various other officials, and with trumpets blasting invited the people, who were gathered there for the market, to meet the following day, Whitsun

Spirit, with Rienzi himself acting as the 'Knight of the Holy Spirit'. Preceded by a banner of freedom depicting Roma on the Lion's Throne with orb and palm and bearing the words in golden letters *Roma caput mundi*, the insurrectionists moved toward the capitol that Whitsun morning. A second banner depicted the Apostle Paul, a sword in one hand, the 'Wreath of Justice' in the other; a third the Apostle Peter with the 'Keys of Harmony and Peace'. Onlookers may have assumed that this was a religious procession, when in fact it had to do with hard political issues, though intertwined to be sure with apostolic, early-church associations, which accounted for the religious aura.

A total revolution, one that affected all areas of life, was intended. The apostle princes Peter and Paul, together with the Holy Spirit, served as the patrons of the new constitution. As the silver laurel wreath was being placed on his sovereign head, Rienzi held the palm and the orb in his hands. In a speech at the capitol Rienzi excoriated the intrigues of the barons for having made a robbers' den of the Holy City, and encouraged the citizens to vote on the constitution. Invoking an ancient Roman tradition, as the democratically elected sovereign, Rienzi was crowned as 'Nicolaus the Puissant and Merciful, Tribune of Freedom, Peace, and Justice, Liberator of the Holy Roman Empire'.

The task before him now was to marshal the whole nation behind the unification effort. As Rienzi saw it, with the failure of the German emperors, sovereign authority had devolved again upon the Roman people. All Italian towns were declared free, all Italians Roman citizens. Necessary now was the definitive constitutional dissolution from the Holy Roman Empire of the German Nation, followed by independence for a single Italian nation. It was decreed that no foreign emperor, king, or prince should henceforth set foot on Italian soil with an armed force, except with the agreement of the Roman people. At the top of the empire an Italian was to be placed who believed in Italy's sovereign destiny. Much of this lofty goal was met within six months.[15] Two years later, however, the pope, in league with the powerful noble families, was able to drive out the usurper.

Failure though it was, what is of interest to us here are the intellectual and historical reasons behind the attempt at liberation, traditionally ridiculed as delirium pure and simple. They have been eloquently explained elsewhere by

---

Sunday, unarmed, at the sound of the capitol bell, for a ceremonial "Parliament", in order to pass a resolution on the new constitution.'

[15] Rienzi boasted, in a later letter to Pope Clement VI that, 'in a few months, the whole Roman province had been subdued and occupied, thereby accomplishing a feat that had eluded the emperors and popes over many years and with enormous sums of money. In September of 1347, the dominion of the city of Rome stretched over an area that almost completely realized centuries of dreams of political power and in some areas to the north, east, and south even exceeded them. The new dating: "in the first year of the liberated Roman Republic", which the Tribune used after 1 July in posting his public and private writings throughout the empire – much to the delight of Petrarch – was hardly unjustified' (Piur, *Cola di Rienzo* 65–6).

Konrad Burdach.[16] The decisive point is that the contractual peace between empire and papacy was transferred to the nation-state, very much as Dante had conceived it. The extraordinary longevity within humanist thought of the interdependent concepts of nation and peace cannot be explained outside of this framework of ideas and events. Transfigured through the image and memory of ancient Rome, a new political dream of unification, cooperation, and the guarantee of shared ideals among all peoples in one nation of citizens was first articulated here. This is the national hope that the humanists held out for the city-states in memory of the ancient Roman Republic and Athenian democracy. The humanists held that *virtus* has the power to bring citizens together in pursuit of a common political goal, resulting in freedom for the republic, self-determination in foreign as well as domestic affairs, renunciation of tyrants and other strongmen, and the determination of city affairs by an autonomous citizenry. The renowned Florentine chancellors, from Salutati to Poggio and Bruni to Machiavelli, agreed in principle, thus affirming what dynamic power they perceived in the images of the ancient polis and the empire, whose powers were being reawakened now in the dawn of early modern Italy.[17] Hans Baron observed that this 'civic humanism' constituted the securest defense against tyranny and was most likely to guarantee peace among the republican city-states.[18]

In a letter to the Roman nation in the fall of 1352, Rienzi claims credit for having

> resurrected for the whole world a matter of great importance, which had been in a dormant stupor, yes, even buried, for many centuries, and which alone paved the way for the reformation of the state and the advent of the golden age. 'Remember in what condition you found your country,' Petrarch admonished [the Italians], 'and how quickly not only Rome but all of Italy was elevated in hope through the plans and deeds of this one man; how great the name of Italy suddenly became; how the glory of

---

[16] Burdach, *Rienzo und die geistige Wandlung seiner Zeit*, vol. 2 of *Vom Mittelalter zur Reformation: Forschung zur Geschichte der deutschen Bildung* (Berlin: Weidmann, 1928). Burdach's influence was unfortunately diminished as a result of the severe criticism of a number of historians, among them Paul Joachimsen, Karl Brandi, and Gerhard Ritter, who had little understanding for his interdisciplinary view of cultural history, involving both iconography and the history of ideas. A major reassessment of Burdach in our day is needed. Initially, see my article in *Literaturlexikon: Autoren und Werke deutscher Sprache*, ed. Walther Killy, 2:325–6 (Gütersloh: Bertelsmann Lexikon, 1989).

[17] Herfried Münkler, *Machiavelli: Die Begründung des politischen Denkens der Neuzeit aus der Krise der Republik Florenz* (Frankfurt a.M.: Europäische Verlagsanstalt, 1984).

[18] Baron, *The Crisis of the Early Italian Renaissance: Civic Humanism and Republican Liberty in an Age of Classicism and Tyranny* (1955; revised edn, Princeton: Princeton University Press, 1966).

> Rome was renewed and made to shine again; how great terror and pain befell our enemies; how our friends were inspired by joy and nations by hope; how the very essence of everything changed; how the face of the earth and the minds of men were altered; how nothing that existed under heaven remained the same!'[19]

This is the same spirit that informs the patriotic Roman letters and poems of Petrarch, the first great humanist, in which he re-enlivened the Horatian political ode and bequeathed it to the European humanists. Within their circles the suffering image of widowed Roma was formed, mourning the loss of pope and emperor, lamenting the devastated city, imploring an end to the self-mutilation, praying that Rome become again what it had been in antiquity: *caput mundi*.[20]

Amid such hopes, the nation entered the political and intellectual history of modern Europe. Its task was to end the antagonism between the secular and spiritual powers, not only between pope and emperor, but also between republics and principalities, rivaling families, nobility and middle class, rich and poor. With respect to establishing national bonds between people of differing classes, the nation was the first and the most effective authority of post-medieval Europe, and has largely remained so down to the present day. This idea has been so completely discredited in the twentieth century, however, that it can never again be restored to its absolute status. But in the social history of European humanism it was viewed, as late as the eighteenth century, as the decisive agent of peace. Its success prior to the atrocities in the twentieth century suggests that a political bond between people in the form of concrete moral values must be fostered if a dangerous vacuum is not to form, in which irrational and inhuman violence can suddenly occur.

In this sense, the decision to look back to humanism's aspirations for peace under the aegis of the nation is in itself an anticipatory act: its aim is to discover standards by which to recognize and correct the deviant paths taken by modernity since the civil revolutions at the end of the eighteenth century.

III Humanism in the Religious Wars

A common misconception is that humanism reached its zenith with Erasmus and began to decline even during his lifetime. According to this view, the reformers captured the hearts and minds of contemporaries and thereby assumed the moral leadership from humanism, which had allegedly become rigid, indulging in the

---

[19] Burdach, *Rienzo und die geistige Wandlung*.
[20] See Burdach's chapters on Rome as Holy Bride (chapter 2, esp. pp. 34–41, 46–51) and on Rome's two *sponsi* as carriers of the universal principate (61–94), in *Rienzo und die geistige Wandlung*.

very scholasticism it once opposed, and blind to current reality. This view is inconsistent with the facts. Our return to humanist origins is thus also justified in that only in this way can we hope to clarify how initial impulses survived, were adopted, and productively adjusted to the circumstances of the times.

To risk a paradox, it may be said that humanism was not put to the decisive historical test until the occurrence of that earth-shattering event, the Reformation. This is true in several respects. For example, the precepts of humanism, formed upon a classical basis, had to stand the serious scrutiny of a radicalized spirituality. The extreme religious and ideological views that arose with the Reformation constituted another test of the mediating capacity of humanist thought. Above all, however, humanism had to demonstrate that it could produce workable answers to the deadly confessional-political crises of the second half of the sixteenth century, which threatened general disaster.[21]

One country after the other was ignited by the torch of religious fanaticism, which had been meant to bring illumination but nearly always ended in the embers of the auto-da-fé, the bloodbaths of radicals egged on by ecclesiastical or political authorities whose goals were incongruent with the genuine cause of faith. Even Italy's radical Franciscan Spiritualists suffered persecution and excommunication by the papal church. The first conflagration to engulf an entire country broke out in Bohemia, sparked by flames from John Wyclif's England, at the newly founded University of Prague, where Jan Huss and his followers preached strict adherence to the pure Word of God, unadulterated by tradition and dogma:

---

[21] Early modern cultural historians must at last produce a complete discussion of the shared history, which lasted for more than a century, of humanism and confessionalism. For points of orientation on the concept of confessionalization, see esp. Heinz Schilling (ed.), *Die reformierte Konfessionalisierung in Deutschland: Das Problem der 'Zweiten Reformation'* (Gütersloh: Mohn, 1986); R. Po-chia Hsia, *Social Discipline in the Reformation: Central Europe 1550–1750* (London: Routledge, 1989); and Georg Schmidt, 'Konfessionalisierung, Reich und deutsche Nation', in *Die Territorien des Reichs im Zeitalter der Reformation und Konfessionalisierung: Land und Konfession 1500–1650*, ed. Anton Schindling and Walter Ziegler, 7:171–200 (Münster: Aschendorff, 1997). The most fruitful attempt at a European synthesis remains Friedrich Heer, whose *Die dritte Kraft: der europäische Humanismus zwischen den Fronten des konfessionellen Zeitalters* (Frankfurt a.M.: Fischer, 1959), though now more than forty years old, has yet to be fully appreciated. Joseph Lecler, *Toleration and the Reformation*, 2 vols, trans. T.L. Westow (New York: Association Press; London: Longmans, 1960), is a key documentary source. In addition to the classic study by Stupperich 1936, see Hans-Joachim Diesner, *Stimmen zu Krieg und Frieden im Renaissance-Humanismus* (Göttingen: Vandenhoeck & Ruprecht, 1990). For insight into the current state of discussion, see Ingo Broer and Richard Schlüter (eds), *Christentum und Toleranz* (Darmstadt: Wissenschaftliche Buchgesellschaft, 1996), which also contains a comprehensive bibliography.

> Devout Christian, seek the truth, hear the truth, learn the truth, love the truth, speak the truth, hold the truth fast, defend the truth unto death, for the truth delivers you from sin, from the devil, from the death of the soul, and finally from eternal death, that eternal absence from God's grace and all happiness.[22]

Possessed of this conviction, Huss mounted to the stake in 1415, having been condemned by the Council of Constance. His death galvanized the Hussites into a cohesive group, though even they soon enough split into moderates and radicals; the latter, the Taborites, dared violence and open conflict even with state authority. The struggles lasted for decades and reached far beyond Bohemia.

Thus Europe witnessed the risks that accompanied the new expressions of faith. And thus Erasmus instinctively hesitated to side with Luther and sought rather to employ all means at his disposal to help heal the religious schism. Unlike Erasmus, Luther was unconcerned about political consequences, aspiring solely towards a pure articulation of the experience of faith. Only the political and social exploitation of Luther's ideas during the Peasants' War (1524–5) forced him to seek princely protection for his teachings. This move, intentionally or not, turned Luther's work into a political affair.

The first major military conflict over faith, if we disregard for the moment its related political causes, was the Schmalkaldic War (1546), less than thirty years after Luther posted his theses. No sooner had this conflict found formal resolution in the Religious Peace of Augsburg (1555) than the struggle erupted again in German lands, now between Lutherans, Zwinglians, and Calvinists, and soon surpassed in violence and bitterness the earlier one between Protestants and Catholics. The new Calvinist faith worked its way westward from its birthplace in Geneva to France, the Netherlands, and England. In France the consequences of the politicized religious struggles were played out with particular cruelty, reaching a dreadful climax on the Eve of St Bartholomew's Day in 1572 with the massacre, at the command of Catherine de'Médici and reluctant approval of Charles IX, of many thousands of Huguenots, and giving new life to the Wars of Religion (1562–98). In the neighboring Netherlands Philip II sought, with the aid of his brutal governor Alba, to stamp out the sparks of the new faith. For thirteen years the struggle raged between the unequal opponents; still the Spanish failed to subdue the rebels. A partition was agreed upon in 1579 with the Union of Utrecht: the seven northern provinces would maintain their Calvinist belief, while the south, today's Belgium, would remain Catholic. Thus allies for the new confession emerged in the west, a circumstance of particular interest to the Reformed principalities of Germany. On both sides, fronts continued to proliferate until the Defenestration of Prague (1618) triggered the savagery of the Thirty Years' War. In England a moderate national church appeared to embody

---

[22] Huss, *Schriften zur Glaubensreform und Briefe der Jahre 1414–1415*, ed. Walter Schamschula (Frankfurt a.M.: Insel, 1969), 95–6.

the spirit of toleration and compromise. But appearances were deceptive. The Anglican Church too turned increasingly radical. When the Puritan parliament forced Charles I to the scaffold in 1649, an earthquake shook Europe.

The early modern history of the European civil and religious wars briefly summarized here comprises the background for the political engagement of the humanist search for a path to peace. Only a few names can be mentioned for this period stretching from the final expulsion of the Jews and Moors from Spain to the English 'Bill of Rights'; from Luther's first public appearance to Gottfried Arnold's compendious monument to the victims of ecclesiastical injustice.[23]

Humanists across Europe perceived Spain to be the main force in the Catholics' struggle to regain church unity, and indeed the political fortunes of Spain were inextricably tied to the religious goal of ensuring purity of the faith, both at home, in the empire, and in the Netherlandish provinces. For centuries large areas of the Iberian Peninsula populated by Arabs had been a refuge for non-Christians, including Jews. This tradition of tolerance ended, however, in the wake of the *Reconquista*, which drove the Arabs back to their last stronghold in Granada. The years 1478–80 saw the introduction of the Inquisition in Castile, 1487 its expansion to include Aragon; in 1492 Isabella of Castile and Ferdinand of Aragon made their entry into Granada, and the *Reconquista* was complete. The ambition to reach out to Africa followed on its heels. Supported by the Inquisition, the crown began to force Jews and Muslims to adopt the Christian faith or be expelled. Under these conditions over half a million Jews and Moors left or were driven from the country. Such violent uniformity heralded the precedence of the state's interests over the heterogeneous religions of its mixed population, formerly a badge of honor for Spain. Aside from the Prague prelude, state's interest in Europe had never showed its face so crassly; Spain became the feared vicar of religious suppression. Because the conversion of these thousands of Jews and Muslims was mere pretense, the Inquisition was suddenly confronted with the phenomenon of heresy, particularly in the guise of Crypto-Judaism.

In the name and spirit of Erasmus, Spanish protesters of these abuses soon incurred the mistrust of church and state. The University of Alcalá, founded in 1498 by Cardinal Cisneros, became one of the strongholds of Erasmianism in Spain.[24] The other existed for a time at the court of Charles V, where professorial

---

[23] Fall of Granada and expulsion of Moors and Jews, 1492; English Bill of Rights, 1689; Luther's first major public appearance, 1517; Arnold's *Unpartheyische Kirchen- und Ketzer-Historie*, 1699–1700.

[24] On Erasmianism in golden age Spain, see esp. Marcel Bataillon, *Erasme et l'Espagne* (1937), 3 vols, ed. Charles Amiel (Geneva: Droz, 1991), and Ángel Valbuena Prat, *Historia de la Literatura Española*, 1:418–41 (Barcelona: Gustavo Gili, 1968); more generally, Americo Castro, *Spanien: Vision und Wirklichkeit* (Cologne, 1957); Wolfgang Otto, *Conquista, Kultur und Ketzerwahn: Spanien im Jahrhundert seiner Weltherrschaft* (Göttingen: Vandenhoeck & Ruprecht, 1992); of the wealth of literature on Vives, esp. Christoph Strosetzki (ed.), *Juan Luis Vives: sein Werk und seine Bedeutung für Spanien und Deutschland* (Frankfurt a.M.: Vervuert, 1995).

chairs for Greek, Hebrew, Arabic, and Syrian were established, thus facilitating biblical studies in the original languages and leading to a polyglot edition of the Bible in 1517. In Alcalá the printer Miguel de Eguia, a dedicated 'apóstol del iluminismo erasmista',[25] was active in publishing Erasmus's religious writings; Alfonso and Juan de Valdés, Francisco de Bergara, Fra Alonso de Virues and, most notably, Juan Luis Vives stepped forward as advocates of Erasmian toleration, the simple Christian life of faith, the dignity of marriage and women, and, above all, peace. The *Diálogo de doctrina cristiana* of Juan de Valdés appeared in 1529, repeating Erasmus's message of charity and devotion in the dialogue form of which he was so fond. Juan's brother Alfonso, secretary to Charles V, and himself a devoted Erasmian, interpreted the *sacco di Roma* as God's punishment of the secularized city. What is the cruelty of the imperial soldiers, he asks, ironically,

> compared with the scandals of the whoring cardinals and all the other horrors of the curia? Is it so terrible that Rome was plundered and the relics carried off, when most of them exist in the world many times over? I myself have seen the Christ child's foreskin in Rome, Burgos, and Antwerp; in France alone there are more than five hundred teeth from his mouth; the milk of the Mother of God is preserved in many places. The same is true of the feathers of the Holy Spirit.[26]

His *Diálogo de Mercurio y Carón*, published about the same time, revolves around the two elliptical foci of world peace and imperial politics, the latter as the executor of the former. Having related some of his many adventures among the Christians, Mercury asks them during the trip across Styx, 'Are you not ashamed to call yourselves Christians, you who live worse than Arabs and wild animals?'[27] – an Erasmian thought transposed into the Spanish milieu. Is it any wonder that Alfonso de Valdés was on friendly terms with Melanchthon? With the deaths of Chancellor Gattinara and Valdés, the auspicious Erasmian blossom, nourished by the hope that the emperor would establish peace, soon withered.

Spain's competing power, France, less fixed on imperial aspirations, took a wholly different path. French humanists generally pursued goals that benefited the state, widening instead of narrowing its scope of action, and paving thereby the road into the modern age. Early modern France's rise owed in no small part to the contributions of the great parlementary jurists of the sixteenth century, all of whom were touched by the spirit of humanism and helped to effect a certain

---

[25] Prat, *Historia* 429.
[26] In his *Diálogo de las cosas ocurridas en Roma*; quoted in Heer, *Die dritte Kraft* 326.
[27] Quoted in Heer, *Die dritte Kraft* 328.

check on state's sovereignty that was missing in Spain.[28] Michel de L'Hôpital was chancellor, Jacques Auguste de Thou the nation's leading historian; the president of the Parlement, Philippe Duplessis-Morney, was a publicist.[29] Although they came from differing social and intellectual backgrounds, they shared the unifying experience of civil war in their country.

France had its own renowned Erasmians, starting with the noted jurist Guillaume Budé. Bishop Guillaume Briçonnet founded the 'School of Meaux', together with Lefèvre d'Estaples and Gérard Roussel, later to be joined by such worthies as the king's own sister, Margarete of Navarre, the Bishop of Bayonne, and Jean du Bellay and his brother Guillaume.[30] All favored reform, as long as it did not divide the One Church. In the surviving work of Guillaume Postel, as in the earlier work of Nicholas of Cusa, confessional synthesis was proposed.[31] And yet, despite their best efforts to reconcile the Catholics and the Huguenots, the irenicists ultimately failed. Fanatical hatred prevailed at even the highest, monarchial level.

The conclusion drawn by the group of moderate jurists, the *politiques* – Jean Bodin's *Six livres de la République* (1576) is its finest expression – was unequivocal, bearing the clarity and stringency of French thought: If the religious parties themselves are incapable of producing solutions on behalf of peaceful coexistence, then it is the duty of the state to impose such measures. To undertake mediation of this kind, the state must avoid siding with any one group and maintain neutrality in religious matters. Commissioned with the task of pacification, enforceable by its monopoly on power, the state guarantees the right of all religious and philosophical communities to pursue individual interests, as long as they refrain from violence and do not prevent others from exercising the same right. In other words, the state privatizes the convictions of its citizens, withdraws from its former role as agent of a given religion, and assumes the role of protector of all citizens. Thus as early as the mid-sixteenth century a concept of the modern state was formed, as monarchy, of course, but flanked by the powerful legal institutions of the parlements. The will, born of the humanist spirit, to employ state's protection was resolutely expressed in 1598 under Henry IV in the Edict of Nantes, which guaranteed all citizens the free exercise of

---

[28] Roman Schnur, *Die französischen Juristen im konfessionellen Bürgerkrieg des 16. Jahrhunderts: Ein Beitrag zur Entstehungsgeschichte des modernen Staates* (Berlin: Duncker & Humblot, 1962).

[29] Discussed at length in Chapter 4 below, 'Paris, Capital of European Late Humanism.'

[30] Augustin Renaudet, *Préréforme et humanisme à Paris pendant les premières guerres d'Italie, 1494–1517* (Paris: Librairie d'Argences, 1953).

[31] Still highly useful for Postel is William James Bouwsma, *Concordia mundi: The Career and Thought of Guillaume Postel, 1510–1581* (Cambridge, Mass.: Harvard University Press, 1957). Also the conference volume, *Guillaume Postel, 1581–1981: Actes du colloque international d'Avranches* (Paris: Editions de la Maisnie, 1985).

religion. When it was retracted less than 100 years later (1685) under Louis XIV, the absolutist state relinquished one of its most significant achievements.

In the Netherlands the assertion of the new faith went hand in hand with the attainment of state's autonomy. This double purpose inspired the Netherlands' rise to become the leading Protestant power, both politically and culturally, in the last third of the sixteenth and first half of the seventeenth century. To the country's most lucid minds, kindred souls to the *politiques*, the casting-off of Spanish domination was to be accompanied by a declaration of religious freedom, which would provide an assertion of the young republic's clear identity vis-à-vis Spain. This farsighted philosophy of *Religionsfrid* had to be defended in light of the failure to maintain the unity of the provinces. Calvinists formed the dominant church. But there were also Catholic as well as Lutheran congregations, and Anabaptists, not to mention Arminians. Once again it was the humanistically schooled experts who took up the cause of tolerance.

Today, however, who knows the name of Dirck Volckertzoon Coornhert, with whom Wilhelm Dilthey inaugurated his 'natural system of the human sciences in the seventeenth century'?[32] While never abandoning the Catholic faith, Coornhert – like Erasmus, he was concerned primarily with ethics and its vital basis, freedom – stood between the fronts both politically and confessionally. The Holy Spirit, as one of Luther's opponents, Sebastian Franck, taught, is also free in the manner in which it takes possession of man. Active tolerance meant in the first place acknowledgment of the minorities, and thus Coornhert's conflict with the Calvinists was inevitable. In his view, it was under no circumstances the state's place to act as the defender and protector of a single confession. We find in his family book an entry to this effect against his fellow countryman Justus Lipsius, a convinced advocate of state's authority: 'The rulers of this world boast of being the protectors of the Christian Church. But no weapon can protect the church, since the kingdom of Christ is not of this world.'[33]

Shortly thereafter the Calvinist Church itself was threatened by schism when Jacob Arminius, wholly in the spirit of Coornhert, advanced his criticism of the doctrine of predestination. Although Hugo Grotius and Gerard Vossius, among other humanists, appealed for mutual tolerance, the Synod of Dordrecht (1619) condemned Arminianism and sacrificed one of the leading political minds of the republic, the seventy-two-year-old Johan van Oldenbarnevelt, to the scaffold.[34] A

---

[32] Dilthey, *Weltanschauung und Analyse des Menschen seit Renaissance und Reformation*, vol. 2 of *Gesammelte Schriften*, 3rd edn (Leipzig: Teubner, 1923), 90–245, here 95 ff.

[33] Coornhert, *Proces van 't Ketter-dooden onder dwangh der Conscientien tusschen Justum Lipsium* (Gouda 1590), in *Werke* (Amsterdam, 1630), 2: bk 1, no. 133, f. 61.

[34] Along with Oldenbarneveldt, Grotius too was under suspicion of bribery and collusion with the Spanish and thus of betraying the true faith. Jan den Tex, *Oldenbarneveldt*, trans. R.B. Powell (Cambridge: Cambridge University Press, 1973).

dark shadow thus fell over the young nation. Having fled his fatherland, Grotius drew upon this experience in writing *De Jure belli et pacis* (1625), a work of profound religious tolerance and a foundational document of human rights. Like Erasmus before and Leibniz after him, Grotius dreamed of the restoration of church unity. The Netherlands succeeded in loosening the rigid control of the Calvinists and, on the eve of the Enlightenment, was the most liberal country in Europe – like Poland two centuries earlier – a place where the persecuted could find refuge and their suppressed writings could be published. The major editions of Erasmus, Jakob Böhme, Abraham von Franckenberg, Quirinus Kuhlmann, and so many other provocative minds, were openly printed here. It was in the Netherlands that the first critical encyclopedia was produced (Rotterdam, 1697), the *Dictionnaire historique et critique* of Pierre Bayle, who had fled religious persecution in France.[35]

The circumstances in England were quite different again. The fact that ideas and arguments known to us from the Continent also appear in England only confirms, of course, that we are dealing with a common European commodity and testifies to the versatility and utility of humanist thought. Three of Erasmus's closest friends lived in England. Two were executed, at the command of Henry VIII, during Erasmus's lifetime: John Fisher, Bishop of Rochester, who defended Catherine of Aragon against the king's petition for divorce (1535); and fourteen days later, Thomas More, for refusing to recognize Henry's supreme authority over the church. Dean John Colet established St Paul's School in London as a center of Christian humanist culture, introduced Greek as a language of scholarship to England, and contributed to the fruitful revival of Platonic thought at Cambridge. The publication of Thomas More's *Utopia* in 1516, facilitated by Erasmus, exemplifies the kind of affinity that existed among these humanists. More's work is often characterized as a 'utopia of state'; yet more precisely it is an ideal vision of community, praising the blessing of life as a precious gift to be tended in understanding and leniency rather than strangled by intellectual and spiritual regimentation. The love and worship of God, different the world over, is essentially always the same. 'Him they call father, and to him alone they attribute the origin, increase, progress, change, and end of all visible things.'[36] Thus the cheerful and wise confession of a man who went to his death in the calm assurance of life in the hereafter.

By subjecting ecclesiastical and spiritual concerns to monarchical authority, Henry VIII had revoked a long-standing humanist principle, one that dated back to Dante, as we have seen. This act was roundly criticized, first by the Catholics, who were immediately affected by it, then by the increasingly radical Protestants. Later in the century the work of the controversial Jesuit publicist Robert Persons

---

[35] Paul Hazard, *The European Mind: The Critical Years 1680–1715*, trans. J. Lewis May (New York: Fordham University Press, 1990).

[36] More, *Utopia*, trans. and ed. Robert M. Adams (New York: Norton, 1992), 73.

reflected the thought of the French *politiques*, especially their sentiment that tolerance for religious plurality in no way compromised or endangered the state.[37] At the end of the sixteenth century, intellectuals recognized the need for mutual liberation to the benefit of all. The willingness of the High Church to compromise, however, was a thorn in the side of the Puritans emerging from Calvinism: the repudiation of the blasphemous relicts of the old faith, they believed, should be total, and spiritual power belonged to the congregations. Samuel Rutherford's tract, *A free disputation against pretended liberty of conscience* (1649), bears witness to the struggle belatedly facing insular England. While life on the Continent was finally beginning to calm down, Charles I was being sent to the scaffold by Cromwell's rebellious Puritan parliament. Freedom of conscience? Free development of heterogeneous confessions? Hardly. Magistrates and pastors alike were charged with supervising confessional purity and enforcing it as necessary with violence.

To the credit of men like John Goodwin, Roger Williams, and so many other English sectarians, they reacted to these practices without delay, attacking the state with no less fervor than the Anglican Church. If the secular hand was in fact empowered to intervene in religious matters, then it made sense that Christ should be installed on the throne; the whole business amounted to brazen usurpation of divine right. 'Yet ought we to be led into this unity by the hand of an Angel of light, not to be frighted into it by an evil angel of fear and terror'[38] – a humanist conviction, spoken by an Arminian in flight from the Puritans. Or the voices of two Baptists: 'Let them be heretics, Turks, Jews, or whatsoever, it appertains not to the earthly power to punish them in the least measure.'[39] 'All these bishops that force princes and peoples to receive their faith and discipline by persecution, do, with Judas, go against Christ, in his members, with swords, staves and halberds.'[40] These outcries still echo the life-affirmative philosophy of Erasmus and his fellow humanists. In the end, out of the many sects there arose the common and firm commitment to the coexistence of all and the abstinence of the state. This was most radically and consistently expressed by Roger Williams, founder of the Rhode Island colony, in whose view it was the confusion of the spiritual and the temporal realms that was behind the real 'mystery of Iniquity'.[41]

---

[37] Persons, *Treatise tending to mitigation towardes Catholicke-Subjects in England* (1607), in which he counters Thomas Morton, a chaplain to James I, for his hounding of Catholics as traitors.

[38] Goodwin, *A reply of two of the Brethren to A.S. . . . with a plea for Libertie of conscience* (London, 1644); quoted in Lecler, *Toleration* 459.

[39] Thomas Helwys, *A short Declaration of the mistery of Iniquity* (1612), 69; quoted in Lecler, *Toleration* 463.

[40] Leonard Busher, *Religious Peace: or a plea for liberty of conscience* (1646; reprint in *Tracts on Liberty of Conscience and Persecution (1614–1661)*, ed. Hanserd Knollys Society [London, 1846]), 23; quoted in Lecler, *Toleration* 463.

[41] Williams, *The Bloody Tenent washed and made white in the Blood of the Lamb* (London, 1647), 103.

This confusion, as Williams saw it, began with Constantine's well-intended but misguided protection of the Christians. It now exists among the Catholics: the pope is the Beast of the Apocalypse. But in truth the Protestants themselves have nothing to boast, given their fascination with worldly power; Elizabeth indeed is the 'Popess' of the Anglican Church. Williams uncompromisingly reaffirms the necessity of the separation of powers, advocated by humanists since Dante, and puts it into practice in the New World. But it was in the area of political philosophy that Williams's contemporary John Locke, in his *Letters on Tolerance* (1689–92), which themselves resonate with thoughts and images from Milton, helped to place England at the head of political Europe. The impact of these letters was enhanced by their timely appearance, simultaneously with the English Bill of Rights (1689), which articulated a farsighted political compromise between parliament and monarchy.[42]

Italy now became the stage for the long-running Council of Trent, beginning in 1545, at which Catholicism joined forces with the Society of Jesus, founded by Ignatius of Loyola, to arm itself for the spiritual, moral, and military reconquest of Europe. Once again in Italy an experiment in radical religious thought, the most sagacious of its time, was conducted. And once again it provoked the unforeseeable consequences of a vision for making God accessible to reason. As a consequence of breaking with orthodoxy, it was subjected to severe persecution.[43] 'What times do we live in?' cried Sebastian Castellio, formerly Calvin's handpicked schoolmaster, in reaction to the Protestant brutality. He was especially horrified to learn of the death sentence urged by Calvin on Michael Servetus, who opposed the doctrine of the Trinity. 'We are becoming bloodthirsty killers out of zeal for Christ, who shed his own blood to save that of others.'[44] Or, as Giorgio Siculo of Ferrara pointedly asks, 'Why do the Protestants so humiliate reason and place human nature lower than that of a horse . . . [when Holy Scripture] glorifies human nature, revealing to us its greatness and divine dignity?'[45] It was in this positive anthropological interpretation of Scripture that the Socinians found a connection between the philosophy of the Renaissance, as expressed by Ficino, Lorenzo de Médici, Pico della Mirandola and others, and the

---

[42] Walter Euchner, *John Locke zur Einführung* (Hamburg: Junius, 1996).

[43] Delio Cantimori, *Italienische Haeretiker der Spätrenaissance*, trans. Werner Kaegi (Basel: Schwabe, 1949), is the classic work on this subject. See also Silvana Seidel Menchi, 'Humanismus und Reformation im Spiegel der italienischen Inquisitionsakten', in *Renaissance – Reformation: Gegensätze und Gemeinsamkeiten*, ed. August Buck, 47–64 (Wiesbaden: Harrassowitz, 1984).

[44] Sebastian Castellio, preface to his 1551 Latin translation of the Bible; quoted in Lecler, *Toleration* 338. See Hans R. Guggisberg, *Sebastian Castellio 1515–1563: Humanist und Verteidiger der religiösen Toleranz im konfessionellen Zeitalter* (Göttingen: Vandenhoeck & Ruprecht, 1997).

[45] Quoted in Heer, *Die dritte Kraft* 490. Siculo had been executed two years before Servetus for his outspoken opposition to the doctrine of predestination. Calvin hailed the execution of Siculo for ridding the world of a 'satanic' influence (Heer 489).

gospel of Christ. Italians like Camillo Renato, Lelio Sozzini and his nephew Fausto (promoter of Unitarianism, sometimes called 'Socinianism'), Bernardino Ochino, and Celio Secundo Curione found temporary refuge in Basel and the Grisons before they and their descendants were compelled to move on, eastward to Poland, Transylvania, and Russia, then westward to the Netherlands, England, and America. Sixteenth-century Poland offered asylum to Anti-Trinitarians, Socinians, the Bohemian Brothers, and the Polish Brotherhood, among others. As late as the seventeenth century, Silesian, Bohemian, and Hungarian humanists found protection there.[46]

In Germany it was Philipp Melanchthon, more than any other individual, who for longer than a generation bore the prodigious burden of wrestling with the consequences of Luther's Reformation. Above all this meant keeping solidarity with the humanists after the breach between Luther and Erasmus over the doctrine of free will. In Erasmus's view, man enjoyed self-determination guided by human reason and participated in the act of divine grace; to this Luther responded with his harsh avowal to God's sole disposition of man.[47] The formulation of the 'correct' Lutheran confession was entrusted to Melanchthon, and in this matter the sworn adherents of Luther accepted no compromise, refusing the Zwinglians or Calvinists, the 'zealots' or 'spiritualists', even the slightest concession. The more obscure Luther became and the more rigid his orthodox followers, the greater was the affinity of many humanists for the doctrines of the 'competitor' confessions, which they often found to be more reasonable and humane.

How is it that bitter disputes could rage for more than a century over relatively minor issues, such as the interpretation of the Holy Communion? In fact the struggle implied much more than disagreement over the question of the sacrament as such; at the heart of the matter lay the philosophical difference concerning the dignity and autonomy of man, and the human ability to comprehend the mysteries of faith. A doctrine that emphasized the symbolic character of the Holy Communion as a commemorative act had a better chance of acceptance among the educated than one that insisted on the transformation of bread and wine into the real body and blood of Christ through their pious intake. Melanchthon, who was imbued, perhaps more deeply than any other humanist of his generation, with the Erasmian conviction that the first Christian duty was conciliation, found himself in the increasingly uncomfortable position of having to mediate in irreconcilable disputes. If the breach with the Catholic Church was now irreversible, a thought that troubled him as deeply as it did Erasmus, then it

---

[46] Janusz Tazbir, *A State without Stakes: Polish Religious Toleration in the Sixteenth and Seventeenth Centuries*, trans. A.T. Jordan (New York: Kościuszko Foundation, 1973).

[47] Erasmus, *De libero arbitrio diatribe* (1524; A Disquisition on Free Will); Luther's response, *De servo arbitrio* (1525; On the Bondage of the Will).

became a simple matter of survival for Protestants to seek peace. This commonsense conclusion held good, both as a matter of Christian doctrine and of practical everyday life, all the way up to the highest level of politics. Melanchthon lived and fought for this worthy goal, only ultimately to fail, much as Erasmus had failed in another way.

The fronts between the Lutherans, Zwinglians, and Calvinists could not be made to yield; on the contrary, they grew increasingly rigid. An adherent of a given Protestant confession was commonly regarded as more despicable and dangerous than an orthodox Catholic. As a result, most humanists turned away in disgust from this kind of intolerance;[48] many ultimately returned to the old belief and were lost to Lutheranism, as Melanchthon painfully realized. But did he not also foresee the consequences to the Christian faith itself if all of this hair-splitting did not end? In Germany as elsewhere in Europe, wherever skepticism took root in humanism – in the end this led to the Enlightenment, with its search for the true, natural religion capable of satisfying the demands of reason – deeply religious seekers took refuge in the confession-free realms of divine inspiration and experience, finding there a more steadfast security than in dogmatic casuistry.

It was in these humanist circles that the doctrine of irenicism took shape.[49] The illustrious spectrum of irenic personalities in early modern Germany ranges from Paracelsus and Sebastian Franck to Caspar Schwenckfeld, Valentin Weigel, and Jakob Böhme, and further to Friedrich Spee, Johann Scheffler (Angelus Silesius), and Christian Breckling. At the end of the seventeenth century Gottfried Arnold would commemorate them in his *History of the Church and Its Heretics*.[50] Is it any coincidence that outsiders have made the deepest mark on the history of German thought, whether in the literary works of Hamann or Herder, Goethe, or Jean Paul, the Romantics from Novalis to Eichendorff, or in the philosophical thought of Schelling and Hegel, Bloch and Benjamin? Every peace movement, no matter how small, can take comfort and encouragement in the thought and hopes of their predecessors on the margins of society. To remember them is to ensure their survival, whatever the future may bring.*

---

[48] Ole Peter Grell and Bob Scribner (eds), *Tolerance and Intolerance in the European Reformation* (Cambridge: Cambridge University Press, 1996).

[49] Of the vast literature on this subject, see esp. Siegfried Wollgast, *Philosophie in Deutschland zwischen Reformation und Aufklärung 1550–1650*, 2nd edn (Berlin: Akademie, 1993).

[50] Arnold will be discussed at length below in Chapter 7, 'Begin with Goethe?'

* Permission to use the English translation of parts I and III of the exhibition text is kindly provided by the Westfälisches Landesmuseum für Kunst und Kulturgeschichte, Münster; the translation has been adapted stylistically and otherwise for use here. Part II was translated by Michael Swisher.

Chapter 3

The Republic of Letters and the Absolutist State: Nine Theses

Humanism was not an institution in the sense that some agenda existed that enjoyed the universal consensus of all self-professed humanists throughout Europe; nor did these men and women as a group behave according to laws that were in some sense higher or better than those of other people.[1] That said, however, powerful traditions, both political as well as intellectual, did exist that gave definite corporate identity to early modern Europe's learned elite. The perception of these shared mental and historical bases led in turn to the deliberate formation of organizational structures in which wide-based humanistic activities and ideas were fostered. Foremost among these were the sodalities, the intellectual societies. It is important to see their rise as in part negatively motivated by dissatisfaction with existing institutions:

> In schools and universities, courts and churches, [humanists] encountered social institutions that they had had no hand in forming but to which they were obligated to conform. In their academies, language and literature societies, and sodalities, however, they could act according to rules that they themselves had devised. No institution therefore was more suited to the self-expression of the humanists of Europe than these *sodalitates literariae*. The forms of communication that the learned members created in these sodalities offer a picture of how they understood their social roles, what hopes of social recognition they entertained, in what regard they held intellectual achievement, and how they valued the levels of rational activity . . . [T]he sodalities represented, as a whole, the most important agency within the European movement of national languages and literatures.[2]

The rise of intellectual societies cannot be appreciated apart from that of the nation-state, sometimes in a relationship of dependence, sometimes one of

---

[1] The welcome recent scholarly tendency towards a more differentiated view of humanists and humanism may be followed in the studies by Anthony Grafton and Lisa Jardine, sometimes in collaboration. See, e.g., their essays in *From Humanism to the Humanities: Education and Liberal Arts in Fifteenth- and Sixteenth-Century Europe* (Cambridge, Mass.: Harvard University Press, 1986), or Grafton's *Commerce with the Classics: Ancient Books & Renaissance Readers*, Jerome Lectures, 20 (Ann Arbor: University of Michigan Press, 1997).

[2] Klaus Garber, 'Sozietäten, Akademien, Sprachgesellschaften', in *Europäische Enzyklopädie zu Philosophie und Wissenschaften*, ed. Hans Jörg Sandkühler (Hamburg: Meiner, 1990), 366.

opposition. The following 'theses' are offered in an attempt to clarify the social and political context of their origins and development in early modern Europe.

Thesis 1: The Social Roots of the European Learned Aristocracy

The first crucial moment of change in the paradigm that defines early modern European literature occurred in Italian early humanism and was as much a socioeconomic as a literary phenomenon. The high bourgeoisie of the thirteenth and fourteenth centuries, in establishing its social and political dominance through trade, finance, and manufacture in the northern Italian city-states, forced the feudal aristocracy either into direct participation in the new cities or out into the countryside away from urban social and economic life.[3] In any reconstruction of early bourgeois culture, particular attention must be paid to the humanists, who constituted the European learned aristocracy. This *nobilitas literaria*, which began to develop independently in the fourteenth century and was consolidated over the course of the fifteenth in the cities and at the courts, occupied from the beginning a clearly discernible position between the high bourgeoisie and the guilds. The argument, however, that humanism gained its own sociocultural profile by distancing itself equally from the high bourgeoisie and the guilds, is misleading.[4] The European learned aristocracy was socially anchored both in the cities, especially in the patrician estate, as well as later at the courts. Humanists responded to the historical ferment through the medium of ancient literary genres, exploiting them as expressive vehicles for forging an identity independent of the institutions and universities of the Middle Ages. Early modern literature was part of a general cultural system driven by powerful conflicts between competing claims of authority and freedom in the political and aesthetic spheres.[5]

---

[3] *Pipers Handbuch der Politischen Ideen*, ed. Iring Fetscher and Herfried Münkler, vol. 2 (Munich: Piper, 1990). The older standard work on the economic history of Italy is Alfred Doren, *Italienische Wirtschaftsgeschichte*, vol. 1 of *Handbuch der Wirtschaftsgeschichte* (Jena: Fischer, 1934).

[4] Karl Mannheim's thesis of a 'socially free-floating' intellectual estate took this view as its presumptive basis; it was canonized and popularized in 1932 in Alfred von Martin's *Sociology of the Renaissance*, trans. W.L. Luetkens (1944; reprint, New York: Harper & Row, 1963), and taken up again in the Hanser series *Sozialgeschichte der Kunst und Literatur vom 16. Jahrhundert bis zur Gegenwart*, ed. Rolf Grimminger (Munich: Hanser, 1979–); cf. Arnhelm Neusüss, *Utopisches Bewußtsein und freischwebende Intelligenz: zur Struktur der Wissenssoziologie Karl Mannheims* (Meisenheim am Glan: Hain, 1968).

[5] The groundwork for further investigation into a social history of early modern Europe was prepared in the mid-1970s in the former GDR. See Robert Weimann, Werner Lenk, and J.J. Slomka (eds), *Renaissanceliteratur und frühbürgerliche Revolution: Studien zu den sozial- und ideologiegeschichtlichen Grundlagen europäischer Nationalliteraturen* (Berlin: Aufbau, 1976).

Thesis 2: The Transformative Ideology of 'True Nobility'

In this regard a certain body of literature deserves special attention: the treatises on the topos *de vera nobilitate* 'on true nobility'. It is astonishing that this corpus has never been thoroughly scrutinized, for it is loaded with arguments that dominate literature from antiquity through the Middle Ages.[6] This scholarly lacuna is probably symptomatic of a general lack of enthusiasm for the political side of humanism, as though humanist logical and poetic forms can have only antiquarian interest.[7] The use of true nobility as a literary topos was rehabilitated by Dante, most notably in his *Convivio*, and was expanded markedly during the fifteenth century by Buonaccorso da Montemagno, Poggio Bracciolini, Bartolomeo Sacchi Platina, and Cristoforo Landino.[8] The literature gathered its force by intellectually marginalizing or discrediting certain groups, especially the high bourgeoisie with its fixation on wealth, accumulation of capital, and monetary acquisition of social and political prestige. Measured against the learned ideals of *otium* 'leisure' and the *studia humaniora* 'humanistic studies', materialistic goals could only arouse contempt. The social differentiation of the early modern cities and city-states is also reflected in this literature. Evidence, however, clearly militates against assuming a basic opposition between bourgeois and educated norms. The treatises emphasized reason and virtue as essential not only to the acquisition of knowledge but also to the exercise of civil responsibility. While the argument in itself is specific to no particular class or estate, it is encoded with an emphatic anti-feudal signature unknown to the Middle Ages. Guided by reason and virtue, its egalitarian plea accompanied the rise of the new burgher class, which included the humanist grouping. Once reason

---

[6] For an orientation, see the introduction by Manfred Lentzen, *Christoforo Landino: De vera nobilitate* (Geneva: Droz, 1970); with respect to early modern Germany, see Volker Sinemus, *Poetik und Rhetorik im frühmodernen deutschen Staat: Sozialgeschichtliche Bedingungen des Normenwandels im 17. Jahrhundert* (Göttingen: Vandenhoeck & Ruprecht, 1978); further, Klaus Bleeck and Jörn Garber, 'Nobilitas: Standes- und Privilegienlegitimation in deutschen Adelstheorien des 16. und 17. Jahrhunderts', in *Hof, Staat und Gesellschaft in der Literatur des 17. Jahrhunderts*, ed. Elger Blühm et al., 49–114 (Amsterdam: Rodopi, 1982), as well as my study in the same volume, 'Zur Statuskonkurrenz von Adel und gelehrtem Bürgertum im theoretischen Schrifttum des 17. Jahrhunderts: Veit Ludwig von Seckendorffs *Teutscher Fürstenstaat* und die deutsche "Barockliteratur"', 115–43.

[7] Karl-Heinz Borck, 'Adel, Tugend und Geblüt: Thesen und Beobachtungen zur Vorstellung des Tugendadels in der deutschen Literatur des 12. und 13. Jahrhunderts', *Beiträge zur Geschichte der deutschen Sprache und Literatur* 100 (1978): 423–57, has proposed a number of useful theses for a similar problem of relating the question of virtue with that of society for scholarship on the twelfth and thirteenth centuries.

[8] Among the classical texts from this period: Buonaccorso's *De nobilitate* (1428); Bracciolini's *De nobilitate* (1428); Giannozzo Manetti's *De dignitate et excellentia hominis* (1452); Platina's *De vera nobilitate* (1475); and Pico della Mirandola's *Oratio de hominis dignitate* (1486).

and virtue had been established as the preeminent human qualities, former social distinctions could be relegated to secondary importance. A universal system of norms – a 'system' to the extent that they were shared by the learned aristocracy across the entire geographical face of Europe – revolutionized, at least theoretically, time-bound social hierarchies and had demonstrably profound influence on the later middle-class appropriation of natural law. Heredity could claim no more than the authority of custom; principles of competence and merit were proposed in its place. The decisive question became simply: What use shall human beings make of their innate ability? Rumblings of a future social upheaval may be detected, always supported by reference to ancient authorities, in the humanist praise of reason and virtue and in the uncompromising devaluation of the aristocracy's inherited privileges. Society was lastingly shaken by this bourgeois appropriation of the classical aristocratic code of conduct. It led in the Enlightenment to the idea, based upon presumably transhistorical norms, of the general perfectibility of human kind.

Thesis 3: The Humanist – Republican Connection

The literature of true nobility is rich in republican allusions and implications. From Coluccio Salutati to Bracciolini to Machiavelli, the great political theoreticians of Florence were also chancellary officials. Nowhere did the principle of merit have greater political significance than in the new city-states. The Greek *polis* as well as the Roman *res publica* were repeatedly cited in attempts to rationalize modern ideas within the framework of old feudal ones. It was through humanist political philosophy that the northern Italian city-state experienced this transformation as a transfiguration, namely, in the light of antiquity.[9] In this transfiguration the cities were refeudalized in the shadows, as it were, away from the central arena of high-bourgeois action. Political participation and social prestige were restored, consequently, despite opposing constitutional models, to the hands of only a few powerful families. The crucial point is that it was the humanists who documented the collapse of feudalism and the establishment of republican government. The most lasting contribution of the early Italian humanists to intellectual history may have been their dialectical view of the causalities between social and economic revolution on the one hand and personal competence and merit on the other. Related to this theory was the certainty that the practice of these high ethical qualities would bear fruit both in

---

[9] This moment is repeatedly described by the liberal school of Renaissance historiography, culminating in the concept of 'civic humanism' proposed by Hans Baron, *The Crisis of the Early Italian Renaissance: Civic Humanism and Republican Liberty in an Age of Classicism and Tyranny* (1955; revised edition, Princeton: Princeton University Press, 1966).

improved governmental institutions as well as in enhanced opportunities for people of virtue to participate directly in the republican commonwealth. In this humanistically stylized version of social transformation, which borrowed heavily on classical antecedents, the concept of true nobility was passed on to the early modern learned aristocracy. It inspired social theory throughout the course of national and territorial absolutism down to the French Revolution.

Thesis 4: Intellectual Societies and their Noble Benefactors

As an institution the nobilitas literaria had its roots in Italian early humanism. The sociocultural history of the intellectual societies, which sprang up wherever learned communities existed, has been investigated as little as the intellectual history of the learned aristocracy.[10] The possibility that a, if not *the*, cardinal problem of early modern culture lies buried here has been vastly underappreciated. In the exchange of pastoral letters between Dante and Giovanni del Virgilio we find decisive confirmation of an affinity between the nobility and learned society. The movement of intellectual societies arose in fourteenth-century Bologna and over the subsequent centuries led to the founding of such renowned sodalities as the Accademia Platonica in Florence, the Accademia Pontaniana in Naples, the Accademia Pomponia in Rome, the Accademia degli Orti Oricellari, also in Florence, the Accademia Aldina in Venice, and finally, likewise in Florence, the Accademia Fiorentina and the

---

[10] Modern scholarship on this aspect of sodalities outside of Italy began with R.J.W. Evans and August Buck. Evans: *Rudolf II and his World: A Study in Intellectual History 1576–1612* (Oxford: Clarendon Press, 1973), and 'Learned Societies in Germany in the Seventeenth Century', *European Studies Review* 7 (1977): 129–51; Buck: 'Die humanistischen Akademien in Italien', in *Der Akademiegedanke im 17. und 18. Jahrhundert*, ed. Fritz Hartmann and Rudolf Vierhaus, 11–25 (Bremen: Jacobi, 1977). See also the two-volume collection edited by Sebastian Neumeister and Conrad Wiedemann, *Res Publica Litteraria: Die Institutionen der Gelehrsamkeit in der frühen Neuzeit* (Wiesbaden: Harrasowitz, 1987), esp. vol. 1, sect. 1, 'Institutionen und Organisationsformen der Gelehrsamkeit' (35–151). Specific to Germany, Jörg Jochen Berns, 'Zur Tradition der deutschen Sozietätsbewegung im 17. Jahrhundert', in *Sprachgesellschaften, Societäten, und Dichtergruppen*, ed. Martin Bircher and Ferdinand van Ingen, 53–73 (Hamburg: Hauswedell, 1978), and the editions by Klaus Conermann on the Fruchtbringende Gesellschaft, esp. *Der Fruchtbringenden Gesellschaft geöffneter Erzschrein: das Köthener Gesellschaftsbuch Furst Ludwig I. von Anhalt-Köthen 1617–1650*, 3 vols (Tübingen: Niemeyer, 1985). F.W. Barthold, *Geschichte der Fruchtbringenden Gesellschaft: Sitten, Geschmacksbildung und schöne Redekünste deutscher Vornehmen vom Ende des XVI. bis über die Mitte des XVII. Jahrhunderts* (1848; reprint, Hildesheim: Olms, 1969), remains an indispensable early history of the sodality. Italian and German sodalities are treated together by Laetitia Boehm and Ezio Raimondi (eds), *Università, Accademie e Società scientifiche in Italia e in Germania dal Cinquecento al Settecento* (Bologna: Mulino, 1981).

Accademia della Crusca. Reasons for the brisk proliferation of intellectual societies are readily apparent. In Catholic countries in particular, church and university constituted oppositions that forced humanists to gather into discrete organizations. Elsewhere, influential patrons like Alemanno Rinuccini and Bernardo Rucellai in Florence stepped forward from the ranks of the *potentes*, the ruling or wealthy patrician families.[11] It is significant that Italian seigneurs assumed protectorship of the sodalities as early as the fifteenth century (Cosimo and Lorenzo de' Médici's supportive participation in the Accademia Platonica is only one conspicuous example),[12] since it was from the *uomini nuovi* 'new men' out of the ranks of the seigneurs that the fledgling learned aristocracy found its most important partners. The movement of northern national literatures, which began in the early sixteenth century, owed its most lasting impulses to these sodalities, which remained viable within the monarchies and territories of western Europe as an institution of sociocultural intercourse until well into the eighteenth century. The sodalities also made a more direct political contribution in reaction to Charles VIII's invasion of Italy (1494). In response to this threat from outside, sodalities from the Accademia Pontaniana in Naples to the Orti Oricellari in Florence, among others, helped to inspire a second and more active politicization of the learned aristocracy, as compared with the initial phase of civic humanism.

Thesis 5: The Sodalities and Absolutism: Dependence and Opposition[13]

One need think only of the sodalities in Heidelberg, Mainz, Vienna, Nuremberg, Munich, and Augsburg to be reminded that princely, imperial, noble, and patrician sources of patronage were available in Germany as well. Two concepts have sweeping implications here: 1) *gedechtnus* 'commendation', the practice of extolling the deeds of powerful and noble patrons (in the most famous case, it was imperially sponsored and strategically exploited by the circle of learned men at

---

[11] Still indispensable is Felix Gilbert, 'Bernardo Rucellai and the Orti Oricellari: A Study on the Origin of Modern Political Thought', *Journal of the Warburg and Courtauld Institutes* 12 (1949): 101–31.

[12] See the standard studies of the Florentine sodality by Arnaldo della Torre, *Storia dell'Accademia platonica di Firenze* (Torino: Bottega d'Erasmo, 1968), and Armand L. Gaetano, 'The Florentine Academy and the Advancement of Learning Through the Vernacular: The Orti Oricellari and the Sacra Accademia', *Bibliothèque d'Humanisme et Renaissance* 30 (1968): 19–52.

[13] The ideas in this thesis are indebted in part to Reinhart Koselleck, *Critique and Crisis* (Cambridge, Mass.: MIT Press, 1988), as well as to Jürgen Habermas, *The Theory of Communicative Action*, trans. Thomas McCarthy (Boston: Beacon Press, 1984), and *The Structural Transformation of the Public Sphere: An Inquiry into a Category of Bourgeois Society*, trans. Thomas Burger (Cambridge, Mass.: MIT Press, 1989).

the court of Maximilian I in Bavaria);[14] and 2) feudal legitimation, which had been eroded during the transition to early modernity but was now being widely and vigorously restored by territorial princes through representative literature and art. The lines connecting this process to the German societal movement of the seventeenth century are obscure; only the one extending from the Italian sodalities, especially the Accademia della Crusca, has been traced thoroughly. The political origins, kept under prudent wraps in that volatile age, of the most important seventeenth-century German sodality, the Fruchtbringende Gesellschaft (founded 1617), have begun to emerge since the mid-1980s. Only within the context of Europe's confessional fragmentation will we be able to understand how broad strategies and goals were mustered into a coherent plan, particularly by the Calvinist princes who promoted political and cultural unification.[15] This unifying purpose was inherent in the Protestant Union's Bohemian policy under Palatine and Anhaltian leadership and consequently suffered when that policy failed. Questions regarding confessional differences and the degree of political latitude allowed in the urban sodalities founded after the Fruchtbringende Gesellschaft are only now beginning to be answered.[16] Nor do we adequately understand what caused the dissolution of the older humanist sodalities or the motivations behind the idea of a national academy of sciences, such as the one Leibniz established in Germany at the turn of the century.[17] That

---

[14] Jan-Dirk Müller, *Gedechtnus: Literatur und Hofgesellschaft um Maximilian I.* (Munich: Fink, 1982); cf. Franz Josef Worstbrock, 'Über das geschichtliche Selbstverständnis des deutschen Humanismus', in *Historizität in Sprach- und Literaturwissenschaft: Vorträge und Berichte der Stuttgarter Germanistentagung 1972*, ed. Walter Müller-Seidel, 499–519 (Munich: Fink, 1974).

[15] For a starting point, see my study 'Zentraleuropäischer Calvinismus und deutsche "Barock"-Literatur: Zu den konfessionspolitischen Ursprüngen der deutschen Nationalliteratur', in *Die reformierte Konfessionalisierung in Deutschland – Das Problem der 'Zweiten Reformation'*, ed. Heinz Schilling, 317–48 (Gütersloh: Mohn, 1986). Also Günther Hoppe, 'Fürst Ludwig I. von Anhalt-Köthen', in *Die Fruchtbringende Gesellschaft und ihr Köthener Gesellschaftsbuch: Eine Einleitung*, vol. 2 of Conermann's *Der Fruchtbringenden Gesellschaft geöffneter Erzschrein* 131–70.

[16] Georg Philipp Harsdörffer's *Japeta* (1643), a translation of the French play *Europe, Comédie héroique* by Jean Desmarets (with possible collaboration of Richelieu), demonstrates that a highly sophisticated form of political allegory thrived in the urban Protestant sodalities. This was first investigated by Ferdinand Josef Schneider, *Japeta (1643): Ein Beitrag zur Geschichte des französischen Klassizismus in Deutschland* (Stuttgart: Metzler, 1927). On the sensitive position of the learned estate relative to the increasingly conservative political trend in the seventeenth century, see Max Reinhart, 'Poets and Politics: The Transgressive Turn of History in Seventeenth-Century Nürnberg', *Daphnis* 20, no. 1 (1991): 199–229. This is discussed at length below in Chapter 6, 'Nuremberg, Arcadia on the Pegnitz.'

[17] Werner Schneiders, 'Gottesreich und gelehrte Gesellschaft: Zwei politische Modelle bei G.W. Leibniz', in *Università, Accademie e Società scientifiche in Italia e in Germania dal Cinquecento al Settecento*, ed. Laetitia Boehm and Ezio Raimondi, 395–419 (Bologna: Il Mulino, 1981), proposes two such political models. Leibniz is discussed in Chapter 7 below, 'Begin with Goethe?'.

a fundamental shift occurred in the direction of the natural sciences is clear.[18] But to what extent was this *via moderna* already anticipated in the hermetic practices of the older sodalities in the tradition of the Accademia Platonica?[19] What relationship obtained between the theological reform sodality, such as Nuremberg's Societas Christiana, founded by Johann Valentin Andreae in 1620, and its secular counterpart in Rostock, the Societas Ereunetica, founded shortly before by Joachim Jungius?[20] What elements, if any, were carried over from the older type of sodality into the Leibnizian model? And finally, to what degree, if at all, did the German sodalities of the eighteenth century make use of sixteenth- and seventeenth-century models? That such connections existed can be attested from the programmatic and historical writings of Johann Christoph Gottsched, in which problems of continuity for the early modern European societal movement converge in an eighteenth-century viewpoint. In the earlier sodalities external concerns about social hierarchy were consciously recast in favor of internal ones about egalitarian representation. Membership and participation were accorded, regardless of social standing, to all who had distinguished themselves in education, art, character, and the qualities of a virtuous life. Although that pious hope did not advance far beyond good intentions, the sodalities did at least aspire to a kind of intellectual organization in whose anti-feudal features we cannot fail to see the ideal of *vera nobilitas*. It is true that the sodalities found support in the principalities and monarchies because of the utilitarian nature of their knowledge and skills for the early modern state; ultimately, however, once the state-building process had been completed, they stood at cross purposes with absolutist practices. Ever since the second half of the sixteenth century, the emperor had been trying, for obvious reasons, to cement the corporate order of society, especially by reprivileging nobility; in the face of this refeudalization, the sodalities held fast to the meritocratic principle of competence.[21] They therefore represent, in

---

[18] Jürgen Voss, 'Die Akademien als Organisationsträger der Wissenschaften im 18. Jahrhundert', *Historische Zeitschrift* 231 (1980): 43–74.

[19] See Frances A. Yates, *Giordano Bruno and the Hermetic Tradition* (Chicago: University of Chicago Press, 1964). Fritz Krafft reviews scholarship between 1945–75 on Renaissance natural science in 'Renaissance der Naturwissenschaften – Naturwissenschaften der Renaissance', in *Humanismusforschung seit 1945: Ein Bericht aus interdisziplinärer Sicht*, ed. Deutsche Forschungsgemeinschaft, 111–83 (Boppard: Boldt, 1975).

[20] Richard van Dülmen, 'Sozietätsbewegung in Nürnberg im 17. Jahrhundert', in *Gesellschaft und Herrschaft*, ed. Dülmen, 153–90 (Munich: Beck, 1969), and *Die Utopie einer christlichen Gesellschaft: Johann Valentin Andreae (1586–1654)*, pt. 1 (Stuttgart: Frommann-Holzboog, 1978). On the group around Andreae, see Donald R. Dickson, 'Johannes Saubert, Johann Valentin Andreae and the *Unio Christiana*', *German Life and Letters* 49, no. 1 (1996): 18–31. What little is known about the short-lived Rostock group may be found in Gottschalk Eduard Guhrauer, *Joachim Jungius und sein Zeitalter: nebst Goethes Fragmenten über Jungius* (Stuttgart: Cotta, 1850).

[21] Reinhart, 'Poets and Politics' 210, describes an example of the conflict between the poetic-intellectual order and the ruling patriciate in Nuremberg during this period of refeudalization. There the 'process of refeudalization culminated in the imperial

however rudimentary a fashion, crystallization points in learned bourgeois counter-culture, perhaps even an incipient public sphere, within the absolutist state. As such they are authentic manifestations of the European learned aristocracy.

Thesis 6: The Politicization of Late Humanism

A social history of the early modern learned aristocracy is little served by starting from religious categories. The old debate about pagan elements in early humanism is a tired one and purely academic; the same may be said about the debate over the relationship between humanism and Christianity, or between humanism and the Reformation. What is important rather is the political turn of humanism in the wake of confessional party formation in the second half of the sixteenth century.[22] Contrary to what is sometimes asserted, humanist thought around 1600 in Europe was far from ossifying into a pedantic institution.[23] Quite the opposite was true. In no phase of its history was humanism more vital or did it enjoy greater public regard than between 1570 and 1620.[24] Now, for the first time, humanism's reputed aloofness from confessional partisanship turned into political action as political theoreticians, especially French jurists, and other proponents of the modern, confessionally neutral, secular state began to emerge from leading humanist circles.[25] In France the idea of a sovereign nation unbeholden to confessional

---

privilege of 1696, whereby the patriciate was at last granted equal status with imperial aristocracy and the Council was empowered to appoint its own to the Richteramt, formerly reserved for the jurists by the constitutional bifurcation of judiciary and administration ... [F]or all intents and purposes, the Rat now possessed absolute power.'

[22] English historians in particular have contributed to research in this area. Among others, Frances A. Yates, 'Italian Liberals and Rosicrucian Manifestos', in *The Rosicrucian Enlightenment*, 130–39 (London: Routledge and Kegan Paul, 1972); Hugh Trevor-Roper, *Religion, the Reformation and Social Change*, 2nd edn (London: Macmillan, 1972); and Evans, *Rudolf II*. For Germany, see Bernd Roeck, 'Aufklärung und Kritik: Tendenzen der Politisierung', pt 1, ch. 9.3 of *Lebenswelt und Kultur des Bürgertums in der Frühen Neuzeit*, Enzyklopädie Deutscher Geschichte, 9 (Munich: Oldenbourg, 1991). The political tendency identified by Roeck in the early eighteenth century did not suddenly come into existence but was prepared already in late humanism.

[23] Erich Trunz made the vitality of late humanism emphatically clear in his classic study 'Der deutsche Späthumanismus um 1600 als Standeskultur' (1931; reprint in *Deutsche Barockforschung: Dokumentation einer Epoche*, 2nd edn, ed. Richard Alewyn, 147–81 (Cologne: Kiepenheuer & Witsch, 1966). As Trunz argues, the opposite view mistakes the late humanists' fundamental belief in *ordo* for moribundity.

[24] Wilhelm Kühlmann, *Gelehrtenrepublik und Fürstenstaat: Entwicklung und Kritik des deutschen Späthumanismus in der Literatur des Barockzeitalters* (Tübingen: Niemeyer, 1982); esp. pt 2, on the intellectual in society.

[25] Roman Schnur, *Die französischen Juristen im konfessionellen Bürgerkrieg des 16. Jahrhunderts: Ein Beitrag zur Entstehungsgeschichte des modernen Staates* (Berlin: Duncker & Humblot, 1962), and Schnur (ed.), *Die Rolle der Juristen bei der Entstehung des modernen Staates* (Berlin: Duncker & Humblot, 1986).

interests was conceived by the party of the *politiques*.[26] Here again, humanism's connection to the crown is confirmed. All the way up the social ladder to Louis XIII's chief minister, Cardinal Richelieu, who wielded the instrument with greater prudence than perhaps anyone before or after, the nation's intellectual elite were repeatedly enlisted in the service of defending the monarchy's rights against Spain and the pope and of promoting the doctrine of absolute monarchy.[27] After Richelieu, attempts by confessional interests to enforce their respective agendas were clearly anachronistic, if not downright obsolete. For a social history of the European learned aristocracy, it would be much more instructive to examine the inner workings of the radical transformation of political thought around 1600. This examination would involve an analysis of late humanism's affinities with neo-Stoicism, separatism, and Calvinism.

Thesis 7: Humanist Affinities with Calvinism and Other Reformisms

Neo-Stoicism's contribution to reason of state and the princely ethos, as well as to the creation of social discipline, has long been recognized.[28] By contrast, the interrelationship between late humanism and alternative reformisms – the Socinians, Arians, Anti-Trinitarians, Baptists, Spiritualists, Rosicrucians, and others – has received little attention;[29] this applies especially to their political implications. In point of fact, the interconfessional activities of the humanists were motivated by contact with just such alternative currents. Moreover, humanist institutions were deeply influenced by the utopian conception, promulgated by the separatist movement, of *una societas christiana*, which served as an alternative idea to the Catholic universalism championed by Charles V. To state it rather too simply, humanists and separatists spearheaded the drive towards more general political participation, an initiative that was thinkable only within the sphere of the Calvinist courts. Particular attention must therefore be

---

[26] The *politiques* were moderate Catholics who supported the king over the more militant Catholic League.

[27] The older studies by Maximin Deloche, *Autour de la plume du Cardinal Richelieu* (Paris: Société française, 1920), and Rudolf von Albertini, *Das politische Denken in Frankreich zur Zeit Richelieus* (Marburg: Simons, 1951), remain basic to understanding Richelieu's exploitation of French intellectuals. More recently, W.F. Church, *Richelieu and Reason of State* (Princeton: Princeton University Press, 1972).

[28] Since at least the late 1960s in the studies of Gerhard Oestreich, some of the most important of which are collected in *Neostoicism and the Early Modern State*, trans. David McLintock, ed. Brigitta Oestreich and Helmut Georg Koenigsberger (Cambridge: Cambridge University Press, 1982).

[29] The notable exceptions to this claim are the classic studies by Yates: *Giordano Bruno and the Hermetic Tradition* and *The Rosicrucian Movement*, and Evans, *Rudolf II*, and 'Learned Societies'.

directed to what political views were shared by the humanists, the separatists, and the Calvinists. Calvinism exerted great attraction on intellectual circles, since, as the most sophisticated among the confessional-political movements, it not only kept humanists alerted to the dangers emanating from a strengthened, post-Tridentine Catholicism, but also proved capable of organizing the various alternative political interests around Europe.[30] Furthermore, owing to its minority status in most European lands, Calvinism manifested a distinctly irenic and cooperative spirit, which combined with its militant anti-Catholicism to form an appealing symbiosis. In practice Calvinism presented a veritable melting pot of oppositional forces to Spain, Rome, or the Habsburgs. Many late humanists demonstrated loyalty to Calvinism and continued to articulate positions that, following Calvinism's collapse in Central Europe, kept them marginalized politically. Not until the Enlightenment were such positions again adopted and promoted.

Thesis 8: The Humanist Symbiosis of Republicanism, Sovereignty, and Nationalism

Roman republican influence on the new urban organizations can hardly be overstated; indeed, it reached far beyond humanist circles. And yet, in spite of republicanism's acknowledged contribution to the evolution of the learned aristocracy in early modern Europe, little is known about its political features. A useful point of departure in this investigation would be towards the end of the period of late humanism, which we may advisedly set at the year 1620.[31] Republicanism was by no means thought of in all instances as antithetical to monarchical absolutism. No early humanist invoked the idea of republican Rome

---

[30] See Hans Sturmberger's classic monograph on dissidence in the Counter-Reformation, *Georg Erasmus Tschernembl: Religion, Libertät und Widerstand: ein Beitrag zur Geschichte der Gegenreformation und des Landes ob der Ems* (Graz: Böhlau, 1953).

[31] To take Germany as our example, one need only compare Opitz's rhapsodic *Aristarchus* of 1617 with his scholastic foreword to the *Teutsche Poemata* in the 1625 edition to appreciate the historical caesura running between these two dates. Opitz, who had been in residence at the Calvinist court in Heidelberg, was profoundly affected – as were so many others with intellectual and personal ties to the cultural crossroads of Heidelberg – by the disastrous fortune of Friedrich V in 1620. See the pertinent chapter in Ingeborg Spriewald et al. (eds), *Grundpositionen der deutschen Literatur im 16. Jahrhundert* (Berlin: Aufbau, 1975), as well as my career biography of Opitz, 'Martin Opitz', in *Deutsche Dichter des 17. Jahrhunderts: Ihr Leben und Werk*, ed. Harald Steinhagen and Benno von Wiese, 116–84 (Berlin: Erich Schmidt, 1984). On the implications of Friedrich's defeat, specifically for Opitz, who had shortly before composed an *Oratio ad Fridericem*, see my study 'Der Autor im 17. Jahrhundert', *Lili* 42 (1981): 29–45, esp. 31.

more cogently than Petrarch; and yet, it was this same Petrarch who encouraged alliance with the seigneurs.[32] The nobilitas literaria abetted as no other social group the advance of the early modern sovereign state. But finally, we must not lose sight of a related factor, present in humanism since Dante, which pointed far beyond the particularism of the Italian city-states and the later German territorial states, and which, in the Enlightenment, became a key concept in oppositional thinking regarding the *ancien régime*. That factor was nationalism. This nationalism, however, must be unburdened of its late-nineteenth-century chauvinistic distortions if we are to appreciate its pre-revolutionary, early-bourgeois form.

Thesis 9: The Rise and Fall of the Idea of a National Literature

The European learned aristocracy, in developing an ideology of *renovatio Romae* 'Rome restored', gave transhistorical legitimation to the idea of a national literature.[33] But in the specific national literature and the specific standardized language, the learned aristocracy simultaneously anticipated the idea of national political unity, an idea from antiquity that had resonated more or less loudly in cultural-political reform movements since Dante.[34] In the case of Germany, the tension between territorial self-interest on the one hand and national aspirations on the other reached an acute crisis. For a brief time early in the seventeenth century a 'small German' national solution appeared imminent in the Calvinist confederation.[35] This conception, to which broad universalist and monarchical hopes were attached, especially as articulated in Rosicrucianism, gave the reform movement around 1600 its dynamic quality. Political participation by the German learned aristocracy was never more vigorous than during the early Bohemian-Palatine phase. At the same time, a lively brand of journalism began to be practiced in the Southwest that made use of popular forms of agitation, signaling yet another post-Reformation opportunity for the intellectuals to expand their role in political affairs.[36] The opportunity miscarried. The learned aristocracy entered

---

[32] Konrad Burdach, *Vom Mittelalter zur Reformation: Forschungen zur Geschichte der deutschen Bildung* (Halle: Niemeyer, 1893–1939), emphatically stresses the centrality of the idea of Rome in Petrarch and the early humanists.

[33] Werner Bahner, 'Die nationale Funktion der Literatur im Blickpunkt des volkssprachlichen Humanismus', in *Formen, Ideen, Prozesse in den Literaturen der romanischen Völker*, 11–26 (Berlin: Akademie, 1977); also Garber, 'Zur Konstitution der europäischen Nationalliteraturen: Implikationen und Perspektiven', in *Nation und Literatur im Europa der Frühen Neuzeit*, 1–55, esp. 11–26 (Tübingen: Niemeyer, 1989).

[34] Garber, 'Zur Konstitution' 26–55.

[35] Hans Sturmberger, *Aufstand in Böhmen: der Beginn des Dreißigjährigen Krieges* (Munich: Oldenbourg, 1959).

[36] Dieter Mertens was the first to make this thesis, in 'Zu Heidelberger Dichtern von Schede bis Zincgref', *Zeitschrift für deutsches Altertum* 103 (1974): 200–41.

the northeastern Lutheran cities and Protestant courts under conditions fundamentally different from those prior to 1620 and entirely unsuited to entertaining national, not to mention European, goals. It was only logical, therefore, that Gottsched and his disciples should return to the beginnings of the Opitzian reform in their effort to reestablish a sound theoretical and historical basis for modern German literature.[37] Late-nineteenth-century critics demolished these historical connections by construing an artificial opposition between the concepts *Baroque* on the one hand and *Renaissance and Enlightenment* on the other. To reintegrate the original connections between Renaissance, Baroque, and Enlightenment into the early modern European national literary movement, together with its cultural and institutional manifestations between early Renaissance and late Enlightenment, should be the primary goal of a social history of the early modern learned aristocracy. The following sketch of operations in the Parisian Cabinet Dupuy may serve as an example.*

---

[37] Klaus Garber, 'Opitz als Garant frühbürgerlicher Öffentlichkeit: Gottsched', in *Martin Opitz, 'der Vater der deutschen Dichtung': eine kritische Studie zur Wissenschaftsgeschichte der Germanistik*, 45–55 (Stuttgart: Metzler, 1976).

* Translated by Max Reinhart.

Chapter 4

Paris, Capital of European Late Humanism: Jacques Auguste de Thou and the Cabinet Dupuy

Without knowledge of late humanism the entrance is blocked to German literature of the seventeenth century. For, by the time Martin Opitz [see Plate 1] presented his reform poetics, *Buch von der Deutschen Poeterey* (1624; Book of German Poetry), the great European debates on vernacular poetic reform had been completed. Opitz was merely summarizing. The period in which these debates took place, late humanism, was a time of vigorous and creative production of ideas, though this assertion was not generally accepted by German literary studies until very recently, so powerful was the sway of opinions to the contrary espoused by an arrogant *Geistesgeschichte*. The statement made in 1935 by the venerable Baroque literary historian Paul Hankamer may serve as an example, as it is representative of the attitude that has prevailed with respect to German Baroque studies:

> In its final phase, late humanism at the end of the sixteenth and beginning of the seventeenth century demonstrated a form of learned existence that was completely alienated from real life. It was a fictive world, built upon nothing but artificial vacuities, whose values exhausted themselves in the pretense of self-importance within its practitioners' otherwise uneventful lives. In this void they composed often virtuosic congratulations and avowals of friendship and elegant epistles to one another, the dreadful emptiness of which could only be supplemented by mutual assurances of their literary immortality, which simply made things more grotesque. In late humanism a communal form evolved that existed entirely outside of the estates and the realm of real society in which they performed their offices. They turned a kind of college camaraderie as it were into an ideal value, and thus they lived. From this there arose a republic of letters. This by no means consisted of large intellectual values but only of the self-involved pleasures of personal merit, which they guaranteed themselves through possession of a formal humanist education.[1]

---

[1] *Deutsche Gegenreformation und deutsches Barock: Die deutsche Literatur im Zeitraum des 17. Jahrhunderts*, 3rd edn (Stuttgart: Metzler, 1964), 43–4.

Plate 1   Martin Opitz (1597–1639). Engraved portrait by J.v.d. Heyden. Frontispiece to *Umständliche Nachricht von des weltberühmten Schlesiers, Martin Opitz von Boberfeld, Leben, Tode und Schriften, nebst einigen alten und neuen Lobgedichten auf Ihn*. Part I. Edited by Kaspar Gottlieb Lindner. Hirschberg: Immanuel Krahn, 1740.

It is my wish in this study to add my voice to the growing number of scholarly corrections to this misguided view of European late humanism.[2] I take as my subject the Parisian intellectual society known as the Cabinet Dupuy, among the most important and influential orders in Europe in the period of late humanism.

The first order of business for late humanists visiting Paris was to pay their respects at a meeting of the Cabinet Dupuy.[3] Here they could expect to meet men from many other orders of Europe's learned aristocracy and carry home a great deal more than just the latest in academic gossip. The Cabinet Dupuy was situated in the capital of a country at the forefront in nation-building, confessional politics, and the operations of absolutist government. Documents pertaining to the previous 150 years of European diplomacy were managed here, a fact that set the Cabinet Dupuy apart from other learned societies in early-seventeenth-century Europe. In short, the Cabinet Dupuy was reputed to be the major clearinghouse for information on current affairs in Europe.

---

[2] Scholarship on the positive view of late humanism must begin with the classic study by Erich Trunz, 'Der deutsche Späthumanismus um 1600 als Standeskultur' (1931; reprint in *Deutsche Barockforschung*, 2nd edn, ed. Richard Alewyn, 147–81 (Cologne: Kiepenheuer & Witsch, 1966), and include recent work by, among others, R.J.W. Evans, *Rudolf II and his World: A Study in Intellectual History 1576–1612* (Oxford: Clarendon Press, 1973); Wilhelm Kühlmann, *Gelehrtenrepublik und Fürstenstaat: Entwicklung und Kritik des deutschen Späthumanismus in der Literatur des Barockzeitalters* (Tübingen: Niemeyer, 1982); and Roman Schnur (ed.), *Die Rolle der Juristen bei der Entstehung des modernen Staates* (Berlin: Duncker & Humblot, 1986).

[3] Also known as the 'Académie Putéane' (Latinized Dupuy = *Puteanus*). Meetings were regularly held at the house of the brothers Jacques and Pierre. See esp. Pierre Gassendi, *Peiresc, 1580–1637: vie de l'illustre Nicolas-Claude Fabride Peiresc, conseiller au Parlement d'Aix* (1655), trans. Roger Lassalle (Paris: Belin, 1992); Claude Nicaise, *Les Sirènes, ou discours sur leur forme et figure* (Paris: Anisson, 1691), 4–14; Isaac Uri, *Un cercle savant au XVIIe siècle: François Guyot (1575–1655) d'après des documents inédits* (Paris: Hachette, 1886), 8–63; Harcourt Brown, *Scientific Organizations in Seventeenth-Century France (1620–1680)* (1934; reprint, New York: Russel and Russel, 1967), 6–16; Josephine de Boer, 'Men's Literary Circles in Paris 1610–1660', *Publications of the Modern Language Association* 63 (1938): 730–36; Gerhard Hess, *Pierre Gassendi: der französische Späthumanismus und das Problem von Wissen und Glauben* (Jena: Gronau, 1939), 1 ff.; René Pintard, *Le libertinage érudit pendant la première moitié du XVIIe siècle* (Paris: Boivin, 1943), 1:92 ff.; Frances A. Yates, *The French Academies of the Sixteenth Century* (London: Warburg Institute, 1947), 284 n. 5; Schnur, *Die französischen Juristen* (1962), 29–30; Antoine Adam, *Les Libertins au XVIIe siècle* (Paris: Buchet and Castel, 1964), 12 ff.; Henri-Jean Martin, *Livre: pouvoirs et société à Paris au XVIIe siècle (1598–1701)*, 2 vols. (Geneva: Droz, 1969); Jürgen Voss, *Das Mittelalter im historischen Denken Frankreichs: Untersuchungen zur Geschichte des Mittelalterbegriffs und der Mittelalterbewertung von der zweiten Hälfte des 16. bis zur Mitte des 19. Jahrhunderts* (Munich: Fink, 1972), 145–55; and Marc Fumaroli, *L'Âge de l'éloquence, rhétorique et 'res literaria' de la Renaissance au seuil de l'époque classique* (Geneva: Droz, 1980), 576 ff.

The historical and intellectual roots of the Cabinet Dupuy extended back into the sixteenth century.[4] The universal historian and former president of the Parisian Parlement Jacques Auguste de Thou was one of its guiding lights [see Plate 2]. His personality and scholarship could still be discerned at the heart of the Académie Française, which took shape a generation later under Cardinal Richelieu. De Thou's influence rested mainly on Parlement;[5] in fact, the pool of parlementary jurists formed the backbone of French humanism. While it is true that only men of substantial means could attain to Parlement, this did not preclude the evolution from within its ranks of a pronounced mentality of officialdom, which was further deepened by bonds of kinship. To belong to Parlement meant ultimately having to abandon the ties of one's high-bourgeois origins in favor of adopting and conforming to a nationalist mentality. The formation of a corresponding estatist mentality among the *noblesse de robe*, as distinct from the old feudal nobility, occurred largely from inside the institution of Parlement, whereby the older humanist ethos of true nobility survived among the jurists

---

[4] Among the many works relevant to the question of continuity between sixteenth- and seventeenth-century humanism, see esp. Friedrich Heer, *Die dritte Kraft: der europäische Humanismus zwischen den Fronten des konfessionellen Zeitalters* (Frankfurt a.M.: Fischer, 1959), and Leonid M. Batkin, *Die italienische Renaissance: Versuch einer Charakterisierung eines Kulturtyps* (Basel: Stroemfeld; Frankfurt a.M.: Roter Stern, 1981). The political background, including the tolerance movement, is memorably portrayed by Joseph Lecler in the introduction to vol. 2 of his monumental *Histoire de la Tolérance au siècle de la Réforme*, trans. T. L. Westow as *Toleration and the Reformation* (New York: Association Press, 1960). See also André Bourde, 'Frankreich vom Ende des Hundertjährigen Krieges bis zum Beginn der Selbstherrschaft Ludwigs XIV. (1453–1661)', in *Handbuch der Europäischen Geschichte*, ed. Theodor Schieder, 3:714–850 (Stuttgart: Union, 1971); Franco Simone, *Culture et politique en France à l'époque de l'humanisme et de la Renaissance* (Turin: Accademia delle scienze, 1974); Natalie Zemon Davis, *Society and Culture in Early Modern France* (Stanford: University of California Press, 1975); John Hearsey Salmon, *Society in Crisis: France in the Sixteenth Century* (London: Benn, 1975); Donald Stone, *France in the Sixteenth Century: A Medieval Society Transformed* (Westport, Conn.: Greenwood Press, 1976); Robin Briggs, *Early Modern France 1560–1715* (Oxford: Oxford University Press, 1977); and Jürgen Voss, *Von der frühneuzeitlichen Monarchie zur Ersten Republik 1500–1800*, vol. 2 of *Geschichte Frankreichs* (Munich: Beck, 1980).

[5] Schnur, *Die französischen Juristen*. The older studies on Parlement by Ernest Désiré Glasson, *Le parlement de Paris; son rôle politique depuis le règne de Charles VII jusqu'à la revolution* (1901; reprint, Geneva: Slatkine-Megariotis, 1974), and Edouard Maugis, *Histoire du Parlement de Paris de l'avenement des rois Valois à la mort d'Henri IV*, 3 vols. (1913–16; reprint, New York: B. Franklin, 1967), are still indispensable; more recent investigations by J.H. Shennan, *The Parlement of Paris* (London: Eyre and Spottiswoode, 1968), and Roland Mousnier, *The Institutions of France Under the Absolute Monarchy, 1598–1798*, 2 vols., trans. Arthur Goldhammer and Brian Pearce (Chicago: University of Chicago Press, 1979–84), esp. 2:253 ff., 318 ff., 594 ff. The studies by Roger Doucet, *Les institutions de la France au XVIe siècle* (Paris: A. et J. Picard, 1948), and Gaston Zeller, *Les institutions de la France au XVIe siècle*, 2nd edition (Paris: Presses universitaires de France, 1987), deal with Parlement as institution.

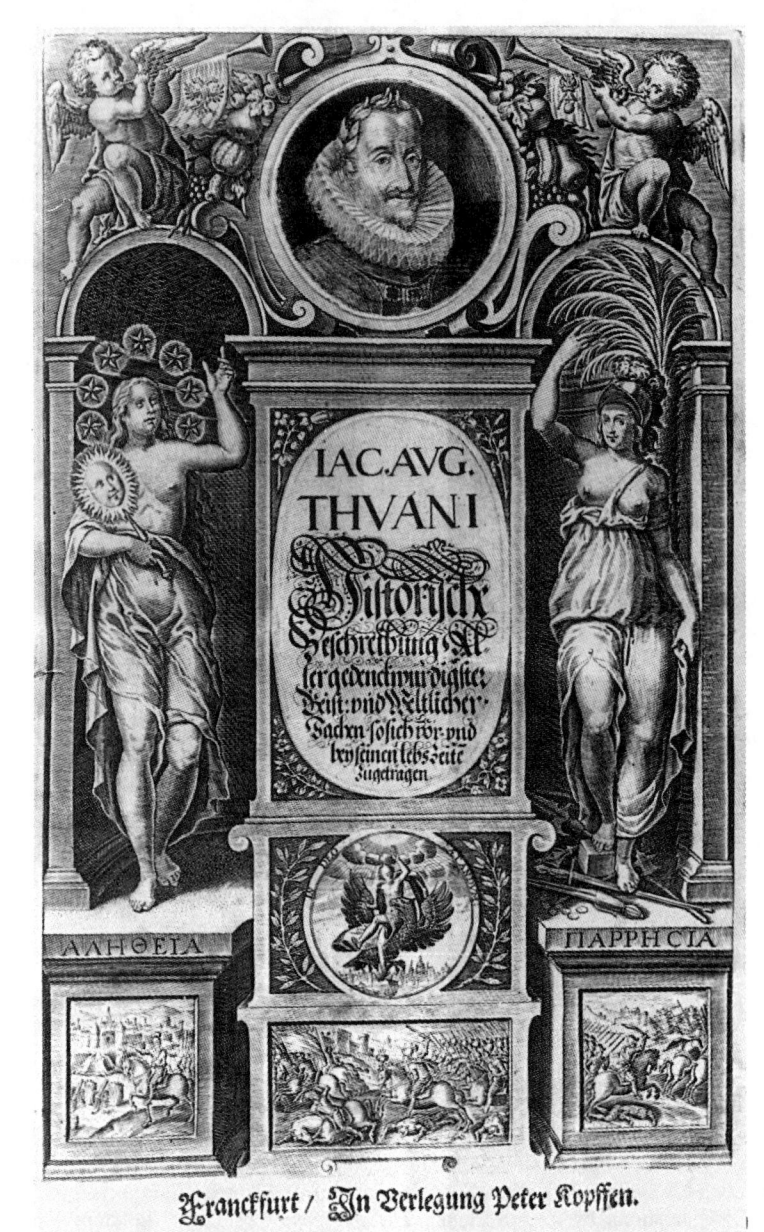

Plate 2   Jacques Auguste de Thou (1553–1617). Frontispiece to JACOBI AVGVSTI THVANI, *Historische Beschreibung deren Namhaffigsten/ Geistlichen vnd Weltlichen Geschichte so sich beydes in- vnd ausser dem Römischen Reich/ [. . .] nun vber die 100. Jahr [. . .] zugetragen.* Frankfurt a.M.: Egenolff Emmel (printer), Peter Kopff (publisher), 1671.

under new conditions. The leading members of Parlement were well aware that they constituted the indispensable foundation for French monarchical expansion and never failed to support the monarchy in times of crisis. Royalism, Gallicanism, and inter-confessionalism became the hallmarks of this mostly moderate Catholic group, whose efforts on behalf of the 'Rise and Triumph of the Modern Idea of State in France', as Martin Göhring characterized it, cannot be overestimated.[6]

All of this is well illustrated by the life of Jacques Auguste de Thou.[7] His father, Christofle, had risen to become the first president of the Parisian Parlement, though he never achieved the intellectual and political renown of the mature Michel de l'Hôpital.[8] L'Hôpital ultimately arrived at an ecumenical theory of shared power, restricted only by his insistence that monarchical authority be respected by the various bodies. Christofle de Thou, on the other hand, maintained loyalty to his estate as to the one true religion, which he considered the *sine qua non* of a sound political system. Thus he opposed the creation of a Catholic League under Henry III as well as the repeated attempts by the curia to influence the policies of the crown. Maintaining contact with the humanist poets of the Pléiade as well as with the jurist-poets of Jean Morel's circle[9] seemed reasonable to him, as it did later to his son, Jacques Auguste. The younger de Thou was personally acquainted with the poets Pierre de Ronsard, Jean-Antoine de Baïf, and Joachim du Bellay, and cultivated ties to important jurists and champions of religious tolerance, including Jacques Cujas, Joseph Scaliger, and

---

[6] Göhring, *Weg und Sieg der modernen Staatsidee in Frankreich*, 2nd edn (Tübingen: Mohr, 1947).

[7] No modern biography exists for J.A. de Thou. That planned by Samuel Kinser, announced in Ernst Hinrichs, *Fürstenlehre und politisches Handeln im Frankreich Heinrichs IV.: Untersuchungen über die politischen Denk- und Handlungsformen im Späthumanismus* (Göttingen: Vandenhoeck & Ruprecht, 1969), 150 n. 64, never appeared. All relevant materials, including the modestly useful commemorative literature, are collected in Alexandre Cioranescu, *Bibliographie de la littérature française du dix-septième siècle*, 3 vols (Paris: Editions du Centre national de la recherche scientifique, 1965–66), and Schnur, *Die französischen Juristen* 29 n. 14. The most exhaustive biographical work was done in the early nineteenth century by John Collinson, *The Life of Thuanus, with some Account of his Writings and a Translation of the Preface to his History* (London: Longman, 1807), and Heinrich Düntzer, *Jacques Auguste de Thou's Leben, Schriften und historische Kunst verglichen mit den Alten* (Darmstadt: Leske, 1837). Henry Harisse's broad study, *Le Président de Thou et ses descendantes, leur celèbre bibliothèque, leurs armoiries et les traductions françaises de J.-A. Thuani historiarum sui temporis d'après des documents nouveaux* (Paris: Leclerc, 1905), includes much valuable genealogical data.

[8] There exist a multitude of under-utilized sources that could provide the substance for biographies of early modern public servants. French humanism is one exception to the rule that early modern political biography is largely undeveloped, and L'Hôpital is a case in point. See the exemplary monograph by René Filhol, *Le Premier Président Christofle de Thou et la Réformation des Coutumes* (Paris: Recueil Sirey, 1937).

[9] Morel was *curé* of the parish of Saint-Saturnin around 1640.

especially Paul de Foix. He nourished relationships in Venice and Rome with the French tragedian Marc-Antoine Muret, the Orsini family, the Venetian publisher Aldus Manutius, and the mechanical scientist Girolamo Cardano. It was also there that he became acquainted with militant Catholicism – a galvanizing experience of his entire generation, in fact. This experience inspired his unconditional commitment to the French monarchy, to an independent path for French Catholicism, and to the idea of religious toleration within a unified nation.

Given these facts, it is understandable that he and certain of his friends, including François Pithou, Claude Dupuy (father of Jacques and Pierre), and Antoine Loisel, would be members of the august Chambre de Guyenne, which had the task of replacing the deadlocked Parlement of Bordeaux and moderating between the Catholics and Huguenots. The wrath of the Guise faction in Paris, culminating in the Day of the Barricades,[10] also strongly affected Jacques Auguste de Thou. As an untiring ambassador of royal authority in a country steering towards misery, especially in Normandy, he stood by his king, who was forced to flee Paris for Chartres and then Tours. The reconciliation of Henry III shortly before his death in 1589 with Henry of Navarre can be traced to the influence of de Thou and his friends. On the one hand, de Thou opposed the anti-Huguenot propaganda, though on the other he unconditionally supported the opportune conversion of Henry IV to Catholicism (1593), inasmuch as it buttressed the *politiques*[11] and served the interests of the state, that is, the French nation. The Edict of Nantes,[12] the crowning edict of the sixteenth century, embodied the political convictions of de Thou and the modern jurist faction of the *politiques*.

---

[10] This popular uprising occurred in Paris on 12 May 1588 at the instigation of the Catholic League. The League opposed Henry III's attempt to rally Paris away from support of Henry Guise, the leader of the anti-Huguenot movement. The public was incited by the League's rumor that Henry was planning a massacre. Barricades were erected by stretching chains across the street corners.

[11] Unlike the Leaguers, the *politiques* exhibited willingness to extend toleration to Protestants as a way of ending confessional strife. The most important older studies of the *politiques* are Georges Weill, *Les theories sur le pouvoir royal en France pendant les guerres de religion* (1891; reprint, New York: B. Franklin, 1967), and Francis de Stoutz de Crue, *Le partides politiques au lendemain de la Saint-Barthólemy* (Paris: Plon, 1892); studies by Henri Sée, *Les idées politiques en France au XVIIe siècle* (Paris: Giard, 1923), 18–81, and W. J. Stankiewicz, *Politics and Religion in seventeenth-century France* (Berkeley: University of California Press, 1960), are relevant for the development of the political theory of the *politiques*; cf. also Göhring, *Weg und Sieg*; Schnur, *Die französischen Juristen*; and W.F. Church, *Constitutional Thought in Sixteenth-Century France: A Study in the Evolution of Ideas* (New York: Octagon Books, 1969), esp. 194 ff., 205 ff., 243 ff. Joseph Lecler, *Toleration and the Reformation*, and Heer, *Die dritte Kraft*, provide in-depth bibliographies.

[12] The accord reached in April 1598 between Henry IV and the Huguenots gave at least temporary legal recognition to the religious, political, and military organizations of the Reformed communities within France. A first history of the edict was published in 1695 by Elie Benoit, *Histoire de l'Edit de Nantes* (Delft: Beman).

Jacques Auguste de Thou is remembered less as a politician, however, than as a historian,[13] though for him the one was inseparable from the other. For de Thou *historia* was a *magistra vitae* 'teacher of life' in the sense that the actors on the stage of history fashion the image of the contemporary world according to personal experience and conviction. De Thou began his historical account with the middle of the sixteenth century and brought it up only to the year 1607, though originally he had intended to end it at 1610 with the assassination of Henry IV. Undertaken with the purpose of advancing the concepts of national sovereignty and religious tolerance, de Thou's work was placed on the Index of Forbidden Books in 1609, probably because his high-placed friends in Rome, Cardinals Joyeuse and d'Ossat, were no longer in a position to act on his behalf.[14] The entire 138 volumes of his *Historia sui temporis*, arguably the greatest contemporary history of the second half of the sixteenth century, appeared posthumously in 1620.[15]

Like the popular courtly novel by Honoré d'Urfé, *L'Astrée*, de Thou's *Historia* was dedicated to Henry IV for his role as a peacemaker. The dedicatory address appeals to moderation in dealing with religious differences:

> All other things are ordered according to secular authority, which is to say, according to the protocol of princes and rulers. Only religion cannot and will not tolerate force; it must be poured into predisposed minds out of the existing word of truth through the hidden workings of God's grace. Force would only cause hearts to be hardened rather than broken or convicted . . . I therefore say straight out that war is not the proper way to root out religious divisions, since the Protestants among us, whose numbers and reputation in times of peace diminished daily, now increase in time of war and have, either out of the current anti-religious fanaticism or out of an arrogant desire for change, unfortunately alienated themselves from us. They repeatedly kindle perilous war, which so often has been waged against themselves, and this has spelled the terrible ruin of French prosperity and become a clear and present danger for religion itself.[16]

---

[13] The most recent complete evaluation of de Thou's scholarship is Samuel Kinser, *The Works of Jacques-Auguste de Thou* (The Hague: Nijhoff, 1966).

[14] Alfred Soman, *De Thou and the Index: Letters from Christoph Dupuy (1603–1607)* (Geneva: Droz, 1972). A related study by Kinser on 'The Condemnation of Jacques-Auguste de Thou's *History of his Time*' was announced in 1966 but never appeared.

[15] Later translated into French as *Histoire universelle*, it is an invaluable resource work on the French Wars of Religion. Edition: *J.-A. de Thou: son Histoire universelle et ses demeles avec Rome*, ed. A.-J. Rance-Bourrey (Geneva: Slatkine, 1970).

[16] The Latin version of the Dedication was reprinted many times, often in translation, including into German. Elie Benoit translated the entire work into French in 1693 ('Dedication' on leaves h2^r–i4^v). The passage in the anonymously translated German text – the basis for the present English translation – reads as follows: 'All andere ding werden nach weltlicher Obrigkeit/ und also der Fürsten und Regenten gutachten verordnet/ allein die Religion kan und will keinen zwang leyden/ sondern muß auß vorgeschriebener meynung der warheit durch verborgene mitwürckung Gottlicher Gnaden/ den verbereyteten Gemütern gleichsamb eingeschüttet werden: hierzu vermag keinerley bezwang/ daß

This statement may be interpreted as a call for toleration of the Huguenots in the interest of preserving religious traditions. As the book itself emphasizes at every turn, religion concerns the private relationship between man and God and therefore escapes the reach of the state. Henry IV allows honest and open speech in his kingdom, and, according to de Thou, France's new prosperity is directly attributable to the right to exercise personal faith and thought. The king rewards the state's willingness to steer clear of confessional matters by promising general security once religion *qua* confession shall have ceased to be the unifying medium of the country, and offers himself as the consolidating element for all of France's citizens. The concept of religion allows for absolutely no extension of the church into the sphere of the state; politics and religion occupy fundamentally different realms.[17] De Thou interprets Henry IV's conversion, therefore, as an act of wisdom, a vote for tradition, and, more importantly, as a clear retreat, in the national interest, from confessional fanaticism. Here as elsewhere de Thou's motivation is to strengthen and secure the authority of the state, which explains why he had by 1600 become one of the leading elder statesmen in the eyes of the younger generation, including the Dupuy brothers.

Jacques and Pierre Dupuy belonged to the post-war generation that helped to guide the solidification of the French monarchy under Richelieu. This they did not so much as active politicians and diplomats, but as writers, especially as historians.[18] After having served briefly as parlementary lawyers, they found

---

dardurch die Hertzen nicht viel mehr gehalsstarrigt/ dann gebrochen/ oder beredet werden . . . sage demnach mit kurtzen worten/ daß der Krieg nicht ein gebürliche weise/ die spaltungen auß der Kirchen zu reutten/ sintemahlen die Protestirenden bey uns/ welche zu Friedenszeitten in zahl und ansehen täglichs sich verminderten/ im Krieg und widerwillen allwegen gewachsen und haben indessen die unserigen/ entweders/ auß allzu zeitigem eyffer gegen der Religion/ oder hochfahrt/ und begierde zu newerungen/ mit sehr schädlichem Irrthumb sich verstossen/ indem sie den gefährlichen Krieg/ so wider die Protestirenden offtmahls angefangen/ und hernach hingelegt geweßen/ mit so unsehlichem fortgang Frantzösischen wolstandts/ und mercklicher gefahr/ der Religion selbsten/ so manchmahl ernewert haben.' Quoted after Garber, 'Paris, die Hauptstadt des europäischen Späthumanismus', in *Res Publica Litteraria: Die Institutionen der Gelehrsamkeit in der frühen Neuzeit*, ed. Sebastian Neumeister and Conrad Wiedemann (Wiesbaden: Harrassowitz, 1987), 75.

[17] Hinrichs, *Fürstenlehre und politisches Handeln* 279, 301. This valuable study also contains an interpretation of the dedication and two other relevant epistolary documents by de Thou (150–55).

[18] No modern biography of the Dupuy brothers exists aside from Solente's sketch, 'Les manuscripts des Dupuy à la Bibliothèque Nationale', in *Bibliothèque de l'Ecole des chartes* 88 (1927). The material compiled by Nicolas Rigault, *Viri eximii Petri Puteani, regi christianissimo a consiliis et bibliothecis vita* (Paris: Cramosiana, 1652) [Bibliothèque Nationale: Rés. Ln[27] 6862α], is therefore indispensable; included are two commemorative poems by Hadrianus Valesius and an elegy to Pierre Dupuy, as well as reproductions and further documentation. For Pierre's historical writings in Périgord, see Albert Dujarric-Descombes, *Recherches sur le historiens du Périgord au XVIIe siècle* (reprint, Geneva: Slatkine, 1971). A commemoration of Jacques is found in the Dupuy-

optimal conditions under Richelieu for their scholarship. Directly appointed to their publicist duties by the first minister, they carried out their activities on behalf of the crown in a fashion different from their fathers.[19] In 1615 Pierre Dupuy collaborated with Théodore Godefroy in cataloguing and reorganizing the *Trésor des Chartes*,[20] as a result of which he was granted the privilege to undertake assignments on supreme royal commission. Following the death of François Pithou, he and Godefroy were entrusted in 1621 with the inspection and evaluation of the documents in Troyes, which were thought to justify royal prerogatives.[21] The *lois fondamentales*, which were based on principles of dynasty and dominion, had long been invoked against claims to special regional rights and privileges. Under Richelieu, however, these fundamental laws were not only mined for their justification of royal power over feudal nobility, but also of foreign annexations. This ideological base was laid mainly by the Dupuys and

---

Papers in the Bibliothèque Nationale, 'Eligia in obitum illustrissimi viri Puteani S. Salvatoris Abbatis, Regique Christianissimo a Consiliis et Bibliothecis effusa: Ac Illustrissimo Excelentissimoque Viro Jacobo Augusto Thuano Jacobi Augusti . . . filio' [Dupuy-Papers: M. Fr. 16793:380–97] (Paris: Martinus, 1657). On their correspondence with Joseph Scaliger, see Philippe Tamizey de Larroque, *Lettres, de Peiresc aux frères Dupuy*, 3 vols (Paris: Imprimeur Nationale, 1888–92). A copy of a poem by the German Calvinist poet Paul Melissus-Schede to Claude Dupuy is contained in Pierre de Nolhac, *Un poète rhénan ami de la Pléiade: Paul Melissus* (Paris: Champion, 1923), 86-8. Epicedia for Claude Dupuy are found in the 1607 volume, *V. amplissimi Claudii Puteani tumulus* (Bibliothèque Nationale: Ln[27] 6853). For poems written by the Dupuys, both in print and in manuscript, see Frédéric Lachèvre, *Bibliographie des Recueils collectifs de poésies du XVIe siècle* (Paris: Champion, 1922), 267–8, and Solente, 'Les manuscripts des Dupuy' 177–250.

[19] Deloche, *Autour de la plume du Cardinal Richelieu*; cf. W.F. Church, *Richelieu and Reason of State* (Princeton: Princeton University Press, 1972), 361–71; on the Cardinal's understanding of reason of state, see Fritz Dickmann, 'Reichtsgedanke und Machtpolitik bei Richelieu: Studien aus neu entdeckten Quellen', *Historische Zeitschrift* 196 (1963): 265–319, and *Der Westphälische Frieden*, 3rd edn (Münster: Aschendorff, 1972), 505–6; letters of Richelieu in *Lettres du Cardinal de Richelieu à MM. Du Puy et Godefroy* (Paris: Bulletin de la Société de l'Histoire de France, 1851–2), esp. 304–6.

[20] This is a collection of records and other documents relating to the older monarchy; later conserved under the rubric 'Archives impériales', for which see H.-François Delaborde, 'Les travaux de Dupuy sur le Trésor de chartes et les origines du supplément', *Bibliothèque de l'Ecole des Chartes* 58 (1897): 126–54. On Godefroy, see D.-C. Godefroy-Méniglaise, *Les savants Godefroy: Mémoires d'une famille pendant les XVIe, XVIIe et XVIIIe siècles* (reprint, Geneva: Slatkine, 1971), 109–39. Most of the documents pertaining to the Dupuy-Godefroy collaboration are contained in either the Dupuy papers (Bibliothèque Nationale) or the Godefroy papers (Institut de France, Paris).

[21] P. Dupuy, *Traité de la maiorité de nos rois, et des régences du royaume* (Paris: Mathurin Du Puis, 1655) [Bibliothèque Nationale: 4° Rés. Le[5] 2], and *Traitez touchant les droits du Roy* (Paris: Courbe, 1655) [Bibliothèque Nationale: Fol. Lb[37] 3257]. Important studies on royal prerogatives and protections: Albertini, *Das politische Denken in Frankreich* 146–59; Dickmann, 'Reichsgedanke' 284–308; Church, *Richelieu and Reason of State* 361–72; and Hans-Wolfgang Stein, *Protection Royale: eine Untersuchung zu den Protektionsverhältnissen im Elsaß zur Zeit Richelieus, 1622–1643* (Münster: Aschendorff, 1978).

Godefroy; their continued efforts to work out a historical basis for Gallicanism was related to this project.[22]

In this effort the Dupuys took up the life-long work of Pithou, editing and providing it with commentary.[23] The Gallicans, anchored firmly in Parlement, cooperated with the crown in seeking to establish one nation as the home of all good French people, irrespective of partisan or social divisions.[24] Opposition to the crown was prohibited as emphatically as papal supremacy over the king. The national policy of unification, which called for independence from Rome, Madrid, and Vienna, found its staunchest supporters in Gallicanism. Royal approval of the acts of legitimation followed in short order: in 1623 Pierre Dupuy was named 'Charge de Conseiller en ses Conseils d'Etat et privé' and was eventually promoted by Richelieu to the office of national historian.

All of these responsibilities fell within the sphere of the official state. The Dupuys, however, found their place within the history of Europe's learned aristocracy by undertaking a different kind of work – simultaneously negotiated with and withheld from Richelieu – for which they garnered wide admiration from Stockholm to Istanbul: the curatorship and continuation of Jacques Auguste de Thou's project in modern history. By the turn of the seventeenth century de Thou had collected a universal library acclaimed for its more than 12,000 volumes and precious manuscripts.[25] The Dupuy brothers were appointed by

---

[22] P. Dupuy, *Traitez des droits et libertez de l'église gallicane* (1639) [Bibliothèque Nationale: Fol. Rés. Ld^{10} 7]; *Preuves des libertez de l'église gallicane* (1639) [Bibliothèque Nationale: Fol. Rés. Ld^{10} 7]; *Commentaire sur le Traité des libertez de l'église gallicane* (Paris: Cramoisy, 1652) [Bibliothèque Nationale: 4° Rés. Ld^{10} 52]. A review of the editions of Pierre Dupuy's works was undertaken in the mid-nineteenth century by Gabriel Demante, 'Histoire de la publication des livres de Pierre Du Puy sur les libertés de l'église gallicane', *Bibliothèque de l'Ecole des Chartes* 5 (1843–4): 585–606.

[23] The first review of the works of Pithou was undertaken by Jacques Lelong, *Die Quellenschriften bei Jacques Lelong: Bibliothèque historique de la France* (Paris: Herissant, 1768), 1:468–519.

[24] Modern scholarship on sociological implications in Gallicanism proceeds from Lucien Romier, *Le Royaume de Catherine de Médicis: la France à la veille des guerres de religion* (Paris: Perrin, 1922), 2:89–150; Joseph Lecler, 'Qu'est-ce que les libertés de l'église gallicane?' *Recherches de science religieuse* 23 (1933): 385–410, 542–68, and 'Qu'est-ce que les libertés de l'église gallicane?' *Recherches de science religieuse* 24 (1934): 47–85; and H.-J. Martin, *Livre* 180 ff.; more recently, see Aimé-George Martimort, *Le gallicanisme* (Paris: Presse Universitaire de France, 1973).

[25] Harisse, *Le Président de Thou*, esp. pt. 1, 'Histoire et catalogues originaux de la bibliothèque' (1–82). See also Ap. Briquet, 'Notes sur la bibliothèque et les armoiries de J.-Aug. de Thou', *Bulletin du Bibliophile* (1860): 896–903; Léopold Delisle, *Le Cabinet des Manuscripts de la Bibliothèque Impériale*, 3 vols (Paris: Imprimeur Nationale, 1868–81); Comte L. Ris, 'Les amateurs d'autrefois XVI: Jacques-Auguste de Thou (1553–1617)', *Bulletin du Bibliophile* (1875): 225–43; Samuel Kinser, 'An Unknown Manuscript Catalogue of the Library of J. A. de Thou', *The Book Collector* 173 (1968): 168–76; and Emmanuel Poulle, *Index-Supplémentaire* [to Delisle] (Paris: Imprimeur Municipal, 1977).

testament as its trustees and proved to be excellent curators. For nearly thirty years they occupied the Hôtel de Thou, which became the preferred gathering place for Europe's learned aristocracy and where de Thou's work was carried on. Some of late humanism's finest minds collaborated in this undertaking; the name of Georg Michael Lingelsheim, under whose pseudonym the first complete edition of de Thou's *Historia sui temporis* appeared in 1620, deserves special mention. This publishing event attested to the work's undiminished appeal and is a monument to the singular achievement of the Dupuys and Nicolas Rigault, the librarian of the Bibliothèque Royale.[26] Here in the Hôtel de Thou the fight against the work's prohibition was organized, expert opinions in defense of de Thou's irenicism were commissioned,[27] and pamphlets composed against the execution in 1642 of François Auguste de Thou.[28] Finally, it was in this residence that the Dupuy brothers meticulously copied the catalogue of de Thou's library. This copy provided the model for the splendid two-volume catalogue compiled in 1679,

---

[26] Jacques de Thou, *Illustris viri Jacobi Augusti Thuani Historiarum sui temporis ab anno Domini 1543. usque ad annum 1607. Libri CXXXIII*, 5 vols. (Geneva, 1620) [Bibliothèque Nationale: Rés. Fol. La[20] 8], and Alexander Reifferscheid (ed.), *Briefe G. M. Lingelsheims, M. Berneggers und ihrer Freunde, nach Handschriften* (Heilbronn: Henninger, 1889). The reference in Reifferscheid is to the *Vorrede* (735–6) by the pseudonymous Lingelsheim; related letters can be determined with help of the *Register*. Petrus Denaisius was among the contributors to the front matter.

[27] The defense of de Thou's irenicism is documented brilliantly in Buckley's London edition of 1733, *Jac. Augusti Thuani Historiarum sui temporis*. A French version appeared in 1734, for which see Alfred Soman, 'The London Edition of de Thou's History: A Critique of Some Well-Documented Legends', *Renaissance Quarterly* 24 (1971): 1–12. Related: the anonymous *Apologie pour l'Histoire de Monsieur de Thou, traduite d'un poème latin dédié à la postérité* (Amsterdam: Desbordes, 1705). The text of de Thou's satirical poem on the Jesuits, 'Posteritati', is contained in his 1620 *Historiarum sui temporis* 1:81-7, as well as separately as *Posteritati: J. Aug. Thuani Poematium, in quo argutias quorundam importunorum criticorum in ipsius Historias propalatas refellit, opus huc usque fere sepultum, nunc redivivum notisque perpetuis illustratum opera atque studio I. Melanchthonis* (Amsterdam: Elzevier, 1678), 1–12, with Melanchthon's exegesis on 13–14. A French version exists in the *Apologia*; English version in Collinson, *The Life of Thuanus* 76–81; German version in David Christoph Seybold, *Thuanus*, vol. 1 of *Selbstbiographien berühmter Männer, ein Pendant zu J.G. Müllers Selbstbekenntnissen* (Winterthur: Steiner, 1796), 470–97.

[28] François Auguste was Jacques Auguste's oldest son; he ended up on the fringe of the Cinq-Mars conspiracy and was eventually beheaded in Lyons in 1641 on Richelieu's orders; see Buckley, *Historiarum*: 'Memoires et instructions pour servir à justifier l'innocence de Messire François-Auguste de Thou, Conseiller du Roi en son Conseil d'Etat' (7:6–100). Also of relevance in Buckley's *Historiarum*: 'Histoire universelle de Jacques-Auguste de Thou depuis 1543 jusqu'en 1607' (15:1–188). Church, *Richelieu and Reason of State* 322 ff., comments on this event; see A. Lloyd Moote, *The Revolt of the Judges: The Parlement of Paris and the Fronde, 1643–1652* (Princeton: Princeton University Press, 1971), for the context.

which makes it possible for us today to visualize how the library was organized.[29] The original is no longer intact, having been sold at public auction in 1677 in order to settle accounts with creditors after the death of the younger Jacques Auguste de Thou.[30] Only the manuscript collection could be salvaged for the Bibliothèque Royale, thanks to the mediation of chief financial officer Jean-Baptiste Colbert. Fortunately, the Dupuy brothers, having been appointed in 1645 to succeed Rigault as royal librarians in the *rue de la Harpe*, saw to it that the library, which their father had helped to establish and which contained so many precious manuscripts, became the possession of the Royal Library.[31] The main corpus (known as the 'Collection Dupuy'),[32] which today constitutes one of the centerpieces of the Salle de Manuscripts in the Bibliothèque Nationale in Paris, was also entrusted to the younger Jacques Auguste de Thou and thereby likewise ended up in the auction.[33]

It is impossible even to begin to give an account of all the thematic focuses of the Collection Dupuy.[34] Nevertheless, a general overview of its organization would be useful, since the collection provides conclusive evidence of the

---

[29] The handwritten catalogues of the de Thou library are contained in vols. 879 and 880 of the Collection Dupuy. Whether and to what degree the two-volume unprinted 'Catalogue Bibliothecae Thuanae' is based on the work of the Dupuys is uncertain; cf. Solente, 'Les manuscripts des Dupuy' 186. The manuscripts of the de Thou library were first inventoried by the Dupuys about 1617; see Cabinet Dupuy, vol. 653, and Delisle, *Le Cabinet des Manuscripts* (1868–81), 1:470 n. 6. In general, consult pt 1 of Harisse, *Le Président de Thou*, and Antoine Coron, 'Note sur les Cotes dites de la Bibliothèque de Thou', *Bulletin du Bibliophile*, n.s. 3 (1982): 339–57.

[30] Like his father, he had tried his hand at politics on the grand scale, only barely to escape death as a *frondeur*. (In a word, the Fronde [1648–52] was a civil war to challenge absolutism as it had been practiced by Richelieu.)

[31] A large two-volume folio catalogue of the printed books and manuscripts of the Dupuy library (in addition to the Collection Dupuy) has been preserved in the Bibliothèque Nationale (Mss. latins 10372 and 10373); the mss. are indexed in 2:668–81. An inventory of the 'Manuscripts de Pierre et Jacques Dupuy (1657)' is contained in vol. 4 of Henri Auguste Omont, *Manuscripts de Pierre et Jacques Dupuy (1657)* (Paris: Leroux, 1908–21), 187–211. Omont, 'Inventaire des manuscrits de Claude Dupuy (1595)', *Bibliothèque de l'Ecole des Chartes* 76 (1915): 526–31, provided a further index to the manuscripts from the collection of Claude Dupuy's father. Solente, 'Les manuscripts des Dupuy' 192–9, also comments on the manuscript collections of the Dupuys and others.

[32] This collection is distinct from the Dupuys' library and manuscript collection. See Léon Dorez, *Introduction à la table alphabétique du catalogue de la collection Dupuy* (Paris: Leroux, 1928), i–xxiv. On the collection's lacunae, see Solente, 'Les manuscripts des Dupuy' xiii–xx and 218–19, as well as Deslisle, *Le Cabinet des Manuscripts* 422–4, and Harisse, *Le Président de Thou* 14 ff.

[33] Solente, 'Les manuscripts des Dupuy' 199 ff., describes how it was at last returned, less than intact, to the Royal Library in 1754 after a series of adventurous detours.

[34] The modern printed catalogue of the collection was systematized by Léon Dorez, *Catalogue de la Collection Dupuy*, 2 vols (Paris: Leroux, 1899), and further developed by Solente. On the older catalogues of the collection, see Delisle, *Le Cabinet des Manuscripts* 422–4 and Solente 214 ff.

intentions of the scholars gathered around the Dupuys. In describing this collection, however, one does best to ignore the organizing principles of most known humanist collections and literary remains. Even the greatest collections – the Uffenbach-Wolf Collection in Hamburg or the Böllinger Collection in Copenhagen or the Rhediger Collection in Wroclaw – focus on international scholarly communication in the form of letters. Epistolary literature is more than amply represented in the Collection Dupuy, to be sure; but in comparison with the wealth of other kinds of materials amassed there, the letters are of less significance than one might assume. The collection is in every way an encyclopedically conceived archive of sources that document European history in its broadest parameters, roughly equivalent in proportion to de Thou's *Historia sui temporis*.[35] In fact, it is reasonable to assume that many of the documents used in de Thou's history ended up in the Collection Dupuy, and even that the *Historia* may have constituted its base. As the collection exists today, however, it appears to represent the work of the Dupuys, who expended enormous energy in compiling and systematizing it, especially during the 1630s.

I offer the following categories as a possible model of organization for this immense collection:

1. *Early Modern France (c.1500–1650)*. Royal policy from about the time of Francis I is superbly documented by a great variety of transcripts, briefs, judgments, decrees, letters, etc. Conspicuous interest is accorded Henry IV, particularly his conversion. The important institutional and domestic policy subjects – demesne, finance, Parlement, Estates General, Gallicanism, monarchomachism, etc. – are all present here.
2. *The French Provinces*. Almost all are richly documented.
3. *Europe*. For nearly all European countries there are numerous large volumes of embassy reports, travel logs, and other types of sources. Catholic and Protestant domains are covered in equal share. The collector's fervor extends to the Near East and its connections with European politics.
4. *Religion and Confessional Politics*. A strong preference is shown for this category. Of the sources on Catholicism, it is not surprising that those on the Jesuit order and the Council of Trent predominate. Given the special importance that reform Catholicism in Italy held for the older generation of de Thous and Dupuys and what hope they invested in the anti-papal movement, it makes sense that there should be a wealth of related testimonies, especially those concerning the great Venetian Paolo Sarpi.[36] On balance,

---

[35] Non-European sources are substantially present, as well, though in considerably less quantity.

[36] On Sarpi's relationship with de Thou, see Manlio D. Busnelli, 'Les relations de Fra Paolo Sarpi et du Président J.-A. de Thou d'après leur correspondance inédite Venise – Paris MDCIV – MDCVVII', in *Annales de l'Université de Grenoble*, Lettres – Droit, n.s. III/1 (1926): 1–30; Giovanni Getto, *Paolo Sarpi* (Florence: Olschki, 1967); and Cazzi Gaetano, *Paolo Sarpi tra Venezia e l'Europa* (Turin: Einaudi, 1979). The larger context of the question of Italian liberalism is the subject of Yates, 'Italian Liberals.'

however, interest in Protestantism dominates, particularly the currents that directly affected contemporary French history, such as Philipism, Zwinglianism, and Calvinism. Letters and other documents concerning John Calvin, Théodore de Bèze, Philipp Melanchthon, the Condé family, Philippe Duplessis-Mornay, as well as religious conditions in Geneva, La Rochelle, and Sédan, among other centers, are plentiful.

5. *European Late Humanism.* In this category the collection is nearly inexhaustible. As the elder Dupuy and de Thou before them had done, Jacques and Pierre Dupuy and their colleagues in the Parisian circle kept up a lively exchange with Europe's entire learned aristocracy. Thanks to their efforts, letters and other documents from and about all the humanist greats around 1600 – L'Hôpital, Saumaise, Casaubon, Joseph Scaliger, Daniel Heinsius, Grotius, Janus Gruter, Lingelsheim, and dozens of others – are preserved in the archives. This is not to mention de Thou's personal collections and the literary writings of the Dupuys themselves.

Intellectual life in France around the turn of the seventeenth century has sometimes been characterized as a form of libertinism.[37] This concept – ultimately fashioned by Third Republic laicism and typically accompanied by labels such as 'religious skepticism', 'defeatism', 'political quietism', 'attentivism', or 'moral free thinking' – bears the obvious signature of the mid-nineteenth century.[38] It has proven less than useful for investigating the historical specifics of late humanism.

Efforts to define late humanism in terms of its own philological methods have been equally fruitless,[39] as is obvious from an analysis of the types of scholars surrounding the Dupuys, first in the Hôtel de Thou, then in the Royal Library.[40] Two main groups may be identified. In the first, French linguists such as Guillaume Du Vair (also a statesman and neo-Stoic philosopher), Saumaise

---

[37] Hess, *Pierre Gassendi* n. 28, and Gerhard Schneider, *Der Libertin: Zur Geistes- und Sozialgeschichte des Bürgertums im 16. und 17. Jahrhundert* (Stuttgart: Metzler, 1970), 9–34, offer opposing views on this tradition of criticism.

[38] This tradition of interpretation began with Jean Denis Long, *La Reforme et les guerres de religion au Dauphine de 1560 à l'edit de Nantes (1598)* (reprint, Geneva: Slatkine, 1970), and François-Thommy Perrens, *Les libertines en France au XVIIe siècle* (reprint, New York: B. Franklin, 1973). It includes the many studies by Ferdinand Buisson, e.g., *Sebastien Castellion: sa vie et son œuvre (1515–1563)*, 2 vols (1892; reprint, Nieukoop: B. de Graaf, 1964), and extends all the way to Antoine Adam, e.g., *Histoire de la littérature française au XVIIe siècle: L'époque d'Henri IV et de Louis XIII* (Paris: Domat, 1948), *Les Libertins au XVIIe siècle* (1964), and *Grandeur and Illusion: French Literature and Society, 1600–1715*, trans. Herbert Tint (London: Weidenfeld and Nicolson, 1972), and René Pintard's two-volume summary *Le libertinage érudit dans la première moitiè du xviie siècle* (Paris: Boivin, 1943).

[39] The attempt by Uri, *Un cercle savant au XVIIe siècle*, is just one such example.

[40] The sketch that follows is based upon the still unsurpassed studies of Josephine de Boer, esp. 'Men's Literary Circles in Paris 1610–1660', and René Pintard, *Le libertinage érudit.*

(better known as Salmasius), Charles Du Fresne Du Cange, and François Guyot, belonged to the Cabinet Dupuy in significant numbers. This group also included a wide circle of external contact persons and visitors, such as the philologists Heinsius, Joannes Fredericus Gronovius, Lucas Holstenius, Isaac Vossius, Gruter, Grotius, Peter Lambeck, Matthias Bernegger, and Johann Heinrich Boecler. To these must be added the lawyers and historians, including Jacques and Pierre Dupuy, Rigault, Godefroy, and André Duchesne. The second main group consisted of distinguished natural scientists: Nicolas-Claude de Fabride Peiresc in Aix (Peiresc maintained a lively correspondence with the Dupuys), Marin Mersenne, Guy Patin, and, most notably, Pierre Gassendi.[41] It was precisely this symbiosis of philological and scientific interests that gave the Cabinet Dupuy its distinctive character and anticipated the rise of the natural sciences within the national academies of the second half of the seventeenth century. Finally, statesmen such as Jean Hotman, military dignitaries, and church delegates (such as the bishops of Chartre, Marseille, and Toulouse) sought admittance into the Cabinet Dupuy.

Obviously, more was at stake here than merely the academic interests of a learned elite. It is true, of course, that the Cabinet Dupuy cultivated primarily scholarly exchange in its private gatherings and even occasionally in public. Great philological ventures of the seventeenth century, such as Du Cange's *Glossarium mediae et infimae latinitatis*, Ménage's *Les Origines de la Langue Françoise*, or Chapelain's *Dictionnaire*, all owed a substantial debt to the holdings of the Dupuy-de Thou library and the cooperation of a wide range of experts. In the Cabinet Dupuy, as in Europe's other intellectual societies, working drafts were routinely submitted for critique before being published, a practice that extended to the fine arts as well. The poets Chapelain, Jean-Louis Guez de Balzac, the literary critic Ménage, the sculptor Jacques Sarazin, and the theologian Jacques Bénigne Bossuet, among others, were welcomed here; books by François de Malherbe, Girard de Saint-Amant, Tristan l'Hermite, and Gabriel Naudé found a receptive audience in this circle, which bore a striking resemblance to the contemporaneous drawing-room culture surrounding Madame de Rambouillet. It is probable that the scientific and mathematical discoveries by Peiresc and Gassendi as well as the philosophical abstracts of Naudé and François de La Mothe Le Vayer were subjected here to their first crucial test at the hands of a highly schooled intelligentsia. Descartes himself solicited the opinions of the Cabinet Dupuy.

---

[41] See the compilations by Jacques Dupuy, e.g., *Correspondance de Jacques Dupuy et de Nicolas Heinsius*, ed. Hans Bots (La Haye: Nijhoff, 1646–56); Larroque, *Lettres de Peiresc aux frères Dupuy*; Pélissier, 'Les amis d'Holstenius, II: Les frères Dupuy', *Mélanges d'Archéologie et d'Histoire, Ecole Française de Rome* 7 (1887): 62–128, and *Lettres inédites de Lucas Holstenius aux frères Dupuy et à d'autres correspondants*, Miscellanea Nuziale Rossi-Teiss (Bergamo, 1897), 511–50. More recently, Philip Wolfe (ed.), *Lettres de Gabriel Naudé à Jacques Dupuy, 1632–1652* (Edmonton, Alberta: Léalta Alta, 1982).

Questions remain, of course. What, for instance, can have prompted the Dupuys to invest the greater part of their energies in the creation and systematization of their book and manuscript collection? It was surely more than just a matter of satisfying the bibliophile's passion. In gathering the latest political news from every country in Europe, in documenting every important current and recent political trend, and in organizing a comprehensive system of European correspondents and informants, their interest was focused less on the past than on the present. The Dupuys responded to the requests of both Louis and Richelieu for legal-historical findings. Parallel to their efforts on behalf of the crown and the official state archives, however, the Dupuys sought to reach independent and broad-based judgments that reflected the position of the learned aristocracy. Such activities were never announced openly, of course. An undisciplined public sphere, after all, was hardly desirable.

Harcourt Brown, who is one of the few modern scholars with an eye for these implied connections, cites an interesting passage from Abraham Wicquefort's *Mémoires touchant les Ambassadeurs* (1677). Wicquefort makes it clear that the Cabinet Dupuy also served as a meeting place for ambassadors and diplomats, with the only concern being that secrecy be guaranteed.[42] One could gain the kind of insight here into high diplomacy that was rarely available elsewhere in Europe or that had the same degree of reliability. This would explain the measures sometimes taken in the Cabinet Dupuy to ensure secrecy – a precaution that was, in fact, customary in other humanist sodalities as well under the early absolutist state, all royalist sentiment notwithstanding. We see in many of these intellectual groups a pronounced tendency towards non-conformity, perhaps even in the direction of a counter-sphere of public opinion.

Thanks to the lively Parisian journal of Christoph Coler, an admiring young friend of the Silesian poet and ambassador Martin Opitz, we have a fairly detailed record of one foreign visitor's experience in Paris at the Cabinet Dupuy.[43] By order of the Catholic governor in Silesia, Karl Hannibal von Dohna, Opitz set out in 1630 from Wroclaw for Paris via Strasbourg. His mission was not on behalf of the Habsburgs or of Spain, as it may have appeared to some.[44] Richelieu had just

---

[42] Brown, *Scientific Organizations in Seventeenth-Century France* 6–16.

[43] English translation follows the German version, *Umständliche Nachricht von des weltberühmten Schlesiers Martin Opitz von Boberfeld, Leben, Tode und Schriften*, trans. in 2 vols by Kaspar Gottlieb Lindner (Hirschberg 1740–41), 1:201 ff.; the quotations below from this journal come from pp. 201 ff. It was common at the time for German scholars and diplomats, primarily from Silesia, the Palatinate, and the Upper Rhine, to visit Paris on either scholarly or ambassadorial missions.

[44] See Klaus Garber, 'Martin Opitz' "Schäferei von der Nymphe Hercinie"' and 'Martin Opitz'. Wilhelm Kühlmann and Walter E. Schäfer discuss the political expectations of Johann Michael Moscherosch, a poet from the Upper Rhine, as he journeyed to Paris in 1624, at the time of Strasbourg's impending encirclement by Karl von Lothringen's troops: *Frühbarocke Stadtkultur am Oberrhein: Studien zum literarischen Werdegang J.M. Moscheroschs (1601–1669)* (Berlin: Erich Schmidt, 1983), 46–86.

successfully concluded his negotiations in the conflict between Sweden and Poland;[45] at home he had captured the last bastion of the Huguenots at La Rochelle;[46] in Italy he had deepened the conflict with Spain by interfering in the Mantuan problem of succession.[47] Coler's account begins in praise of the Parisian Parlement and continues with a reflection on how Opitz proceeded to familiarize himself with the Cabinet Dupuy:

> [Opitz] examined this political arena very carefully, becoming acquainted with the leading statesmen, familiarizing himself with the crucial questions and learning how to assess them, and keeping everything fresh in his mind in order to give his homeland a full report . . . At this time his primary goal was to become privy to classified information. In particular, he sought to understand the balance of power in Europe, which country would dominate the other in the event of a shift.[48]

Grotius served as host to Opitz. Describing the Parisian house of the renowned lawyer, Coler writes that it was 'like a Delphic oracle to which the emissaries of the greatest kings and princes, members of Parlement, and councilors of the royal and imperial courts paid regular visits. Our Opitz too was a most welcome guest there.' Through Grotius Opitz was introduced into the house of the Puteani, the Dupuy brothers:

> Nearly every day there was a meeting of various individuals in the house of the Puteani in Paris where one could think, deliberate, and express opinions freely with respect to the entire European political realm. Grotius himself enjoyed attending as often as his considerable duties would allow. And on one occasion he did not come alone but brought our Opitz along, commending him highly before the entire distinguished assemblage.[49]

---

[45] With the Treaty of Altmark (29 Sept. 1629), which ended the long dynastic struggle between Gustav Adolph and Sigismund III.

[46] The Peace of Alais in June 1929 terminated the Huguenot Wars.

[47] In early 1630 the French moved into Savoy and captured Pinerolo, a hasty action that was overturned in July with the Treaty of Cherasco.

[48] '[Opitz] sahe sich auf diesem politischen Schauplatze sehr genau um. Er wurde mit den größten Staatsmännern bekannt. Er erfuhr die wichtigsten Dinge, er lernte sie beurteilen, und behielt alles in frischem Andenken, damit er seinem Vaterlande völlige Nachricht davon geben könnte . . . Itzo wollte er eigentlich nur von den Geheimnissen des Staats Nachricht einziehen. Besonders ging sein Absehen dahin, wie es um das Gleichgewicht von Europa beschaffen sey, und welches Land dem andern überwichtig wäre, wenn es in Bewegung kommen sollte?'

[49] 'Es wurde damals zu Pariß in dem Hause der Puteanen von unterschiedenen Privatpersonen fast täglich eine Zusammenkunft gehalten, darinnen man von dem ganzen Europäischen Staate frey gedachte, frey urtheilte, und frey seine Gegenmeynungen fürtrug. So oft die vielen und wichtigen Geschäfte dem Grotio zuliessen, auch daselbst zu erscheinen; so oft that er es sehr willig. Doch itzt kam er nicht allein, sondern brachte unsern Opitz mit sich, und wußte ihn der gesammten ansehnlichen Gesellschaft mit sehr vielem Lobe anzupreisen.'

Here in the Cabinet Dupuy Opitz made the acquaintance of many important figures, including Saumaise, Rigault, Hotman, Daniel Thilenus of Silesia, 'and other erudite men whom one met in great numbers in Paris back then', including one of Jacques Auguste de Thou's sons.

The first leg of his return trip involved a debriefing at the Castle of Dohna. Did Opitz have knowledge at this point of the French coalition being formed with the Protestants, and especially with Sweden, with whom Richelieu conspired to sacrifice Catholicism on the altar of French reason of state? We do not know. But one thing we may be sure of: his journey was no mere *peregrinatio academica*. Opitz's first biographer correctly underscores the private status of the individuals who met in the Cabinet Dupuy. Supported by the archive's holdings, these learned men availed themselves of the opportunity afforded them by the early absolutist state to expand their competence, expertise, and insight into European affairs, in order thereby to exert the greatest possible influence over the course of events. Parlementary jurists, who often found themselves in conflict with the monarchy, did the same. It is true that the pressure to conform increased markedly under Richelieu; certainly historiographers during this time were increasingly pressed into the role of servants of power. But the Cabinet Dupuy, which was also sought out by government officials in their capacity as private individuals, remained beyond the direct reach of the state's control. This remove allowed for relatively liberal scholarly discourse, even as it provided the participants with a certain safety zone against political danger.

The modern state was conceived in France, the Mecca of modern diplomacy. As a general breakdown of national order occurred elsewhere throughout Old Europe, the modern state could be studied in action in Paris for the first time. For several critical decades in the Hôtel de Thou and in the Bibliothèque Royale, the ideal observation post was the Cabinet Dupuy. During this time the very heart of European late humanism beat within it.*

---

* Translated by Joe G. Delap.

Chapter 5

Utopia and the Green World: Critique and Anticipation in Pastoral Poetry

If there was a single literary genre that gave ideal expression to the self-understanding of the nobilitas literaria as it was organized in intellectual societies throughout Europe, then it was surely pastoral. It is impossible to separate the social and political influence emanating from the societies from the influence of pastoral poetry as genre upon the societies. This reciprocity, as we shall see, owed above all to the utopian strain inherent in both the philosophical base of the societies (egalitarian, meritocratic, 'truly noble') and the formal elements of the genre as handed down from Vergil.[1]

It is curious then, that pastoral has never been seriously investigated as an independent type of utopian literature.[2] After having enjoyed popularity for some 2,000 years, pastoral commenced to decline around the middle of the eighteenth century. It was about this time that a distinctly middle-class aesthetic arose in opposition to two related traditions, one literary, the other social. The practitioners of this aesthetics rejected the classical, or normative, conception of genre; their opposition owed in part to the association of certain kinds of writing, among them pastoral, with the dominant courtly culture. This anti-classical, anti-courtly attitude initially fueled a certain progressivist thinking in both the literary and political spheres, and in this pre-revolutionary phase,[3] pastoral received fresh inspiration from the new aesthetic tendency.

This phase was short-lived, however, and was replaced by a psychologizing aesthetics, the effect of which was to sanitize pastoral of its negative elements and thus its critical potential. There was little appreciation in nineteenth-century aesthetics, despite its ideological basis in nature, for classical and humanist pastoral forms. The late-bourgeois idealization of nature rejected pastoral as it

---

[1] 'Above all, societal thinking puts its stamp on their artistic creations far more than has been appreciated so far, and none more deeply than the Arcadian Utopia, which may be considered as the aesthetic and fictional codification of the societies.' Klaus Garber, 'Sozietäten, Akademien, Sprachgesellschaften', in *Europäische Enzyklopädie zu Philosophie und Wissenschaften*, ed. H.J. Sandkühler (Hamburg: Meiner, 1990), 366–7.

[2] The twentieth-century studies relevant to such an investigation, including an extensive bibliography for all major European literatures, are collected in Klaus Garber (ed.), *Europäische Bukolik und Georgik*, Wege der Forschung, 355 (Darmstadt: Wissenschaftliche Buchgesellschaft, 1976).

[3] That is, the years immediately preceding the French Revolution.

had been practiced between Dante and Fontenelle. Frustrated in their search for 'nature' to discover only what seemed to them to be 'un-nature', the new aestheticians expressed their discontent in a steady stream of anti-pastoral denunciations. This tendency continued far into the twentieth century. What the critics of pastoral objected to more than anything else was its allegorism. In repudiating its basis in allegory, they stripped pastoral of its utopian, which is to say sociocritical, function. It is my purpose here to try to restore an appreciation for pastoral as a utopian vehicle. This will involve revisiting the question of allegory as it is used in a certain corpus of texts, some of them well-known, others obscure, and always in terms of broader social and political contexts.

Eclogue, Idyll, and Pastoral Novel: from Theocritus to d'Urfé

There is no utopian dimension in Theocritus, the architect of the idyll.[4] For utopia to be present, two conditions are necessary: a negation of existing historical, political, and social structures; and the presence of contrasting places and times. Theocritus's pastoral world differs from that constructed in the eighteenth century, which employed realistic techniques to free itself of the learned courtly styles modeled on Vergil's *Eclogues*. Theocritean pastoral is a self-conscious product of a highly refined aesthetic sensibility; this pertains as well to the related pastoral mimic plays (*mimoi*), whose fictitious Hellenic origins influenced the development of European pastoral. The modern motif of longing for nature, with its implied social discontent, is foreign to this artificial world. Theocritus's best-known idyll, *Thalysia*, begins with a stroll from the city into the country and has not the slightest hint of social criticism.[5] The nature scenery, adapted to the festive cult of Demeter, is rich in Mediterranean delights:

> Overhead, many elms
> and poplars rustled, and nearby
> the sacred waters splashed down
> from the Nymphs' cave. Brown cicadas
> shrilled from the shady branches,
> and far off the tree-frog whined
> in the heavy underbrush.

---

[4] This fact has often been discussed, most notably in Gilbert Lawell, *Theocritus' Coan Pastorals: A Poetry Book* (Cambridge, Mass.: Harvard University Press, 1967); Thomas G. Rosenmeyer, *The Green Cabinet: Theocritus and the European Pastoral Lyric* (Berkeley: University of California Press, 1969); and Bernd Effe, *Die Genese einer literarischen Gattung: Die Bukolik* (Constance: Universitätsverlag, 1977).

[5] Josef-Hans Kühn, 'Die Thalysien des Theocritus (id. 7)', *Hermes* 86 (1958): 40–79; also G. Weingart, 'Theocritus' Seventh Idyll' (PhD diss., University of Freiburg, 1966), and Charles Segal, 'Theocritus's Seventh Idyll and Lycidas', *Wiener Studien*, N.F. 8 (1974): 20–76.

Larks and finches sang, doves crooned,
and bees hummed about the spring.
Everything smelled of rich summer
and rich fruits.[6]

Theocritus's idylls honor the aristocratic hosts for the natural beauty of their island of Kos. Nature does not represent some contrastive space to the deficient reality of society. The only dichotomy is that which exists between the destructive passion of eros and the moderation cultivated among the simple shepherds to whom the pastoral song is entrusted. One searches in vain for political implications. The *political* as a pastoral component has its birth in Vergil.[7]

Vergil's *Eclogues* rely continuously on Theocritus even as they expand the idyll's expressive range, exemplifying how the renewal of one tradition may generate new ones. My particular concern, however, is to demonstrate how Vergil infused utopian thought into pastoral.

The opening of *Eclogue* 1 establishes an archetype. The shepherd Tityrus, playing his flute in the shade of a beech tree, embodies the leisurely musical life. Vergil does not, however, bind *otium* ontologically to pastoral, but is concerned to reveal its historical contingency. Tityrus owes his leisure to the intervention of the 'god' whom contemporaries readily identified as Octavian; the expatriate shepherd Meliboeus, on the other hand, has received no favor from this god. And thus in the pastoral world of Vergil conflicts arise that were unknown to Theocritus. A shepherd who is homeless is contrasted with one who is secure and happy. Nature mirrors the difference in their fates: familiar and pleasant in the

---

[6] Theoc., *Id.* 7.135–43. Translation: Barriss Mills, *The Idylls of Theokritos* (West Lafayette, Ind.: Purdue University Studies, 1963).
πολλαὶ δ' ἄμμιν ὕπερθε κατὰ κρατὸς δονέοντο
αἴγειροι πτελέαι τε· τὸ δ' ἐγγύθεν ἱερὸν ὕδωρ
Νυμφᾶν ἐξ ἄντροιο κατειβόμενον κελάρυζε.
τοὶ δὲ ποτὶ σκιαραῖς ὀροδαμνίσιν αἰθαλίωνες
τέττιγες λαλαγεῦντες ἔχον πόνον· ἁ δ' ὀλολυγών
τηλόθεν ἐν πυκιναῖσι βάτων τρύζεσκεν ἀκάνθαις·
ἄειδον κόρυδοι καὶ ἀκανθίδες, ἔστενε τρυγών,
πωτῶντο ξουθαὶ περὶ πίδακας ἀμφὶ μέλισσαι.
πάντ' ὦσδεν θέρεος μάλα πίονος, ὦσδε δ' ὀπώρας.

[7] See esp. Werner Suerbaum, 'Vergil 1980: Hundert Jahre Vergil-Forschung', in *Aufstieg und Niedergang der Römischen Welt: Geschichte und Kultur Roms im Spiegel der neueren Forschung*, ed. Hildegard Temporini and Wolfgang Haase, 31.1:3–358, 1359–99 (Berlin: Walter de Gruyter, 1980); also Friedrich Klinger, *Virgil: Bucolica, Georgica, Aeneis* (Zürich: Artemis, 1967); and E.A. Schmidt, *Poetische Reflexion: Vergils Bukolik* (Munich: Fink, 1972). My interpretation builds upon the foundation laid by H.J. Schneider, 'Bürgerliche Idylle: Studien zu einer literarischen Gattung des 18. Jahrhunderts am Beispiel von Johann Heinrich Voss' (PhD diss., University of Bonn, 1975); my earliest application of these ideas came in a study of Nuremberg pastoral, 'Vergil und das "Pegnesische Schäfergedicht"', in *Deutsche Barockliteratur und europäische Kultur*, ed. Martin Bircher and Eberhard Mannack, 168–203 (Hamburg: Hauswedell, 1977).

case of Tityrus; barren, stony, and swampy in the case of Meliboeus. Details are politically coded. This integration of political concerns into the eclogue prepares the utopian dimension of a fictional work of art.

Importantly, neither in Vergil nor his successors is this political component exploited in literalistic fashion as a means of presenting an ideally engineered society. Pastoral discourse is indirect discourse. The purpose of the shepherd's departure for Octavian's Rome is concealed in bucolic images, but the story's goal is far from being coterminous with the bucolic sphere. In Rome Tityrus receives the freedom that was denied him in love. The lowly pastoral art form (*genus humile*) takes on the epic dignity of political prophecy. Octavian tells the shepherd, 'Graze your cattle again and put your bulls to stud.'[8] This is the disguised promise that had been given to the shepherd by the godly youth in Rome. By the time Meliboeus meets Tityrus, the promise has been fulfilled:

> Fortunate old man, here between the rivers
> you know and the sacred springs you'll lie in the cool shade.
> Here your hedge, as it always has, at your neighbor's line
> will pasture on willow buds those Hyblaean bees,
> which soon will coax you to sleep with their light murmuring hum.
> There beneath the high rock the vinedresser
> will sing to the breeze and all the while your hoarse pigeons
> and your turtle dove, high in the elm, will murmur and coo.[9]

Such a life is starkly different from the fate of his disconsolate fellow shepherd:

> But the rest of us must go to thirsty Africa
> or Scythia and the rapid Oaxes's chalky stream,
> or else to Britain, cut off from us by the width of the world.
> Oh, will I ever in any time to come, look
> with wonder at a land I can at last call
> my own, see my modest cottage, its roof heaped
> with turf, and after a while, behold my kingdom, my rows
> of grain? Is some rough soldier to have these furrowed fields?

---

[8] *Ecl.* 1.45. 'Pascite ut ante boues, pueri, submittite tauros.' Translation: Barbara Hughes Fowler, *Vergil's Eclogues* (Chapel Hill: University of North Carolina Press, 1997).

[9] *Ecl.* 1.51–8.
> Fortunate senex, hic inter flumina nota
> et fontis sacros frigus captabis opacum;
> hinc tibi, quae semper, uicino ab limite saepes
> Hyblaeis apibus florem depasta salicti
> saepe leui somnum suadebit inire susurro;
> hinc alta sub rupe canet frondator ad auras,
> nec tamen interea raucae, tua cura, palumbes
> nec gemere aeria cessabit turtur ab ulmo.

Some foreigner these crops? What misery civil strife
has brought to us Romans! For such as these have we sown this land![10]

The fiction has a dialectical structure. To replace deficiencies in the world Vergil prophesies a new condition. The old world knew only division and civil wars; in the new world, unity and harmony will reign. The two shepherds are universal symbols of past and present: one (Meliboeus) exists as historical reality; the other (Tityrus) is a poetic anticipation of the future liberated shepherd, who represents not only the poet but also the common people of the Roman Empire. To be sure, liberation still awaits a divine youth; nevertheless, *Eclogue* 1 is not merely reducible to a praise-of-ruler topos. It anticipates a political order in which the kind of life that Tityrus now enjoys will be universally possible. By having bound his pastoral vision to imperial government Vergil profoundly influenced the direction of later pastoral literature. Historically and personally, Vergil's anti-republican sentiment may be understandable enough. As interpreters, however, we must not overlook the liberating function that Vergil assigns to pastoral life, that is, to the life of poets.

'Pastoral literature does not deal with shepherds as such, but with singing shepherds. Singing shepherds and their songs are the real subjects of pastoral.'[11] The role of the syrinx thus also assumes political implications unknown to Theocritus. In *Eclogue* 9, the second great Roman eclogue, the shepherds are again affected by wider political events, in this instance by the imperial policy of land redistribution. The special privilege enjoyed by the shepherd poet in *Eclogue* 1 is threatened in *Eclogue* 9 where, like so many of his countrymen, he is forcefully expelled from his homeland. That Menalcas may have saved the land with his song is nothing but rumor. The shepherd's song threatens to fall silent:

> Alas, can such wickedness be anyone's?
> Alas for your comfort nearly lost to us with you,
> Menalcas! Who would sing the nymphs – who would strew
> the earth with flowering herbs or canopy the springs
> with green shade – or the songs I lately picked up from you

---

[10] *Ecl.* 1.64–73.
> At nos hinc alii sitientis ibimus Afros,
> pars Scythiam et rapidum cretae ueniemus Oaxen
> et penitus toto diuissos orbe Britannos.
> en umquam patrios longo post tempore finis
> pauperis et tuguri congestum caespite culmen,
> post aliquot, mea regna, uidens mirabor aristas?
> impius haec tam culta noualia miles habebit,
> barbarus has segetes. en quo discordia ciuis
> produxit miseros; his nos conseuimus agros!
> insere nunc, Meliboee, piros, pone ordine uites.

[11] Schmidt, *Poetische Reflexion* 17.

> when you were on your way to darling Amaryllis?
> 'Tityrus, until I return, pasture the goats . . .'[12]

The shepherds are left only with quotation.[13] The older shepherd refuses the younger's invitation to join him in singing in the quiet of the evening (*Eclogue* 9.66-7). Singing is a sign that the shepherd lives in harmony with himself and his environment. Vergil implies, given that the song may end and the shepherd be left with nothing but memory, that singing is not for all seasons but depends on the precondition of peace.

The shepherd's song retains an Orphic quality in Vergil; nature is in sympathy with the singer. Pastoral thrives on this harmony, or reconciliation, between man and nature as no other genre prior to the eighteenth century.

It is symptomatic of the engineered social utopia, beginning with Thomas More's *Utopia* (1516), that human participation is not possible in the natural world, and that the imagination focuses therefore exclusively on the regulation of social mechanisms. No realm exists beyond society, nothing escapes planned control; even nature is subject to the imperative of social utility. By contrast to the engineered social utopia, Vergilian pastoral does not apply totalizing norms of political, economic, cultural, and behavioral theory. At the same time – and herein lies Vergil's unique importance – politics has an effective role in pastoral and is made visible through its opposite, nature. As a satirical function of pastoral, politics is measured according to the standard of the primitive shepherd life, a technique that reveals the origin of the critical, or negative, power of pastoral. Politics is obligated to serve the regulative principles of the genre: leisure and song, unrestricted interaction with beautiful nature, humane communication with one's fellow man.

The classical design of the social utopia eventually wore out, having been enslaved too long to the realistic details of particular times even as they sought critical distance from them. The idea of a totally engineered utopia, where spontaneity, subjectivity, and other differences are quashed, was discredited by history and replaced by dystopia. On the other hand, the unique aversion of

---

[12] *Ecl.* 9.17-23.
> Heu, cadit in quemquam tantum scelus? heu, tua nobis
> paene simul tecum solacia rapta, Menalca!
> quis caneret Nymphas? quis humum florentibus herbis
> spargeret aut uiridi fontes induceret umbra?
> uel quae sublegi tacitus tibi carmina nuper,
> cum te ad delicias ferres Amaryllida nostras?
> 'Tityre, dum redeo – breuis est uia – pasce capellas . . .'

[13] Theoc., *Id.* 3.3-5.
> Τίτυρ', ἐμὶν τὸ καλὸν πεφιλημένε, βόσκε τὰς αἶγας,
> καὶ ποτὶ τὰν κράναν ἄγε, Τίτυρε·
> [Tityros, good friend, feed the she-goats,
> and lead them to the spring.]

pastoral poetry to institutionalized society, and its concentration of the aesthetic imagination on nature as the locus of human perfectibility, provided it with a luminance that is visible even today in the idyllic citations of modern poetry. The goal of the engineered utopia, of course, is to subjugate nature; history has made it clear, however, that human survival itself depends on protecting nature from the harmful incursion of society. Thus it may have practical value to make an effort to recover a greater appreciation of a genre whose promise of happiness is linked to the release of powers in nature that benefit the human race. Seen in this way, Arcadia is the symbol of an aesthetic experiment, initiated by Vergil through pastoral poetry, whose goal is a humane model of 'shepherd' life in beautiful nature; it simultaneously obligates to its own terms the managers of political and social power. The shepherd who sings of nature's beauty anticipates such a harmony.

Although in *Eclogue* 4, with its messianic view of Octavian, Vergil may appear to have transgressed the limits of the bucolic, he in fact remains true to its classical conventions. For the evolution of pastoral in general and of pastoral as a utopian medium in particular, two innovations were essential: a new temporal structure focused on the future, and the incorporation of the Golden Age (*aetas aurea*). *Eclogue* 1 knows of the promise; *Eclogue* 4 lives upon it. Thus Vergil infuses the eclogue with the force of a temporal utopia.

It is one of the ironies in the history of the genre that this potential was realized in the mid-eighteenth century at the very time when Vergil was being rejected by the new aesthetics. The sentimental idyll of the Swiss poet and painter Solomon Gessner is as unthinkable as the sociocritical idyll of the Storm and Stress if Vergilian anticipation is missing. Vergilian pastoral's critical contrasts, especially in the use of spatial structuring, also motivated the historical structuring of the eighteenth-century idyll. The *Eclogues* had their roots in the transition from Republic to Empire and rose upon the hope that a prince of peace would put an end to the civil wars. Similarly, the eighteenth-century idyll depended for its effectiveness upon an opposition to courtly pastoral: no negative, anticipatory component existed in courtly pastoral, since its function was only to mirror the positive face of courtly culture. In Vergil the prophecy of the divine youth, the royal agent of peace, contains the attributes of the return of the Golden Age:

> For you, little child, spontaneously, as first gifts,
> the earth will lavish creeping ivy and foxglove,
> everywhere, and Egyptian lilies with smiling acanthus.
> Goats will come home by themselves with udders full
> of milk, nor will the oxen fear the lion's might.
> Your very cradle will flower with buds to caress you.
> The serpent will die as well as poison's treacherous plant,
> and everywhere Assyrian balsam will come to bloom.
> And when you have learned to read the praises of heroes and deeds

of your own father and know what manhood is, the plain,
little by little, will grow gold with waving grain,
and grapes will redden on the untended vine of the thorn,
and the hard oaks distill honey-dew from their barks.[14]

The Golden Age is integrated into pastoral literature as part of a ruler panegyric. It is an appropriate motif here insofar as it shares the elements of pastoral's sympathetic connection between humanity and nature, and for Vergil to return to the bucolic sphere at the conclusion of the messianic *Eclogue* 4 is a consciously artistic gesture. Contentment now within what was formerly a hostile animal world, and the restraint on human intrusion into nature in the knowledge that nature will respond on its own to the needs of humanity: these are essential elements of the Vergilian vision. The fairy-tale ending typically found in myth is the ultimate goal of pastoral as well: a return, that is, to the unitary condition between man and nature. Only in his eclogues can we find the adequate representation of Vergil's conception of the utopia of peace.[15]

The Neronian pastoral of Calpurnius, on the other hand, is interesting only for the way in which it reflects the early reception of Vergil.[16] It has none of the mystery of Vergil's eclogues; its language, while often reminiscent of Vergil, is literalistic and incapable of the master's nuances. Three of Calpurnius's seven

---

[14] *Ecl.* 4.18–30.
   At tibi prima, puer, nullo munuscula cultu
   errantis hederas passim cum baccare tellus
   mixtaque ridenti colocasia fundet acantho.
   ipsae lacte domum referent distenta capellae
   ubera nec magnos metuent armenta leones;
   ipsa tibi blandos fundent cunabula flores.
   occidet et serpens et fallax herba ueneni
   occidet; Assyrium uolgo nascetur amomum.
   At simul heroum laudes et facta parentis
   iam legere et quae sit poteris cognoscere uirtus,
   molli paulatim flauescet campus arista
   incultisque rubens pendebit sentibus uua
   et durae quercus sudabunt roscida mella.

[15] Thomas Metscher, 'Poets of Peace: Vergil – Dante – Erasmus', *Kultur und Gesellschaft* 12 (1981): 3–8, reviews the long tradition of poets writing about peace, in which Vergil is the chief classical source, and which culminates in the early modern humanists.

[16] The term 'Neronian' bespeaks the intent of Calpurnius to praise the young Nero as the restorer of the Golden Age. On Neronian pastoral, see esp. Wolfgang Schmid, 'Panegyrik und Bukolik in der neronischen Epoche: Ein Beitrag zur Erklärung der Carmina Einsidlensia', *Bonner Jahrbücher* 153 (1953): 63–96; Gunther Scheda, *Studien zur bukolischen Dichtung der neronischen Epoche* (Bonn: Habelt, 1969); and Eleanor Leach, 'Corydon Revisited: An Interpretation of the Political Eclogues of Calpurnius Siculus', *Ramus* 2 (1973): 53–97, and 'Neronian Pastoral and the World of Power', *Ramus* 4 (1975): 204–30.

eclogues, placed strategically at the beginning, middle, and end of the collection, praise the young Nero. The later commonplace that pastoral was mainly an affirmative genre and fixed uncritically on praise has its origin in these poems, a bias that is typically, and wrongly, dated back to Vergil.[17]

Whereas Vergil merely alludes to the civil wars as historical backdrop for his Roman pastoral utopia, Calpurnius rewrites in a more specific vein:

> Fair peace shall come, fair not in visage alone – such as she often was when, though free from open war, and with distant foe subdued, she yet 'mid the riot of arms spread national strife with secret steel. Clemency has commanded every vice that wears the disguise of peace to betake itself afar: she has broken every maddened sword-blade. No more shall the funereal procession of a fettered senate weary the headsman at his task; no more will crowded prison leave only a senator here and there for the unhappy Curia to count. Peace in her fullness shall come; knowing not the drawn sword, she shall renew once more the reign of Saturn in Latium.[18]

A passage of this nature communicates some measure of the historical experiences out of which imperial ideology was construed. The polar structure given the eclogue by Vergil serves Calpurnius's technique of portraying the cruelty of the preceding age with great immediacy. In Calpurnius's view, the Neronian empire, by contrast with the disorderly Republic, is one of harmony. In

---

[17] Richard Faber discusses the problematical identification – by twentieth-century adherents of so-called Occident-ideology or state-metaphysics – of Vergil as 'father of the Occident'. In his *Politische Idyllik: Zur sozialen Mythologie Arkadiens* (Stuttgart: Klett, 1976), Faber summarizes: 'With Vergil . . . the history of poetry as political affirmation begins in all seriousness: henceforth, rulers strive to ensure their place in history so that history reads as they wish. To this end they have to employ the services of the poet. Thus a new genre of political poetry arises that continues as a literary institution to the present day . . ., the so-called praise-of-ruler' (8). This thesis derives from Hans Magnus Enzensberger, *Einzelheiten*, no. 2 (Frankfurt a.M.: Suhrkamp, 1967). Applied to the social mythology of Arcadia, however, it is less than convincing. Even for a second-rate poet like Calpurnius the problem of affirmation is far more complex than this.

[18] *Buc.* 1.54–64. Edition: *Calpurnius Siculus – Bucolica*, in *Minor Latin Poets*, trans. J. Wight Duff and Arnold M. Duff, 207–85 (Cambridge, Mass.: Harvard University Press, 1935).

> candida pax aderit; nec solum candida vultu,
> qualis saepe fuit quae libera Marte professo,
> quae domito procul hoste tamen grassantibus armis
> publica diffudit tacito discordia ferro:
> omne procul vitium simulatae cedere pacis
> iussit et insanos Clementia contudit enses.
> nulla catenati feralis pompa senatus
> carnificum lassabit opus, nec carcere pleno
> infelix raros numerabit Curia patres.
> plena quies aderit, quae stricti nescia ferri
> altera Saturni referet Latialia regna.

Bucolics 4 and 7 the background of civil war fades measurably, thereby reducing the need to apostrophize the empire as a force for peace; the promises contained in the myth of the Golden Age have been fulfilled under Nero. This motif of fulfillment in the early imperial period remained formulaic through the Carolingian eclogue and into the Renaissance. Although pastoral's anticipatory function was thereby largely paralyzed, the eclogue nevertheless continued to function as more than a mere vehicle of cultural affirmation.

The place of utopia in medieval pastoral is somewhat puzzling, especially with respect to allegory, which is applied only to selected motifs.[19] Together with related panegyrical forms practiced by Metellus of Tegernsee and Marcus Valerius, the eclogue was typically if not universally esteemed in the Middle Ages for its moral content.[20] The full Christianization of pastoral, which utilized the well-established symbolism of the Bible, was not achieved until the early modern spiritual pastoral. Early medieval theoreticians like Tertullian, Gregory of Nazianus, and Jerome, had warned against the practice of this profane genre with its commitment to ἡδονή: 'pleasure'.[21] Their caution surely contributed to the theologization of the genre. The shepherd now became a preacher, though the pastoral environment itself was not Christianized. When Endelechius attributes the rescue of Tityrus's diseased herd to divine intervention, or when Theodulus in the tenth century renews the ancient amoeboean contest between Pseustis and Alithia as a pretext for demonstrating the Christian defeat of pagan ideas, classical form still functions as the allegorical vessel. The conversion of the Arcadian Golden Age into a Christian Paradise, or of Vergilian prophecy into spiritual eclogue, or of the eclogue's messianism into Christian eschatology – none of these uses existed in the medieval pastoral. Nor was the utopian dimension of pastoral revived until early humanism's return to the classical eclogue.

The pastoral correspondence of 1319 between Dante and the Bolognese grammarian Giovanni del Virgilio belonged more to the Renaissance than to the Middle Ages.[22] A convinced Latinist, Del Virgilio had reproached Dante, who was living at the time in exile in Ravenna, for his plan to write his *Divina Commedia* in the vernacular. Dante replied with an allegorical eclogue modeled on Vergil in

---

[19] The groundbreaking work was done by Schmid, 'Panegyrik', and developed by Dietmar Korzeniewski (ed.), *Hirtengedichte aus spätrömischer und karolingischer Zeit* (Darmstadt: Wissenschaftliche Buchgesellschaft, 1976), and Helen Cooper, *Pastoral: Medieval into Renaissance* (Ipswich: Brewer, 1977).

[20] 'The "pastoral" motifs in the seminal Christian ideas had to be formulated poetically outside of the pastoral genre, if at all; to make use of them for the purpose of inspiring a renewal of the traditional idyll was simply out of the question.' Schmid, 'Panegyrik' 60–61.

[21] 'It is therefore not surprising to encounter allusions to the antagonism that arose occasionally between the expressive world of pastoral and presumably true Christian spirituality.' Schmid, 'Panegyrik' 48–9.

[22] Konrad Krautter, *Die Renaissance der Bukolik in der lateinischen Literatur des 14. Jahrhunderts: Von Dante bis Petrarca* (Munich: Fink, 1983).

which he expresses the hope that, in creating a vernacular poetic language, he has in fact elevated the *genus humile*.[23] Humble pastoral form and the idea of a non-Latin 'national' language are two sides of a single coin. Dante transformed the eclogue into an instrument that would prove capable of supporting the humanist literary and social utopia.

At the very outset of the early modern period, then, the possibilities inherent in the pastoral-allegorical mode of communication were exploited in these two eclogues by Dante. The choice of the humble pastoral genre implied more than simply making use of an allegorical instrument; it both demonstrated Dante's commitment to the *lingua volgata* and reinforced his claim to being the people's poet. His criticism of the educated class is well known. For the educated estate, represented here by Del Vergilio, writing an eclogue in the vulgar language amounted to a descent into the literary lowlands; Dante openly confesses his devotion to the vernacular and initially ignores the epic (thus following Vergil's pattern). Whereas Del Virgilio sees the humanist society as a hermetic guild of Latin-language poets, Dante envisions a literary society distinguished by nobility of intellect, soul, and morality, charged with the responsibility of creating a vernacular culture.[24] As a result, allegorical pastoral became the genre most suited to representing the utopia of the intellectual aristocracy, the 'pastoral community'.

The intellectual and poetic arguments for such a community were introduced by Petrarch in *De vita solitaria*, which he began in Vaucluse in 1346. Petrarch developed the eclogue into the ultimate model of learned culture, and his idea of a solitary intellectual life nourished humanism until well into the eighteenth century. If there is one eclogue besides Vergil's first that had unquestioned canonical status in humanism, it was Petrarch's own first eclogue, *Parthenias*. As all of his eclogues, it springs from the experience of *solitudo*, the opposite of *occupatio*:

> What devalues occupatio is not activity as such, but rather the self-alienation and moral deprivation of people whose lives are entangled in the materialistic and egotistical interests of an indulgent society. The picture that Petrarch draws of homines occupati is a caricature of a society that is morally bankrupt . . . The choice of the pastoral mode is consistent with his dedication to the vita solitaria – a dedication that further implies criticism of the values of the dominant social class.[25]

---

[23] Del Vergilio renewed his complaint, and Dante in turn reiterated his stand with a second eclogue in Italian. Werner Bahner, 'Dantes theoretische Bemühungen um die Emanzipation der italienischen Literatursprache', in *Formen, Ideen, Prozesse in den Literaturen der romanischen Völker* (Berlin: Akademie, 1977), investigates the roots of this problem in *De Convivio* and *De lingua volgata*.

[24] 'An aristocracy of education replaced the feudal aristocracy. Just as the bourgeois view of the individual in the city-states rested on ability and performance, the intellectual view rested on knowledge and literary competence. The term for this social, intellectual, and ethical stature is *gentilezza*.' Hugo Friedrich, *Epochen der italienischen Lyrik* (Milan: Mursia, 1964), 51.

[25] Krautter, *Renaissance* 108–9.

Petrarch felt that the papal court at Avignon bore chief responsibility for this corrupted state of affairs. The literary realization of this belief, however, is manifested in pastoral through the creation of a counter-world. The shepherd poet Silvius seeks solitude, knowing that it is only by retreating from society that he can get on with the immense task of restoring the conditions of antiquity; a direct return to classical origins implies opposition to Christian ecclesiastical culture. The resulting political consequences can be articulated only through allegorical discourse.

In Petrarch's eclogue Homer appears together with Vergil. Thus it is as a hero that Silvius embarks upon his poetic career, an epic theme, once again integrated into pastoral, with political consequences. By avoiding exclusively biblical themes, as the interlocutor Monicus recommends, insisting instead on the dignity and sufficiency of classical form and content, entry is made into the political sphere through the medium of poetry alone. Silvius refuses to allow his brother to tell the story of David, insisting that he keep to the epic of *Africa*, a political subject that gives the eclogue an exclusively secular character. Six of the twelve eclogues have political themes: two (3 and 6) castigate the curia in Avignon directly, two (8 and 12) indirectly; one (2) applies to Naples; and one (5) to the Rome of Rienzi. As in his literary epistles Petrarch presents the figure of a widowed and helpless *Roma*, an image that resonates politically as late as the Thirty Years' War.[26] Criticism and anticipation are interrelated in Petrarch's eclogues. Because the Avignon Curia is the main cause of Rome's weakness and decadence, the solitary poet, absorbed in antiquity, rouses himself to devise a new political goal: to establish the idea of ancient Rome as the ingress to national unity. As Vergil before him, Petrarch combines poetic self-representation and political engagement in eclogue form, thereby opening up an expressive range for humanist pastoral to explore throughout the Renaissance in both neo-Latin and vernacular literatures.[27]

---

[26] 'Rome appears as the representative of the Italian nation. The poet views it as the old, historical metropolis of Italy, on whose fate the future of the fatherland depends ... Neither ecclesiastical nor secular rulers were able to forge the holy alliance from this point forward; this was done, instead, by the rising third empire, the intellectual empire of Latin learning, renewed by Italian nationalism reborn of antiquity.' Konrad Burdach and Paul Piur (eds), *Briefwechsel des Cola di Rienzo* (Berlin: Weidmann, 1912–29), pt 1:76; cf. Piur's commentary, pt 5:173–86. Concerning Petrarch's enigmatic allegorical language as a medium of poetic criticism, see Piur, *Petrarchas 'Buch ohne Namen' und die päpstliche Kurie: Ein Beitrag zur Geistesgeschichte der Frührenaissance* (Halle: Niemeyer, 1925).

[27] The individual stages of the eclogue during the Quattrocento cannot be clearly distinguished. See Walter Greg, *Pastoral Poetry and Pastoral Drama: A Literary Inquiry, with Special Reference to the Pre-Restoration Stage in England* (New York: Russell & Russell, 1959), 30–31, 423–4; cf. Enrico Carrara, *La poesia pastorale* (Milan: Vallardi, 1936), 167–8, 205–6; and Cecil Grayson, 'Alberti and the Vernacular Eclogue in the Quattrocento', *Italian Studies* 11 (1956): 16–29. For the neo-Latin eclogue, see W. Leonard Grant, *Neo-Latin Literature and the Pastoral* (Chapel Hill: University of North Carolina Press, 1965).

A new pastoral form appeared in the *Arcadia* (1502, 1504) of Jacopo Sannazaro. The first major pastoral novel, *Arcadia* displays a coherent structure having a prose frame and containing a cycle of twelve eclogues.[28] As I see it, the pastoral novel can be properly appreciated only within the long tradition of political eclogues.[29]

Naples and the Neapolitan court provide the political background to Sannazaro's *Arcadia*.[30] An Aragonese collateral line had come into power with Ferrante I, whose reign (1458–94) was overshadowed by repeated uprisings of the barons, culminating in a major conspiracy and its bloody suppression. Ferrante relied on the nobilitas literaria of the city for assistance. Giovanni Pontano, the most important poet of Italian humanism and head of the Neapolitan academy, presided on occasion over the administrative law court. In 1494 Charles VIII of France campaigned victoriously through Italy with the support of the Sforza in Milan. In February 1495 he marched on Naples, where he was met by a jubilant public and lauded in a magnificent speech by Pontano. A few years later, with Spain's ad hoc alliance with the pope in southern Italy, the fate of Naples was sealed together with that of Italy. Federigo, the last king in Naples,

---

[28] The 1502 original edition contained only ten eclogues. On the structure of *Arcadia*, see Reinhold Grimm, 'Arcadia und Utopia: Interferenzen im neuzeitlichen Hirtenroman', *Utopieforschung: Interdisziplinäre Studien zur neuzeitlichen Utopie*, ed. Wilhelm Voßkamp, 2:82–100 (Stuttgart: Suhrkamp, 1982).

[29] Hellmuth Petriconi, 'Das neue Arkadien' (1948; reprint in Garber, *Europäische Bukolik* 181–201), summarizes Sannazaro's use of Arcadia: 'For Sannazaro, the Golden Age embodies the original idea of shepherding . . . and the new Arcadia, while imperfect, resembles the Golden Age when freedom of love was the rule. In other words, shepherding, i.e., the shepherd's garb, is the literary cloak for representing love and lovers without regard for moral, social, or other constraints lacking in that world' (189). Typically, scholars have stressed the elegiac or sentimental element, which arose out of the conditions described by Petriconi. E.A. Schmidt, 'Arkadien: Abendland und Antike', *Antike und Abendland* 21 (1975): 46–7, comments: 'This type of poetry is characterized by the utmost gentleness and sweetness, by sentimentality and a poignant atmosphere. Tears, sighs, and lamentations are its dominant motifs, the touching amorous lament a main theme . . . Sorrow and pain are enjoyed as a tender mood in which the distress and pangs of grief disappear behind a veil of deep melancholy.' In an attempt to reconstruct the true Vergilian Arcadia, Schmidt has examined a number of the assumptions that underlie twentieth-century Vergil scholarship. A corresponding study of Sannazaro's *Arcadia* remains to be done; only then will we know whether the distinction that Schmidt claims existed between ancient and early modern pastoral is tenable. If the presence of a utopian dimension in Vergil's eclogues can be attested, then the renewal of Vergil in Sannazaro derives not from some productive misunderstanding, as some think, but rather from the very core of the Vergilian work.

[30] Ernesto Pontieri's 11-volume *Storia de Napoli* (Naples: Società editrice Storia de Napoli, 1967–78) should be consulted here, esp. vols 3 and 4. For the political and cultural background to the *Arcadia*, see Francesco Tateo, 'La crisi culturale di Jacopo Sannazaro', in *Tradizione e realtà nell'umanesimo italiano*, 11–109 (Bari: Dedalo libri, 1967); and Eduardo Saccone, 'L'Arcadia di Iacobo Sannazaro: Storia e delineamento di una struttura', *Modern Language Notes* 84 (1969): 46–97.

capitulated in 1501 and died in exile in France, accompanied by Sannazaro, one of the staunchest loyalists of the royal court. The French victory and the exploits of Charles VIII called down harsh invectives from Sannazaro. The great century of Italian humanism had ended, and the nation itself degenerated into a mere strategic objective of foreign powers. The period of the Counter-Reformation and Baroque now began. Sannazaro's *Arcadia*, begun in the 1480s and reworked and expanded in the 1490s, was written in a moment of historical transition that ended catastrophically.

Sannazaro is justified in alluding to himself as the modern successor to Vergil, inasmuch as he succeeds in demonstrating, allegorically, of course, the political motivations behind the modern renewal of the classical motifs. Every eclogue in *Arcadia* contributes in some way to the political semantics of the work. The prose sections, for their part, function chiefly to reintegrate the allegory into the Arcadian frame. Sannazaro begins his narrative with the ancient motif of the amorous lament, a practice imitated by subsequent writers of pastoral novel. The renown of *Arcadia* is due at least in part to the incorporation of misfortune and sorrow, hopelessness and resignation, into the bucolic tradition; indeed, it is effected with an intensity and radicality that recalls Vergil. Sannazaro's reiteration of the ancient erotic repertoire, far from being capricious, conjures up the political world. From the first eclogue on, Arcadia appears to be under some threat, a sense that is heightened by the animal allegory running through the entire work. In fact, the expected catastrophe in Arcadia has already occurred, as represented in the figure of the unrequited lover. The relationship between Arcadia, contemporary reality, and Golden Age may be elucidated as follows: 1) Arcadia is the fictional space in which the literary restoration of antiquity is to be brought about. 2) Over this space hangs the cloud of an unhappy present, which provides the rationale for the historical semantics and the arsenal of classical motifs. 3) Consequently, the Golden Age functions antithetically to Arcadia: Arcadia reflects the reality of political disorder; the Golden Age represents an age of mythical tranquillity, the utopian counter-image in which justice rules and to which Astraea has returned. Thus Sannazaro projects into the primordial past what the future political goal should be. But even in Arcadia, relief from reality is possible. In terms of the pastoral code, events can be understood, alternatives weighed, precautions taken. In this sense the *aetas aurea* eclogue sung by Opicio is replete with historical drama. To say that this eclogue exists only to glorify free love would be banal.

As an example of how this interrelationship operates between Arcadia, reality, and Golden Age, we may consider the final eclogue (no. 12). Its addressee is identifiable as the deceased wife of Pontano, and the occasion is transfigured by rich allegory. The shepherd narrator Sincero, who first appeared in the Golden Age eclogue, decides to leave Arcadia and return to Naples. Arcadian life, after all, is determined by Neapolitan life, and it is the memory of the city that keeps the shepherds under its spell.[31] Earlier, in reply to Sincero's autobiographical narrative (Prose 7), the consoling shepherds had reassured the poet that he was in no danger and that his property (in Naples) was safe. Prose 8 introduces the motif of *voluntario esilio*, with repeated allusions to Sannazaro's personal experiences in France. Arcadia is a freely sought exile, a sympathetic refuge, and must ultimately be abandoned, even in the absence of liberty at home.

Arcadia is not some amorous, escapist paradise. Behind the curtain of pastoral innocence there emerges a world of lamentation and despair, of pain over the destructive political strife.

> Will there ever be a day, that I can say among free men
> 'Thanks be to Heaven, we have escaped great peril?'[32]

This question haunts *Arcadia* throughout. In returning to Naples from the shepherd world the poet evinces his loyalty to his lost fatherland. In a final dream Sincero sees himself separated from the Arcadian shepherds and alone among desolate graves. This ghostly realm of the dead is the locus of mediation between the Arcadian and historical worlds. He hears the bitter sobbing of the Siren – it can only be Parthenope; an orange tree she once tended is torn from its roots and scattered to the four winds. 'Where then shall I take my repose? under what shade now shall I sing my verses?'[33] The invasion by foreign powers has broken the Aragonese dynasty in Naples and stripped the poet of his support. Arriving at the shores of his homeland he is greeted by weeping nymphs. His beloved is dead, Naples has fallen. The work closes with a lamentation:

> How many shepherds, Sebeto, and how many peoples
> will you see dying, of those that are settled beside you,
> before your banks are elmed or poplared?[34]

Naples is no longer Naples, and *Arcadia* is ultimately a political elegy in which Sannazaro's old homeland is recollected as the ideal place to have lived.

---

[31] At the end of the story the poet's homeland of Sebeto appears as a vision arising behind the Arcadian landscape.

[32] *Arcadia*, in *Opere Volgari*, ed. Alfredo Mauro (Bari: Laterza & Figli, 1961), Poem 8.29–30. Translation: Ralph Nash, *Arcadia and Piscatorial Eclogues* (Detroit: Wayne State University Press, 1966).
sarà mai dì ch'io possa dir fra'liberi:
'Mercé del ciel, dal gran periglio evasimo'?

[33] Prose 12. 'Ove dunque mi riposerò io? sotto qual ombra omai canterò i miei versi?'

[34] Poem 12.103–5.
Quanti pastor, Sebeto, e quanti populi
morir vedrai di quei che in te s'annidano,
pria che la riva tua si inolmi o impopuli!

The most common pastoral form in Europe in the sixteenth and seventeenth centuries was the eclogue in praise of rulers, which reached its high point in Spain with Garcilaso de la Vega and in France with Pierre de Ronsard.[35] The *laus regentis* was mainly concerned with glorifying the monarchy; the pejorative label of 'affirmative function' so often attached to it, however, is misplaced to say the least. Many of these panegyrical eclogues are filled with the same humanistic ethos that informs the medieval mirror of princes, the purpose of which was to obligate the ruler to a high standard of conduct and to the cause of peace. When we consider, for instance, how many 'political' humanists held advisory offices as state servants among the confessional factions, the evidence is convincing that pastoral praise of rulership intended an outcome that was much more than merely affirmative; its strategy was often subtly critical, even utopian, in anticipating outcomes. Use of the form cannot be judged as a whole but must be taken case by case. One remarkable development, particularly visible in the work of Garcilaso in Spain and the Pléiade in France, was the attention given to the private features of eclogue during the formative phase of absolutism. Here too differentiation is called for. The incorporation of personal elements into the genre may simply have been a logical human response to the general fixation on the state, contributing little to political thinking. On the other hand, alternative models arose within the private sphere that either offered or anticipated models for a society beyond absolutism.

Finally, a type of explicitly political eclogue also flourished in the sixteenth and seventeenth centuries, the greatest of which was doubtless *The Shepheardes Calendar* (1579) of Edmund Spenser.[36] Like Philip Sidney, the other major English pastoral poet, Spenser warned the Protestant Queen Elizabeth about the dangers of enlarging the sphere of Catholic influence through marriage to the Duke of Alençon. Wolfgang Iser has shown that Spenser's eclogues presented Elizabeth with alternative choices and their probable result.[37] Spenser thus aligns

---

[35] For the Spanish eclogue, see Doris Lessig, *Ursprung und Entwicklung der spanischen Ekloge bis 1650 (mit Anhang eines Eklogenkataloges)* (Geneva: Droz, 1962); Marcia Jose Bayo, *Virgilio y la pastoral española del Renacimiento (1480–1550)* (Madrid: Gredos, 1970); and Francesco Lopez Estrada, *Los libros de pastores en la literatura española: La órbita previa*, 2 vols (Madrid: Gredos, 1974). For the French eclogue, esp. Alice Hulubei, *L'Églogue en France au XVIe siècle: Epoque des Valois (1515–1589)* (Paris: Droz, 1938).

[36] Simone Dorangeon, *L'églogue anglaise de Spenser à Milton* (Paris: Didier, 1974), and Raimund Borgmeier, *The Dying Shepherd: Die Tradition der englischen Ekloge von Pope bis Wordsworth* (Tübingen: Niemeyer, 1976).

[37] 'Every example demands that the essential quality of each event be considered; that means finding case by case the "secret meaning" hidden by the poet in his interplay with the pastoral requisites. So that the intended reader of the *Shepherdes Calendar* be forced to discover it, the answer itself must not be explicit.' Iser, 'Spensers Arkadien: Fiktion und Geschichte in der englischen Renaissance' (1970; reprint in Garber, *Europäische Bukolik* 260–61).

himself with the tradition of political allegory formed in antiquity and developed by Dante, Petrarch, and Sannazaro. This observation is basic to understanding the eclogue as a utopian medium.

Not only the eclogue but also amorous pastoral poetry and praise of country life (*laus ruris*) enjoyed a renewal, particularly in Petrarchan style, in the age of humanism. The *laus ruris*, in particular, contains specific utopian features.[38] The idyll and eclogue of early modern Europe may be said to have transcended space, time, and genre, in the sense that they could be adapted to larger dramatic and novellistic forms. Pastoral drama had no classical antecedents, aside from the mimic play.[39] The novel, for its part, evolved out of autochthonous forces, that is, independently of the poetological tradition of Longus's bucolic romance, *Daphnis and Chloë*. Within the rising controversy between antiquity and modernity, the new novel was celebrated by some as an advance over antiquity, as an example of modernity's equality with, if not superiority to, Longus. Pastoral drama and opera were Italian creations; the pastoral novel assumed individual characteristics from country to country. The dramatists Torquato Tasso and Battista Guarini, together with the late-sixteenth-century novelists Jorge de Montemayor, Félix Lope de Vega, Miguel de Cervantes, and Honoré d'Urfé, represent the culmination of the two genres in which pastoral reached the European courts and offered the aristocracy an attractive medium for cultural interaction.

Tasso's *Aminta* (1573)[40] preserved the genre's satirical dowry for the Cinquecento, as witnessed in the praise of 'O bella età de l'oro' (O beauteous Golden Age) at the end of the first act, which includes the famous adage 'S'ei piace, ei lice' (What delights, is lawful).[41] What Vergil in *Eclogue* 1 had presented

---

[38] More will be said about the *laus ruris* as a vehicle of utopian thought when we turn to the German prose eclogue.

[39] On pastoral drama in Italy, see in addition to Carrara and Greg, Louise George Clubb, 'The Making of the Pastoral Play: Some Italian Experiments between 1573 and 1590', in *Petrarch to Pirandello: Studies in Italian Literature in Honour of Beatrice Corrigan*, ed. Julius A. Molinaro, 45–72 (Toronto: University of Toronto Press, 1973); for the Spanish counterpart, besides Estrada, *Los libros*, the older but very insightful book by James P.W. Crawford, *The Spanish Pastoral Drama* (Philadelphia: University of Pennsylvania, 1915); for the French, the unpublished dissertation by Jules Marsan, 'La pastorale dramatique en France à la fin du XVIe et au commencement du XVIIe siècle' (PhD diss., University of Paris, 1905), is still useful.

[40] *Aminta* will be discussed here solely with respect to its author's successor and rival, Guarini.

[41] *Aminta*, in *Opere di Torquato Tasso*, 2nd edn, ed. Bortolo Tommaso Sozzi, 2:179–271 (Torino: Unione Tipographico-Editrice Torinese, 1964), act 1, sc. 2, ll. 656 and 681. Translation: Leigh Hunt, as *Amyntas*, in *The Genius of the Italian Theater*, ed. Eric Bentley, 143–93 (New York: New American Library, 1964). On satire in *Aminta*, see Mario Sansone, *L'Aminta di Torquato Tasso* (Milan: Principato, 1941), and Richard Cody, *The Landscape of the Mind: Pastoralism and Platonic Theory in Tasso's Aminta and Shakespeare's Early Comedies* (Oxford: Clarendon Press, 1969).

as an individual's experience takes place in *Aminta* openly before the court. Tasso radicalizes *onor* 'honor' as the central concept of modernity: 'idolo d'errori, idol d'inganno' (the idol of error and deceit).[42] Rivalry is the driving motivation among the honor-addicted, and their victim is the shepherd. The influence of both early capitalism and the court is felt here, both of which stimulated more regulations and stricter codification of behavior – a *dura legge*, as Coro describes it.[43] Against this 'harsh law' the Arcadian promise of wholeness appears in a vision of liberated love, a figurative expression of the poet's alternative to confessional fanaticism, particularly that of the Counter-Reformation. Honor would be foreign to this amorous vision. The court, as Tasso characterizes it, most flagrantly abuses the Arcadian ideal. To the restrictive courtly practice of love as mere etiquette, of pretense and denial, discretion and duplicity – in general, the tendency towards self-concern and self-reflection – Tasso raises the critical mirror of the Golden Age in the name of the common people. He does not simply dismiss the court as regressivist, however, but views it rather through the prism of nature, which enables him, in the words of courtier shepherds like Thyrsis and Daphne and especially the wise poet Elpine, to explore avenues of compromise between apparently irreconcilable extremes:

> There is no need of death
> To bind a great heart fast:
> Faith is enough at first, and Love at last.
> Nor does a fond desert
> Pursue so hard a fame
> In following its sweet aim;
> Since Love is paid with its own loving heart.
> And oftentimes, ere it work out its story,
> It finds itself clasp glory.[44]

This is the very message that Lope and, especially, Cervantes will keep alive within the desolate landscape of their tragic Arcadian stories.

In Guarini's *Il Pastor fido* (1590) the historical wave of the future dominates, which had much to do with the work's extraordinary resonance in the sixteenth

---

[42] *Aminta*, act 1, sc. 2, l. 671.
[43] Ibid., 678.
[44] *Aminta*, act 3, sc. 2, ll. 1470–78.
> Non bisogna la morte,
> ch'a stringer nobil core
> prima basta la fede, e poi l'amore.
> Né quella che si cerca
> è sì difficil fama
> seguendo chi ben ama,
> ch'amore è merce, e con amar si merca.
> E cercando l'amor si trova spesso
> gloria immortal appresso.

and seventeenth centuries.[45] Its only precedent in pastoral literature was Guevara's anti-courtly *Menosprecio de corte y alabanza de aldea* (1553; Deprecation of the Court and Praise of the Village). In Guarini, Arcadia presents a sequential pattern of guilt, forgiveness, and reconciliation. An overt act of fidelity is required for absolution. Hence the attribute: il Pastor *fido*. Sensuous love, embodied in woman and condemned as a moral flaw, must be overcome through discipline. This mistrust of nature, with its correlative faith in the dominance of reason, was alien to Tasso, but it made Guarini's drama an ideal fit within the ideological world of monarchical absolutism. The poet sketches a picture of hero and world that legitimizes monarchism and sanctions *legge* as the key to state power. Law has universal implications, and these are symbolized in the loyalty that exists between the protagonists. Loyalty prevailed in the Golden Age, in contrast to the present. With Guarini, the operative modern dichotomy is not between love and honor, as in Tasso, but between being and appearance. *Il Pastor fido* is a drama of exposure that transforms knowledge acquired through insight into a genuine virtue. Thus the concept of *onor* impugned by Tasso is restored in Guarini. The loyal shepherdess Amarilli ultimately comes to rely on honor, not conventional social honor, but the unassailable honor within herself, which struggles against her fate. The hope she invests in this private honor is the theme of the final chorus, when the oracle's prophecy has been fulfilled in Mirtillo's voluntary sacrifice for Amarilli and when the maiden tribute has been removed from Arcadia:

> O happy pair that sowed in tears
> A harvest which in smiles appears,
> How many bitter hours you spent
> To taste the sweets of true content.
> From hence, you blinded mortals, know
> Sincere delights and real woe.
> Nor think unmixed all present joy,
> Nor all pure evils which annoy.
> The truest joy that here is found
> Is when wronged innocence is crowned.[46]

---

[45] Nicolas Perella, *The Critical Fortune of Battista Guarini's 'Il Pastor fido'* (Florence: Olschki, 1973), and 'Heroic Virtue and Love in the "Pastor fido"', *Atti dell'Istituto Veneto di scienze, lettere ed arti: Classe di scienze morali, lettere ed arti* 132 (1973–4): 653–706.

[46] *Pastor*, act 5, sc. 10, Chorus. *Il Pastor fido*, in *Opere di Battista Guarini*, 2nd edn, ed. Marziano Guglielminetti, 473–716 (Turin: Unione Tipografico-Editrice Torinese, 1971). Translation: *The Faithful Shepherd: A Translation of Battista Guarini's 'Il Pastor fido' by Dr. Thomas Sheridan*, ed. and completed by Robert Hogan and Edward A. Nickerson (Newark: University of Delaware Press; London: Associated University Presses, 1989).

> Oh fortunata coppia,
> che pianto ha seminato e riso accoglie!

It is likely that Guarini intended his description of the oracle's terrible consequences for the lovers to be understood as cultural criticism.[47] That did not, however, lessen the utility of his work for both church and state. While the happy ending may have been abetted in part by the lovers' own actions, as in the later heroic novel, all hope for salvation remained in the hands of a divine Providence that exercised sole authority over oracle and law. Baroque heroism notwithstanding – the emotional power of the work in fact rests upon this heroism – the destiny of the heroes is ultimately determined from above. Were it not for the possibility of divine intervention in their misery, the heroes would remain nothing but playthings of fortune. It is in this sense that *Il Pastor fido* contributes to the mythification of absolute sovereignty; absolutism finds here its aesthetic counterpart.

Just as pastoral drama and opera remain the proper domain of Italy, the pastoral novel belongs chiefly to Spain.[48] In the Spanish pastoral novel between Montemayor's *Diana* (1559) and Lope's *Arcadia* (1598) we observe a markedly increased focus on the utopian promise of happiness in Arcadia. The tragic aspect of love, relentlessly foregrounded in classical pastoral since Theocritus, informs the Spanish pastoral novel, where it experiences in the prose interludes – this feature owes much to developments in European narrative fiction – a drastically heightened intensity. Montemayor was compelled in *Diana* to adduce stock pastoral motifs, later codified in the Garcilaso commentary by Francisco Manuel de Herrera, in a totally unarcadian manner, namely, through the life histories of

---

> Con quante amare doglie
> hai raddolciti tu gli affetti tuoi!
> Quinci imparate voi,
> o ciechi e troppo teneri mortali,
> i sinceri diletti e i veri mali.
> Non è sana ogni gioia,
> né mal ciò che v'annoia.
> Quello è vero gioire,
> che nasce da virtù dopo il soffrire.

[47] Elida Maria Szarota, 'Deutsche "Pastor-Fido"-Übersetzungen und europäische Tradition', in *Europäische Tradition und deutscher Literaturbarock: Internationale Beiträge zum Problem von Überlieferung und Umgestaltung*, ed. Gerhart Hoffmeister, 305–27, here 309–10 (Bern: Francke, 1973).

[48] The historical understanding of the Spanish pastoral novel owes much to the groundbreaking studies of Erich Köhler, esp. 'Absolutismus und Schäferroman' (1966; reprint in Garber, *Europäische Bukolik* 266–70), 'Wandlungen Arkadiens' (1961; reprint in Garber, *Europäische Bukolik* 181–201), and 'Über die Möglichkeiten historisch-soziologischer Interpretation', in *Esprit und arkadische Freiheit: Aufsätze aus der Welt der Romania*, 3rd edn, 83–103 (Munich: Fink, 1984). Also from the Köhler school: Annemarie Rahn-Gassert, 'Et in Arcadia ego: Studien zum spanischen Schäferroman' (PhD diss., University of Heidelberg, 1967).

the shepherds.[49] Simple shepherd's love, overburdened by the formalistic reiteration of set material, is restored finally through the fairy-tale-like figure of Felicia. While Montemayor may have been melodramatic, these effects doubtless accounted in part for *Diana*'s great popularity.

The two works in which the Spanish pastoral novel achieved greatness, however, Cervantes' *Galatea* and Lope's *Arcadia*, show that a historical problem, not merely an aesthetic one, needed to be solved.[50]

In *Galatea* (1585),[51] a profound and perhaps the most difficult pastoral novel in all literature, Cervantes repeatedly leads his figures, under the spell of Amor, into the very abyss of love. The novel begins in fact with the unforgettable image of a deathly pale shepherd who has stabbed his rival to death. Thus the fatalistic quality of love arises even before the appearance of Galatea, the embodiment of perfect beauty, who is capable of arousing sublime feelings within her lovers. The pastoral novel obligates its author to an unceasing search for resolutions to the many and, as in *Don Quixote*, often unresolvable, conflicts.[52] In his examples of proper amorous conduct, which he always bases on knowledge and moderation, Cervantes suggests how traditional pastoral values may be preserved. In one remarkable episode, for instance, Marcela's insistence on having uninhibited freedom prohibits a harmonious reconciliation in the Arcadian community: absolute freedom (represented by Marcela) and absolute passion (represented by Grisostemos) are irreconcilable. In *Don Quixote*, with the collision of these two absolute and therefore life-threatening principles, Arcadia falls apart.

Lope conceptualizes this experience as *desengaño* 'disillusionment' and obligates his protagonist to seek after knowledge and virtue rather than chimerical Arcadian pleasures.[53] In no other place or time did this Arcadia-Utopia

---

[49] Bruce Wardropper, 'The Diana of Montemayor: Revaluation and Interpretation', *Studies in Modern Philology* 48 (1951): 126–44; C.B. Johnson, 'Montemayor's Diana: A Novel Pastoral', *Bulletin of Hispanic Studies* 48 (1971): 20–35; and Gerhart Hoffmeister, *Die spanische Diana in Deutschland; vergleichende Untersuchungen zu Stilwandel und Weltbild des Schäferromans im 17. Jahrhundert* (Berlin: Erich Schmidt, 1972), all of which remain indispensable general studies. Edition: *Los Siete Libros de la Diana*, ed. Francisco López Estrada and Teresa López García-Berdoy (Madrid: Espasa Calpe, 1993). Translation: *The Diana by Jorge de Montemayor*, trans. RoseAnna M. Mueller (Lewiston, NY: Edwin Mellen Press, 1989).

[50] Francesco López Estrada, *Estudio Critico de 'Galateo' de Miguel de Cervantes* (La Laguna de Tenerife: Universidad de La Laguna, 1948), and Rafael Osuna, 'La critica y la erudición del siglo XX ante La Galatea de Cervantes', *The Romanic Review* 54 (1963): 241–51.

[51] *La Galatea*, ed. Juan Bautista Avalle-Arce (Madrid: Espasa-Calpe, 1987).

[52] Köhler, 'Wandlungen', an analysis of the Marcela episode in *Don Quixote*, provides an exemplary study of this complexity, which is also found in *Galatea* (esp. 217–30).

[53] Lope de Vega, *Arcadia*, ed. Edwin S. Morby (Madrid: Editorial Castalia, 1975). This point is made repeatedly in Jole Scudieri Ruggieri, *Stilistica e stile nell' 'Arcadia' di Lope* (Turin, 1965), and Rafael Osuna, *La Arcadia de Lope de Vega: Genesis, estructura y originalidad* (Madrid: Fundacion Conde de Cartagena, 1972).

dialectic unfold as spectacularly as in late-sixteenth and early-seventeenth-century Spain. In the end it failed. Historical contradictions undermined the classical symbol of pastoral itself: Arcadia.

The pastoral novel attained its highest courtly refinement in the immensely popular *L'Astrée* of Honoré d'Urfé, published in installments between 1607 and 1625.[54] Its disguised political scenario, transposed back to the fifth century, was never properly appreciated before Norbert Elias. In his now standard work *The Court Society*, Elias argues that the fictional opposition between the pastoral and courtly worlds in *L'Astrée* is reflective of the political opposition that obtained between the monarchy, then on the rise, and the increasingly threatened noble estate, to which the d'Urfé family belonged:

> But even though d'Urfé, like many other people after the civil wars, having fought vainly against the man who is now crowned and at the center of the court and probably against the growing power of the monarchy as well, lays down his sword and creates a dream image of peaceful and simple pastoral existence for war-weary people, nevertheless, on the ideological level he continues the struggle in his novel. The simple, good, free life of the lower-ranking shepherds and shepherdesses is contrasted again and again to the customs and morals of the higher-ranking lords and ladies of the court, the actual wielders of power in this world. And the repeated stress on the difference in the amorous behavior of the two groups shows particularly clearly the continuation of the struggle on a different level, as a conflict between two different sets of values, a protest against the encroachment of the court that is becoming increasingly inescapable.[55]

This process, however, can be subsumed only artificially under what Elias calls 'aristocratic romanticism'. For Elias the term characterizes a process of 'courtization', such that courtly mechanisms remained operative even within the anti-courtly utopia, in other words, in the very teeth of criticism. But *L'Astrée* took the European courts by storm precisely because its shepherds (much as the true lovers in *Il Pastor fido*) exemplify heroic self-control and loyalty. In the characters Celadon and Astrée the neo-Stoic ideal of constancy is transfigured in a way that makes it possible for nobles and princes alike to identify with it.

---

[54] *L'Astrée*, 5 vols, ed. Hugues Vaganay (Geneva: Slatkine, 1966). Of particular use for the present study are Köhler, 'Absolutismus'; Norbert Elias, *The Court Society*, trans. Edmund Jephcott (New York: Pantheon Books, 1983); and Eckhart Schroeder, 'D'Urfé: L'Astrée', in *Der französische Roman vom Mittelalter bis zur Gegenwart*, ed. Klaus Heitmann, 1:95–119 (Düsseldorf: Bagel, 1975); Renate Jürgensen, *Die deutschen Übersetzungen der 'Astrée' des Honoré d'Urfé* (Tübingen: Niemeyer, 1990).

[55] Elias, *Court Society* 256–7; orthography slightly adapted.

Pastoral in Early Modern Germany: From Martin Opitz to J.H. Voss

In antiquity, then again in Renaissance southern Europe and England, pastoral rose to the stature of world literature, whereas in seventeenth-century Germany it remained only a local phenomenon. Many great German writers, including Andreas Gryphius and Hans Jakob Christoffel von Grimmelshausen, either ignored or parodied the genre; not surprisingly, Germany made very little contribution to the courtly pastoral. This is not to say, however, that pastoral found no welcome in Germany. Martin Opitz, the foremost name in the seventeenth-century literary reform, encouraged courtly pastoral through his translation of Sidney's *Arcadia* (1629) and Rinuccini's pastoral tragi-comedy *Dafne* (1627). In the Fruchtbringende Gesellschaft, Baroque Germany's first and most important intellectual society,[56] pastoral was also cultivated through translation. Vergil and Sidney, Tasso and Guarini, Montemayor and d'Urfé were all made available in German. A central purpose of the Fruchtbringende Gesellschaft was, after all, to establish a comprehensive canon of European literature in German. Pastoral figured prominently among the translations, not only because of its traditionally privileged place in literature, but especially because of its more recently evolved possibilities for noble and princely self-representation. The correspondence carried on between this aristocratic society of *vraits amants* in Anhalt-Köthen and the author of *L'Astrée* reveals the German fascination with the French image of the *honnête homme* in shepherd's garb.[57] At the time only the *laus regentis* type of pastoral was actively practiced in Germany. Educated members of the professional middle class, such as Georg Neumark, secretary of the Fruchtbringende Gesellschaft, and Sigmund von Birken, second president of Nuremberg's Pegnesischer Blumenorden, exploited the *laus regentis* pastoral to further their own careers as courtly literati.[58]

The German pastoral novel clearly reflects the cultural gap between the western European nation-states and the German territorial states.[59] The earliest

---

[56] 'Fruitbearing Society', founded 1617 by Prince Ludwig of Anhalt-Köthen (near Weimar), whose territory was officially Reformed but had significant Calvinist sympathies.

[57] Heinrich Welti's older study, 'Die Astrée des Honoré d'Urfé und ihre deutschen Verehrer', *Zeitschrift für neufranzösische Sprache und Literatur* 5 (1883): 107–19, remains the standard on this topic.

[58] G. Kretschmer, 'Georg Neumark, ein Weimarer Bibliothekar und Dichter des 17. Jahrhunderts', *Zeitschrift für Bibliothekswesen* 91 (1977): 91–101. On Birken's role as sodality president, see Klaus Garber, 'Sigmund von Birken: Städtischer Ordenspräsident und höfischer Dichter: Historisch-soziologischer Umriß seiner Gestalt, Analyse seines Nachlasses und Prolegomenon zur Edition seines Werkes', in *Sprachgesellschaften, Societäten, Dichtergruppen*, ed. Martin Bircher and Ferdinand van Ingen, 223–54 (Hamburg: Hauswedell, 1978).

[59] Wilhelm Voßkamp, 'Der deutsche Schäferroman des 17. Jahrhunderts', in *Handbuch des deutschen Romans*, ed. Helmut Koopmann, 105–16 (Düsseldorf: Bagel, 1983).

works in this form date back to the 1630s and are concerned with aristocratic life. Philipp von Zesen's *Adriatischer Rosemund* (1645) introduced middle-class characters into the genre.[60] Elsewhere in Europe the pastoral novel provided the upper middle class and nobility with norms and images of social behavior, codifying standards of interaction among noble and patrician families, as part of the effort to establish an aristocratic profile distinct from a monarchical profile. In Germany, on the other hand, the pastoral aristocratic novel focused less on public and more on private aspects of culture. Behind the versatile shepherd's mask, situations and problems from a largely aristocratic milieu could be brought to light. Because the German writers had at their disposal no ceremonial form for representing the mannered intercourse of European aristocratic families, their literary gestures often appear forced and overly stylized, betraying technical and behavioral uncertainty, even a crudeness that borders at times on vulgarity. In the first German pastoral novel the female character Amoena violates etiquette by taking the initiative in love; in the second novel of the type, Leoriander, a member of the landed aristocracy, sinks deeper and deeper into the permissive milieu of a city tavern. As these examples suggest, the German pastoral novel was first filled with real-life experiences that allowed only the narrowest range of moral and social options. Nowhere do we find there the grand social designs of the foreign pastoral novel. For literature of that rank in Germany one must look to the late-century courtly heroic novel, in which lovers are ultimately reunited as an optimistic sign of moral and social vindication. The early pastoral novel in Germany evinced resignation, melancholy, and an utter lack of future social perspective; it was hardly suited to the task of rekindling the utopian spark of the Vergilian pastoral form.

Germany's genuine contribution to the pastoral of the seventeenth century came from neither the courtly nor the aristocratic sphere but rather from the educated middle class. It was here that the real designs for a utopian social order in pastoral were proposed. Opitz standardized the basic repertoire of motifs for the pastoral, much as he did for other genres. His early *Teutsche Poemata* (1624), a collection of poems that attained wide popularity over the century, included pastoral love songs with Petrarchan elements.[61] There are endless variations in Opitz of the praise of country life; particularly his Horace imitations inspired scores of emulators over the following decades. Somewhat against expectations perhaps, his rural didactic poem *Zlatna* (1623), one of his aesthetically and

---

[60] Arnold Hirsch, *Bürgertum und Barock im deutschen Roman: Ein Beitrag zur Entstehungsgeschichte des bürgerlichen Weltbildes*, 2nd edn, ed. Herbert Singer (Cologne: Böhlau, 1957), 89–90.

[61] The song collection made late in the nineteenth century by Max Freiherr von Waldberg, *Die deutsche Renaissance-Lyrik* (Berlin: Hertz, 1888), is still a useful resource for the investigation of pastoral love songs.

technically most refined works, found little contemporary resonance.[62] With respect to the eclogue, the domain of German humanist poets since the late fifteenth century, Opitz chose to work only in Latin.

His genuinely independent contribution to European pastoral integrates elements from two long traditions. Like the southern pastoral novel, it consists of alternating verse and prose sections; and like the classical Vergilian eclogue, it is composed in response to a social occasion and dedicated to some patron or other worthy. It was essentially by combining these two traditions in his *Schäfferey von der Nimfen Hercinie* (1630; Pastoral of the Nymph Hercinie) that Opitz created the genre of prose eclogue.[63] The tremendous popularity of this new pastoral form over the course of the century, imitated in nearly all of Germany's literary centers by mostly middle-class authors, owed especially to its suitability as a medium for the poetic transformation of social occasions.[64] The authors of these extraordinarily wide-ranging and colorful works, protected by the bucolic mask, freely articulate ethical, cultural, social, and political positions as a means of asserting their own identity vis-à-vis the aristocracy or patriciate, emphasizing their moral and intellectual qualifications for undertaking the tasks demanded by the cities and territorial states. The language and literature societies (*Sprachgesellschaften*) that provided the poets with this corporate identity stressed, in their egalitarian charters, the fact that their members were intellectual and moral peers; they contributed in this fashion to the undermining of the traditional social hierarchy.[65] The idea gradually took shape that the social order

---

[62] Anke-Marie Lohmeier, *Beatus ille: Studien zum 'Lob des Landlebens' in der Literatur des absolutistischen Zeitalters* (Tübingen: Niemeyer, 1981).

[63] [Ed. note: Traditionally called *Schäferei* 'pastoral', German scholarship now regularly employs the prosimetric term *Prosaekloge* 'prose eclogue', which has the advantage of alluding to both literary traditions. It was Garber who coined the term and first began to investigate it as a distinct form of early modern German pastoral, in *Der locus amoenus und der locus terribilis: Bild und Funktion der Natur in der deutschen Schäfer- u. Landlebendichtung des 17. Jahrhunderts* (Cologne: Böhlau, 1974), esp. 26–38.]

[64] The structure and other features of the genre are described in detail in Garber, *Locus amoenus*, and 'Martin Opitz' "Schäferei von der Nymphe Hercinie" als Ursprung der Prosaekloge und des Schäferromans in Deutschland', *Daphnis* 11 (1982): 547–603; Max Reinhart discusses the formal and social aspects of prose eclogue in *Johann Hellwig's 'Die Nymphe Noris' (1650): A Critical Edition* (Columbia, SC: Camden House, 1994), xxviii–xxxiii. A comprehensive bibliography of prose eclogue has been compiled by Garber and Renate Jürgensen, *Bibliographie der deutschen Schäfer- und Landlebendichtung des 17. Jahrhunderts* (Stuttgart: Hiersemann, 1998).

[65] Many studies since the early 1980s have explored this problem. To name only a few: Bircher and van Ingen, *Sprachgesellschaften*; Garber, 'Gibt es eine bürgerliche Literatur im Deutschland des 17. Jahrhunderts?' *Germanisch-romanische Monatsschrift* 31 (1981): 462–70; Erika A. Metzger and Richard E. Schade (eds), *Sprachgesellschaften – Galante Poetinnen (Literary Societies/Literary Women)* (Amsterdam: Rodopi, 1989); Max Reinhart, 'Poets and Politics: The Transgressive Turn of History in Seventeenth-Century Nürnberg', *Daphnis* 20, no. 1 (1991): 199–229.

adapted in these elite societies should one day become general social reality. This utopianism was especially propagated through prose eclogue, and it was no coincidence that German poetic organizations were founded ritualistically as pastoral societies.[66]

In the prose eclogues of Sigmund von Birken [see Plate 3], the most prolific writer of pastoral literature in seventeenth-century Germany, the sheer wealth of ideas related to society and culture shatter the traditionally narrow thematic boundaries of pastoral.[67] Among the issues of interest to Birken is the role of women in intellectual societies. During his long term as president of the Blumenorden (1658–81), Birken succeeded in recruiting several extraordinarily gifted women poets, including Catharina Margaretha Dobeneck and Maria Catharina Stockfleth, and maintained a long and fruitful correspondence with Catharina von Greiffenberg, an exile in Nuremberg from Catholic Austria and one of Baroque Germany's most gifted poets.[68] With respect to the admittance of women into this traditionally male institution, Birken felt obliged at last to act upon the well-seasoned theory of meritocratic nobility. In order to become more than an empty formula, real action was necessary. Birken found the vehicle of the prose eclogue well suited to deliberating on the problem.

Birken's *Fürtrefflichkeit des Liebloblichen Frauenzimmers* (1669; The Merits of an Excellent Woman), a prose eclogue in the form of a conversation between four 'gifted and virtuous shepherdesses', succinctly defines the order's attitude with regard to women in the second half of the seventeenth century:

> Our most laudable and charming shepherdesses do not sparkle merely with outer physical beauty; the radiance of virtue arises from their hearts, and wisdom from their souls. We recognize their excellence not only by the aura that surrounds them, but by their manners and speech, as well.[69]

---

[66] Garber, 'Sozietäten, Akademien, Sprachgesellschaften', in *Europäische Enzyklopädie zu Philosophie und Wissenschaften*, ed. Hans Jörg Sandkühler, 4:366–84 (Hamburg: Meiner, 1990).

[67] Nuremberg prose eclogue will be treated at length below in Chapter 6, 'Nuremberg, Arcadia on the Pegnitz.'

[68] On Dobenecker, see Joachim Kröll, 'Die Ehre des Gebirges und der hohen Wälder: Catharina Margaretha Dobenecker, geborene Schweser', *Daphnis* 7 (1978): 287–339; on Stockfleth, Volker Meid, 'Ungleichheit gleich Ordnung: Zur "Macarie" (1669–1673) von Heinrich Arnold und Maria Katharina Stockfleth', in *Schäferdichtung*, ed. Wilhelm Voßkamp, 59–66 (Hamburg: Hauswedell,1977); and on Greiffenberg, Louise Gnädinger, 'Ister-Clio, Teutsche Uranie, Coris die Tapfere: Catharina Regina von Greiffenberg (1633–1694): Ein Portrait', in *Deutsche Literatur von Frauen*, ed. Gisela Brinker-Gabler, 1:248–64 (Munich: Beck, 1988).

[69] *Fürtrefflichkeit* (Nuremberg, 1669), 13. 'Unsre lob- und liebwürdigste Schäferinnen/ gläntzen nicht allein von äuserlicher Schönheit des Leibes/ sondern auch Tugend leuchtet aus ihrem Herzen/ und Weißheit aus der Seele/ wie wir an ihren Sitten und Reden/ als an den Stralen/ erkennen.'

Plate 3   Sigmund von Birken (1626–1681). Engraved portrait by J. von Sandrart. Frontispiece from *Festschrift zur 250jährigen Jubelfeier des Pegnesischen Blumenordens gegründet in Nürnberg am 16. Oktober 1644.* Edited by Th. Bischoff and Aug. Schmidt. Nürnberg: Johann Leonhard Schrag, 1894.

The voice of Heinrich Arnold Stockfleth, husband of Maria Catharina, expressly rejects as 'delusion' and 'male tyranny' the widely held prejudice of male intellectual superiority. Dorilis, as Maria Catharina was called, is herself a living example:

> In her manners there is nothing but nobility and no trace of vanity. Her memory, filled with her extensive reading, and her wit, sharpened by mature judgment, make her an eloquent conversationalist. Her mind penetrates at once to the crux of the matter and positions itself centrally so as to have a view of everything.[70]

This statement amounts to more than simple flattery of the talented Maria Catharina. It rests on a humanist theology of creation, according to which the authority of natural law may be ascertained behind the biblical account. The first principle to be recognized is that 'the woman was in fact created in every way, other than in gender, exactly as the man' (32). Dorilis probes further, asking ironically how this innate potential can be developed, when on every hand society hinders women's intellectual advancement:

> How can we achieve our potential when our abilities are nipped in the bud? We are virtually imprisoned in our own homes, where, as in a prison, we are trained only for mean labor, such as spinning and weaving. We are rushed into learning to cook and do housework. Many a woman is forced to become Martha when she would prefer to be Mary. Indeed, we are condemned to such barbarity and ignorance that not only men, but even most other women, having so degenerated in vanity and ignorance, despise and deride the few of us who engage ourselves with learning. No one respects an educated woman.[71]

In the light of creation these social rules are exposed as foolishness. Society withholds from women the opportunities to acquire the kind of reason and knowledge that would make them truly virtuous:

---

[70] *Fürtrefflichkeit* 14–15. 'In ihren Sitten/ ist nichts als Adel: und welches das seltsamste/ ohne alle Eitelkeit. Ihr Gedächtnis/ von der Vielbelesenheit erfüllet/ und mit dem reifsten Urtheil allemal vergesellschaftet/ machet sie höchst-redseelig. Ihr Verstand/ sihet allen Sachen auf den Grund/ und setzet sein Aug in den Mitteldupf/ alle Umstände auf einmal zu überschauen.'

[71] *Fürtrefflichkeit* 36–7. '[W]ie solten wir zur Vollkommenheit gelangen/ da man unsere Fähigkeit in der Blüte sterbet/ uns zuhaus gleichsam gefangen setzet/ und/ als wie in einem Zuchthause/ zu schlechter Arbeit/ zur Nadel und Spindel/ angewöhnet? Man eilet mit uns zur Küche und Haushaltung/ und wird manche gezwungen/ eine Martha zu werden/ die doch etwas lieber Maria seyn möchte. Ja so gar sind wir zur Barbarey und Unwissenheit verdammet/ daß nicht allein die Manns-Personen/ sondern auch die meisten von unserem Geschlecht selber/ weil sie in der Eitelkeit und Unwissenheit verwildert sind/ uns verachten und verlachen/ wann eine und andere auf löbliche Wissenschaft sich befleissiget/ und nichtes auf Gelehrte Weibspersonen halten.'

> We are told . . . to be virtuous. But how are we to become so when we are forbidden to read the very books from which virtue is to be learned? Shall virtue simply fly to us like the roasted birds in Utopia? Rational and virtuous actions follow from the practice of reason and the knowledge of virtue.[72]

She continues this line of reasoning in terms of classical moral philosophy:

> Why must we languish in this forced ignorance and innocently endure the name of simplicity? Are we not just as human as men? Indeed, are not reason and speech the unique characteristics that separate humans from unintelligent animals? Why should we not be allowed to exercise our reason? And how are our conversations to be judged useful, when we are barred from learning anything? Are we lower than . . . the mindless beasts that are taught all manner of tricks and trained to talk?[73]

Prior to about 1600, certain ethical implications of the classical discourse of true nobility had been largely passed over by humanists. By the seventeenth century, however, the utopian community of shepherds could no longer in good conscience ignore the practical question concerning women and other non-privileged members of society.[74] Their response was more significant than is generally known in literary studies. As Arnold Hirsch argues in his study of the

---

[72] *Fürtrefflichkeit* 37–8. 'Man . . . will/ daß wir Tugendsam seyn: wie können wir es aber werden/ wann man uns das Lesen der Bücher verbietet/ aus welchen die Tugend muß erlernet werden? Soll uns dann dieselbe/ wie die gebratene Tauben in Utopien/ aus der Luft zufliegen? Auf Verstand-übung und Tugend-erkenntnis/ folgen vernünftige tugendhafte Werke.'

[73] *Fürtrefflichkeit* 38–9. 'Warum müssen wir also in einer aufgedrungenen Unwissenheit verderben/ und den Namen der Einfalt ohne Schuld erdulden? Sind wir dann nicht sowol Menschen/ als die Männer? Nun ist/ der Verstand und die Rede/ des Menschen Eigenschaft/ die ihn von den unvernünftigen Thieren unterscheidet: warüm sollen wir dann unsern Verstand nit ausüben dörfen? Und wovon sollen wir nutzlich reden/ wann man uns verbietet/ etwas zu lernen? Sollen wir dann geringer seyn/ als . . . verstandlose Thiere/ denen man allerley Künste lehret/ und sie zum Reden angewöhnet?'

[74] [Ed. note: Garber's discussion (pp. 60–62) at this point of Heinrich and Maria Catharina Stockfleth's *Kunst- und Tugend-gezierte Macarie* (1669–73), omitted from the translation, extends his remarks on Birken. His observations are elegantly confirmed in an independent study by Elena Ciletti, 'Patriarchal Ideology in the Renaissance Iconography of Judith', in *Refiguring Women: Perspectives on Gender and the Italian Renaissance*, ed. Marilyn Migiel and Juliana Schiesari, 35–70 (Ithaca: Cornell University Press, 1991), 52–3: 'Important scholarship has made it increasingly apparent that on the subject of women, the humanist recuperation of and reverence for classical authors cannot simply be counted among the intellectual felicities of the age . . . It is true, of course, that humanism did evolve a "liberal" discourse of gender, the most familiar Italian contributor to which is Castiglione, but this development was fitful at best and largely the exception to the rule.' Birken's efforts on behalf of women are therefore the more impressive.]

Stockfleths' pastoral novel *Macarie* (1673),[75] the greater portion of which was written by Maria Catharina, the appeal to virtue in the literature of seventeenth-century Nuremberg helped to open up a new cultural space, not only for women, but for the middle class in general:

> The *honor* of the courtier is overcome by the *virtue* of the shepherd. With this concept the bourgeoisie creates for itself an ethical means to equalize existing class distinctions ... As the good-spirited Pegnitz shepherds strive to better themselves through education, a modern world of moral education takes shape, a spiritual domain toward which large numbers of burghers will strive in the eighteenth century. [It indicates] the beginning of a push in the social space, a forward movement of the bourgeoisie -- just as the movement's definitive isolation and strengthening in the eighteenth century represents the first maturation of middle-class identity.[76]

Hirsch's insight provides an important key to understanding the learned middle-class sodalities and their pastoral subgroups. In these Arcadian societies the true inheritance of utopia, the effective combination of critical negation and optimistic anticipation, was preserved. In both institutional and literary form the prevailing social order was revoked and replaced, symbolically, by a counter-image. It was this utopian call that inspired the finest German pastoral works of the seventeenth century.

The middle-class pastoral novel of the late-seventeenth century is best represented by Johann Thomas's autobiographical *Damon und Lisille* (1663–72).[77] The 'shepherd trade', Thomas writes, has flourished again after the Thirty Years' War due to the Peace of Westphalia, which restored 'security' to the 'subjects' of the land. Young men and women are once again free to fall in love, as this short pastoral novel relates in the story of one couple's first encounter, courtship, marriage, conjugal bliss, and shared pain, ending at last with the death of the beautiful and beloved wife. Open since the early Renaissance to biographical elements, the pastoral novel encouraged allegorical treatment of personal experiences of all kinds, from the intellectual to the amorous. This capability to give form to personal intimacy, to justify the literary representation of individual experience, to permit the recollection of personal lives, made the pastoral novel especially attractive as a narrative medium. It is capable of

---

[75] *Die Kunst- und Tugend-gezierte Macarie*, ed. Volker Meid (Bern: P. Lang, 1978). This remarkable novel was all but forgotten until Hirsch discovered a copy in 1929.

[76] Hirsch, *Bürgertum und Barock* 113–14.

[77] *Damon und Lisille 1663 und 1665*, ed. Herbert Singer and Horst Gronemeyer (Hamburg: Maximillian- Gesellschaft, 1966). The afterword by Singer and Gronemeyer is the starting point for any study of this pastoral novel. The reflection of middle-class life in late-seventeenth-century German pastoral is treated in Herbert Jaumann, 'Bürgerlicher Alltag im barocken Schäferroman? Gattungsgeschichtliche Thesen zu "Damon und Lisille"', in Voßkamp, *Schäferdichtung* 39–58.

UTOPIA AND THE GREEN WORLD

expressing remarkable tenderness and beauty, as in the following passage from *Damon und Lisille*:

> Meanwhile, the people had decided to dance, and Damon with his Lisille joined in as well. He led her more in his arms than by the hand, and they inclined their heads so closely together that, as they paused near the hedges while the dancers made their round, he was able to kiss her for the very first time. (To which she responded simply by warmly pressing his hand.) But after the dance had ended, Lisille, embarrassed at having allowed Damon such liberty and having compromised herself so soon, stole away from the garden. Damon was the first to notice that she was gone, and at once he began a diligent search for her . . . First, he looked for her at the fountain, the one they call the Crystal Fountain for its crystal clear water. When he did not find her there, he hurried on to the wooded park nearby, calling her name, until finally, after much searching, he caught sight of her lying beneath a wild pear tree. Her lap was full of flowers, and in one hand she held a half-formed wreath that she had been weaving when, lulled by the soft sound of the leaves sighing in the breeze, she fell asleep.[78]

In this lovely scene of first sexual desire, despite all peripheral anxieties, the ideal of happiness is briefly fulfilled for two young burghers, as surely as in earlier courtly pastoral novels. The element of courtly criticism typical of learned middle-class writing in the seventeenth century is completely absent here.

German pastoral novel and prose eclogue disappeared after having flourished for only a few decades. Verse eclogue and the spiritual pastoral survived here and there, and pastoral opera appeared in the eighteenth century alongside the rococo pastoral play; but the small occasional forms of pastoral held little interest beyond 1700. The rather sudden freeze on conventional works-on-commission seems to have been a necessary precondition for the eighteenth-century transformation of pastoral into a vehicle ideally suited to the expression of nature and the natural

---

[78] *Damon und Lisille* 13–14. 'In dessen hatten sich jene beredt/ einen Tantz anzufangen/ und muste Damon mit seiner Lisillen auch herbey. Er führte sie mehr in seinen Armen/ als an der Hand/ und kamen sie mit den Häuptern so nahe zusammen/ daß er ihr im Gepüsch/ da der Reygen durchgieng/ den ersten Kuß beybracht. Welches sie gegen ihn anders nicht als mit einem Handtrücken rechete. Aber nach geendigtem Tantz/ als ob sie sich schämete/ dem Damon zu viel Freyheit zugelassen/ und sich selbst ihm zu zeitliche verrathen zu haben/ verlohr sie sich auß dem Garten hinweg/ und ward am ersten von dem Damon vermist/ der sich nicht säumte sie allen Fleisses zusuchen . . . Er suchte sie also zu erst bey dem Brunnen/ den man wegen seiner frischen und lautern Quell den Crystallbrunnen zu nennen pflegt/ und als er sie da nicht fand/ lieff er weiter in das darbey gelegene Lustwäldlein/ ruffte hier und dar der Lisillen/ biß er ihrer endlich nach langem suchen ansichtig ward. Sie lag unter einem wilden Birnbaum/ hatte den Schoß voller Blumen/ und hielt in der einen Hand einen halb außgemachten Krantz/ den sie zu winden angefangen/ aber über solcher Arbeit/ und dem sachten Geräusch der Blätter in Schlaff gesuncken war.'

life. Pastoral began to discard its former dependence on panegyrical occasions, though it did retain to a degree the panegyrical formula as a tool for social and political criticism. It was in the rural poem and the idyll, closely related in their forms and motifs, in which nature poetry thrived and the critical potential of pastoral continued to be viable deep into the eighteenth century.[79]

Nature is featured most prominently in the poem *Die Alpen* (1729; The Alps) by the Swiss anatomist and physiologist Albrecht von Haller.[80] *Die Alpen* is a didactic work that appeared at about the same time as the nature poetry of the Hamburg poets Barthold Heinrich Brockes and Friedrich von Hagedorn. Essential components from both the bucolic and the georgic traditions are contained in equal measure in *Die Alpen*;[81] the poem's sociopolitical criticism is intense.[82] Dispensing with the conventional nature exordium, Haller launches into a weighty satire employing imagery evocative of the courtly sphere. Invoking 'moderate nature' he raises an emphatic objection to the human incursion into nature that is so typical of courtly society:

---

[79] Renate Böschenstein-Schäfer, *Idylle*, 2nd edn (Stuttgart: Metzler, 1977), esp. 15–16, 73–4, 152–3, as well as her related Goethe study, 'Arbeit und Muße in der Idyllendichtung des 18. Jahrhunderts', in *Goethezeit: Studien zur Erkenntnis und Rezeption Goethes und seiner Zeitgenossen*, ed. Gerhart Hoffmeister, 9–30 (Bern: Francke, 1981). The categories of 'naivete' and 'nostalgia' were introduced in the mid-1970s into the investigation of middle-class pastoral by Hella Jäger, *Naivität: Eine kritisch-utopische Kategorie in der bürgerlichen Literatur und Ästhetik des 18. Jahrhunderts* (Kronberg, Czech.: Scriptor, 1975), and Thomas Lange, *Idyllische und exotische Sehnsucht: Formen bürgerlicher Nostalgie in der deutschen Literatur des 18. Jahrhunderts* (Kronberg, Czech.: Scriptor, 1976). These arguments came under fire in Gerhard Kaiser, *Wandrer und Idylle: Goethe und die Phänomenologie der Natur in der deutschen Dichtung von Geßner bis Gottfried Keller* (Göttingen: Vandenhoeck & Ruprecht, 1977). Of particular relevance to my views are three studies by H.J. Schneider: 'Die sanfte Utopie: Zu einer bürgerlichen Tradition literarischer Glücksbilder', in *Idyllen der Deutschen: Texte und Illustrationen*, ed. Schneider, 353–442 (Frankfurt a.M.: Insel, 1978), 'Naturerfahrung und Idylle in der deutschen Aufklärung', in *Erforschung der deutschen Aufklärung*, ed. Peter Pütz, 289–315 (Kronberg, Czech.: Scriptor, 1980), and *Deutsche Idyllentheorien im 18. Jahrhundert* (Tübingen: Narr, 1988).

[80] Haller, *Gedichte*, ed. Ludwig Hirzel (Frauenfeld: Huber, 1882).

[81] The distinction between bucolic and georgic goes back to the two pastoral forms of Vergil, the *Eclogues* (or *Bucolics*, idyllic songs of cow- or goatherds) and the *Georgics* (a poem devoted to agricultural husbandry; this form was also highly cultivated by Horace, esp. his second epode, 'Beatus ille').

[82] First attempts to articulate the sociopolitical content in Haller were made by Werner Kohlschmidt, 'Hallers Gedichte und die Tradition', in *Dichter, Tradition und Zeitgeist: Gesammelte Studien zur Literaturgeschichte*, 206–21 (Bern: Francke, 1965); Leif Ludwig Albertsen, *Das Lehrgedicht: Eine Geschichte der antikisierenden Sachepik in der neueren deutschen Literatur mit einem unbekannten Gedicht Albrecht von Hallers* (Aarhus: Arkona, 1967), 159–60; and Hans Christoph Buch, *Ut pictura poesis: Die Beschreibungsliteratur und ihre Kritiker von Lessing bis Lukács* (Munich: Hanser, 1972), 97–8.

Endeavor, o mortals, to improve your lot; use all that Art has invented and Nature endowed; enliven the flowery meadow with irrigation, carve away the cliffs according to the decrees of Corinth; drape the marble wall with Persian carpets, feast on Tutankamin's nest of gold, imbibe of emerald pearls, fall asleep to the sounds of the lute, awaken to trumpets, remove mountains from your path, fence the fields for hunting. After fate itself has acquiesced to your desire, you shall remain poor in your happiness, and miserable in your riches![83]

Haller's citation of the Golden Age, in clear imitation of Tasso, amounts to a denunciation of the vices of surplus and wantonness of high society.

The question, veiled yet hardly ambiguous, arises: 'What right does a prince have that a shepherd does not?' (l. 15) A description of shepherd life on the mountain, as well as of the Alps themselves, leads to a perfunctory castigation of injustice. The georgic tradition did not typically accentuate the toils of the shepherd's life to the degree found in Haller, whose purpose is to demonstrate, by the example of the shepherds, these 'students of Nature' (l. 31), that excess is incompatible with nature properly understood. The Alps, after all, are 'no Tempe' (l. 35). Haller too wishes happiness for his shepherds, but it is to be discovered in the midst of natural scarcity – not because he advocates poverty, but because he is appalled by the court's wastefulness. Precisely because pristine nature is beautiful, sublime, and purposeful, its disfigurement by courtly society is sinful. Haller occasionally aims explicit criticism at the city, but he soon enough again turns back upon 'the wild princes'.[84]

Courtly criticism, which is an organizing principle of *Die Alpen*, is not intended simply as moral criticism, however. The sublime Alpine world reinforces Haller's political messages as well. Thinking of the Swiss republican tradition Haller directs his criticism, on behalf of the 'quiet contentment of the common folk' (l. 445) as symbolized by the Alpine shepherds, against the system of monarchical absolutism. At several points he adduces the concept of freedom to express not only individual moral autonomy but the very absence of an unnatural social hierarchy:

---

[83] *Alpen*, ll. 1–10.
  Versuchts, ihr Sterbliche, macht euren Zustand besser,
  Braucht, was die Kunst erfand und die Natur euch gab;
  Belebt die Blumen-Flur mit steigendem Gewässer,
  Theilt nach Korinths Gesetz gehaune Felsen ab;
  Umhängt die Marmor-Wand mit persischen Tapeten,
  Speist Tunkins Nest aus Gold, trinkt Perlen aus Smaragd,
  Schlaft ein beim Saitenspiel, erwachet bei Trompeten,
  Räumt Klippen aus der Bahn, schließt Länder ein zur Jagd;
  Wird schon, was ihr gewünscht, das Schicksal unterschreiben,
  Ihr werdet arm im Glück, im Reichthum elend bleiben!
[84] *Alpen*, e.g., ll. 451–61.

> Here rules no difference invented by cunning pride, that subjugates virtue and ennobles vice; no tedious toil makes the hours seem long, work fills out the day and quiet enwraps the night; here no lofty spirit is blinded by ambition, the morning sun steals not an ounce of day's delight. Freedom grants every person, as from a gentle mother's hands, in ever equal portions, pleasure, peace, and rest.[85]

The commemoration of 'hero-ancestors' (l. 285) also has a place in Haller's concept of freedom. In the wintery tale of a wise old shepherd, for example, this theme is struck in a moment unlike any other in earlier German pastoral:

> Another man, his head covered with the same snow, a living law, his people's guide and conscience, teaches how the craven world bends its neck to the yoke, how vain princes' opulence sucks dry their countries' marrow, how Tell, with defiant courage, trampled the bitter yoke, the yoke that half of Europe wears; how in chains all about us many suffer poverty and starvation, and even France's paradise harbors its own broken beggars; how harmony, loyalty, and courage, with undivided strength, cling steadfastly to the wings of happiness.[86]

The sentimental idyll, perfected by Salomon Gessner, suffered for a long time under the negative verdicts of Herder and the young Goethe, later of A.W. and Friedrich Schlegel, and finally Hegel. Nor did eighteenth-century thinking about bourgeois 'melancholy' result in a deeper appreciation of the genre.[87] The idyll,

---

[85] *Alpen*, ll. 71–8.
  Hier herrscht kein Unterschied, den schlauer Stolz erfunden,
  Der Tugend unterthan und Laster edel macht;
  Kein müßiger Verdruß verlängert hier die Stunden,
  Die Arbeit füllt den Tag und Ruh besetzt die Nacht;
  Hier lässt kein hoher Geist sich von der Ehrsucht blenden,
  Des morgens Sonne frisst des heutes Freude nie.
  Die Freiheit theilt dem Volk, aus milden Mutter-Händen,
  Mit immer gleichem Maaß Vergnügen, Ruh und Müh.

[86] Ibid., 291–300.
  Ein andrer, dessen Haupt mit gleichem Schnee bedecket,
  Ein lebendes Gesetz, des Volkes Richtschnur ist,
  Lehrt, wie die feige Welt ins Joch den Nacken strecket,
  Wie eitler Fürsten Pracht das Mark der Länder frisst,
  Wie Tell mit kühnem Muth das harte Joch zertreten,
  Das Joch, das heute noch Europens Hälfte trägt;
  Wie um uns alles darbt und hungert in den Ketten
  Und Welschlands Paradies gebogne Bettler hegt;
  Wie Eintracht, Treu und Muth, mit unzertrennten Kräften,
  An eine kleine Macht des Glückes Flügel heften.

[87] Wolfram Mauser's 'Melancholieforschung des 18. Jahrhunderts zwischen Ikonographie und Ideologiekritik: Auseinandersetzung mit den bisherigen Ergebnissen und Thesen zu einem Neuansatz', *Lessing Yearbook* 13 (1981): 255–77, reinvigorated the investigation on the social reflection of bourgeois 'melancholy'.

as Gessner explains in his remarkable foreword to the *Idyllen* of 1756,[88] makes the Golden Age present by stimulating three necessary preconditions: 'Einbildungs-Kraft' (imagination = aesthetic category); 'stiller Gemüth' (a tranquil spirit = moral category); and distance from 'unsere Sitten' (our customs = sociocultural category). This exposition contrasts sharply with the traditional theory of the idyll. In Gessner the opposition between the Golden Age and the present is radical, but it is not total; in fact, the two dimensions are closer to each other in Gessner than ever before. Scenes from the Golden Age, summoned through the poetic imagination, 'remind us . . . of the sweetest hours we have ever known'. The Golden Age is not qualitatively different from the present and can be recreated under certain circumstances in the life of each individual. One creates the precondition for the individual's separation from urban society by undertaking a solitary sojourn into uninhabited nature. It is also essential that one possess a spirit that is sensitive to and respectful of the beauty of nature. 'Wholly delighted, wholly attuned to its beauty, I am happy there, like a shepherd in the Golden Age, and richer than a king.'

On the other hand, the Golden Age cannot be restored in the environment of the countryside, 'where the subservient farmer must deliver his profit to his prince and the cities, and where oppression and poverty have made him uncouth, cunning, and mean.' The restoration must be the work rather of 'worthy inhabitants' who are capable of pleasing 'people of noble mind'. Gessner gives his shepherds this tranquil spirit and moral sensibility.

Both Herder and Goethe felt that the Gessnerian aesthetic synthesis lacked natural truth. Their criticism, however, cannot distract from the very real shift that Gessner's work represents within the genre's nearly two-thousand-year-old allegorical tradition. In post-Gessnerian Sentimentalism, such as in the poetry of Christian Ewald von Kleist, the Golden Age or Arcadia became associated with life in nature, since it was now felt that personal fulfillment depended on being able to release emotions in the natural realm. Gessner's productive misunderstanding of Theocritus in his foreword to the *Idyllen*, which generated his entire pastoral poetics, resulted from his determination to loosen the allegorical content of Vergilian pastoral, particularly in its degraded courtly

---

[88] Gessner, *Idyllen: Kritische Ausgabe*, ed. Ernst Theodor Voß, Universal-Bibliothek, 9431–5 (Stuttgart: Reclam, 1973), 15–18. On Gessner and the idyll, see Voss's foreword to the critical edition of Gessner, as well as his biographical study, 'Salomon Gessner', in *Deutsche Dichter des 18. Jahrhunderts: Ihr Leben und Werk*, ed. Benno von Wiese, 249–75 (Berlin: Erich Schmidt, 1977); cf. Heidemarie Kesselmann, *Die Idyllen Salomon Geßners im Beziehungsfeld von Ästhetik und Geschichte im 18. Jahrhundert: Ein Beitrag zur Gattungsgeschichte der Idylle* (Kronberg, Czech.: Scriptor, 1976); and Barthold Burk, *Elemente idyllischen Lebens: Studien zu Salomon Geßner und Jean-Jacques Rousseau* (Frankfurt a.M.: P. Lang, 1981). A related discussion in Gerhart Hoffmeister, 'Gessners "Daphnis" – das Ende des europäischen Schäferromans', *Studia Neophilologica* 44 (1972): 127–41.

forms, by returning to the sentimental experience in nature that he presumed to find in Theocritus.

And so the return of the Golden Age in the present – no longer understood as the exclusive preserve of allegory – rests upon the belief that it once existed in reality. Stated another way, the Golden Age is the prefiguration of the utopian enclave in the present; Golden Age and present time become compatible through the shared experience of a sentimental life in nature. The role of the Golden Age is to guarantee a kind of existence that can never be a certainty in the real present. 'Separation from nature', Gessner emphatically states, inevitably 'results in enslavement.' Morality and natural pleasure, along with the liberation of the inner nature and an emotional connection to the external beauty of nature, are mutually dependent. While the Gessnerian shepherd is always an allegorical representation of the sophisticated and sentimental city dweller, pastoral nature has evolved from an essentially exchangeable property into a space of experience with life-altering consequences.

The bucolic and georgic traditions overlap in Gessner's idylls. *Der Wunsch*, significantly the final idyll of the 1756 collection, inclines toward the rural-life pastoral.[89] Neither shepherds nor country folk speak; nor does the poet take to the country, as Opitz did in *Zlatna*, but only imagines a stay there. In this respect *Der Wunsch* is a counter-piece to C.E. von Kleist's *Der Frühling* (1749). Gessner remarks in his foreword to the collection, 'An den Leser' (To the Reader), that the city represents society at large, and it is only in getting away from society that one can find fulfillment of one's wishes. The person who speaks honestly has no chance of survival in the city, where 'inescapable webs of danger' hang about everywhere. That is not an ontological view of the world, but a contingent statement about society, where customs and circumstances are always changing.

Life in the country implies renunciation of wealth and fame, just as it did in the seventeenth century. But now it further implies renunciation of dominion 'over one's brothers', a proposition that would have been unthinkable in the rigidly hierarchical Baroque. Brotherhood cancels dominion. A move to the countryside signifies withdrawal into a realm free of the state. 'Unknown and still', 'unenvied and unnoticed', life flows 'peacefully' in a 'solitary locale'. The image of a cottage 'in the green shade of arching nut trees' contrasts with the tumultuousness of the city; 'gentle quietude beneath the green archway of trees', 'the cool well under the rows of grape vines' at the 'welcome entrance' to the house – this poetic landscape, down to the very details of light-shading, bespeaks seclusion and protection. In the image of the little pond, with its island arbor, the choicest spot of the Rococo, isolation from society finds its most characteristic expression, a place of retreat opening only to nature:

---

[89] *Der Wunsch*, in *Idyllen: Kritische Ausgabe*, ed. E.T. Voss, 66–72, Universal-Bibliothek, 9431–5 (Stuttgart: Reclam, 1973). Because of the brevity of this idyll, page references are deemed unnecessary.

> In the middle of the pond I would build an arbor on a tiny island; were a little hedge of vines to climb upwards along the side there into the distance, by a small field with waving blades of grass, would the richest of kings be as worthy of envy as I?[90]

This landscape is harmoniously tailored to man. There is no sign of dominion anywhere in nature. Birds dwell there in 'undisturbed freedom', and bees where 'peace and quiet is the order of the day'. That is exactly opposite to the court's dominion over nature. Whereas the country poet 'stands ready to assist the pleasant fantasies of nature', the court turns them into a 'serviceable commodity' for 'reshaping into grotesque images'. The pastoral tradition of cooperation with nature is possible only beyond the court.

Once the idyllic locus has been established aesthetically, the poet defines more precisely the social space from which he has withdrawn in search of protective nature. Nature appears as a utopian counter-space within which criticism and social experimentation are possible. The poet's country home differs from that of the nobleman Dorante, in whose home 'society . . . uninterrupted' fairly hums with the business of courtly politics. Dorante hosts the courtly aristocracy, and his well-set table buzzes incessantly with worldly conversation. But this aristocratic culture does not come from the heart. Conversations at Dorante's table are a sham, devoid of honesty: 'majestical manners float before an empty brow'.

The most visible sign of the inner impoverishment of this culture is its disdain for nature. For Orontes, another rural property owner from the upper class,

> nature is beautiful only for the tender morsels flying around in the air, or buzzing about in the woods, or swimming around in the water. He hurries out to the countryside with the sole purpose of being able to charge about undisturbed.[91]

His class is morally corrupt. While the poet goes to the country to discover his inner self, the social lord goes there to avoid having to confront his inner self. A happy experience with external nature can happen only when the correct attitude towards internal nature prevails, as implied in this sarcastic reply to a certain nobleman:

---

[90] '[I]n des Teiches Mitte baut' ich eine Laube auf eine kleine aufgeworfene Insel; zöge sich dann noch ein kleiner Reb-Berg an der Seite in die offene Gegend hinaus, und ein kleines Feld mit winkenden Ähren, wäre der reichste König dann gegen mir beneidens werth?'

[91] '[D]ie Natur [ist] nur schön, weil niedliche Bissen für ihn in der Luft fliegen, oder den Hain durchirren, oder in der Flut schwimmen. Er eilt auf das Land, um ungestöhrt rasen zu können.'

> May you never have a day on which you are left all alone. That would be an intolerable company for you, for you might catch a shocking glimpse of yourself. But no, horses all lathered and snorting bring you their contemptible burdens, who leap cursing from the innocent beasts. A great racket of nonsense and boisterous wit accompanies the party to the table, until the raging scene dies away at last in a lifeless stupor.[92]

The offence is not exclusively moral but has social causes and consequences as well. The wealth of the propertied class derives from the exploitation of the peasants, as in the case of the niggardly Harpax,

> whose doors are watched by haggard dogs that in their hunger rip the tear-soaked bread from the hands of the beggar as he is cursed and sent away. Far and wide, the poor country farmer suffers indebtedness to you; seldom does even a thin wisp of smoke rise from his dilapidated chimney. For why should you go hungry when you can rob the poor weeping man of his wealth![93]

Thus the affinity between pastoral and satire is renewed in the literature of sentimentality. *Der Wunsch* in fact is an immediate precursor to the sociocritical idyll of the Storm and Stress. The various forms of sociability that the poet experiences in the countryside must be viewed against the disgraceful social background of poverty and exploitation.

And yet, harmony reigns in the naive world of the country dweller. The reapers are unified in their singing, joking, and storytelling; the vineyards echo each autumn with the laughter of boys and girls collecting grapes; folks gather at evening for wine and fellowship and dancing in the moonlight. The larger world ranges high above the narrative of this humble but stable rural community – a naive prefiguration of the happiness that, on a higher level, the country poet will be allowed to enjoy within a circle of like-minded individuals. This is expressed in three ways in *Der Wunsch*. First, in its cheerful sociability – a delicate rococo motif – accompanied by sincere conversation, the simple joy of mealtime, the temperate enjoyment of wine, and singing and laughter. These habits typify the relaxed yet self-conscious social behavior of the educated middle class, as depicted so well by Hagedorn in his *Fabeln und Erzählungen* (1738; Fables and

---

[92] 'Dir begegne nie, daß ein einsamer Tag bey dir allein dich lasse, eine unleidliche Gesellschaft für dich, vielleicht entwischt dir ein schauernder Blik in dich selbst. Aber nein, gepeinigte Pferde bringen dir schnaubend ihre unwürdigen Lasten, sie springen fluchend vor dem unschuldigen Thier; Tumult und Unsinn und rasender Witz begleiten die Gesellschaft zur Tafel, und ein ohnmächtiger Rausch endet die tobende Scene.'

[93] 'dessen Thüre hagre Hunde bewachen, die hungernd dem ungestühm abgewiesenen Armen das bethränte Brod rauben. Weit umher ist der arme Landmann dein gepeinigter Schuldner; nur selten steigt der dünne Rauch von deinem umgestürzten Schornstein auf, denn solltest du nicht hungern, da du deinen Reichthum dem weinenden Armen raubest!'

Stories). Second, in the sentimental form of human coexistence, with its deep moral sincerity: the 'good countryman . . . in his brown-shaded cottage' lives next door to the poet in his own simple cottage. They are united by the classical pastoral ethic of concern for one another, expressed here in modern sentimental terms: 'The readiness to help and advise one another makes them smiling, neighborly friends; for what is more blessed than being loved, or the happy greeting of someone for whom you've done something good?' This image contrasts sharply with the reality of rural oppression and urban corruption. Third, finally, in the philosophical variation of country life found in both Kleist and Gessner as heirs of the Scottish poet James Thomson. Whereas high society exploits knowledge as a source of topics for empty chitchat, the country poet delves into the treasure chest of ancestral wisdom, embracing both folk traditions and natural science, economics and history, ethics and metaphysics, and, always, poetry.

For Gessner it is only 'the few' – Klopstock, Bodmer, Gleim, Wieland, and especially C.E. von Kleist – who, drawing on antiquity, know how to break the spell of the courtly art, that 'airy filigree of gold lace and scentless flowers'. The poetic country enclave has its equivalent in the circles of sentimental poets within modern society. Sentimental poetry is appreciated only by the like-minded: 'the spoiled nation does not recognize your worth; your appreciation will come only in a better afterworld.' Moral opposition thus expands into aesthetic opposition, for the sentimental taste is inherently disgusted by the courts. Nature remains the reference point of country existence as it unfolds in the poetic realm. Poetry itself is directly inspired by nature, while courtly convention decays amid nature's abundant disorder:

> Too clever man! Why do you strive to improve on nature with your imitative arts? Go on, build your green-walled labyrinths, let the tips of yews stand erect at precisely measured heights, the paths be of pure sand, with no plant out of place to mislead the wandering foot. I myself like the meadow and the wild grove. Nature has ordered their variety and randomness according to secret rules of harmony and beauty that our souls divine with tender ecstasy![94]

The sudden turn to resignation at the conclusion of *Der Wunsch* is surprising. The way of life expected when the Golden Age returns is in the end nothing but a 'vain wish': it may become reality in 'our most blessed hours' but not

---

[94] 'Zu kühner Mensch! was unterwindest du dich die Natur durch weither nachahmende Künste zu schmüken? Baue Labyrinte von grünen Wänden, und laß den gespizten Taxus in abgemessener Weite empor stehn, die Gänge seyen reiner Sand, daß kein Gesträuchgen den wandelnden Fußtritt verwirre; mir gefällt die ländliche Wiese und der verwilderte Hain, ihre Mannigfaltigkeit und Verwirrung hat die Natur nach geheimen Regeln der Harmonie und Schönheit geordnet, die unsere Seele voll sanften Entzükens empfindt.'

permanently in this present existence. Thus the situation described above, where the Arcadian world of the sentimental poets was indisposed to metaphorical characterization, is ironically inverted here. Their correspondence reveals that these poets in fact considered sentimental life among the like-minded in nature a practical goal. At the conclusion of Gessner's collection, the enlightened teacher takes precautions lest the function of Arcadia in the idyll be misconstrued, as it easily could be, as a desire to abandon society or as the longing for a carefree life in nature, thereby appearing to excuse readers from assuming their social responsibility. The ideal of virtue lies at the heart of the Gessnerian idyll, and this virtue is universally applicable. 'Our true happiness is virtue,' he concludes. Moral sensibility, nowhere more intensely experienced than in nature, must also be capable of standing the test of everyday life. Furthermore, virtue transcends class and must be practiced at all social levels, not least by the non-governing classes. Virtue does not eliminate social class, but it is all that really matters; it also fosters self-awareness and social identity, particularly among those people who may imagine that they are not being addressed by Gessner's criticism. Virtue is the means both to endure social inequality as well as to change it from within.

Gessner's *Der Wunsch* is an excellent aesthetic indicator of the degree to which the sentimental literary vanguard of the eighteenth century saw itself alienated from the society of the *ancien régime*. The work delineates a boundary against court and nobility that signifies more than just literary opposition. Its portrayal of fulfilled existence within beautiful nature diminishes the attractiveness of the ruling classes and arouses mistrust of courtly rule. The reconciliation sometimes achieved in the seventeenth century between the rural-poetic and courtly spheres is no longer conceivable; nor is the conflict resolvable as an academic dispute between nobility and educated bourgeoisie over the concepts of state and social order. Rather, acceptance of the *ancien régime* is terminated and a new general class proposed, one that, by virtue of its appeal to an originary state of nature, erases hierarchical boundaries. Metaphysical opposition turns into social opposition, notwithstanding the fact that conflicts between rival classes, particularly with respect to the issue of social mobility, are not explicitly addressed. Instead, the negative principle in the *genus humile* is renewed in a way that theoretically dislodges the ruling classes from their privileged center; simultaneously, it holds up a contrasting system of norms and values to reveal the superficiality, indeed the vacuity, of courtly culture.

Gessner's *Idyllen* was a European success – the first major German-language success before Goethe's *Werther* – its influence extending even to the French physiocrats[95] around Anne Robert Jacques Turgot and the Jacobins around Robespierre. In Germany its readers were mainly the intellectual pillars of

---

[95] A school of French economists, founded by François Quesnay, that developed the first complete system of economics. The core of their system was the 'economic law' of absolute freedom of trade.

enlightened absolutism who maintained deep ties with their counterparts in the cities.[96] We can easily imagine the interest these groups must have taken in the idyll's critique of court and nobility. It was not imperative that the idyll call for the secession of educated professionals from the court, as long as reasonable hope existed that a systematic reform of territorial absolutism would take place and as long as the territories proved generally receptive to new ideas, such as those proposed by the physiocrats. The sentimental idyll offered intellectuals – considerably greater in number in the eighteenth than in the seventeenth century – a medium of self-understanding and sociocultural consolidation distinct from court and nobility. That *Der Wunsch* should conclude on a note of praise for private virtue in no way detracted from its public message, and it is precisely in this observation that the latent potential of the idyll as a political genre is to be found. Critique lies hidden in an idyllic space where a type of morality can be practiced that is at once distinguishable from that of the court and also applicable beyond the limits of the idyllic enclave. Courtly society is summoned before a critical instance whose moral authority rests upon its willingness to exercise radical refusal and its claim to provide contrastive norms for living.[97]

We have seen how all of this represented a move beyond the seventeenth-century view. Another point remains to be emphasized, however, which has to do with the political history of the genre and the learned institutions. The new experimental thought about class structure, which under absolutism remained essentially untouchable, was a subject of discussion already in late humanism in terms of the idea of the superiority of knowledge over family or class inheritance. Although the sentimental ideal of moral sensibility largely abandoned the humanistic tradition of learning, the notion of virtue's primacy continued to flourish in modified form. The voice of the educated bourgeoisie was at last beginning to be heard, coming from beneath the tier of ruling classes of the *ancien régime* and its own private but increasingly self-conscious sphere. It appealed to a set of reforms that eventually led in Germany to the verge of absolutism and in France to revolution.

With the French Revolution the long history of pastoral reached its conclusion. And yet, precisely at this final moment, its poetic logic and historical

---

[96] Identified by Rudolf Vierhaus in his studies on eighteenth-century sociology and mentality, in his *Deutschland im 18. Jahrhundert: Politische Verfassung, soziales Gefüge, geistige Bewegungen* (Göttingen: Vandenhoeck & Ruprecht, 1987).

[97] In the preface to his study of emerging modernity in the eighteenth century, *Critique and Crisis: Enlightenment and the Pathogenesis of Modern Society* (Cambridge: MIT Press, 1988), 2, Reinhart Kosellek speaks of 'a type of Enlightenment' in which 'camouflage and mystification as well as other indirectly operative modes of behaviour' prevailed among its writers in response to the need to hide their critical messages from sovereign censorship. Leo Strauss identified this phenomenon shortly after World War II in his essay 'Persecution and the Art of Writing', in *Persecution and the Art of Writing*, 22–37 (Glencoe, Ill.: Free Press, 1952). The sentimental idyll shares elements of this self-protective strategy.

dialectic were revealed with special clarity. Nature had always been the common denominator. After the 1770s the realistic idyll in Germany became the primary instrument for the social interpretation of nature. Nature's signification in Gessner as both beautiful landscape and beautiful humanity owed to an idealizing aesthetic synthesis. With the radicalization of the Enlightenment by the Storm and Stress, however, German literature broke through the strictly aesthetic realm to address both peasant life and aristocratic rule, particularly with respect to the laws regulating serfdom that connected the two social groups. Only at this stage did it at last escape the allegorism that had determined pastoral interpretation down through Gessner.

It was this break that mobilized one last time the anticipatory potential of the genre. The move backward by the eighteenth-century 'realists' from Vergil to Theocritus reactivated the sociopolitical thrust of the Vergilian eclogue, as paradoxical as that may sound. To realize the anticipatory potential in this move meant treating the realistic properties of the pastoral world, formerly understood as allegory, as objective reality. In other words, in the very act of abandoning the anticipatory function of the learned moral pastoral, its political viability now became apparent. Laying aside pastoral's classical trappings, that is, its literary fiction, in which, presumably, no real commonalities existed between shepherd, country scholar, and peasant, the sentimental writers reconstructed the genre upon a foundation of rural motifs. Country and country folk, by contrast with their opposite, the court and nobility, continued to be identified directly with nature, thereby ensuring their value as a political subject. In this turn to the folk, presented sometimes as unspoiled by society, sometimes as victimized by society, the utopian principle was activated once again: in the imaginary world of pastoral the socially negative factor must be assumed to exist in nature, even when it is not expressly indicated.

Johann Heinrich Voss is the main representative of the realistic idyll.[98] In *Die Pferdeknechte* (The Horse Grooms) reality consists of a dark world of serfs and masters, which comes as a radical shock to traditional expectations of pastoral form. Arcadia is a longed-for asylum from servitude. It is important to note, however, that the serfs do not necessarily suffer indignities with patience. Michel, for one, demands happiness, and when it does not come about, he vents his disappointment in destructive rage. *Ährenkranz* (The Wreath of Grain) is a different kind of work with a happy outcome reminiscent of Vergil's *Eclogue* 1.

---

[98] Most of Voss's pieces in that genre were published together in his *Idyllen* of 1801. Of the more recent scholarship, see esp. the afterword in the critical edition by Ernst Theodor Voss, *Johann Heinrich Voss: Idyllen* (Heidelberg: Schneider, 1968), 29–92, as well as E.T. Voss's 'Arkadien und Grünau: Johann Heinrich Voss und das innere System seines Idyllenwerkes' (1968; reprint in Garber, *Europäische Bukolik* 391–431); also H.J. Schneider, 'Bürgerliche Idylle: Studien zu einer literarischen Gattung des 18. Jahrhunderts am Beispiel von Johann Heinrich Voss' (PhD diss., University of Bonn, 1975), and 'Johann Heinrich Voss', in von Wiese, *Deutsche Dichter* 782–815.

It contains a 'Meliboeus'- section called 'Die Leibeigenen' (The Serfs) following a 'Tityrus'-section called 'Die Freigelassenen' (The Emancipated). The god in Rome to whom Vergil's Tityrus owed his freedom is here the local baron, whose political generosity brings Arcadia to pass in one emancipated village. The message is that utopia is possible only with the help of an enlightened patriarch. *Die Erleichterten* (The Relieved Ones) provides a bridge between these two idylls. It depicts the transition from serfdom to freedom thanks to an enlightened nobility, through whom middle-class reforms have a chance of being realized. Arcadia functions as the space of exemplary social action. The focus is not on whether the socially disadvantaged are happy or unhappy, but rather on the margin of success flowing from ethically motivated political action from above. *Luise* (1795), Voss's most ambitious idyll, upholds the genre's anticipatory character in the post-revolutionary period.[99] Educated middle-class citizens speak self-confidently with the noble governors in the parsonage at Grünau, while the servant staff and simple village folk are granted at least limited access to the kind pastor's family. Voss thus develops the fictional rural microcosm into a political macrocosm of free individuals, not unlike the one in far-off America, such as he always hoped would come to pass in Europe after the French Revolution.

But the bourgeois adaptation of pastoral had serious consequences for the idyll, whose properties proved all too vulnerable to personal manipulation. The sphere that Voss had conceived as a utopian space for the creation of a classless brotherhood of man, an idea possible only with the rise of the educated middle class, ultimately dissolved into a regressive, anxiety-ridden little corner of the world.

Standing between Voss and the nineteenth-century idyll is Goethe's *Hermann und Dorothea* (1798),[100] a hexameter idyll in nine cantos, which tells the story of the love between a German innkeeper's son and a French refugee girl. It is the first work of the revived pastoral genre in which the French Revolution provides the setting from start to finish. The Revolution transforms the two small-town protagonists into cosmopolitan individuals, which is to say, it helps to complete them as human beings. Goethe accomplishes this transformation by utilizing the full potential of pastoral as an aesthetic and a political vehicle. In *Hermann und Dorothea* the idyllic aesthetic of an originary condition of human and natural purity engenders the revolutionary political zeal to recreate that condition:

> What was later often reduced to a simplistic duality between the spheres
> of home and politics is in Goethe's work a mirror in which, on the one side,

---

[99] The so-called *Luisen-Idyllen* or *Grünauer-Idyllen* first appeared in periodical form; the *Luise* idyll was printed in Wieland's *Teutscher Merkur* in 1784. An English translation was made of the 1795 book in the mid-nineteenth century by James Cochrane, as *Louisa* (Edinburgh: Johnstone, 1852).

[100] *Hermann and Dorothea*, trans. David Luke, in *Goethe's Collected Works*, ed. Victor Lange, et al., 8:247–307 (New York: Suhrkamp, 1987).

the social revolution – depicted in the wave of refugees as a destructive force – makes us aware of the disturbances within the propertied middle class, while, on the other side, the transcendence of petty bourgeois narrow-mindedness is seen as a corollary to the idealistic goals of the political revolution.[101]

However, insofar as Goethe makes the French Revolution into Arcadia, Arcadia threatens to dissolve into a Schillerian aesthetic utopia.[102] Goethe largely ignores actual conditions in Germany, and politics in the abstract makes for a politically neutral myth, possible only in provincialism. Rather like Voss, who turned the family into the ideal sphere of enlightened humanity, Goethe places the private family at the opposite end of revolutionary action, 'thereby laying the groundwork for the later monumentalization of German domesticity as an apolitical space.'[103] The nineteenth century would relentlessly pursue a course by which we may recognize one of the implicit dangers in *Hermann und Dorothea*: Where the idyllic world no longer prefigures a political world, or where the pastoral *societas parva* is no longer the paradigm for the *societas civilis*, there the utopian light is extinguished. It was in this sense that pastoral as a form of European utopian literature came to an end with the French Revolution.*

---

[101] Schneider, 'Die sanfte Utopie' 402.

[102] Schiller, *Werke*, ed. Gerhard Finke and Herbert Georg Göpfert (Munich: Hanser, 1960), 1:474, observed of Germany in 1797: 'As the political empire began to crumble, the spiritual empire established itself ever more firmly and completely.' On the context of this issue in terms of German imperial patriotism, see Michael Stolleis, 'Public Law and Patriotism in the Holy Roman Empire', in *Infinite Boundaries: Order, Disorder, and Reorder in Early Modern German Culture*, ed. Max Reinhart, 11–33, Sixteenth Century Essays & Studies, 40 (Kirksville, Mo.: Sixteenth Century Journal Publishers, 1998).

[103] Schneider, 'Die sanfte Utopie' 407.

* Translated by James F. Ehrman.

Chapter 6

Nuremberg, Arcadia on the Pegnitz: The Self-Stylization of an Urban Sodality*

Let us now turn from the broad historical view of pastoral as a vehicle of utopianism to look more closely at how pastoral poetry in the tradition of Vergil helped to shape the institution of the learned society. Our analysis will proceed as a close reading of three texts, making observations of a social, historical, political, or theoretical nature as the texts themselves suggest the need. To a far greater degree than sociology or historiography, literary analysis is driven by a demand for *Vermittlung* 'mediation', 'connection', 'correlation', 'interpretation'. As Adorno insists, the structure of the texts themselves defines the way in which external connections have meaning.[1] We shall take Nuremberg's Pegnesischer Blumenorden in the decade of the 1640s as our case study.

I. Historical Backgrounds

It was not until the fifth decade of the seventeenth century that the free imperial city of Nuremberg came to participate in the general movement of German literary reform set in motion nearly twenty years earlier by Martin Opitz.[2]

---

* This essay began as a lecture in 1994 on the occasion of the 350th anniversary of the founding of Nuremberg's Pegnesischer Blumenorden [hereafter in notes: P.Bl.O.]. It is dedicated to the memory of Joachim Kröll.

[1] Theodor W. Adorno, 'Thesen zur Kunstsoziologie', in *Ohne Leitbild: Parva Aesthetica* (Frankfurt a.M.: Suhrkamp, 1967), esp. 94–103.

[2] My investigation builds upon the groundbreaking work of Heinrich Meyer, *Der deutsche Schäferroman des 17. Jahrhunderts* (1928; reprint, Hannover-Döhren: Hirschheydt, 1978), and Blake Lee Spahr, 'The Pastoral Works of Sigmund von Birken' (PhD diss., Yale University, 1951). It is impossible here to review the history of scholarship on the subject, though, as a pragmatic starting point, certain studies are indispensable: Josef Nadler, *Literaturgeschichte der deutschen Stämme und Landschaften*, 3rd edn, vol. 2 (Regensburg: Habbel, 1929); *Barock in Nürnberg 1600–1750* (Nuremberg: Germanisches Nationalmuseum, 1962); Horst Brunner and Erich Strasser, 'Nürnberger Literatur um 1600', in *Nürnberg – Geschichte einer europäischen Stadt*, ed. Gerhard Pfeiffer, 1:283–7 (Munich: Beck, 1971); Dietrich Jöns, 'Literaten in Nürnberg und ihr Verhältnis zum Stadtregiment in den Jahren 1643–1650 nach den Zeugnissen der Ratsverlässe', in *Stadt – Schule – Universität – Buchwesen*, ed. Albrecht Schöne, 84–98 (Munich: Beck, 1976); B.L. Spahr, 'Nürnbergs Stellung im literarischen Leben des 17. Jahrhunderts', in Schöne, *Stadt* 73–83; Irmgard Böttcher, 'Der Nürnberger Georg Philipp

Hamburg, Leipzig, Breslau, and Königsberg had led the way as urban literary centers in the late fifteenth and early sixteenth centuries, much as Strasbourg, the so-called 'second cradle' of late medieval and early humanist culture, had done in the old Reich. The geographical shift from the southwest and southeast to the north and northeast that marked the spread of late humanism in Germany meant that Nuremberg, a middle-German city, was located at the center of the new cultural geography. One of the jewels of the old empire, Nuremberg had its meistersinger, whose popularity continued into the seventeenth century, and its *Spruchsprecher*, the official city poet, ready on cue to deliver an appropriate verse for any formal event. The cultivation of music in Nuremberg remained vital through the seventeenth century; the same was true of the theater, which was vitalized in part by troupes of itinerant and foreign players. Other staged spectacles, such as the singspiel or lyrical drama, also flourished. With the elevation of the local academy into the Universität Altdorf in 1622, Nuremberg had joined Strasbourg as a city of higher education, though it still had no professor of the stature of Strasbourg's Matthias Bernegger, who commanded respect across Europe. The local high schools served primarily the transmission of the neo-Latin repertoire into German literature and did not become innovative educational institutions until after 1642, when Johann Michael Dilherr arrived in Nuremberg to found the Auditorium publicum at the Egidien School.[3]

In the 1640s Nuremberg faced massive problems that had accumulated over the course of two decades of war.[4] The Protestant Union, which Nuremberg had largely managed to steer clear of, was dissolved in 1621 and the city again could avow its allegiance to the emperor. Still, it could not escape being implicated as part of the Protestant opposition and had to bear its share of punishment in the

---

Harsdörffer', in *Deutsche Dichter des 17. Jahrhunderts: Ihr Leben und Werk*, ed. Harald Steinhagen and Benno von Wiese, 289–346 (Berlin: Erich Schmidt, 1984); Max Reinhart, 'Welt und Gegenwelt im Nürnberg des 17. Jahrhunderts: Ein einleitendes Wort zur sozialkritischen Funktion der Prosaekloge im Pegnesischen Blumenorden', in *Pegnesischer Blumenorden in Nürnberg: Festschrift zum 350jährigen Jubiläum*, ed. Werner Kügel, 1–6 (Nuremberg: Tümmel, 1994); John Roger Paas (ed.), *der Franken Rom: Nürnbergs Blütezeit in der zweiten Hälfte des 17. Jahrhunderts* (Wiesbaden: Harrassowitz, 1995).

[3] Hellmut Rössler and Günther Franz (eds), *Universität und Gelehrtenstand 1400–1800* (Limburg, Lahn: Starke, 1970).

[4] Pfeiffer, *Nürnberg* 265–302; Rudolf Endres, 'Nürnberg in der Frühzeit', in *Europäische Städte im Zeitalter des Barock*, ed. Kersten Krüger, 141–67 (Cologne: Böhlau, 1988), and 'Verfassung und Verfassungswirklichkeit in Nürnberg im späten Mittelalter und in der Frühen Neuzeit', in *Verwaltung und Politik in Städten Mitteleuropas*, ed. Wilfried Ehbrecht, 207–19 (Cologne: Böhlau, 1994). Bibliography to 1945 in *Fränkische Bibliographie*, ed. G. Pfeiffer, vol. 2, pt 2 (Würzburg: Schöningh, 1970); between 1945 and 1975, and then after 1990, see the reviews in *Mitteilungen des Vereins für Geschichte der Stadt Nürnberg* [hereafter: *MVGN*]; between 1975 and 1990, *Nürnberg Bibliographie*, 3 vols (Nuremberg: Stadtbibliothek Nürnberg, 1983, 1988, 1992). Also 'Nürnberg', in *Bayerisches Städtebuch*, pt 1, ed. Erich Keyser and Heinz Stoob (Stuttgart: Kohlhammer, 1971), as well as the articles in *Handbuch der bayerischen Geschichte*, vol. 3, pt 1, ed. Max Spindler (Munich: Beck, 1971).

harsh terms of the Edict of Restitution (1629).⁵ The relief felt initially at the arrival of the Swedish general Gustav Adolf in 1632 did not last. The city council took pains to avoid the impression that it was cooperating with Gustav Adolf, as that could have provoked the hand of the emperor as a sworn treaty partner. After the disastrous defeat of the Protestant army at the Battle of Nördlingen in September 1634, Nuremberg was fortunate, thanks to a separate treaty negotiated by Saxony (Treaty of Prague, 1635), to reclaim its privilege of religious self-determination. Having been a party in the Heilbronn League,⁶ however, Nuremberg and the other participants were excluded by the Habsburgs from the imperial amnesty after Nördlingen. Two Nuremberg diplomats were singled out as key personalities in the later literary representation of these events: Jobst Christoph Kreß and Johann Jacob Tetzel. For the time being, however, no literary response was forthcoming to Gustav Adolf's entry into the city on 31 March, despite all the fanfare of the official welcome led by Christoph Fürer and Georg Christoph Volkamer. This may seem surprising, given that the young poet Georg Philipp Harsdörffer, in his role as a junior city diplomat to the Heilbronn League, was an eyewitness to the spectacular event. Not even the disaster at Nördlingen, though close to Nuremberg, occasioned poetic lamentations. Apparently, the new reformed poetry required still another decade of incubation before it would reach maturity as a literary language in Nuremberg.

In addition to local and more recent problems, structural crises that had been developing over many years came to a head in the seventeenth century. Although it had been the most affluent and advanced of all the free cities, Nuremberg was powerless in the mid-sixteenth century to withstand the onslaught of margravial Brandenburg-Ansbach and Brandenburg-Kulmbach (Bayreuth), both flourishing territorial states.⁷ As Gerhard Pfeiffer succinctly observes, 'Nuremberg's great

---

⁵ '[Ferdinand II] claimed the cities as patrimonial properties. This meant that the cities lost their territorial sovereignty and, as a consequence, their right of religious self-determination. The entire religious identity of the city, as it had existed for the last hundred years, as well as the city's social identity, which was based on it, were threatened by the implementation of the imperial Restitution.' Theodor Bischoff, *Georg Philipp Harsdörfer: Ein Zeitbild aus dem 17. Jahrhundert* (Nuremberg: Schrag, 1894), 21.

⁶ Formed in 1633 under Swedish (Protestant) leadership with the cooperation of the Franconian, Swabian, and Rhenish Circles as a defensive league. The league began to fail as early as spring 1634.

⁷ In the years 1552–4 Margrave Albrecht Alcibiades subjected the outlying lands of Nuremberg to devastating attacks. The economic impact of this depradation and the subsequent reparations were such that Nuremberg never fully recovered. See Hanns Hubert Hofmann, 'Ansbach: Physiognomie eines Territoriums und seiner Städte', *Zeitschrift für Bayerische Landesgeschichte* [hereafter: *ZfBL*] 36 (1973): 645–61; also Heinz Quirin, 'Markgraf Albrecht Achilles von Brandenburg-Ansbach als Politiker: ein Beitrag zur Vorgeschichte des Süddeutschen Städtekriegs', *ZfBL* 31 (1971): 261–308; Richard Kölbel, 'Der erste Markgrafenkrieg 1449–1453', *MVGN* 65 (1978): 91–123; Heinz-Joachim Neubauer, 'Der Bau der großen Bastei hinter der Veste 1538–1545', *MVGN* 69 (1982): 196–263, esp. 232 ff. Gerald Strauss's *Nuremberg in the Sixteenth Century* (New York: Wiley, 1966), provides the relevant background.

century (1450–1550), which had seen the acquisition of its modern lands, ended with the Margrave Wars.'[8] The Reformation too, in its own way, was as debilitating an influence as the Margrave Wars on Nuremberg's political energies.[9] On the one hand, Nuremberg was convinced that the Reformation was the right path to the future; on the other hand, the city remained politically obligated to the emperor.[10] This required a delicate balancing act that profoundly affected the political history of Protestantism over the next two centuries. It had an equally profound effect on literary developments, particularly in generating a type of urban 'occasional' literature that gave allegorical expression to social and political events. The steady flow of social-disciplining ordinances regarding titles, clothing, and social hierarchy between the later sixteenth century and about 1672[11] helped to motivate this subtle literature. In the 1990s this critical literary response has at last begun to receive adequate interpretation.[12]

The sociopolitical crisis developed in the wake of the deterioration of the city's mercantile system and the consequent heavy dependence on foreign trade. This decline was reflected in the seventeenth century by the steady emigration of the patrician *ratsfähig* 'governing' families into the countryside, where they merged with the Franconian rural aristocracy.[13] In Nuremberg, *doctores juris* 'doctors of jurisprudence' were excluded by law from participation in the small

---

[8] Pfeiffer, *Nürnberg* 170. The economic impact is assessed by Martha White Paas, 'Nürnbergs Wirtschaft im 17. Jahrhundert', in Paas, *der Franken Rom* 46–61.

[9] Anton Schindling, 'Nürnberg', in *Die Territorien des Reichs im Zeitalter der Reformation und Konfessionalisierung: Land und Konfession 1500–1650*, ed. Schindling and Walter Ziegler, 1:32–42 (Münster: Aschendorff, 1989).

[10] Brigitte Altherr, 'Das Verhältnis von Kaiser und Reichsstadt in der 2. Hälfte des 15. Jahrhunderts dargestellt am Beispiel Nürnbergs und Augsburgs' (matriculation paper, Universität Erlangen-Nürnberg, 1981); also the exhibition catalogue of the Staatsarchiv Nürnberg, *Nürnberg – Kaiser und Reich* (Neustadt, Aisch: Degener, 1986); and Franz Willax, '"Gefährliche Patrioten und schädliche Leuth": antischwedischer Widerstand in Nürnberg 1631–1635', *MVGN* 78 (1991): 123–73.

[11] Liselotte Constanze Eisenbart, *Kleiderordnungen der deutschen Städte zwischen 1350 und 1700: ein Beitrag zur Kulturgeschichte des deutschen Bürgertums* (Göttingen: Musterschmidt, 1962).

[12] See esp. Max Reinhart, 'Poets and Politics: The Transgressive Turn of History in Seventeenth-Century Nürnberg', *Daphnis* 20 (1991): 199–229.

[13] Hanns Hubert Hofmann, 'Nobiles Norimbergenses: Beobachtungen zur Struktur der reichsstädtischen Oberschichte', in *ZfBL* 28 (1965): 114–50, and 'Der Adel in Franken', in *Deutsches Patriziat 1430–1740*, ed. Hellmuth Rössler, 95–126 (Limburg, Lahn: Starke, 1968). See also Gerhard Pfeiffer, 'Nürnberger Patriziat und fränkische Reichsritterschaft', in *Norica: Beiträge zur Nürnberger Geschichte* (Nuremberg: Stadtbibliothek, 1961), 35–55; Gerhard Hirschmann, 'Das Nürnberger Patriziat', in Rössler, *Deutsches Patriziat* 257–76 and, somewhat more broadly, *Das Nürnberger Patriziat im Königreich Bayern* (Nuremberg: Edelmann, 1971); also Rolf Endres, 'Adel und Patriziat in Oberdeutschland', in *Ständische Gesellschaft und soziale Mobilität*, ed. Winfried Schulze, 221–38 (Munich: Oldenbourg, 1988).

council, the city's main governing body.[14] The governing families, which since the mid-sixteenth century had sought to legalize social exclusivity pursuant to solidifying their oligarchical position, encouraged their sons to forego the doctoral degree in order not to forfeit political options. The high office of consul, on the other hand, which Nuremberg considered essential to its political existence, was dignified by the doctor's cap; notable examples from the 1630s were Drs Fetzer, Heinrich Hüls, and Georg Richter.

By about 1640 the strength of the urban bourgeoisie had waned significantly, and Nuremberg's literary life began to flourish again in a new way. Structurally, it rested on three interactive social groupings: the traditional urban patriciate; the upwardly mobile, though no longer governing, trade, corporate, and financial bourgeoisie; and the learned estate, whose exact position on the social scale is more difficult to fix.

The key to grasping the importance of this complex relationship for literature lies in the phenomenon of the *Gelegenheitsgedicht* 'occasional poem'.[15] The

---

[14] Hans Liermann, 'Nürnberg als Mittelpunkt deutschen Rechtslebens', *Jahrbuch für Fränkische Landesforschung* [hereafter: *JfFL*] 2 (1936): 1–17; Ottmar Böhm, 'Die Nürnberger Anwaltschaft um 1500 bis 1806' (Diss. jur., Erlangen, 1949); Friedrich Wolfgang Ellinger, 'Die Juristen der Reichsstadt Nürnberg vom 15. bis 17. Jahrhundert', in *Genealogica, Heraldica, Juridica: Reichsstadt Nürnberg, Altdorf und Hersbruck* (Nürnberg: Die Egge, 1954); Andreas Gedeon, *Zur Rezeption des römischen Privatrechts in Nürnberg* (Nürnberg: Abraham, 1957). On the challenge to the reputation and social position of the Nuremberg lawyers, Ferdinand Elsener, 'Die Doktorwürde in einem "Consilium" der Tübinger Juristenfakultät des 18. Jahrhunderts: ein Beitrag zur Geschichte der Stände im "Imperium Romano-Germanicum"', in *Mélanges Philippe Meylan: Recueil de travaux publiés par la Faculté de droit* 2:25–40 (Lausanne: Impr. Centrale, 1963); also Hermann Lange, 'Vom Adel des Doctor', in *Das Profil des Juristen in der europäischen Tradition*, ed. Klaus Luig and Detlef Liebs, 279–94 (Ebelsbach: Gremer, 1980), and Winfried Theiss, '"Nur die Narren und Halßstarrigen die Rechtsgelehrte ernehren . . .": zur Soziologie der Figuren und Normen in G. Ph. Harsdörffers Schauplatz-Anthologien von 1650', in *Literatur und Volk im 17. Jahrhundert*, ed. Wolfgang Brückner, Peter Blickle, and Dieter Breuer, 89 ff. (Wiesbaden: Harrassowitz, 1987). For the broader context, Heinz Lieberich, 'Die gelehrten Räte: Staat und Juristen in Bayern in der Frühzeit der Rezeption', in *Land und Volk: Herrschaft und Staat in der Geschichte und Geschichtsforschung Bayerns*, 120–89 (Munich: Beck, 1964). On the implications for the poets as part of the intellectual estate, see Reinhart, 'Poets and Politics'.

[15] A full-scale social study of occasional poetry in the vernacular for Nuremberg, as for Germany itself, remains one of the chief desiderata of early modern German literary history. The repertoire, most of it in the form of pastoral literature, is huge. See Klaus Garber and Renate Jürgensen, *Bibliographie der deutschen Schäfer- und Landlebendichtung des 17. Jahrhunderts* (Stuttgart: Hiersemann, 1998), and Gerhard Dünnhaupt, *Personalbibliographien zu den Drucken des Barock*, 6 vols (Stuttgart: Hiersemann, 1990–93). With respect to the primary figures with whom we are concerned here, Harsdörffer, Klaj, Birken, and Hellwig, research is far from complete, but must include Blake Lee Spahr, *The Archives of the Pegnesischer Blumenorden: A Survey and Reference Guide* (Berkeley: University of California Press, 1960); Garber, 'Sigmund von Birken: Städtischer Ordenspräsident und höfischer Dichter: historisch-soziologischer Umriß seiner Gestalt, Analyse seines Nachlasses und Prolegomenon zur Edition seines Werkes', in

possibility of reconstructing the literary scene in Nuremberg prior to the founding of the Pegnesischer Blumenorden in 1644 is more favorable than for many cities, since Nuremberg managed to salvage most of its official, as well as minor literary, documents out of the destruction of World War II.[16] Within a single decade of the 1640s, Nuremberg made huge strides towards regaining its former cultural leadership within the empire. The literary revival was accompanied by a flourishing musical life on the one side and a vital Reformed theology on the other.[17]

It is true, of course, that Nuremberg's literary quality remained very much dependent on the genius of certain outstanding individuals, most notably Georg Philipp Harsdörffer.[18] Harsdörffer started his literary career as a rather enigmatic writer and translator of political pamphlets concerned especially with the growing effect of French policy emanating from Richelieu in Paris. These emblematic pamphlets are only now beginning to be analyzed in detail.[19] It is impossible to

---

Sprachgesellschaften, Sozietäten, Dichtergruppen, ed. Martin Bircher and Ferdinand van Ingen, 223–54; Jeremy Adler, 'Pastoral Topography: Sigmund von Birken and the "Picture-Rhymes" of Johann Helwig', *Visible Language* 20 (1986): 121–35; Wilhelm Kühlmann, 'Kunst als Spiel: das Technopaegnium in der Poetik des 17. Jahrhunderts', *Daphnis* 20 (1991): 505–29; Max Reinhart, *Johann Hellwig: A Descriptive Bibliography* (Columbia, SC: Camden House, 1993).

[16] Renate Jürgensen, 'Norimberga Literata', in *Stadt und Literatur im deutschen Sprachraum der Frühen Neuzeit*, ed. Klaus Garber, 1:425–90 (Tübingen: Niemeyer, 1998).

[17] This has been emphasized recently in Paas, *der Franken Rom*. Besides the standard bibliography by Franz Krautwurst, *Das Schrifttum zur Musikgeschichte der Stadt Nürnberg* (Nuremberg: Schul- und Kulturreferat von der Stadtbibliothek, 1964), see also Heinz Zirnbauer, *Musik in der alten Reichsstadt Nürnberg* (Nuremberg: Gaa-Verlag, 1966), Willi Kahl, 'Das Nürnberger historische Konzert von 1643 und sein Geschichtsbild', *Archiv für Musikwissenschaft* 14 (1957): 281–303, and Hermann Harrassowitz, 'Das historische Konzert vom 31. Mai 1643', *MVGN* 75 (1988): 61–75, which has an updated bibliography. On Reformed theology in church practice in Nuremberg, see Hans Leube, *Die Reformideen in der deutschen lutherischen Kirche zur Zeit der Orthodoxie* (Leipzig: Dörffling und Francke, 1924).

[18] Of the recent studies on Harsdörffer, see esp. Italo Michele Battafarano (ed.), *Georg Philipp Harsdörffer: Ein deutscher Dichter und europäischer Gelehrter* (Bern: Francke, 1991), and his essays 'Harsdörffers Beitrag zu Entprovinzialisierung deutscher Kultur', in *Nürnberg und Italien: Begegnungen, Einflüsse und Ideen*, ed. Volker Kapp and Frank-Rutger Hausmann, 213–26 (Tübingen: Stauffenburg, 1991), and 'Der Nürnberger Georg Philipp Harsdörffer – ein Sohn Europas', in Paas, *der Franken Rom* 196–212. The most accessible introduction in English to Harsdörffer is Peter Hess, 'Georg Philipp Harsdörffer', in *German Baroque Writers, 1580–1660*, vol. 164 of *Dictionary of Literary Biography*, ed. James Hardin, 145–60 (Detroit: Gale, 1996).

[19] Max Reinhart, 'Battle of the Tapestries, A War-Time Debate in Anhalt-Köthen: Georg Philipp Harsdörffer's *Peristromata Turcica* and *Aulaea Romana*, 1641–1642', *Daphnis* 27, nos 2–3 (1998): 291–333; pt 3 discusses Harsdörffer's relation to France and Richelieu; also Reinhart's 'Text and Simultext: Borrowing Claudian in Seventeenth-Century Germany (A Case from the Fruchtbringende Gesellschaft', *German Life and Letters* 52, no. 3 (1999): 281–96. An edition with translation by Reinhart is forthcoming in P. Lang, *'Lamentation for France' and Other Polemics on War and Peace (The Latin Pamphlets of 1641–1642)*. Previously the pamphlets had been treated, briefly, by only

understand seventeenth-century Nuremberg writing outside of the history of the free imperial cities, for only thus does one gain an appreciation for the danger to the old empire represented by the new power west of the Rhine that had arisen out of long civil wars. With his political writings Harsdörffer renewed the tradition of civic humanism in his hometown.[20] In fact, however, Harsdörffer's writings, like those of the universally trained humanists first found in Trecento Italy, demonstrate affinities with multiple traditions and discourses. One thinks of his infusion of literature with current knowledge from the natural sciences – put another way, his adaptation of scientific ideas in literary form. Or of his insistence on the writer's responsibility to avoid subjects and styles that could provoke political or confessional tempers. In general, the writer is to maintain a European perspective on events by staying above the immediate fray, and to attempt through instruction and education to cultivate enlightened attitudes among readers.[21] His most famous work, the *Frauenzimmer Gesprächspiele* (eight volumes, 1641–9),[22] proves that the city itself and the new cultural segment of society in the empire – nobility, courts, and the urban upper classes – were capable of assimilating refined European taste.

With the arrival in 1644 of the young theologian Johann Klaj, an immensely gifted poet as well as a convinced irenicist and ecumenicist, the third great literary pillar was established in Nuremberg.[23] Dilherr's Egidien Church now became the stage for Klaj's experimental *Redeoratorien* 'declamatory oratorios', unlike anything written to date in the German literary reform.[24] By the end of the

Theodor Bischoff, *Georg Philipp Harsdörfer* 30–33, and Ferdinand Josef Schneider, *'Japeta' (1643): Ein Beitrag zur Geschichte des französischen Klassizismus in Deutschland* (Stuttgart: Metzler, 1927), 32–6.

[20] Studies on humanism in Nuremberg began in earnest with Max Hermann, *Die Rezeption des Humanismus in Nürnberg* (Berlin: Weidmann, 1898), and Gustav Bauch, 'Die Nürnberger Poetenschule 1499–1509', *MVGN* 14 (1900): 1–64. More recently, Anton Schindling, 'Die humanistische Bildungsreform in den Reichsstädten Straßburg, Nürnberg und Augsburg', in *Humanismus im Bildungswesen des 15. und 16. Jahrhunderts*, ed. Wolfgang Reinhard, 107–20 (Weinheim: Acta humaniora, 1984).

[21] See the introduction by Jörg Jochen Berns to his reprint edition of Harsdörffer and Schwenter's *Deliciae Physico-Mathematicae* (Frankfurt a.M.: Keip, 1991). On the ecclesiopolitical aspect of Harsdörffer's work, Jean-Daniel Krebs, *Georg Philipp Harsdörffer (1607–1658): Poétique et Poésie* (Bern: Lang, 1983), 1:329 ff., and Oliver Pfefferkorn, *Georg Philipp Harsdörffer: Studien zur Textdifferenzierung unter besonderer Berücksichtigung seines Erbauungsschrifttums* (Stuttgart: Heinz, 1991); also Dieter Merzbacher, 'Der Abendmahlstreit zwischen dem Vielgekörnten und dem Spielenden, geschlichtet vom Unveränderlichen', *Daphnis* 22 (1993): 347–92, which explains the 'Reformed' element in the Fruchtbringende Gesellschaft.

[22] *Frauenzimmer Gesprächspiele* [hereafter in notes: *FzG*], 8 vols, ed. Irmgard Böttcher, Deutsche Neudrucke: Barock, 13–20 (Tübingen: Niemeyer, 1968).

[23] That is, after Harsdörffer and Johann Michael Dilherr, Nuremberg's leading pastor and educator.

[24] *Redeoratorium*, neither drama nor epic nor lyric, a virtuosic musical-lyrical performance genre that establishes a close relationship between meter and personality

1640s, thanks to these three leaders and the ancillary talents assembled in and around the Blumenorden, Nuremberg had reached a new peak of literary culture. This development culminated in the literary, musical, and dramatic festivities – these included the performance of declamations, plays, ballets, and operas – in celebration of the peace treaties signed in Nuremberg in 1649 and 1650.[25]

So sudden an outpouring of creativity seems to defy explanation. However, an awareness of historical conditions, especially of the confessional and political forces to which Nuremberg owed its unique existence at midcentury, removes some of the mystery. Being situated at the northern tip of Catholic Bavaria, where it was much dependent on Habsburg authority, Nuremberg was exposed as no other city, except perhaps Regensburg, to the ecclesiopolitical dangers of the Thirty Years' War. As the European powers moved towards peace, however, conditions improved markedly for Nuremberg. Previously beset as a refuge, especially for persecuted Protestant aristocrats from Lower Austria, Nuremberg at last began to reap the benefits of its central location between the Protestant and Catholic regions.[26] Nuremberg profited from this shift even more than Opitz and his early followers had, given its close historical association with the northern Italian cities. In Harsdörffer, the Italian influence combined with his exceptional knowledge of Spanish and French literature and society to produce conditions in Nuremberg more favorable than in any other German city to adopting European culture.[27] As a result, Nuremberg succeeded where other cities failed in moving away from the attitudes and methods of late humanism and towards a new kind of formal practice inspired by the acoustical and metaphorical semantics of vernacular German. In Nuremberg the level of experimentation in these areas was unparalleled in contemporary Germany, unmatched later on even in re-Catholicized Silesia. Nuremberg's affinity for the modern evolution of prose fiction, including prose drama, owed directly to its cultural connections with Italy, France, and Spain.

(dactyls for joy, trochees for pain, etc.). See esp. Conrad Wiedemann, *Johann Klaj und seine Redeoratorien: Untersuchungen zur Dichtung eines deutschen Barockmanieristen* (Nuremberg: Carl, 1966); also Max Reinhart, 'Johann Klaj', in Hardin, *German Baroque Writers* 195–205.

[25] On Nuremberg peace poetry at the close of the Thirty Years' War, see Hartmut Laufhütte, 'Der gebändigte Mars: Kriegsallegorie und Kriegsverständnis im deutschen Schauspiel um 1648', in *Ares und Dionysos: das Furchtbare und das Lächerliche in der europäischen Literatur*, ed. Laufhütte and Hans-Jürgen Horn, 121–35 (Heidelberg: Winter, 1981); Gerd Dethlefs, 'Die Nürnberger Dichterschule und die Friedensmedaillen 1648/50', *Wolfenbütteler Barock Nachrichten* [hereafter: *WBN*] 16 (1989): 1–18; John Roger Paas, 'Sigmund von Birken's "Des Friedens Vermählung mit Teutschland"', *WBN* 17 (1990): 82–9; Antje Oschmann, *Der Nürnberger Exekutionstag 1649–1650: das Ende des Dreißigjährigen Krieges in Deutschland* (Münster: Aschendorff, 1991).

[26] Werner Schnabel, *Österreichische Exulanten in oberdeutschen Reichsstädten: zur Migration von Führungsschichten im 17. Jahrhundert* (Munich: Beck, 1992).

[27] Battafarano, 'Harsdörffers Beitrag zur Entprovinzialisierung deutscher Kultur.'

My major concern in this study is to show how the highly developed artistry of southern Europe was assimilated in the sodality of one imperial city in terms of the thematic and formal arsenal of the Opitzian literary reform. I shall focus on pastoral, which at this particular time in Germany, and especially in Nuremberg, proved to be an extraordinarily versatile genre of literary self-expression. The adaptation of pastoral in seventeenth-century Nuremberg reveals how one important group of urban learned poets understood their role in both literary history and society. The most important of these writers, besides Harsdörffer and Klaj, were Sigmund von Birken and Johann Hellwig.

II. The Pastoral Archetype of the Nuremberg Sodality

Curiously, the mythical history of the founding of the Pegnesischer Blumenorden was spun out of the sodality's second major pastoral work, the *Fortsetzung der Pegnitz-Schäferey* (1645; Continuation of the Pegnitz Pastoral), written by Birken with Klaj's collaboration. By alluding in the title to the earlier *Pegnesisches Schäfergedicht* (Pegnitz Pastoral) of Harsdörffer and Klaj, Birken was able to place his own work within the aura of the founding document.[28] The formal date of the sodality's founding is assumed to have been fall 1644, since this is when the *Pegnesisches Schäfergedicht* was printed, though nothing is said in the work itself about having been written for a founding. It is dedicated to the composition of social poems by Strefon (Harsdörffer) and Klajus (Klaj). The front matter of volume 4 of Harsdörffer's *Frauenzimmer Gesprächspiele*, which likewise appeared in 1644, mentions no other colleagues. One year later the 'Pegnitz shepherds' joined their counterparts from the Fruchtbringende Gesellschaft in praise of *der Spielende* 'the Playful One' (Harsdörffer's sobriquet in the renowned sodality) in the introduction to volume 5 of the *Gesprächspiele*. The genre that they employed for the occasion was that of the sodality's mythological founding work, a prose eclogue.[29] Pastoral was by now emblematic of the Nuremberg sodality.[30]

---

[28] Klaus Garber, 'Vergil und das "Pegnesische Schäfergedicht"', *Deutsche Barockliteratur und europäische Kultur*, ed. Martin Bircher and Eberhard Mannack, 168–203 (Hamburg: Hauswedell, 1977); also Silvia S. Tschopp, 'Friedensentwurf: zum Verhältnis von poetischer Struktur und historischem Gehalt im "Pegnesischen Schäfergedicht" von G. Ph. Harsdörffer und J. Klaj', *Compar(a)ison* (1993): 217–37. Both the *Pegnesisches Schäfergedicht* (hereafter in notes: *PS*) and the *Fortsetzung der Pegnitz-Schäferey* (hereafter in notes: *FPS*) are reprinted in Klaus Garber (ed.), *Pegnesisches Schäfergedicht 1644–1645*, Deutsche Neudrucke, Reihe: Barock, 8 (Tübingen: Niemeyer, 1966).

[29] Prose eclogue was described above in Chapter 5, pp. 95–116, in the section 'Pastoral in Early Modern Germany: From Martin Opitz to J.H. Voss.'

[30] The figure of a shepherd with staff and flock in a park-with-river landscape appears in vol. 5 for the first time in the *FzG* series on the title-page engraving.

Poetology and Allegory

Technically, the *Pegnesisches Schäfergedicht* [see Plate 4] is an epithalamium on the occasion of a patrician double-wedding (so indicated on the verso of the title-page). The title-page portrays Nuremberg from the perspective of the Haller meadow along the Pegnitz River and includes the figures of a peasant and a shepherd. These are the specific symbols of location (rural pleasance) and genre (pastoral) within which the social event is to take place. Even before the narrative begins, a dedicatory poem thematizing the effort on behalf of German poetry displays the dactylic and onomatopoeic features peculiar to the Nuremberg sodality:

> St. Ihr wisset/ daß unsere Hütten nicht haben
> Auf Stättisch mit Schminke beschmükete Gaben.
> Kl. Wir bringen hier Bäurische Hirtengedichte
> Bey unseren Heerden erwachsene Früchte.
> St. Ihr werdet die Fehler vielgünstig ersetzen/
> Und unsere Felder euch lassen ergetzen.
> Kl. Empfahet die Erstlinge hiesiges Flusses/
> Empfahet die Lieder gebierliches Grusses.
> . . .
> St. Wir wollen euch reichere Schenkungen bringen/
> Wenn unsere Flöten sich höher aufschwingen.[31]

These 'first fruits of the river we know' are, like the majority of later writings of this society, 'rude' pastoral poems in the *genus humile* mode, which allows for a certain license for imperfection ('mistakes that you see'); on the other hand, they aspire, recalling Vergil's opening lines to *Eclogue* 4, to epic dignity ('. . . as our flutes learn much higher to sing').

---

[31] *PS* 3. Running references to page numbers in this explication will be provided in the main text in parentheses; references are omitted for any subsequent quotations from the same page. Longer set-off quotations of verse will be given in the original German in the text and followed, in the footnote, by a working English translation.
> St. You know that our cottages nothing possess
> Of ornamentation and citified dress.
> Kl. We offer our shepherding verse rudely wrought,
> Which ripens apace in tending our flock.
> St. Mistakes that you see you will kindly set right,
> And find in our meadows a source of delight.
> Kl. Accept these first fruits of the river we know,
> Accept in our verses the honor we owe.
> . . .
> St. Off'rings more precious than these we will bring,
> In time, as our flutes learn much higher to sing.

Plate 4   *PEGNESISCHES SCHAEFERGEDICHT/ in den BERINORGISCHEN GEFILDEN/* angestimmet von *STREFON* und *CLAIUS*. Nürnberg: Wolfgang Endter, 1644. Title-page engraving. From *Pegnesisches Schäfergedicht 1644–1645*. Edited by Klaus Garber. Deutsche Neudrucke, Reihe: Barock, 8. Tübingen: Niemeyer, 1966.

The unique connection between rude style and intellectual aspiration, between the everyday and the poetic, is an early modern concettist phenomenon that forces extremes into proximity. The glorification of the highest members of urban society occurs in a mode that is conceptualized as the lowest in poetic handbooks. This playful incongruity is corrected in actual poetic practice, where the finesse and virtuosity of the lower mode match the aesthetic standard for adulation of higher things. As in all publications of the Pegnesischer Blumenorden, stylistic opposition implies social opposition; this tension is felt in pastoral poetry as in no other genre. The gifts do not come in 'citified dress' but are 'rudely wrought', as befits an unaspiring genre; they are nonetheless products of a highly schooled aesthetics. But the image transcends *poiesis* as such. Poetic activity as well as pastoral life outside the city gates are both unadorned, undisguised, humanly unimproved; they are natural, primitive, closer to original creation.

That neither the social nor the poetic dualism should be taken at face value is obvious. The unadorned, 'un-citified' pastoral world is endowed with a certain license. The apparent simplicity, whether with respect to ethics or to manners, represents an empty space that is specific to pastoral and to be filled by either an individual or a social construct. This operation, however, is never addressed frontally. One has only to refer to the last page of the preface to see this. There a pastoral poetics is offered in nuce, not as an objective discussion but in the figurative style of a *Gesprächspiel* 'playful conversation'. In this indirect way we not only are alerted about how to read the text, but we also discover the historical and poetological, indeed the moral and theological, boundaries within which the action takes place. A pastoral poet from each major national literary culture is invoked: Theocritus, Vergil, Ronsard, Tasso, Lope de Vega, and Sidney;[32] to this group the Germans Opitz, Fleming, and Zesen are joined. The only surprise here to the genre historian is the substitution of Tasso for Sannazaro, probably indicative of the preference for the late Cinquecento over the Quattrocento, again reflecting Opitz's tastes. All the great national poets wrote pastoral, 'because the carefree shepherd's life is an ancient, useful, and innocent occupation, and also pleasing to the greatest God' (4). The greater potential of the genre is implied (Yahwe and David, Christ and Peter, as prefigurations of governing and ecclesiastical orders), which the Nuremberg poets fully explore.

But do the poet shepherds not far exceed the limits of their worldly radius, and thus poetic probability, in operating at this level of ultimate things?

> To this we answer that in the description of their rude conversations and raw manners there is in fact more irritation than enjoyment. But these shepherds perhaps mean for the sheep to stand for their books, the sheep's

---

[32] As we learn in the preface, the pastoral names have been taken from Sidney's *Arcadia*.

wool for their poems, the dogs for the leisurely hours of their deep studies. This fact should not be withheld from the reader from the very start.[33]

Nothing would be more ill-advised, however, than to search for the precise references of these allegories in pastoral, as the allegories are themselves the encryption of traditional pastoral practice. For pastoral began as companion to the epic, concealing its poetic secrets in lowly discourse, all the while referring to multiple levels of meaning. The dialectic between the highest and the lowest is the key to appreciating pastoral allegory. Its mimetic critics in Sentimentalism saw this as a failure, whereas to its practitioners it denoted maturity and dignity. It is significant that peasant and shepherd are pictured together three times in the *Pegnesisches Schäfergedicht*: in the copper engraving, in the dedicatory poem, and in the theoretical remark. The totalizing law of pastoral is represented in this synonymity of peasant and shepherd, of lowest social class and highest poetic aspiration. Pastoral seeks to make its motifs obvious to its readers in rustic songs. Nuremberg *Gesprächspiel* appears in pastoral clothing now perspicaciously, now as a puzzle, now allegorically; but it always appears casually, open to all topics, and unrestrictive of its readers.

In the three Nuremberg prose eclogues with which we are concerned, three specific areas – use of space, experience of time, and the logic of the genre itself – are interconnected and affect interpretation at every step. Behind all of this is the ultimate panegyrical purpose of the work.

Arcadian Space and History

The pre-sentimental pastoral landscape of the seventeenth century is overgrown with signs and script. Even when the landscape does not enter directly into the text or imagery, it is always somehow present at the margin, often explicitly so in the marginalia. The sometimes anagrammatic rendering of locale, which is decoded in the marginal notes, directs us to the fact of its unique character as pastoral. The technique for establishing the bucolic locale is typically that of opposition. The classical requisites of pastoral locale are song, erudition, and love; in the introductory words of the *Pegnesisches Schäfergedicht* (in slight variation of Opitz's *Hercinie*): 'a habitat of pleasures, a garden house of field nymphs, an abode of forest gods, a refuge for shepherds, a learned retreat for poets, and a lovely strolling place for amorous spirits' (5). This conventional lowly mythology sets up the allegorical frame of interpretation for the rustic 'nobility' of pastoral. But man-made war threatens to put an end to the originary,

---

[33] *PS* 4. 'Hierauf wird geantwortet/ daß bey Beschreibung ihrer Bäurischen Gespräche unnd groben Sitten/ mehr Verdrus als Belustigung zu befahren: und diese Schäfer durch die Schafe ihre Bücher/ durch derselben Wolle ihre Gedichte/ durch die Hunde ihre von wichtigen Studieren müssige Stunden bemerket haben: Welches sie dem Leser Eingangs anzumelden nicht ümgehen sollen.'

creationist model of life. The *Schäfergedicht* balances these contrastive spheres. Although the war has totally replowed the pastoral landscape in Meissen, replaced its allegorical world with the emblemata of Mars, forced the shepherd Klajus to emigrate, nevertheless, the old imperial city, reminiscent of Tityrus's enclave on the Mincio in *Eclogue* 1, has remained intact. From now on, however, the pleasance on the Pegnitz will be affected by the war-ravaged here and now, which threatens to come crashing into the pastoral reserve at any time. This explains the occasional eschatological overtones.

Arriving at the gates of Nuremberg, Klajus hears Echo's cryptic promise that he will be allowed to continue his pastoral art here. This stirs him to apostrophize the city – though not before reciting a sonnet in praise of the Pegnitz river. In pastoral it is typical protocol to approach a city by way of its river; water and Naiads are integral components of the pastoral world. From Boccaccio to Sannazaro, Montemayor to d'Urfé, water functions in part as a mythico-theological counter-image to modern civilization.

Before considering the details of the presentation, however, let us observe the three ways in which context affects the interpretation of praise. First, praise enables Klajus, a stranger to the city, to be introduced into the new milieu. Second, it gives him the opportunity to pay homage to the hometown of the renowned Harsdörffer. And third, his praise (like the later landscape panegyrics) glorifies the patrician wedding couples and the upper stratum of Nuremberg society. Through the words of the refugee poet, Nuremberg ('beautiful empress', 'paragon of German soil', 'princess of this land', 'sun of this world . . . never subdued by the enemy') receives acknowledgment of her beauty, power, and privilege within the imperial federation (8). Topographical description refers in this way to the highest levels of city government. For a moment, moreover, the emigrant is able to seize the opportunity to express a Protestant sentiment: 'How loved you were by that great hero of the North!'[34] though he is careful immediately to signal his confessional neutrality: 'Honored empire-wide by every native folk'. Finally, he lifts his eyes to the future and raises the pastoral toast 'Peace and quiet' as the unique expression of Nuremberg's own 'heart's desire'.

The once common practice among the 'brown shepherds of Meissen' of singing 'while the wolves slept' (9) is taken up now in the city that has been spared ruin. Strefon provides its finest expression; overheard by the refugee, it offers a vignette of the way in which the Pegnitz shepherds understand themselves and the role they are obliged to play. His praise is steeped in contrasts, though to interpret them literally would do violence to the poetic art. In no other German sodality was it more imperative than in Nuremberg's Blumenorden under Harsdörffer's presidency that poetry prove its goodness and dignity by creating deep levels of meaning. Praise of the lowly must be read in terms of the universal dignity of man, whereby ostentation and pomp, riches and court, are negative

---

[34] Probably in reference to the Swedish general Gustav Adolf, though possibly Luther (Wittenberg).

images of haughtiness. On the face of it, of course, this is simply a direction to appreciate and participate in the lower 'carefree herdsman's life', as Klajus and Strefon will do. Only the penultimate strophe avoids any contrastive reference:

> Ich liebe die Flutgeschmoltzne Crystallen/
> Betaueter Erden triefendes Haar/
> Wenn reichlich bereiffte Früchte gefallen/
> Und lieget in Wochen das heurige Jahr.[35]

The first words exchanged between the penniless student of theology and the wealthy patrician touch on social differences and their possible equalization. At midday, with the sun at its zenith and the Pegnitz landscape, cast in rich shadows, at its most delightful, Klajus happens upon some poems signed by the 'unworthy Playful One'. He 'humbly' approaches the renowned Strefon, who greets him heartily:

> 'Good,' said Strefon, 'good! Klajus (for he had recognized the name on his shepherd staff) is a most welcome guest in these parts, although the elevated greetings and courtly words to which he is accustomed are not the language of our lowly huts, which is rather kind simplicity and open-hearted German honesty. If he cares to follow me on my rounds with the flock, I will find his company a pleasure, as his masterful pastoral poems already resound from the Elbe to the Pegnitz.'[36]

In the fictional world of the shepherds outside the gates of Nuremberg, social equality becomes possible, as implied in the attention given to the pastoral nicknames.

Harsdörffer's egalitarian greeting is reminiscent of the earliest programmatic documents from the Fruchtbringende Gesellschaft and provides one of the social keys to the German sodality movement of the seventeenth century. By contrast to the so-called 'higher places' where 'elevated greetings and courtly words' signify false social distinction, a spirit of equality exists on the banks of the Pegnitz. It is not a particular individual but rather a collective 'we' that speaks 'in these parts' for the guardians of these cherished ideals. To confess loyalty to the classical

---

[35] *PS* 11.
> The crystalline flakes, quick-melting, I love,
>   Hair that is dripping with fresh-fallen dew,
> When full-ripened fruit falls down from above,
>   The current year waiting to give birth anew.

[36] *PS* 12. 'Wol/ sagte Strefon/ wol/ Klajus (denn er hatte den Namen an seinem Schäferstabe erbliket) müsse hiesiger Orten ein willkommener Gast seyn/ so hohe Begrüssungen und Hofworte/ wie er führet/ wohnen nicht in unseren niederigen Hütten/ sondern die liebe Einfalt/ und offenhertzige Teutsche Redlichkeit: Beliebe demnach meinem Schäfer mit mir der Heerde zu folgen/ hab ich mich seiner Gegenwart zu erfreuen/ weilen seine Geistreiche Hirtengedichte von der Elbe bis an die Pegnitz bereit erschollen.'

values suggests deep devotion to poetry, specifically to erudite poetry. As a writer of learned pastoral poems, the refugee, despite his social inferiority, is not unknown, and he is honored with the invitation to accompany the illustrious Strefon on his pastoral rounds, to join in the singing and exchange of songs. Simplicity and honesty, the values that Tacitus recognized as the essence of the ancient German character, are manifest in this founding work of the Pegnesischer Blumenorden as anything but simplistic in the literal sense: Germanic moral integrity finds its expression in the cultivation of an erudite style of German language and poetry.

The topics for the poems come largely from the landscape traversed during the course of the shepherds' walk. Once again the poetic process aims at a total melding of the familiar with the new. The Pegnitz is a particularly rich source. The mythical home of nymphs, especially the Naiads, it also generates the local paper- and wire-mill industries. City and river depend on one another: 'River profits city, city profits river' (7). The windmills turn the meadows along the Pegnitz 'into rich pastures for fall grazing' (11). And now, as Strefon reveals in his poem of greeting to Klajus, the work done by the watering and fertilizing activities of the mills symbolizes the work of the poets on behalf of the German language. That is not to say that the poem can be read only on the metaphorical level. The Pegnitz shepherds were highly attentive to the realia about them, as in the instance of the wire and paper mills: 'an unfamiliar hammering, pounding, and banging' suddenly fills the countryside (17). The reputed placelessness and timelessness of pastoral, its pure idealization in literary criticism, contributes only to a fairy-tale view of the poets as some perfumed band of enchanting shepherds. The writers of Nuremberg prose eclogue well know that they are the first to have squeezed poems about wire and paper mills from the German language.

> Was jederman verwirfft/ halt ich mit Recht für mein.
>   Höret den Hammer die Lumpen zerklopffen/
> Und durch den Pegnitztrieb zerstampffen auf dem Stein/
>   Sehet/ was brudelt and wudelt im Stopffen!
> Der Flächsinlumpenbrey wil Zeug genennet seyn/
>   Pantschet die Formen und lasset sie tropffen:
> Filtzt jeden Bogen wol und streicht ihn Schlittenein/
>   Diesem Nichts sol man das Wissen einpfroffen.[37]

---

[37] *PS* 18–9.
>   What others toss aside, I rightly keep as mine.
>   Hear how the hammers are smashing the lumps,
>   Which as the Pegnitz churns on stone are trampled fine.
>   Listen to boiling and bubbling of pumps.
>   The lumpy flaxen brew transforms to human ken.
>   Wring out the forms now and leave them to dry:
>   Mat ev'ry papered leaf and slide the carriage in,
>   Into this nothing some meaning imply.

The old free imperial city is still a stronghold of innovation, no less poetic than technological, in the seventeenth century. This too is worthy of praise. Technological wonder is embedded in the ideal landscape, the *locus amoenus*, even as the rays of the first day of Creation continue to shine upon this modern landscape. Paradisiacal, original time is wedded to the historical work of human hands.

Arcadian Time and Historical Time

Pastoral forms are typically divided into two destructive categories: love and war. The amorous motif dominates in pastoral lyric, drama, and prose; that of war in pastoral occasional poetry and cultural criticism, as in the eclogue (including prose eclogue). In the German reform tradition of pastoral writing this was no less true of Opitz, Fleming, and Zesen than it is now of Harsdörffer and Klaj. The fear of this destructive power is inscribed in even the purest nature poem. Klajus has not yet made Strefon's acquaintance when he receives the urgent message that the areas around the Pegnitz are in need of protection:

>   Schöne Linde
>   Deine Rinde
> Nehm den Wunsch von meiner Hand:
>   Kröne mit dem sanfften Schatten
>   Diese stets begrasten Matten/
> Stehe sicher vor dem Brand;
>   Reist die graue Zeit hier nieder
>   Deine Brüder/
> Sol der Lentzen diese Aest'
>   Jedes Jahr belauben wieder
> Und dich hegen Wurtzelfest.[38]

The historical drama itself is wrapped within this allegory. But why do the two poets turn again to Sidney for the allegorical personification, the shepherdess

---

[38] *PS* 11–12.
>   Lovely lime,
>   Here my rhyme
> Upon your trunk from my own hand:
>   Lay a crown of gentle shades
>   Over these green-carpet glades;
> Unscathed by fire, safely stand;
>   Though your comrades here on earth
>   fall in death,
> Yet these limbs at time of spring,
>   Year to year again bud forth,
> Firmly rooted, yours protecting.

Pamela, of 'poor Germany gasping for her last breath' (14)? As always, a poetic problem lies at the bottom. In this case it has to do with challenging the alliterative, onomatopoeic, and metaphorical capacity of the German language, here on the historical theme of war, in the unmistakable Nuremberg manner.[39] Conventional allegorical elaboration, which harkens back by way of its German practitioners, among them Justus Georg Schottel, Jesaias Rompler von Löwenhalt, Johann Rist, and Paul Fleming, to the roots of European humanism in Dante and Petrarch, is of course expected here.[40] As we saw in Chapter 2, it was Konrad Burdach who first showed how the bridal-imagery of the curia was transmitted by Dante and, especially, Petrarch (for example, in the *sponsa*-mysticism surrounding the widowed capital of Rome), as the embodiment of the spiritual and institutional union envisioned between pope and church. The sorrowing mother figure, old before her time and weeping over her warring sons, stands at the beginning of the humanist tradition of national allegorical figures, especially in the programmatic literature calling for the rejuvenation of a national language and literature. Gradually, the situation was transformed into the restitution of the old Roman Principate, and the sense of a national Italian mission began to unfold, contributing directly to the shaping of the Renaissance into a political-cultural movement.[41]

The rather unusual Pamela motif of the *Pegnesisches Schäfergedicht* belongs to this tradition. The insanity of the 'melancholy shepherd Pamela' (14), who in Sidney's *Arcadia* was victimized by the king's obliviousness to his national duties, is brought on by the political madness around her. Her grief springs from the self-flagellation of Germany's peoples, who, instead of seeking unity as in the past, seem to be set on destroying each other. The Tacitean ethical discourse of ancient German nobility is now turned to articulating a political crisis, to sounding a battle cry for Germany to reawaken and turn around. As in Dante and Petrarch it is from a mother's broken heart that the fervent plea is made to her children, especially her sons, to abandon the madness of civil war and heed the

---

[39] Rudolf Drux, 'Sprachspiele gegen den Krieg: ein Beitrag zur poetischen Nachahmung bei Harsdörffer', in Battafarano, *Georg Philipp Harsdörffer* 83–103.

[40] For the German context, see Irmgard Weithase, 'Die Darstellung von Krieg und Frieden in der deutschen Barockdichtung', *Wissenschaftliche Zeitschrift der Friedrich-Schiller-Universität Jena* 2 (1951–2): 47–64. The European context is reflected in James Hutton, *Themes of Peace in Renaissance Poetry*, ed. Rita Guerlac (Ithaca: Cornell University Press, 1984); Franz Josef Worstbrock (ed.), *Frieden im Horizont des Renaissance-Humanismus* (Weinheim: Acta humaniora, 1986); Klaus Garber, 'Die Friedens-Utopie im europäischen Humanismus: Versuch einer geschichtlichen Rekonstruktion', *Modern Language Notes* 101 (1986): 516–52; Hans-Joachim Diesner, *Stimmen zu Krieg und Frieden im Renaissance-Humanismus* (Göttingen: Vandenhoeck & Ruprecht, 1990).

[41] Klaus Garber, 'Zur Konstitution der europäischen Nationalliteraturbewegung: Implikationen und Perspektiven', in *Nation und Literatur im Europa der Frühen Neuzeit*, ed. Garber, 1–55 (Tübingen: Niemeyer, 1989), with an overview of scholarship.

commandment of brotherly love. Formerly unified and impregnable, Germany is now the victim of her own disunity. This note, sounded by Opitz in his *Aristarchus* some quarter-century earlier at the onset of the Thirty Years' War, echoes now in Nuremberg in longing anticipation of the war's end and a return to domestic tranquillity. Thus the creators of Nuremberg prose eclogue join the humanistic discourse on national unity, which had been carried on in much the same way in Renaissance Italy, itself as divided and at war then as Germany is now. At that earlier time too, pacifists and irenicists had stepped forward to criticize the national state of affairs, sometimes openly, sometimes in veiled language, but always resolutely. Early modern pastoral was often the vehicle of this discourse, and indeed its critical potential becomes fully clear only within the political context.

Klajus and Strefon assume the augury role of announcing the signs that point away from desperation and towards hope. In Pamela's eyes, hope is in vain: 'I am enslaved Germany,' she says, 'and your consolation means little to me. If any peace seem to be possible in me, it will surely soon disappear again just as before' (17). On the symbolic plane, however, it is a different story, and Pamela is sanguine about a turning of events. The pleas of poets may seem only to echo hollowly in the political arena, in that 'city graveyard' unnoticed by soldiers; nevertheless, despite the horrors of the world and its fixation on *res gestae*, there is cause for optimism:

> Entzwischen tröstet mich/ daß so viel neue Feben
> Erhalten meine Sprach' und Wolkenan erheben;
> > Was neulich Opitzgeist beginnet auß dem Grund/
> > Ist ruchtbar und am Tag auß vieler Teutschen Mund.[42]

This is how poetic language was understood in humanist circles around Europe: as the vernacular seal and pledge of national unity and greatness, as a supplement for what is absent or endangered in the political world of the young monarchies. The nationalism at work here was the backbone of humanist self-confidence and explains the continued praise of the lowly green world. For, paradoxically, the shepherd is none other than a conservator of the elevated world to which the future is vouchsafed.

Pastoral Concettism

The prosimetric pastoral, based on the model of Sannazaro's *Arcadia* and introduced by Opitz with his *Hercinie* (1630) into seventeenth-century German

---

[42] *PS* 15.
> But how it doth console that new Apollos rise,
> Attending to my language, exalting to the skies;
> > What one man, Opitz, caused to spring from German ground
> > Now's heard from every mouth the entire realm around.

literature, was the preferred form in Nuremberg for poetic experimentation in verse. It is free of the narrative burden of having to motivate change, tension, innovation, tempi, etc., and relatively unconcerned with exposition, peripeteia, and the resolution of dramatic conflict. Nor is the prosimetric pastoral constrained by the conventions of poem collections, which insist on including representative examples in the various lyrical forms. Constructed around the simple narrative strategy of a nature-walk, it is surely the most open form in all of seventeenth-century German literature, enjoying the great poetic license that had evolved from the allegorical identification of the shepherd with the scholar and the poet. As such it found its most complete realization in the prose eclogues of the Nuremberg poets. Brought to fruition by Opitz's generation, prose eclogue was enhanced in Nuremberg through experimentation with the techniques of variety and hyperbole. The *Pegnesisches Schäfergedicht* of 1644 provided the new stylistic model.[43]

Compared to Opitz's *Hercinie*, which has a more stringent narrative structure, the Nuremberg version resembles a casual garland of pearls. The opening pages contain an echo poem, a sonnet, an ode, and several dactylic poems – among them Klaj's oft-anthologized 'Hellgläntzendes Silber' – as well as a figure poem in the form of an anvil. As the *Schäfergedicht* proceeds, stock forms from the pastoral ludic repertoire are adduced: puzzle poems carved in pumpkins, stichomythic role-playing, epigrammatic verses in imitation of Tasso or Lope (his *Arcadia* was especially esteemed in Nuremberg), antiphones on the times of the day or seasons of the year, number and letter poems, multiple-stanza poems with exchangeable lines and half-lines, and so forth.

It is important to observe that the level of aesthetic refinement in these poems in terms of sound, image, metaphor, and rhythm, challenges the prevailing notion that the German language of the seventeenth century lagged far behind other vernaculars and was an inadequate instrument of poetic expression.[44] In fact, the Nuremberg poets took undisputed leadership in developing Opitz's poetics, especially prosody, as mediated by the Wittenberg professor of poetics August

---

[43] See esp. Klaus Garber, 'Nachwort des Herausgebers', in *Pegnesisches Schäfergedicht 1644–1645* (1966) 3*–27*, esp. 15*–18*; also Eberhard Mannack, '"Realistische" und metaphorische Darstellung im *Pegnesischen Schäfergedicht*', *Jahrbuch der Deutschen Schillergesellschaft* 17 (1973): 154–65; Anthony J. Harper, 'In the Nürnberg Manner? Reflections on a 17th. Century Parody', *Neophilologus* 58 (1974): 52–65; Mannack, 'Nachwort', in *Die Pegnitz-Schäfer: Nürnberger Barockdichtung*, Universal-Bibliothek, 8545, ed. Mannack, 275–92 (Stuttgart: Reclam, 1988); and Max Reinhart, 'Textual Introduction', in *Johann Hellwig's 'Die Nymphe Noris' (1650)* (Columbia, SC: Camden House, 1994), esp. xxviii–xli.

[44] This conception has been turned into a kind of law by eminent studies on the rise of modern literary German that establish their *terminus a quo* with the eighteenth century. One thinks esp. of Eric A. Blackall's classic *The Emergence of German as a Literary Language, 1700–1775* (1959), 2nd edn (Ithaca: Cornell University Press, 1978).

Buchner.[45] In their hands German poetry proved capable of rich sensory expression – until the Age of Romanticism German poetry rarely exhibits its equal in playfulness.[46] Precisely for this reason it would be improper to overload the poetic rafts of the Nuremberg poets with allegorical interpretations. Their famous *Klangmalerei* 'sound painting' served in the first instance to create word, number, and letter games pursuant to an aesthetic program to illustrate the genius of the German language, not, as so often asserted, primarily to demonstrate the 'natural' quality of German via cabalistic and spiritualistic speculation. The theoreticians of the early Enlightenment construed this emancipation of the formal aspects of language as anti-mimetic and, in keeping with their reprivileging of the idea of language's direct referentiality and their discouragement of the exploration of multi-referentiality, prohibited its practice. However, that does not mean that Nuremberg prose eclogue was merely a linguistic and poetic exercise having no philosophical underpinning. Historical content in literature often nestles in unlikely corners, and it is always communicated through form, as the panegyrical section that follows demonstrates.

Pastoral as Memorial and Panegyric

After the two shepherds have poetically transformed the Haller meadow, Strefon leaves his flock temporarily in other hands – his cottage, he indicates, is not far from the Haller meadow – and together he and Klajus proceed up the slight hill towards the cemetery of the St Johannis Church in the northwestern sector of the city. From this vantage point they are able to enjoy a panoramic view of Nuremberg and its countryside. A realistic counter-image now appears briefly: a rural scene before the gates of the city, showing its profitable forests, fields, and gardens. Realistic description has a definite place in Nuremberg *laus urbis*. In this case, it is employed as a deliberate rebuttal to a disparaging remark made by Conrad Celtis a century and a half earlier in his own description of the city: 'In your northern sector,' he wrote, 'the fields are so sterile that even grasshoppers cannot live off of them.'[47] 'Little by little,' Strefon counters, 'our countryside has come to vie with that of Italy for its delicious fruits, oranges, lemons,

---

[45] Esp. through his *Kurzer Weg-Weiser der Teutschen Tichtkunst*, which circulated widely in manuscript form. Among its innovative features, Buchner's recommendation of dactylic verse, which he associated with the doctrine of natural imitation, proved to be especially fruitful in Nuremberg, not least because it was handled with mastery by Klaj, who had learned it directly from Buchner in Wittenberg.

[46] See the introduction in Wiedemann, *Johann Klaj und seine Redeoratorien*, as well as his article 'Engel, Geist und Feuer: Zum Dichterselbstverständnis bei Johann Klaj, Catharina von Greiffenberg und Quirinus Kuhlmann', in *Literatur und Geistesgeschichte*, ed. Wiedemann and Reinhold Grimm, 85–109 (Berlin: Schmidt, 1968).

[47] *Conrad Celtis und sein Buch über Nürnberg*, ed. Albert Werminghoff (Freiburg: Bolze, 1921).

pomegranates, and figs. Time, which changes all things, has gradually enriched our formerly infertile sandy soil.' Thus, even the fields of this free imperial city have a role in the humanistic competition between cities, territories, and nations; and Nuremberg's illustrious son, fortuitously positioned between the patrician families and the burgher guild of learned poets, champions his city's achievements.

Gazing upon the sandstone cliffs where old 'Norisburg' once stood, Strefon strikes another favorite humanist theme, the connection to Rome, in this instance the presumed Roman origins of Nuremberg. Klajus interrupts to remind that the memorial work being inaugurated relates directly to the present, and an exchange ensues with respect to the responsibility of historians, especially poets, in preserving and interpreting events and deeds:

> 'If only,' Klajus began, 'our noble, spirited, and upright Germans, whom all nations held in awe, had recorded their heroic deeds as diligently as they carried them out, or had the bloody wars of past centuries not obliterated the memory of Germanic deeds and people, we would have more reports than we do about their bravery, their manly weapons, their colorful shields, their clamorous, storm-raising blitz attacks and glorious victories.' 'That is doubtless regrettable,' said Strefon, 'but I am not convinced that we ought to complain so much as be astonished that, ever since the Germans began to fight with one another, many highly intelligent minds have tried, and continue to try, to enter into the Eternal Register everything that fire consumed, rain and storms washed from the stones, and time scratched from the metals, such that neither fire nor flood will again touch the record, and future generations (assuming there are such) will be able to read it until the final trumpet sounds.'[48]

Once again: the ancient 'upright Germans, whom all nations held in awe', this literary creation out of the pages of Tacitus's *Germania*. What better custodians of this memorial literature can there be than Nuremberg's own shepherd poets?

---

[48] *PS* 21–2. 'Hätten/ fienge Klajus an/ unsere edle/ unverzagte/ und von allen Völkern hochgefürchte Teutsche Biederleute mit solchem Fleiß ihre löbliche Heldenthaten aufgeschrieben/ als sie selbe verrichtet/ oder die blutigen Kriege vor etlich hundert Jahren/ mit den Leuten/ nicht auch zugleich derselben Gedächtnis ausgerottet/ so könten wir von dero tapfern Mannheit/ männlichen Waffen/ buntbemahlten Schilden/ stürmst-schreckenden und wekkenden Lermenschlagen/ rühmlichen Siegen mehr/ als so/ Nachricht haben. Freylich wol/ sagte Strefon/ ist es zu betrauren/ aber doch stehe ich im Zweiffel/ ob jenes mehr zu beklagen/ oder über dem sich mehr zu verwundern/ daß seyther die Teutschen einander selbst in die Haar gerahten/ viel hocherwekte Geister sich dahin bemühet und annoch bemühen/ daß/ was das Feuer aufgefressen/ die Regen und Ungewitter von den Steinen ausgewaschen/ die Zeit aus den Metallen gekratzet/ in das Register der Ewigkeit einzutragen/ und dahin zuschreiben/ da es keine Glut noch Flut belangen kan/ daß es die Nachwelt (so anderst eine zu hoffen) bis zur letzten Posaunen lesen wird.'

Now, however, the Germans are put in charge of an inheritance lacking to their forefathers: the memorializing literature bequeathed to modern Germany by earlier humanists like Celtis, Eobanus Hessus, and Paul Melissus Schede. First practiced by the mythical shepherd Daphnis, the songs of memory entered European literature through Theocritus's first idyll, itself in imitation of the legendary shepherd poet Stesichorus. In the metamorphoses of Daphnis ancient bucolic thinking is endlessly renewed. The shepherd remembers, produces the memorializing words, recounts the *res gestae*, and thus unceasingly retraces the transition into pastoral's complementary genre, the epic, with its heroic, battle-filled world, which he records, interprets, and transmits to posterity.

The *Pegnesisches Schäfergedicht* is no exception. The epic subject par excellence, war, is addressed from the very beginning. A second epic subject is introduced in the middle of the work: the marriage couples and, by implication, Nuremberg's old governing families to which the couples belong. Harsdörffer and Klaj handle this transition as had Opitz, Sidney, Montemayor, Sannazaro, and the rest, using the figure of a nymph to act as guide back into the rich pastoral world of Vergil, thereby connecting the pastoral world (*genus humile*) and heroic world (*genus grande*).[49] The final sections of the *Georgics*, dedicated to the bee colony, portray the descent of the beekeeper Aristaeus, bitterly complaining about his withered beehives, into the underwater world. His mother, Cyrene, alludes repeatedly to the *Iliad* and, in one instance, to Bacchylides' description of the descent of Theseus to Poseidon and his nereid wife Amphitrite.[50] The shepherds' amazement at the wonders of the radiant other-world of the court occurs regularly as a pastoral motif.[51] Harsdörffer was acquainted with it from Opitz and Sannazaro, though perhaps more directly from Montemayor and Lope. The contrast between pastoral and heroic scenery is effectively contrived and marks the transition in pastoral occasional poetry, about half-way through, to the panegyrical section.

In place of the traditional guiding nymph, Harsdörffer and Klaj employ 'Gerücht' (Rumor), in clear allusion to the events of *Aeneid* 4.173–218. Rumor

---

[49] On the history of the descriptions of the nymphs and grottoes and their reception by Opitz, see esp. Alfred Huebner, 'Das erste deutsche Schäferidyll und seine Quellen' (PhD diss., Königsberg, 1910).

[50] Commentary in Will Richter (ed.), *Vergil: Georgica* (Munich: Hueber, 1957), 375 ff. In addition to the older scholarship, e.g., F. Klinger, E.K. Rand, and L.P. Wilkinson, some of the more recent studies influencing my judgments are Michael C.J. Putnam, *Virgil's Poem of the Earth: Studies in the Georgics* (Princeton: Princeton University Press, 1979), David O. Ross, Jr, *Virgil's Elements: Physics and Poetry in the Georgics* (Princeton: Princeton University Press, 1987), and Joseph Farrel, *Virgil's Georgics and the Traditions of Ancient Epic: The Art of Allusion in Literary History* (New York: Oxford University Press, 1991).

[51] 'The amazement experienced when entering a wonderful palace has been part of the supply of epic motifs ever since the description of the gardens of Alkinoos.' Friedrich Klinger, *Virgils Georgica* (Zurich: Artemis, 1963), 205.

promises a laurel wreath to the winner of the poetic contest that she has arranged (23). Unlike Opitz, the two poets give little attention to the path that leads to the central repository, the 'Temple of Honorable Memory'. Dedicated to courage and competence, the temple is situated on a lovely meadow, palm trees to the right, cypresses to the left; between them stands Pallas carrying an open book, a spear, the black-white-red flag in her right hand and the coats of arms of the Tetzel, Haller, and Schlüsselfelder families in her left. The poets reach the temple only after having negotiated 'some nearly impenetrable vegetation'. It is round in shape, interesting mainly for the pedestals bearing life-size 'pictorial columns' inscribed with the names and virtues of the honorees. The poets, awestruck, do not attempt to emulate the rhetorical virtuosity of their predecessors, preferring instead to extrapolate on the virtues inscribed beneath the mottoes. But they need not, says Rumor, 'be shocked by the images of these heroes'.

> Consider instead how Truth, who is as my sister in this place, curates the Temple of Memory on behalf of an uninterrupted succession of exceptionally virtuous and meritorious old Germans and avoids the empty titles with which Hypocrisy commonly outfits herself. Virtue is, after all, immortal through her heirs, and I myself could produce the names of aristocratic forebears from centuries past if time permitted us to remain here long enough. For now, however, you will have enough to read and learn from what you see before you.[52]

Thus begins the central panegyrical section. The renunciation – of social status, titles, and behavior unbecoming to their ancient ethical calling – that dignifies the German shepherds as heirs to the centuries-old pastoral tradition is applied as the measure of worth in the Temple of Honor. The pastoral values, which is to say, the values of the learned sodality, are then transferred to the Nuremberg patrician families; in this way pastoral values mediate between higher and lower social estates, but without prejudicial hierarchization. The Hallers, the Schlüsselfelders, the Tetzels, all fall into a category with the shepherds and 'ancient Germans', who were distinguished solely by reputation, honesty, and merit. While it is true that this does not represent history 'as it really was' (Ranke), in fact the primary function of pastoral is rather to anticipate how things should be. Nobility, *urban* nobility here, becomes the formal carrier of *virtus* and is thus obligated to practice the values of which the literary shepherds are the custodians. This critical mechanism functioned as an essential component of the

---

[52] *PS* 24. '[B]etrachtet vielmehr/ wie die Warheit/ welche mit mir dieses Orts verschwestert/ diesen Tempel der Gedächtnis/ zu stetsbleibender Nachfolge so ansehnlicher/ redlicher/ wolverdienter alten Teutschen aufgeführet/ und allen Titteltand/ den die Heucheley vielmal anzuschmitzen pflegt/ an seinem Ort verbleiben lassen. Einmal ist die Tugend in ihren Erben unsterblich/ und könte ich auch dieser Altadelichen Ahnen von vielen hundert Jahren hero vorweisen/ wann die geschwinde Zeit uns aufzuhalten vergönnete. Dises mal werdet ihr aus gegenwärtigem gnug zu lesen und zu lernen haben.'

European sodalities.[53] What is being praised here has a long history and ensures 'an uninterrupted succession of exceptionally virtuous and meritorious . . . Germans' for the future (24).

With this principle in mind, the portraits of the individual patricians make sense. This is not to suggest that they do not enjoy individuality. Indeed, they are far from atrophying into simplistic allegories of virtue, as the following facts taken from the verses (mainly quatrains) to the portraits make clear.[54] Wilhelm Schlüsselfelder, the sire of his family in Nuremberg, oversaw the city's building construction. Under his son, Wilibald, a member of the city council, 'both town and government in peace and flower stood'. Carl's life was marked by deep piety, in turn related to the Germanic virtues: 'here lie integrity and ancient German faith'. His own son Carl died young, but not before earning a name for himself in the religious and educational life of the city. The earliest known member of the Haller family, Wilhelm, was an advisor to Emperor Maximilian I, a diplomat in Burgundy and Hungary and one of the city's great senators. His son of the same name likewise entered the service of Maximilian I and later that of Charles V; his son Hans was an excellent land superintendent. The son Hans Jacob served as a forester. Jobst Tetzel, the first of his line, was an officer, as was his grandson Friedrich; and while Jobst Tetzel's precise occupation is not clear in the inscription, Carl's life illustrated the classic humanist pairing of pen and sword.

These few observations suffice to show that the panegyrical function of the *Pegnesisches Schäfergedicht* is not consumed with fuzzy generalities of physiognomic portraiture. The ideology of ancient German loyalty and honesty is related specifically to the praise of the virtues of service to the city, just as it had been in Quattrocento Italy and would continue to be in Nuremberg through the middle of the seventeenth century. In this sense Nuremberg prose eclogue contributed to the renewal of a culture of civic behavior within the governing estate, which, owing to the general refeudalizing trend in the empire, had eroded considerably. It follows that the *Schäfergedicht* can only have been welcomed by the leading magistrates of the city. For the literary historian, it offers a reflection on the civic role and attitudes of the learned and patrician *nobilitas literaria*, translated into an urban idiom.

---

[53] Arnold Hirsch, *Bürgertum und Barock im deutschen Roman* (Cologne: Böhlau, 1957), Chapter 6: 'Die Entstehung der modernen Seelenlage im Schäferroman.'

[54] In general for older printed works and manuscripts on Nuremberg families and genealogy, see Georg Andreas Will, *Biblioteca Norica*, 7 vols (Altdorf: Meyer, 1772). See further Will, *Nürnbergisches Gelehrten-Lexicon*, 2 pts (Nuremberg and Altdorf: Schüpfel, 1756), and esp. the enlarged edition by Christian Conrad Nopitsch (Altdorf: Nopitsch, 1805). A wealth of genealogical documents and occasional poetry, including funerary materials, related to the families is collected in Nuremberg's Stadtbibliothek. Interestingly, in the otherwise richly detailed funeral sermons for both the Haller von Hallerstein and the Tetzel von Kirchensittenbach families, no mention is made of the *PS* in context of the marriage of 16 October 1644.

III. Surpassing the Prototype: Birken's 'Fortsetzung der Pegnitz-Schäferey'

In the *Fortsetzung der Pegnitz-Schäferey* (1645), his ambitious sequel to the *Pegnesisches Schäfergedicht*, Sigmund von Birken faced the challenge of finding a judicious balance between continuity and change. He solved the problem by adopting the beginner's approach to success: simply outdoing one's model. Attempts to emulate or surpass a masterwork are rarely successful, for at least two reasons: great works are great precisely because their first loyalty is to their own laws; and their power typically lies more in understated or indirect expression than in self-conscious displays of virtuosity. In his first attempt at prose eclogue, Sigmund Betulius (later: von Birken) pulls out all the stops in an effort to match the accomplishment of Harsdörffer (his mentor and patron) and Klaj. Whether the boldness with which he manipulated the form was appreciated by Harsdörffer, a keen student of genre, if not a formalist in the strict sense, is impossible to say. Klaj, on the other hand, obviously slighted by this newcomer, may well have objected.[55] His own short pastoral,[56] published three years later under the same name as the one he had written with Harsdörffer, has features that distinctly contrast with Birken's *Fortsetzung*, especially its eschewal of virtuosity and complexity, opting instead for a simple rustic style.

Birken's foreword extends to four pages, while the body of the prose eclogue itself swells to over a hundred. His ambition of later years, to demonstrate pastoral's footing on biblical ground, is not yet visible in this work; by contrast, his acumen, reminiscent of Opitz, for strategies of self-promotion, is already highly evolved by 1645. The key is the biographical component, bequeathed to pastoral by Vergil, which he will exploit throughout his remarkable career. Poets assume shepherd names as a means of 'developing their thoughts more freely than within their normal identity',[57] in other words, to mask the autobiographical self. Birken may be alluding to Opitz or Fleming or Rist, even to Schottel or Tscherning or Homburg (curiously, the name of Zesen is missing). The trail of German language classicist literature is particularly bright in prose eclogue. Birken, soon to gain acknowledgment as the leading poetic authority of the post-Opitzian generation, argues that the belated appearance of German writing within

---

[55] Klaj's name originally appeared on the title-page, only to be expunged in the edition printed shortly thereafter in the same year. It is certainly thinkable that Klaj, by this time a respected German poet in his own right, was privately disturbed by the audacity of this young upstart, particularly in view of the minimal role he had been given in the composition of the *Fortsetzung*. It is possible that he discreetly had his name removed from the title-page of the new edition. At any rate, it is unusual to find – following the two congratulatory poems by Harsdörffer and Birken's brother, Christian – a 'Dedication to All Lovers and Notable Patrons of the German Language' signed, not by both authors, but only by Floridan (Birken). But enough of speculation.

[56] *Pegnesisches Schäfergedicht, in den Nördgauer Gefilden, angestimmet von Filanthon und Floridan* (Nuremberg, 1648).

[57] *FPS* leaf)(2^{v}.

the concert of European literatures is compensated for by its special role in what seems to be emerging as the final stage of pastoral.[58] The nineteen-year-old Betulius sums up German pastoral poetry, as well as German language and literature in general, in a daring prognosis: '[It appears], given the sheer volume of excellent writings, that [German] will shortly seize the lead from all other literatures.'[59]

His own first work thus has an exponential position in this program, and the subsequent modesty formula only serves to underscore his awareness of it. The young Nuremberg sodality will first learn of its origins from his work. His claim to have undertaken it at the behest of the other members is precisely calculated. Not Harsdörffer, not Klaj, not even the prominent physician Johann Hellwig (Montano), but rather young Betulius himself pens the legend of the origins of the Pegnesischer Blumenorden. He sets his name to the very first poem in fact, a sonnet that exploits the sodality's flower image and is addressed to all cultivators of the German language. If we associate this theme, first, with the hinted reproach of German for failing to honor its national heroes, and second, with the program of allegorical reformulation of ancient mythology through the medium of pastoral, it is clear that Birken intends to tax this lowly genre with a heavy load of themes and goals.[60] This he does against the satirical backdrop of a 'Thistle Sonnet' dedicated to the notorious abuser of language 'Herr Hasewald Langohr, sonsten genandt Dünkelwitz' (Mr Long-eared Jackrabbit, a.k.a. Dimwit).

Re-citing the Prototype

Whereas the *Pegnesisches Schäfergedicht* had opened with a quatrain concerned with place ('There where the Meissner stream'), the *Fortsetzung* leads with a temporal reference ('The night was now gone by').[61] Consciousness of time is characteristic of the Nuremberg poets; it is used with particular effectiveness here in the reenactment of the founding myth. Birken opens his first prose section by establishing continuity with Harsdörffer and Klaj. His own work he modestly calls an 'inferior poem'; nevertheless, it is a 'continuation of our free-spirited

---

[58] Later on, following in the tracks of Schottel, he will integrate in much the same way biblical origins with the later form of the German pastoral.
[59] *FPS* leaf)(3^r.
[60] Again, the precedent is *Ecl.* 4.1: 'Sicelides Musae, paulo maiora canamus.'
[61] This is emphasized by the abrupt truncation of the last line, where it occurs just before the beginning of the prose section:
'ES war die Nacht vorbey/ das frühe Pferdgetümmel
Gieng vor der Sonnen her/ am liechtbegläntzten Himmel.
Die Welt war von dem Schlaf zur Arbeit aufgewekkt/
Das Feld war mit dem Tau durchsafftet und bedekkt.
Der Tag war jetzt am tag – – –
Als sich FLORIDAN/ mit niemanden/ als seinen freyen Gedanken/ begleitet/ hinter seiner geringen Heerde zu denen gewönlichen Trifften truge . . .' (1).

poems'. The walk taken by Strefon[62] and Klajus had come to an end in the area around the Haller meadow, and it is logical in terms of the literary game that Floridan should begin his own walk there. Thus the description of the Haller meadow becomes a feat of one-upmanship. Birken opts for witty personification of the 'Lovely Meadow'. The poem that follows addresses a Nuremberg landmark, a bridge over the Pegnitz, much as Harsdörffer and Klaj had proceeded from the Haller meadow description to a poem on the wire and paper mills. Birken's choice is clever, for it sets up the use of *Brükkreimen* 'bridge rhyme' (2). He is determined to 'bring new honor' to the Pegnitz landscape by inventing striking forms and metaphors. One innovative example is the introduction of a spiritual morning song of praise and thanksgiving (3), which, at the work's end, is answered by a spiritual evening song (101–2). Spiritual contrafacture will in fact become one of the hallmarks of Birken's oeuvre. Unlike his predecessors, Birken has little sense for landscape as panegyrical object. His genius lies rather in his ability to integrate autobiographical details, which he expands far beyond its use in the *Pegnesisches Schäfergedicht*.

Once again the pleasance on the Pegnitz contrasts favorably with the 'regrettable condition of his fatherland', the Bohemian Sudetenland, where a cruel catholicization has been underway since the late 1620s. 'Unreasonable Fate' has kept this Lutheran pastor's son from seeing his homeland again after having left it at the age of three.[63] The fact that historical misfortune must be transmitted indirectly in encoded form owes less to poetic regulation than to Harsdörffer's injunction that explicit politics be kept out of literature – publication was carefully monitored by the city council – under all circumstances. This does not keep the young Birken from complaining (in a prose passage), however indirectly, that his homeland faces an uncertain future. Behind this cautiously worded observation lies a criticism that the exile of the Protestants had made a mono-confessional state of the Sudetenland: Lutherans are no longer welcome there. His plea for an end to the war is reserved for a lyrical passage:

> Hier sitz' ich an dem Rand/ in deines Ufers Schatten/
>   Du schlanker Pegnitzfluß/ hier nehm ich meine Rast/
>   Hier schau ich deiner Fluht nicht-ungestümmen Brast/
>   Hier seh ich neben dir die frischbegrünten Matten.
> Du aber/ Vatterstrom in meinem Mutterland/
>   Ist dein Geräusche dann von Lust so weit entsessen/

---

[62] Birken uses the spelling 'Strephon'; present practice will be to retain the spelling 'Strefon' of the *PS*, except in direct quotations from the *FPS*.

[63] Floridan reports the expulsion from Bohemia on p. 15, but says only that at the time he was 'noch minderjährig/ ja fast unmündig'. In fact, he was three in 1629, when Ferdinand II issued the Edict of Restitution, which required the return to Catholic jurisdiction of all lands in Protestant possession since the Peace of Augsburg (1555). His parents, Daniel and Veronica Betulius, fled to Hohenberg and Bayreuth, later settling in Nuremberg in 1632.

Daß deiner Ufer mich ein fremdes macht vergessen?
Nein/ Unglükk Unglükk hat dich mir/ mich dir entwandt.
Es schwebet über dir ein schweres Himmelhassen/
Der Weltgemeine Sturm/ des Krieges Jammerglut.
Kürtz'/ O du Wolkengott/ des starken Wetters Wut/
Laß ach! die Eger frey durchrauschen ihre Gassen/
Die manches Thal durchwäscht. Dann soll mir ihre Lust
Stäts eine Wollust seyn/ ein süsser Sinnenmust.[64]

What Birken wishes for the Eger he finds in abundance on the Pegnitz. In pastoral, the future is always represented by some present state, which, for its part, is a continuation of an originary condition. Pastoral exhibits a synoptic temporal structure that includes past, present, and future. The reality of war, which deviates totally from the pastoral ideal, appears as a historically deficient and temporary condition. The poets' awareness of having to pass censorship affects both the rhetoric of the genre as well as the conventions of political expression; the real cause of the pastoral critic's *otium* cannot be explicitly identified. Fortuna and an avenging God ('the heavens' heavy wrath') represent the certainty of historical fate, and hope is left solely in the hands of the 'God of Thunder'. Museful pastoral existence would expire in its own richness were it limited only to tasting the innocent joys of the present. But because its poets are ethically bound to remember history, they must articulate it – in the conventional terms at their disposal, of course.

By analogy to the earlier corresponding poem by Klaj, Birken returns in memory to his student years in Jena, offering a long poem (8–13) of some 168 alexandrine lines. Like Klaj's, it foregrounds the conflict between pastoral life and destructive war. In his manuscript version Birken constructed a scheme having the logic of individual experience: literary reminiscence and its mythological elevation, employing similes, metaphors, synecdoche, word plays, sound painting, inexpressibility topoi, and the like. The printed version returns to

---

[64] *FPS* 7.
  I sit here at the edge, upon your shore, in shadows,
    You slender Pegnitz stream; and here I'll take my stay.
    I see here in your flood the not impetuous spray,
    I see here next to you the freshly greenéd meadows.
  But you, O Father Stream, in this my mother land,
    Has your familiar sound left joy so far away,
    That unfamiliar shores outsing our better days?
    No, 'tis fate that you from me, and me from you has banned.
  Above you grimly sways the heavens' heavy wrath,
    The storms that wrack the world, the misery of war.
    Make short, o God of Thunder, the furious weather's roar.
  O let the Eger rush unchecked along its path
    And flood the valleys round. Then shall your joy e'er be
    For me a pleasure rare: sweet sensuality.

the symbolic world of shepherd life in which the qualities of the institution of the learned sodality are integrated. The university, untouched by the war, functions much as the intellectual societies as a 'refuge for shepherds'. Jena is raised to the heights of Pindus. Birken's activities there, learning, cultivating friendships, and practicing poetry, prepared him for his future in Nuremberg. Here as there the concern is with shepherds, songs, and Mars, who threatens the innocence of shepherd life. Jena defends itself against the enemy of the arts and learning, and the young poet, a modern Maro, takes an active role in this defense. Individual details are woven into the fabric. For example, as of the writing of this poem, it has been six months since he left his beloved Jena; its university, he says, was a home for the Muses, a paradise where he basked in the light of learning. The Luther Fountain symbolizes the ideal spiritual location,

> Der sonsten Luthern hat oft Last und Durst gestillet/
> Dem teuren Gottes-mann/ in dessen küler Krufft/
> Der Schnitter/ halb-verschmacht/ dem Geist herwieder rufft.[65]

Praise of location as homage to the father of Lutheranism is given license here, but only in veiled terms. The Philosophers' Plaza and the St Johannis Tower, known for its echo effects, are further local details to which the young author guarantees enduring fame through the memorializing word. Jena owes its fame to its learned guests ('From guests your glory stems'), into whose ranks the penniless student is accepted as a promising young poet.

Archives: Biography and Sodality

Only now does the meeting occur with the fictive co-author, Klajus. It is wrapped in gently erotic allusions, whereby Birken briefly escapes the shadow of the Nuremberg model and imitates the author of *Hercinie*. In terms of the narrative itself, it amounts to only an intermezzo; then, having introduced Klajus, Floridan begins his second autobiographical presentation. Klajus, however, who has yet to present a poem, now sinks for pages on end to the level of a mute bystander, contrary to all rules of *Gesprächspiel* 'pastoral dialogue'.

Birken exploits the poetic license of the genre to recount the main stations of his life story, right up to the present.[66] Eger too is a 'free city' and home to the

---

[65] *FPS* 11.
Which Luther's thirst and burden formerly had stilled,
That holy man of God, within whose chilly walls
The reaper, deathly thirsting, to spirit life recalls.

[66] This information has served as the basis for his biography from Martin Limburger, *Die Betrübte Pegnesis: Den Leben, Kunst- und Tugend-Wandel des Seelig-Edlen Floridans, H. Sigm. von Birken . . . fürstellend* (Frankfurt a.M.: Funken, 1684), to Johann Herdegen, in *Historische Nachricht von deß löblichen Hirten- und Blumen-Ordens*

'druids schooled in theology' (15) – the Protestant pastors, before, that is, 'brutal revenge and hateful slander embittered the minds of the leading citizens'. Not only 'Glükk' (Fortuna) but also 'Geschikke' (Misfortune) played a role in the forced expulsion of Birken's family from Bohemia. No sooner had he begun to be introduced to the joys of pastoral life (education), than that too was marred, this time by the untimely death of his parents, 'such that I had to believe that a bad star must have poured its influence upon the hour of my birth, or else rose simultaneously with it, because Fate has pursued me relentlessly ever since' (16).

This struggle with unfathomable fate, conventional in pastoral, also serves a didactic purpose insofar as the orphaned child sees his 'destiny' as directed from above ('Yet I finally acquiesced, as was proper, in this my destiny, because I believed that it had been so determined by heaven'). He is 'admitted into the Book of Shepherds according to local custom', which is to say, granted the right of citizenship; his later academic transfer to Jena he also views as 'exclusively the decision of the council of heaven'. The contradictions endemic to the genre are invoked to emphasize 'what comforts there are in living in little huts and simple peasant cottages, free of the vain opulence of cities' buildings and vices', that is, when one undertakes at last to spend one's time in the pursuit of learning. It is the ever uncertain social status of the educated, particularly with respect to the unique role of the university, which existed outside of the social structure as such, that encourages distantiation from court and city alike and gives the nobilitas literaria its unique aura. Once again it is a 'decision of heaven' (17) that compels this student of law and history, theology and philosophy, back to Nuremberg before he has completed his studies and before Mercury, the 'nimble messenger of the gods and the world-traveling husband of Herse', is called into action.

With that, Strefon/Harsdörffer can now be introduced. That this occurs relatively early on is in deference to his great reputation; but narratologically as well, it allows Birken to grapple with his own fate the more intensively, not knowing what he has done to attract the 'fury' of heaven. The mythlike untying of his life's knot belongs to the art of pastoral biography. Against the fateful darkness that characterizes Birken's life, Harsdörffer's star shines all the more brightly. In his farewell poem to Jena (19–21), Birken's enigmatic fate again turns out to be the manifest will of 'heaven's high council'. What follows is a variation on the paradigm of Klaj's departure from Meissen for Jena: the 'Conjuration of Echo' (24–6), the 'Greeting on the Pegnitz' (26), and the 'Sonnet of Praise' to Strefon (27) are all part of it.

These poems are constructed in such a way that the next theme, the sodality's founding, is anticipated in them, though its technique is rather perfunctory. The

---

an der Pegnitz Anfang und Fortgang, 79–158 (Nuremberg: Riegel, 1744), to the twentieth-century biographies, esp. by Joachim Kröll, 'Sigmund von Birken dargestellt aus seinen Tagebüchern', *JfFL* 32 (1972): 111–50, and 'Sigmund Birken (1626–1681)', *Fränkische Lebensbilder* 9 (1980): 187–203. The biographical element was allowed in *Schäferei* as long as it served a poetic, moral, or reflective purpose.

account of the founding is placed in the mouth of Klajus, though it is doubtless Birken's invention. The amoebean singing competition, an essential component of bucolic poetry (*Idyll* 5 and 8; *Eclogue* 3 and 7), is obligatory, but in this case it occurs specifically in response to the contest in the *Pegnesisches Schäfergedicht*, where Fama had promised a wreath for the winner, though ultimately a decision could not be reached. Again Echo mediates the playful competition between the two founders, and again the decision remains open. This exceptionally well-crafted poem (29–31) allows Strefon and Klajus to voice their mockery of Echo at the end, when they do not understand her inconclusiveness; once they have come to their senses, however, they recognize the deeper wisdom of this goddess of grottoes, mountains, and valleys. It is from pastoral nature itself, in its embodiment as the goddess Echo, that the Pegnitz shepherds receive their societal emblem of wild flowers, which have 'crept artfully in among the laurel leaves', along with instructions on how they are to be used. On the one hand, the wild flowers symbolize the social distance between the aristocratic Fruchtbringende Gesellschaft and the urban sodality in Nuremberg, which 'henceforward will be called the Society of Shepherds of the Flowers' (32). On the other, the association that the flowers evoke with the laurel strengthens the urban claim to the privilege of bestowing poetic coronations. Birken will later make prudent use of it for advancing the social status of the sodality, but also his own social mobility. Each new member is granted a wild flower from the sodality's wreath under the condition that he 'work diligently to contribute useful improvements to our mother tongue – pure and elegant rhymed poems and clever inventions – and in general encourage its use.'

But the order on the Pegnitz proposed to do more than cultivate German language and poetry; and this broader aim is encoded in their prose eclogues. The subsequent 'Welcome to Spring' (34–6), each line of which is shared between two speakers, illustrates this purpose. Known for his detailed marginal notes, Birken indicates here that the origins of the society owed in part to Justus Georg Schottel: 'Animals and elements,' he writes, 'even inanimate objects speak German, as will be evident occasionally in this work' (34). No theoretician understood the relevance of the history and theory of language to the cultural and patriotic aims of the *Sprachgesellschaften* more keenly than Schottel. This explains not only his authority within the Fruchtbringende Gesellschaft but also his importance to the Nurembergers' notion of a humanist competition among Europe's poetic languages. In Schottel's view of language, the sounds of nature constitute part of its base, and the practice of onomatopoeic poetry in the vernacular therefore has implications that go far beyond the linguistic level to suggest a vital connection between language and politics.

Recent Political Imposition

No sooner have the shepherds expressed, in *Rükk-Reimlauf* 'mirror-rhyme',[67] thanksgiving for the 'refreshing and peaceful shadows', when the 'hail' and 'thunder' of war sounds in a four-stanza trochaic poem entitled 'The Tears of War': 'Your lead-heavy yoke . . . / . . . presses Mother Earth' (37). The 'harmony' and 'joyful care of peace' that belong to the pastoral world are perverted in a condition of war into 'evil luck', which calls for an outraged condemnation of civil war in Germany. This is expressed in a lengthy dialogue poem, 'Lamentation of War', which reads in part:

> NEhmt war/ wie öde liegt der Teutschen ädler Grund
> Wie macht den Mutterleib das Schwert der Kinder wund/
>   Die Söne balgen sich/ ihr Muht/ erhitzt von Kriegen/
>   Schmältz Städt und Länder ein/ die grimmen Krieger siegen
> In ihrem Mutterland/ vergiessen Brüderblut/
> Und wüten wider sich/ daß nie kein Tiger thut.
>   Wer solt jetzt teutsches Land auf Teutschen Boden finden?
> Das Alte liegt verwüst/ kein Neues gräbt man auf/
>   Es ist mit Brand verheert/ es stäubt noch mit den Winden.
> Kurtzkünftig bleibt ihm gar das Leben in dem Lauf.[68]

This complaint occurs repeatedly in pastoral, the genre-home of the purest, and most easily violated, of worlds. From the time of Vergil, the worst evil within the pastoral world has always been war, especially civil war, which wreaks its havoc on the shepherds, the citizens of the most innocent form of society. Its effect silences singing, causes shepherds to hang up their flutes, and halts all cultural enrichment. Klaj alludes to this tradition in an extraordinary image that illuminates the potential of the genre for historical criticism:

>   Ach! hengt die Flöten auf/
> Ihr Hirten/ brecht kein Rohr. Was ist/ das euch erfreuet/

---

[67] As Birken practices the form, the first line rhymes with the last, the second with the penultimate, and so forth, until eventually they meet in the middle.

[68] *FPS* 38.
> See now, how barren lie the noble German fields,
> How wounded Mother Earth by swords her children wield.
>   The sons, in selfish rage enflamed by war, will fight,
>   Reduce both town and land; grim warriors try their might
> Throughout the mother land, their brothers' blood they spill
> And lay each other waste, as tigers never will.
>   What German land exists in Germany today?
> The old has been destroyed, the new is not in sight.
>   By fire reduced to dust, the dust is blown away.
> And life's own sun runs down and vanishes in night.

>   Nun eure Felder gar mit Knochen überschneiet/
>   An Scheddeln trächtig sind? [. . .][69]

One would not anticipate seeing in pastoral landscape the features of Golgotha. But there they are, especially in the skulls, or in the line 'But where the serpent whistles, the poet tires of singing' (39), or in the reference to 'devilishness'. Only within the metaphorical field of original sin, the fall from the Creator's grace, are we able to see that the murderous war assumes implications beyond human suffering. To read Nuremberg pastoral correctly requires transposing the pagan to the theological realm. 'Here still is golden time': the lament echoes even here. But it is simultaneously an accusation. A vast horizon of meaning is opened up in terms of creation-theology in a threnody:

>   Wo soll es endlich hin? man dekket auch die Zinnen
>   Der Gottes-Tempel ab/ und Rosse wohnen drinnen.
>   Das Weibsvolk gibt man feil/ der Wiegen Unschuldt leidt/
>   (Die Teufel sind doch selbst in Menschen eingekleidt/)
>   Des Alters grauer Witz/ vor Zeiten hochgeehret/
>   Muß mit dem greissen Kopf hin auf die Metzelbank/
>   Offt hat auch eine Wund zwey Leben ausgeleeret/
>   Zwey Leben eines Leibs. Ich werde blaß und krank.[70]

The language and ideas recall Opitz's great consolatory war poem, *Trostgedicht in Widerwärtigkeit des Krieges*. Just how difficult it can be to maintain the proper aesthetic distance to such a realistic theme is obvious in Birken's occasional drift into the personal realm, as when a few lines later he recounts being robbed on the way from Jena to Nuremberg. It is left to Klaj to steer the narrative back onto historical ground with his lamentation of the fall of Magdeburg (40).

---

[69] *FPS* 38.
>   Oh! Hang your flutes up high,
>   You shepherds, break no reed. What cause to be elated,
>   When ev'rywhere your fields like snow with bones are sated,
>   With skulls their richest fruit? [. . .]

[70] *FPS* 40.
>   Where will it ever end? The spires have been pulled down
>   From God's own holy house, a horse's stable now.
>   Our women go for sale, the cradle's darlings weep
>   (And devils ev'rywhere in human fashion creep).
>   Gray wisdom of old age, beforetimes honor's pride,
>   Upon a chopping block its ancient head must lay.
>   A single wound at times has drained two lives of life –
>   One body but two lives. I sicken and grow pale.

Hero Panegyric in Pastoral

The sudden turn, a convention of prose eclogue, to the middle panegyrical section interrupts this development. Birken returns to Opitz's use, borrowed from Sannazaro, of the subterranean setting, but he goes beyond Opitz, and certainly beyond Harsdörffer and Klaj, by calling up ancient details of pastoral mythology on which to base the founding of his society. Suddenly the hillside opens up and Pan himself emerges (41). Pan is no stranger to the shepherds. The 'honorable Thyrsis', that is, Natale Conti ('Natales Comes', as Birken notes in the margin), described him as having a leopard skin thrown over his shoulder, in his left hand the seven-reed pipe, in his right hand the crooked staff, his horned head crowned with spruce leaves, and, of course, speaking the language of shepherds.[71] Pan's message is of the singular, eternal quality of virtue, whether practiced by shepherds or warriors.

> Ihr Hirten/ die ihr klagt und klinget/
> Die ihr den Kriegergreul besinget/
>   Ihr solt nicht also gar verfluchen
>   Den Krieg/ hier unter diesen Buchen.
> Die Tugend würket auch in Waffen/
> Mit Waffen muß man Frieden schaffen.
>   Ein Hertz/ das Löwenmuth bewohnet/
>   Ein dapfres Hertz/ wird auch belohnet.
> Es überlebt ein Held sein Leben/
> Und darf im Zelt der Sternen schweben/
>   Er wandert hoch mit dem Gerüchte/
>   Sein Ruhm wird nimmer nicht zu nichte.
> Kommt/ last/ ihr Hirten/ jetzt die Auen/
> Ich laß' euch Lust und Wunder schauen/
>   Ich/ euer Gott und eurer Heerden:
>   Kommt/ dieser soll gehütet werden.[72]

---

[71] *Natalis Comitis Mythologiae, sive Explicationum fabularum libri decem. In quibus omnia propre naturalis & moralis philosophiae dogmata sub antiquorum fabulis contenta fuisse demonstratur. Cum locuplettissimis indicibus eorum scriptorum, qui in his libris citantur, rerumque notabilium, et multorum nominum ad fabulas pertinentium explicationibus. Opus non tantum humanarum, sed etiam sacrarum literarum et philosophiae studiosis parutile, ac prope necessarium* (Venice, 1551).

[72] FPS 41–2.
> You shepherds who complain and moan,
> Who sing about the battle's woe,
>   Cease to curse of war's increases
>   Here among familiar beeches.
> Virtue lives in arms besides,
> And arms it is that peace-talk guides.
>   Hearts that swell with lion's nerve,
>   Valiant hearts praise too deserve.

The placement of the 'Lamentation of War' directly before the panegyric to the heroes of that war is understandable, since there is no middle ground between the two extremes; the good and the bad simply must be accepted as such, not least because the genre requires it. Guided by Pan, the shepherds leave their meadows in order to enter the heroic grotto. In this locale the pastoral dactyl and four-foot iambic line are replaced by epic alexandrines:

> Hier dieses ist der Ort/ der Held- und Thaten hält/
> Wo mancher Löwenmuht wird preißlich vorgestellt/
> Hier lebt der Tugend Lohn/ den nach dem Sterben erbt
> Der/ welcher rümlich stirbt und löblich hat gelebt:
> Wer so nach Ehren klimmt/ hat überwohl gestrebt/
> Du/ Fremder/ halte Fuß/ ließ/ was der Ruhm gekerbt:
> Sie hat das Lobgerücht nach Würden ausgemahlt/
> Die Feder ihren Geist/ der Pinsel die Gestalt.[73]

The relationship between poet and patron in prose eclogue is a personal one: Opitz honors his patron Hans Ulrich von Schaffgotsch; Fleming his friend from Reval, Rainer Brockmann; Gottfried Finckelthaus, the Leipzig poet of rustic verse, the patrician Schwenkfelder family. Birken abandons this practice in favor of praising the highest subject of the Thirty Years' War, its heroes. An outsider, Birken lacked the local familiarity necessary to address the patrician families of Nuremberg; still, praising the war's heroes was itself hardly less daring. Harsdörffer's consent must have been necessary, and even then only after receiving permission from the political leaders of the city.

The introduction maintains strict political neutrality,

> for, although such a war has thrown our common fatherland into awful destruction, courage nevertheless remains (the glory of which it is the

> A hero lives beyond his time,
> Within the star-filled tent sublime;
> Bestrides in glory heaven's glade,
> His fame to nought will never fade.
> Come, shepherds, now forsake your mead,
> To joys and wonders let me lead.
> I, your god and of your sheep;
> Come, all are safe, away with me.

[73] *FSP* 48.

> Of heroes and their deeds this gallery within
> Besings and calls to mind these lionhearted men.
> Here find their just reward beyond the grave all they
> Who died in honor's cause and lived by truth and faith.
> Who mounted to the sky has more than nobly strived.
> Thou, Stranger, pause and read these words by Fame inscribed,
> For Fame has here portrayed with great and worthy skill
> Their likeness with her brush, their spirit with her quill.

poet's duty to describe) a praiseworthy virtue, whether it exists in the hearts of friend or foe; for which reason we have portrayed it without preference for either side.[74]

On one side stand Philip IV and the Infant Ferdinand of Spain, as well as Louis XIII of France, and Wallenstein; on the other side, Gustav Adolf of Sweden, Prince Ulrich of Denmark, Moritz and William II of Orange, Bethlen Gabor, Christian of Anhalt, and Bernhard of Saxe-Weimar. The Catholic generals Spinola, Tilly, and Pappenheim stand opposite their Protestant counterparts, Counts Charles of Bucquoy and Ernest of Mansfeld, who, according to Birken's description of the portraits, are adorned with laurel wreaths after the fashion of Roman generals. But non-princely and non-aristocratic persons are honored in this pantheon as well, for example, Dietrich Falkenberg of Magdeburg, the royal adviser Johann Panner, and the Bavarian field marshal Franz von Mercy. What these persons lack in social stature is compensated by the transcendental virtue of true nobility. The hero identified only as Colonel Schlang is a good example:

> Obrister Schlang.
> Ich war von schlechtem Stand/ doch grösser am Gemüte
> Und an Verstand/ als der vom Fürstlichen Geblüte:
> Ein Held an Hertz und Witz/ der erste stäts vorm Feind/
> So fand mich auch der Tod. Mich lobet Feind und Freund.
> A. 1642.[75]

Birken takes care, at the end of the panegyrical section, to mesh the personal qualities of the twenty-four honorees with the events of the war. The 'Tablets of Praise' were to be kept in the cave, where they had been brought by nymphs from the home towns of the heroes, 'until the long-remembered flame should at last extinguish itself' (55). Although the horror of war cannot be mitigated by poetic means, the shepherds are nevertheless entrusted with preserving under all conditions historical remembrance against war's onslaught. As memory's agents from the protection of their bucolic refuge, the poets refuse to halt before local, regional, or even national borders; in thus carrying out their historical

---

[74] *FPS*)(3^v. 'dann/ obwohl solcher Krieg unser allgemeines Vatterland in höchstverderblichen Schaden gestürtzet/ so bleibt doch die Dapferkeit/ welcher Ruhmbeschreibung den Poeten oblieget/ an seinem Ort lobwürdig/ sie wohne gleich in Freundes oder Feindes Hertzen; massen wir auch einen ieden beederseits unparteyisch aufgeführet.'

[75] *FPS* 54.
> Colonel Schlang
> From lowly birth I came, but greater were my mind
> And judgment than that one who sprang from princely line.
> Hero in heart and word, first my land to defend:
> Death also found me thus: praised both by foe and friend.
> A.D. 1642.

responsibility, they provide a trust to the cultic centers, both here and elsewhere, now and in the future.[76]

The Allegory of Pan on the Pegnitz

Framing the hero panegyric is the presentation of the subterranean world of Pan and his followers, to which the equally important praise of the sodality is attached. No less a personage than Pan himself, god of shepherds, is made the patron of the order on the Pegnitz, given its devotion to art, virtue, and religious observance. Birken's challenge to his colleagues is provocative and can be advanced only because the Blumenorden had recently become engaged in the discussion of whether and to what degree pagan and Christian elements could justifiably be brought together in a syncretic relationship. At Pan's appearance 'fear so completely paralyzes' the shepherds that they cannot flee (42). From this point forward, under the guardianship of Pan and his faithful, the satyrs and forest gods, the astonished shepherds are simply led and instructed. As was the Gallery of Heroes, Pan's grotto is filled with 'many stories and historical exampla'. At Pan's high bidding, the 'goat-footed men' show 'these particular shepherds' that none in the supernatural world are dearer to the lowly gods of field and meadow than the members of this 'honorable shepherds' society' (43). The portraits in the Gallery of Heroes are of glistening gold; the stories of lower mythology associated with Pan are gracefully inscribed on the round walls of the cave. Here too Thyrsis is the authority. The shepherds are moved by the fate of their unfortunate social counterpart, the satyr Marsyas, who challenged Apollo to a musical competition, failed, and was horribly punished.[77] Pallas, born from the head of Jupiter, and the inventor of the shepherd's horn, is present, as is Mercury, who robbed Apollo of his bow, quiver, and lyre, and Mulcibar of his hammers. And so forth.

That which exists above as the mythical subject of pastoral poetry appears prefigured in the grotto world below. The intimate connection between the two spheres is suggested by the satyrs' acceptance, on behalf of the 'great Pan', of the simple gifts of milk and honey offered by the shepherds, not in some placeless and timeless Arcadia, but on the shores of the Pegnitz in the here and now. With or without its rustic trappings, however, pastoral poetry, like humanist lyric poetry, is typically love poetry. In the present instance this is seen in two Cupid

---

[76] Birken's employment of historical examples demonstrates prose eclogue's further affinity with the mirror of princes genre; indeed, he does so with unsurpassed virtuosity. The dynastic memorial panegric within the medium of prose eclogue was one of the chief literary occupations of his life, developing eventually from an urban into a courtly vehicle.

[77] Ov., *Met.* 6.385–400, describes how Marsyas took Athena's flute to compete with Apollo and, having lost, was skinned alive; the tears shed for him by his friends turned into the clearest river in Phrygia.

figures of clear alabaster and in two nymphs of pure white marble, the verisimilitude of which is so great that the shepherds 'at first glance deemed [them] to be real nymphs and gods' (45). The nymphs in fact are none other than Echo and Syringa (the seven-reeded Pan's pipe seen on the title-page). Their fate is closely bound to that of Pan, to whose 'biography and stories' a particularly elegant passage is devoted (46). In the place where Pan invites his playmates to dance,

> an altar, overgrown with multicolored wild flowers, arose from the earth; numerous gifts from the shepherds already lay upon it. At its four corners there climbed four candle-like firs (trees long holy to Pan), arching up to the ceiling, which was quite high, where their heavily leafed arms offered themselves to each other, as it were, and, in their unity, formed a lovely roof over the altar. To its side could be seen a long slab of earth, rectangular and symmetrical, in the shape of a table, at which, perhaps, Pan and the satyrs would eat and drink.[78]

Not far from the altar reside the three Fates, whose task it is to 'make decisions regarding the life and death of humans' (47). Of these three Clotho is intent on 'spinning pure gold from several learned German men'. Who could these men be?

> 'The reason, however, that Pan came with his three sisters from Arcadia to this place,' said one of the four, 'is because the former location became inhabited by wild and untamed people who knew nothing about worship of the gods; what is more, the newly formed shepherds' society on the Pegnitz had persuaded him to select this place for his home, where he would be best taken care of by the gifts and songs of its members, so he hoped.'[79]

In this hope, the satyr chronicler adds, Pan has not been deceived. 'He is therefore particularly indebted to the founder of that group, as well as to all of its members,

---

[78] *FPS* 46–7. 'ein Altar/ mit mannich färbichen Feldblumen bewachsen von der Erden erhube/ auf welchem allbereit etliche Hirtengeschenke geliefert stunden: An den vier Ekken desselben stiegen vier kertzengerade Fichten (welcher Baum dem grossen Pan von langen Zeiten her heilig gewesen) bis an die Dekke des Gemaches/ welche zimlich hoch sich zeigete/ woselbst sie ihre dikkbelaubten Arme einander gleichsam boten/ und mit Vereinigung derselbigen den Altar fast anmutig überdacheten. Allernächst diesem war ein langes/ vierekkichtes und gleichförmiges Stükk Erde/ in Form einer Tafel/ zu sehen/ woran vielleicht der Pan mit den Satyren Speiß und Trank zu nehmen pflegete.'

[79] *FPS* 47. 'Die Ursach aber/ daß sich Pan mit seinen 3. Schwestern aus Arcadien an dieses Ort begeben/ meldete einer unter den vieren/ diese zu seyn/ weil besagte Gegend der Zeit von wilden und ungezämten Leuten bewohnet würde/ die von Verehrung der Götter gar nichts wüsten/ zu deme so hätte ihn auch/ sein Erdgemache der Orten auszuwälen/ bewogen die an der Pegnitz neu aufgerichtete Hirtengesellschaft/ von deren Mitgliederen seiner mit Geschenken und Liedern am bästen würde gepfleget werden/ er verhoffete.'

and wishes to grant both of you a special favor today in order to inspire you to even greater service and worship' (48). As a sign that 'the great Pan favors you and the members of your society above all others' (57), he gives each shepherd a small jewel having the shape of a reed pipe, 'which he had previously carved from a reed belonging to one of his nymphs', and binds the gift with a promise:

> [H]e will from henceforth be your good Pan: your meadows shall always have fat cattle, your sheep shall give milk twice daily, you shall live securely in your huts, your herds shall be free from the danger of wolves, no accidental illness shall reduce their numbers, and their increase shall exceed the flocks of others from year to year. In short, he will make of you the happiest and most blessed of shepherds and help you in sundry ways; those who are dear to the gods because of their loyalty and devotion shall be richly rewarded.[80]

With an observation (in imitation of *Hercinie*) on the Schwartzbach springs[81] and a description of the Rednitz and Pegnitz rivers along which the shepherds wander as they leave Pan, the subterranean episode ends.

Birken is careful here, in contrast to much of his later practice, not to subject the mythological narrative to explicit allegorical interpretation, giving instead only hidden clues about how to understand the text properly. Only the foreword provides clear indications of the author's intent:

> No one could or should take offense at the interlarded stories of the gods, if it is kept in mind that the learned pagans themselves did not mean things to signify what they really are, but often rather to express with these names and what they imply the highest virtues and the lowest vices in didactic poems (*Apologiae*). What Plinius writes concerning the divine groves bears repeating: 'We do not so much pray to the images on the columns, which are adorned with gold and ivory, as to the groves and the mute silence within them.' By 'Pan' (whom I otherwise avoid) they understood the whole (το πᾶν, *universum*), that is, everything that occurs in nature.[82]

---

[80] *FPS* 57. 'daß er hinfort euch wolle ein gütiger Pan seyn: Eure Auen sollen immerzu fette Weide haben/ Eure Schafe sollen des Tags zwier können gemolken werden/ ihr solt in euren Hürden sicher wohnen/ eure Heerden sollen frey seyn von Gefärden des Wolfes/ keine zufällige Krankheit soll ihre Zahl ringeren/ sondern sie sollen järlich vor andern merklich zunehmen/ und kurtz/ er will aus euch die gesegnetesten unnd seligsten Hirten machen/ unnd an euch vielfältig darthun/ wie hoch beglükket werden die jenigen/ so wegen ihrer Treu und Frömmigkeit den Göttern lieb sind.'

[81] The frequently-occurring motif of the spring derives from the Aristaeus episode of the *Georgics*.

[82] *FPS*)(3ᵛ–4ʳ. 'An denen eingemengtem Göttergeschichten wird und kan sich auch niemand ärgern/ wann er bedenket/ daß sie auch bey den gelehrten Heiden dasselbige nicht/ was sie eigentlich sind/ bedeuten/ sondern oft mi[t] solchen Nahmen/ und was denen zugeeignet/ die schönsten Tugenden und schändlichsten Lastere zu lieben und hassen in (*Apologis*) Lehrgedichten vorgestellet werden[.] Nachdenklich ist/ was von den Götzen-

Birken's *Fortsetzung* aggressively joins in the controversy over the admissibility of classical mythology in modern poetry, specifically German pastoral. His answer is clear. It is not only admissible, it is essential if we moderns are to take advantage of the opportunities available in the renewal of classical poetry. Readers are therefore challenged to familiarize themselves with at least those authorities cited by Birken and to know the allegorical meanings of the mythical names, images, and stories. Armed with this knowledge, the texts in praise of pastoral life can be properly understood.

Interestingly, Birken makes reference to both Natale Conti and Francis Bacon in his foreword but only to Conti in the main text. In the foreword to his *Mythologia* the Venetian Conti offers a sophisticated philosophical decoding of ancient mythology. His primary concern, however, is to produce a new mythology handbook, a compilation and classification of the many attributions and interpretations by the gods in the various traditions. By contrast, Bacon's concern with understanding myth's power to connect the ages before and after the advent of writing revolutionized exegetical method. He argues that all 'original truths' extrapolated from myth are demonstrably components of one's own philosophy. With Bacon a philosophy of myth is no longer just a philosophy; questions of filiation are of value only insofar as they are useful in separating invalid from valid elements of transmission. But neither is Bacon's method reducible to transmission criticism. The *sapientia veterum* 'wisdom of the ancients' is simultaneously present and liquidated in Bacon's philosophies of nature, morals, state, and society. In an overpowering, multi-perspectivist act of appropriation, he achieves a holistic coherence between truth and method, totality and particularity. The disruptions implied in Bacon's analysis of the philosophy of nature appealed to the self-taught and exceptionally open-minded Harsdörffer. Birken, for his part, preferred to rely on the narrative material at hand in Natale Conti's encyclopedia of mythology.

Conti attributes three functions to Pan: nature, sun, and general influence in the world. In conceptualizing Pan as the 'totality of all things', or simply 'nature', Birken, however, shows an affinity with Bacon. To Schottel, Pan is 'all nature, or the universality of all things'. Harsdörffer, who had previously related 'The History, or Poem, of Pan, Pastoral or Forest God of Shepherds' – which, he adds, 'would not be unuseful or inappropriate to the type of poetry that deals with rich green pastures' – calls Pan 'the entire world structure'.[83] All four sources provide detailed descriptions of Pan's body, insignia, and deeds, as well as the interpretation of the members of his retinue. With regard to Pan's birth, Harsdörffer borrows Bacon's theological-materialist explanation: 'Pan is the

---

Häinen Plin. schreibet: wir beten nicht so sehr an die an Gold und Helffenbein zierreiche Seulbilder/ als die Häyne/ und in ihnen das stumme Stillschweigen. Mit dem Pan (daß ich anders vorbeygehe) haben sie dieses Gantze (το πᾶν, *universum*) das ist/ alles/ was in der Natur befindlich/ verstanden.'

[83] *FzG* 4.17.

entire world structure, which came about either from Mercury (the Word of God) or, as some have reasoned, from that minute particle of dust, which, as primeval matter, or stuff, was mixed into a variety of forms.' Harsdörffer goes on to develop the Pan–Mercury affinity in a manner suited to pastoral. 'That [Pan] comes immediately after Mercury may be taken to mean that the world, after the Word of God, is our best preacher, as the Prophet Poet sings: "The heavens declare the glory of God; and the firmament sheweth his handywork."'[84] Birken radically reduces the allegorical pallet by encapsulating Pan's meaning as 'this entirety (τὸ πᾶν, *universum*) . . . everything that occurs in nature' and ignoring, in stark contrast to the extensive allegorizing of his later pastorals, the interpretation of details. All the more important, then, is his rich metaphorical and technical structuring and, accordingly, the integration of Pan's world into that of pastoral.

But let us return now to the text of the *Fortsetzung* itself. The very roundness of the moss-covered cave reminds of the round temple where Pan resides (46). The ceremony involving the 'happy dance' of the 'Napaeae, Orestiads, Dryades, Hamadryades, etc. (which grow young with the oaks and, when these are cut down, die again with them)', recalls the Dionysian cultic dance and sacrifice. The altar of Pan, reserved for the 'gifts' of the shepherds, is decorated with the Pegnitz societal emblem of wild flowers. The spruce trees, also familiar in the Dionysian realm, are apostrophized as 'having been sacred to Pan since time immemorial' (47). The Dionysian affinity continues in the role of the Muses, who are entrusted to the care of the 'learned Germans'. Combined with these Dionysian allusions are biblical ones. For example, the altar table at which Pan eats and drinks with the satyrs evokes association with the Last Supper. But in the most drastic biblical allusion, the fiction nearly breaks down. It occurs in the moment when the shepherds are exhorted to fulfill their poetic mission and are sent forth with Pan's pipe (57), an unavoidable comparison with the paraenetic (Gk. παραινέω) words of St Paul in Acts 27:9 and 22. In fact, even Pan's promise to be a 'good Pan' is properly understandable only in terms of the New Testament, and this is a clear indication that a reversal from pagan to Christian conceptualization in pastoral has taken place in Germany. His promise of protection covers not only learning and poetry, but life itself.

Immediately upon leaving this subterranean world the shepherds offer a poem of praise to Pan. At first he is presented as a woodland wanderer and, in an echo of the Song of Songs (2:14, 5:2), as a cooing dove, filled with desire for his fleeing lover (59). As the poem develops, however, two thematic centers form: the growth of poetry and the escape from war. The 'droning' of Pan's pipe fills the 'udders' of the 'flocks', which is to say, it is the source of the Pegnitz shepherds' songs. The poetry of nature is deeply creative; even the 'trickling brooks' 'whisper with the piping sounds'. By the same token, nature's power can horrify and paralyze – further intimation of the Dionysian sphere – as reflected in the 'Anblikk' (look) that bewitches the enemies of shepherds and poetry (60).

---

[84] *FzG* 4.19.

Evil is incarnate in the pastoral world as the 'gluttonous wolf', the 'furious beast', which 'With blood of lambs besprinkles all our fields / And seeks to swallow all our flocks.'[85] The entire moral universe, creational order itself, which is associated allegorically with Pan, is threatened by the destructive power of evil. Pan's enchanting glance, however, 'can frighten the evil ones' by affecting them with 'cold heat'; it is likened to the 'lightning there that comes from cloudy bank', the instrument of divine punishment of a sinful world. In the lines of Klajus, based on the Typhoeus material in Conti's *Mythologia*, Pan can be a 'bold warrior', not unlike warring Jehovah. His pipe and sacred spruce grove must never fall victim to 'mad Mars', this 'murder-fevered guest'. Thus the pastoral realm asserts itself once again in the laudatory speech to Pan, now a Christian counteractive force to the malignant powers in history that bear the mark of Cain for their outrages against creation.

Orphic Song and Institutional Identity

In the second half of the *Fortsetzung*, the Pegnitz shepherds Birken and Klaj, Harsdörffer and Hellwig, Samuel Hund and Johann Sechst, are united in song; only Christoph Arnold is absent, being away at Altdorf University, though he too is tacitly included in the opening 'Dedication to All Lovers and Notable Patrons of the German Language.'[86] Attention turns first to the wild-flower emblems, which are replete with allusions to the uniqueness of shepherd life. The myrtle of Myrtillus (Hund) is a 'tiny and common but beautiful fruit' (64). The wild rose of Lerian (Arnold) does not scratch the shepherd, who is 'known for duty as for right', but does wound the courtier, who 'considers falsehood right'. The violet of Alcidor (Sechst) reseeds itself in the protected 'shadows dark and brown', where 'decor and thing are joined', in 'heav'nly favor's shadow' (65). Strefon's lilies of the valley blossom, watered by the tears of the nymphs, beneath the 'shadow's wing': 'In the haughty flower garden / Such a thing cannot be found.' The wild carnation of Montano (Dr Hellwig) enlivens the senses with its aroma, and its extract is an antidote to poison: 'And reason too is sharpened by virtue when it rises, / The pois'nous adder's vice is naught to virtuous hearts' (65–6). Klajus's clover, trampled under the feet of Pan, springs back towards the shepherd god, now boldly analogized as a poet: just as he 'signifies the whole of things', so does the poet embrace 'this comprehensive world: / fire and air, earth

---

[85] A history of the wolf allegory in pastoral would be welcome. It was first there in Vergil but entered early modern literature, prepared by the symbolism of the *Divine Comedy*, mainly through Sannazaro's *Arcadia* in reference to the fall of Naples. Cf. Milton: 'Besides what the grim wolf with privy paw / Dayly devours apace, and little sed' (*Lycidas* ll. 128–9).

[86] Samuel Hund, from Meissen (fl. 1650), historian and court adviser; Johann Sechst, from Elnbogen in Bohemia (1636–74), corrector in the Endter printing house in Nuremberg; Christoph Arnold, from Hersbruck near Nuremberg (1627–85), well-traveled (including England) and prolific scholar at the Auditorium Egidianum.

and water'. Finally, Floridan's marigold arises from the blood of the nymphs wounded in the hunt, its velvet filling even emeralds with envy.

Thus pastoral emblematics are interwoven with contrastive signs of above and below. Pan's pipe – gift of the gods, 'symbol of the order' (67, margin), which, along with the wild flowers, 'distinguishes [this sodality] from all the others' – will be used by the shepherds to make such music that 'The wide-rumored fame of our poems like stars in the heavens will shine.' Their motto 'In Usefulness Joyful' can be concretized in the pastoral sphere only in oppositional terms: 'burdensome' money and 'vain' honor are the insignia of society at large; but the shepherds' natural state, under the protection of Pan, is dedicated solely to the mind and creativity.

At this moment Strefon produces from his pocket a verse epistle, called 'Rose Song' (68), which he has received from Lerian, whose silk membership ribbon is adorned with a wild rose. Once again the language of the Song of Songs resonates in the opening stanza. Having established the spiritual connotations of this rose garden, Arnold launches into a game of word associations typical of the Nuremberg manner.[87] Envy exists in the courtly world of *minne* 'love', but it also intrudes into the bucolic realm as a dangerous foreign presence. This paradox seems to have been spun out of language itself. The wild-rose emblem carries within itself its opposite, 'wanton envy'; the perspicacious shepherd transforms it poetically into a positive asset.

> Wiltu/ loser Neid/ dich weiden/
>   Uns aussaugen Blut und Kraft?
> Ha! dein knirschend-tolles Neiden
>   heilt der Rosen Wurtzelsaft.
> Last die Kettenhunde mukken/
> Keiner wird uns gantz verschlukken.[88]

This artful game is now adapted, at Strefon's suggestion, to the Petrarchan theme of pastoral solitude. The choice to employ alexandrine verse owes to the fact that it contains a natural caesura: $\smile /\smile /\smile / \| \smile / \smile / \smile / (\smile)$. This is a particularly useful coincidence in the present instance, since the poetic game is built on the fiction that the page on which the poem was originally written has been torn down the middle, precisely separating the second half-line from the

---

[87] The use of verbal play is a probe for deeper meaning. Such ludic experimentation is often visible in even the tiniest details and gives Nuremberg poetry its unique *utile et dulce* character.

[88] *FPS* 68.
> You, wanton envy, wish to smile,
>   Suck away our strength and blood?
> Ha! your grinding-madd'ning guile's
>   Cured by dose of rose's root.
> Let the chain-dogs bellow freely,
> None will swallow us completely.

first; the three shepherds must restore the missing second half-lines. Their three poems demonstrate different technical, artistic, and intellectual solutions. The first poet has a positive view of solitude:

| Ich liebe diesen Ort/ | | der ferne von Geschrey |
| Mich auf so ödem Weg | | fürt aller Sorgen frey.[89] |

In his dactylic *Abgesang* 'conclusion' he adds a certain cautionary note, however:

Einsamkeit lehret		die lieblichsten Lieder/
Lieder die lauten		in Felsen herwieder.
Aber wir sollen		die Wildnisse hassen
Weil sie verursacht		die Schäfer zu lassen.[90]

For those estranged from society at large, the pastoral world offers full sociability among peers. Its hallmark is honest 'simplicity', the quality generated in the first half-line of the alexandrine: peace and quiet, 'trusting with an open heart', absence of 'false exchange', and 'deep concern and suffering'.

What, the second poet asks, is 'the heaviest torment?' The 'lying mien of truth'. Accordingly, no negative restriction is implied in the dactylic conclusion to this second version. The simple life in all its purity is antithetical to the 'city's splendor':

Ich liebe diesen Ort/		der sonder Hofarts-pracht
Mich auf so ödem Weg		mir selbst selb-eigen macht.
Es überschattet mich		mein unversehrt Gewissen/
Wo sich mit dem Gesang		die Freuden reich ergiessen.[91]

The consistent theme of solitude returns again in the third poem, somewhat modified:

| Einsamkeit krönet | | die Anger und Auen/ |
| Mahnet die Hirten | | und Herden zu schauen. |

---

[89] *FPS* 72.
    This place I dearly love, | which far from human cries,
    By solitary path | my careless footstep guides.

[90] *FPS* 72.
    Solitude teaches | the loveliest airs,
    Airs ever sounding | on cliff faces bare.
    But should the wildness | our hatred inspire,
    Shepherds provoking | from fields to retire.

[91] *FPS* 74.
    This place I dearly love, | which far from splendor vain
    By solitary path | helps self-reliance gain.
    O'ershadowed all the while | by conscience full untroubled,
    Where'r with singing greeted, | my joys of life redoubled.

> Nimmermer werd ich | die Wildnisse hassen/
> Welche reitzt Hürden | die Schäfer zu lassen.[92]

Solitude and sociability are the two halves, which, integrated, complete the pastoral ideal.

A clever 'letter-multiplication' game follows (77–8), in which each shepherd is challenged to use the first letter of his name as often as possible in a quatrain. That done, Montano now joins Strefon in a friendly poetic competition on the subjects of virtue and heroism (79). Whereas Harsdörffer praises heroic courage, Dr. Hellwig, the convinced advocate of civic responsibility, recalls the Golden Age, when virtue was at its height. The 'bygone days' in which 'golden virtue' shone was the time when shepherds populated the world:

> Ein jeder war/ zwar bey geringer Haab/
> > Im Ruhestand/
> Ernehrte sich mit seinem Schäferstab/
> > Und fettem Land.[93]

There was neither 'bronze nor silver', 'war nor soldier's pay'. Against this, who would dare to praise 'steel and iron', the presence of which reminds one of 'the end of time'?

> Man wuste nicht die Wörter Dein und Mein:
> > Das Sorgengeld
> War dazumahl in schlechtem Wehrt und Schein
> > Bey aller Welt.
> Man tauschete nur Wahr üm Wahre/
> Ohn Meucheltrug/ List und Gefahre:
> Zu dieser unsrer Zeit muß Falschheit redlich seyn.[94]

---

[92] *FPS* 76.
> Solitude crowning | the pastures and mead,
> Urges the shepherds | and flocks to give heed.
> Nevermore wildness | our hatred inspire,
> Forcing our flocks | from fields to retire.

[93] *FPS* 79.
> All lived then, though little did they own,
> > In peaceful stand,
> Nourished well by shepherd's staff alone,
> > And fatted land.

[94] *FPS* 80.
> One did not know such words as 'yours' and 'mine':
> > Base currency
> Away back then had neither worth nor shine
> > On land or sea.
> One traded only same for same,
> No false exchange, no subtle game:
> Dishonesty's become a virtue in our time.

These images from Hesiod are not to be taken literally, of course. Nevertheless, they do express regulatory ideas that can be applied critically to real social conditions. Johann Fischart, in the last quarter of the previous century, was the first in Germany to exploit the praise of bourgeois virtues towards critical ends; Hellwig renews the practice here and elsewhere in pastoral form with respect to urban life.[95] The shepherd who is undistracted by societal problems, the scholar who has a sovereign grasp of it all: in both roles he is called upon as speaker and sentinel, as it were, because he acts directly from the center of a specific form of life immune to the temptations of society. As learned shepherd he speaks on behalf of the whole. The contrasting life forms and social spheres allow, in precise analogy to the Christian conversion of values, that which is presumably lower to be understood as that which is higher and nobler. Pastoral *otium*, while always desirable, becomes the neo-Stoic ideal of tranquillity, of *beatitudo* fulfilled.

There was no literary figure that more fully embodied the integration of poetic and learned, moral and religious ideals, than the shepherd. In the literary competitions of the shepherds, such as that between Floridan and Klajus that follows, neither can be said to outdo the other, since their respective positions are equally exemplary statements of pastoral ideals.

>   Klajus
> UNsrer Hürden Hirtenlust ist noch vielen unbewust.
>   Wer in satten Lebens-Tagen
>   Seglet nach der Sorgen Rand
>   Und der Freuden Zeitbehagen/
>   Liebe Schaf und Schäferstand/
> Hasse hochbefürte Dächer und der Städte Goldgemächer.
>
>   Floridan
> Unsrer Hürden Hirtenlust ist noch vielen unbewust.
>   Wo lebt Ruhe sonder rasten/
>   Wo schwebt lieber Freyheit Thron?
>   Wo gläntzt helles Tugend-glasten/
>   Und der Unschuld Perlen-Krohn?
> Freylich freyes Schäferleben kan die wahre Wollust geben.
>
> . . .
>
>   Floridan
> Unsrer Hürden Hirtenlust ist noch vielen unbewust.
>   Es darf Neid und Haß nicht dulden/
>   Weil er Hof und Hofart flieht/

---

[95] See Fischart's *Das Glückhafft Schiff von Zürich: Ein Lobspruch, vonn der Glücklichen und Wolfertigen Schiffart, einer Burgerlichen Geselschafft auß Zürich* (Strasbourg: Jobin, 1577). For Hellwig, see part IV of this essay, pp. 165–204, 'Return to the Urban Community.'

Nicht den scheelen Sorgen hulden/
Weil sein Thun auf Unschuld siht:
Und was sonst für nütze Sachen die aus Schäfern Fürsten machen.[96]

Hylas, Macaronic Pseudo-Shepherd

Curator and innovator of the mother language, the shepherd is always stalked by the macaronic pseudo-shepherd, Hylas, who corrupts pure language by the admixture of barbarisms. Hylas combines the conceits of the ridiculous knight and the à la mode dandy. His home, sometimes the court, is usually the town. Floridan remarks sarcastically that Hylas has 'crawled out of the citizen's coat and into the shepherd's jacket' (87). He is a grotesque figure, like Don Quixote, a dupe who takes words at face value and thereby throws his world into confusion. The classical use of the grotesque in pastoral is Charles Sorel's *Berger Extravagant* (1627). What is lampooned as amorous fantasy in Sorel, however, is treated in German prose eclogue as a travesty on those who corrupt language, who disfigure the vernacular by 'linguistic adulteration'. The Gallicisms in this case mimic courtly usage; the apostrophe to Neride employs Petrarchan clichés with absurd earnestness. Hylas misunderstands learned, particularly erotic and pastoral, literature. A linguistic 'adventurer', he believes 'all the sinful lies of the old poets, as though they were to be taken literally, indeed, as though they were the natural truth itself'. This gross error is an insult to true poets, who have cultivated, ever since Boccaccio and Petrarch, a style of poetry employing complex references.

---

[96] *FPS* 84–6.

Klaj
Joys of flocks we shepherds know in others rarely root and grow.
   Who life's weary journey's measured,
     Sails for where all sorrows fade,
   Where begins unending pleasure:
     Love both sheep and pastor's trade,
Scorn the highly vaulted ceilings and the city's golden chambers.

Floridan
Joys of flocks we shepherds know in others rarely root and grow.
   Where is quiet without flight,
     Or sways the precious freedom throne?
   Where the gleam of virtue bright,
     And innocence's pearly crown?
Unencumbered shepherd's life provides the pleasure that is real.

. . .

Floridan
Joys of flocks we shepherds know in others rarely root and grow.
   Hate and envy come to naught;
     Shepherds flee both court and pride,
   Troubling cares are all forgot,
     Ev'ry act is aimed for right:
All that's said and done for good, this turns shepherds into princes.

The pleasure Birken takes at the end of the *Fortsetzung* in parodying Hylas runs on to an inordinate length and disturbs the work's proportions.[97] This blemish to the form, however, makes his point forcefully. Birken's intention is to present a contrasting image of linguistic abuse to the ancient poetic and mythological tradition by which pastoral shepherds preserved their existence.

The Good Shepherd

The work concludes much as it began, with a devotional song, now of course to Evening (101–2), in four strophes. Pan belongs to the realm of lower mythology; however, as god of learned shepherds and their flocks, he takes on a new role in the intellectual and social history of late humanism. The shepherds accept his protection, knowing their flocks will be safe from the wolves, because they recognize in him *the* shepherd, that is, the Good Shepherd of the Bible. This imagistic cosmos Birken reserves for the concluding spiritual poem. In Birken's view, spiritual poetry represented nothing less than the telos of pastoral allegorical interpretation: the purified expression of poetic humanism.

> Gott/ wir danken deiner Güte/
>   Daß wir frölich treiben ein.
> Uns erfreute dein Gehüte:
>   Unsers unsre Schäfelein.
> Grosser Schäfer/ dich erhebt/
> Was in dunkeln Büschen bebt.
>   Was doch sollen wir dir schenken?
>   Unser Dank ist nur ein Denken.[98]

IV. Return to the Urban Community: Johann Hellwig's 'Die Nymphe Noris'

The connection with the *Pegnesisches Schäfergedicht* is not reestablished by title in the third Nuremberg prose eclogue. With his *Die Nymphe Noris* [see Plate 5] Dr Johann Hellwig, the self-assured son of Nuremberg, joins in the praise-of-city

---

[97] Encompassing some 10 pages (86–95).
[98] *FPS* 101–2.
> Lord, our thanks for thy affection,
>   That our lives in joy we lead.
> We delight in thy protection:
>   Loved ones in the sheep we feed.
> O Great Shepherd, thou art raised
> E'en by lowly creatures' praise.
>   Can we give back what we ought?
>   All our thanks is not but thought.

Plate 5   *Die Nymphe NORIS IN Zweyen Tagzeiten vorgestellet [. . .] DURCH einen Mitgenossen der PegnitzSchäfer etc.* Nürnberg: Jeremia Dümler, 1650. Frontispiece.

tradition through the figure of the nymph who gave the city its name.[99] In his preface, to be sure, Hellwig does indicate at least a chronological, or sequential, connection with the two preceding works:

> Said author has also employed, to his great pleasure, this very style in the present modest work, with the intention thereby of providing the loyal devotees of pure German language the third and fourth continuation, or, the third and fourth part, of the Pegnitz Pastoral, which was begun recently by other noted Pegnitz shepherds (among whose unworthy colleagues he may be counted).[100]

The Poet's Commitment to Civic Humanism

The author has very much his own view of things, however, and an impressive arsenal of stylistic fireworks with which to articulate it. As a physician, Hellwig was not professionally occupied with the life of letters. Nevertheless, at the same time he saw himself, as every learned man did, bound to 'his pledge to do more in the execution of the German heroic language, to investigate its pure sources, and to be an example for others' (4). This ancient German 'heroic language' is not some showy artifact to be constantly and artfully refined and retuned. It is rather a precious yet stable vessel for the forming of pure and noble poetic thoughts, which in turn become a guide to proper moral conduct. The goal of 'well-wrought' writing is 'to put to paper something good and useful and of benefit to the times'. Books of this sort, however, have a difficult fate. Bookshops are full of them, but they have no buyers. Yet they contain something invaluable. One does not write for 'vain honor and one's own name'. In an ingenious trope, Hellwig insists that art not give in to the 'common heap, even when standing in its rotten midst'. The 'sweetened words and wit' intend to reach the 'coarse rabble', and ultimately to 'ban sin and bring true virtue to the citizenry, and allow good people to enjoy soothing diversion and the sinful to feel deep regret'. For the skeptic and realist, the Horatian *utile cum dulce* is shifted in favor of *utile*; the thought-laden didactic language recalls the attitudes of the town watchman of the urban poet Johann Fischart.

---

[99] *Die Nymphe Noris in zweyen Tagzeiten vorgestellet* (Nuremberg: Dümler, 1650). Edition: Max Reinhart, *Johann Hellwig's 'Die Nymphe Noris' (1650): A Critical Edition* (Columbia, SC: Camden House, 1994). Hellwig derived the name from Eobanus Hessus, who resided in Nuremberg between 1526 and 1533. Eobanus (*Epicedia* 11.174) personified Nuremberg as a lovely benefactress of poets. Her prototype in European literature is Boccaccio's *Ninfale fiesolano*.

[100] *Noris* 5. 'Dieser Schreibart nun hat sich besagter Urheber/ mit Ergetzung seiner selbsten/ in diesem Werklein auch gebraucht/ und solcher Massen die dritte und vierdte Fortsetzung/ oder den dritten und vierdten Theil der PegnitzSchäferey/ die von andern wolbelobten PegnitzSchäfern (für derer unwürdigen Mitgenossen er sich auch erkennet) unlangsten angefangen worden/ den treuen Liebhabern der reinen Teutschen Sprache an die Hand geben wollen.'

Hellwig's *Nymphe Noris* teaches that these virtues, grounded on the assumption of a firm class consciousness, had hardly been exhausted by the middle of the seventeenth century. This motivated the cultivation of a type of pastoral composition in which urban poets found a unique voice, different from the Opitzian model, but by no means to be associated with that of 'Spruchsprecher und Fabelhannsen' (5, pundits and anecdotists), whose verse is one-dimensional and whom Hellwig therefore targets for ridicule. True poetry weds inventiveness with what is useful. It is able to 'hide edifying lessons behind such lovely masks'; behind its words 'there exists something greater or higher' that relies on judgment and aesthetic understanding and whose deeper meaning can be apprehended only by the 'perspicacious reader'. At the same time, however, its beautiful appearance entices the reader to embark on certain missions of discovery, such as exploring the playful side of language, which Harsdörffer has adapted from the Spanish. But Hellwig's dominant theme, as he insists, is to offer a description

> of his dear fatherland, to whose honor he has felt especially obliged to undertake this modest work, whereby he has not only depicted, with his poetic brush, its landscape so richly blessed by God, but also sought to paint in lively fashion its highly renowned government, including its noble families, most memorable historical events, and notable buildings, all of this accompanied by suitable instructional commentary, hoping thus to have adequately served those who are yet to come, with encouragement and admonition, to virtue and honorable imitation.[101]

The humanist tradition of praising and commemorating a place is revived now by Hellwig for the urban community. More clearly than his colleagues showed in their pastorals, Hellwig is motivated by a commitment to protect the ethos and maxims of the city, especially of the ruling class, from decay and to pass them on to future generations as a binding legacy. We gain a clear sense from Hellwig's work of the threat to which the city-state was subjected in the middle of the seventeenth century. Hellwig responds by applying the moral and religious values that derive from the spirit of older civic humanism.

It is pastoral, prose eclogue in Nuremberg, with its devotion to history and public affairs, to which this ethos can be ascribed, more so than to heroic and love poetry, in which elevated and ornamental courtly language dominates. For Hellwig, to belong to the 'lowly shepherd's estate' means to prefer 'open-hearted

---

[101] *Noris* 5. 'seines lieben Vatterlands/ zu dessen schuldigsten Ehren meisten Theils Er dieses Werklein unter die Hand genommen/ indem er nicht allein desselben von Gott reichgesegnet Landsart mit Poetischem Grieffel abreisset/ sondern auch zugleich dessen hochrühmliche Regimentsform/ benebenst denen Adelichen Geschlechten/ denkwürdigsten Begebenheiten/ und namhaftesten Gebäuen lebhaft abmahlet/ und mit sonderlichen Lehrberichten auszieret/ vermeinend/ gnugsam gethan zu seyn/ so etwas darinnen denen noch kommenden zur Tugendbringender Anmahnung und löblicher Nachfolge dienen solte.'

simplicity and unadorned, natural conversations' (6). Unadorned speech, however, does not equate with crudeness. He avows that he has included 'nothing that is secretive or harmful' in his work, and he appeals to an august tradition of erudite but honest writings in praise of Nuremberg and its worthies. There are the historians, such as Sleidanus, Chytraeus, Peucerus and Dresserus; there are also other scholars, such as the patrician Carl Nützel and the Altdorf professor of poetry and metaphysics Michael Piccart, who 'have composed beautiful Latin verses on the noble families'. Hellwig acknowledges his indebtedness to these earlier exemplars of 'fatherland' literature dedicated to the honor and glory of Nuremberg. Hellwig's work rings accordingly more patriotic than that of others. But in order to be able to 'give perfect birth to something edifying in the future', he must be able to count on 'sympathetic approval' from his readers – not so much as a reward for his efforts but rather as a confirmation that his instructive message of service to the 'glory of the fatherland' is bearing fruit.

Pastoral Spirituality

The image of the spiritual shepherd stands first and last in *Die Nymphe Noris*. His spirituality is not allegorically hidden but exercised straightforwardly, and existential certainty is basic to all that occurs. Spirituality is one of the columns on which the individual life may rest; the other is the relationship between citizens and their country. Leisurely pastoral existence and the cultivation of poetry are the noblest duties of the shepherd's estate, for they are gifts from God and remain untouched by human influence. By contrast with Birken and Opitz, pastoral as envisioned by Hellwig must be edifying, though this religiosity does not in any way diminish the importance of the public sphere, which, deriving as it does from an older Lutheran social ethos, confirms the here and now of the life of the community. The idea of the Nuremberg fatherland is only a reflection of a higher one that provides a permanence denied here on earth. This thought prepares the spiritual dawn song with which the shepherd's daily activities begin:

> 'Oh, dear Lord!' [Montano] whispered to himself, 'in what danger would our life and deeds not be, were we not surrounded by thy gracious protection? . . . Truly, if thy fatherly hand were not over us, we would vanish like smoke, leaving neither bones nor ashes. Thine is the honor; thine is the glory, o loving God, that we are able to enjoy comfortable rest, to lead our newly sheared flocks to pasture, and to take sweet pleasure in our shepherdly games. We give thee thanks for all of this.' Whereupon the shepherd proceeded to intone this morning song:[102]

---

[102] *Noris* 7–8. 'Ach lieber Gott! sagte er bey sich selbsten/ in was Gefahr stehet doch unser Thun und Leben/ wann es nicht mit deinem Gnadenschutz umzäunet were? . . . Ach ja! wann hier deine Vatterhand nicht were/ würden wir/ wie ein Rauch/ vergehen/ und sich weder Beine/ noch Aschen mehrers finden. Dein ist die Ehre; dein ist der Ruhm/ ô liebreicher Gott/ daß wir noch bißhero dieses alles mit beheglicher Ruhe geniessen/ die jüngst Wollenberaubte Heerde zur Waide führen/ und uns in unseren Schäferspielen so

DEin Lob/ *ô* Gott/ vermehre
   mein Mund an allem Ort;
Dir bleib allein die Ehre/
   Du bist der einig Hort/
des Güte wir vertrauen/
all unser Thun erbauen
   in deinem Gnadenport.

Du hast mich und die Heerden/
   die dein Geschenk und Gab/
beschützet für Gefährden;
   Du segnest meinen Stab/
der Du uns sicher machest/
und mächtiglich bewachest
   all unser Thun und Haab.

Nun diese deine Hulde
   werde' alle Morgen neu;
vergib uns unsre Schulde/
   und stetig um uns sey.
Kein Feind uns nicht berukke/
die Sorgenlast nicht drukke/
   die Nahrung wol gedey.

Dein Lob darum erklinget
   auf grüner Heid und Au/
und mein Mund frölich singet
   bey früem Morgentau/
auf daß dein Nam erschalle/
und aller Ort erhalle/
   wie ich Dir/ Gott/ vertrau.[103]

---

süssiglich vergnügen mögen: darum wir Dir billichen Dank zu sagen haben. Und fienge hierauf an besagter Schäfer folgendes Morgenlied zu singen:'

[103] *Noris* 8–9.

1) My mouth, O Lord, intone
   Thy praise wher'ere I be;
The glory, thine alone;
   Salvation, none but thee;
Trusting in thy goodness,
Doing what thou wouldest,
   In ports of grace and peace.

2) My sheep inside the manger
   (Thy gift, Lord, I confess)
Protectest thou from danger;
   My rod and staff thou bless,
Who voidest all alarm,
And keepest from all harm
   What we do and possess.

3) Now this, thy tender favor,
   Each morning grant anew;
Forgive our debts, O Savior,
   Stay near, whate'er we do.
Let foes not ill oppress,
Nor burdens sore distress;
   Supply our table too.

4) For this our praise shall ring
   O'er verdant meadows' lawn,
And voices joyful sing
   At glorious break of dawn;
To publish wide thy name,
And ev'rywhere proclaim
   How near thou me hast drawn.

The Urban Style

Pastoral activity takes place within these spiritual horizons. Stylistically, the language of Hellwig's *Noris* is less heated than Birken's *Fortsetzung*. Onomatopoeic language is used sparingly; metaphors are avoided almost completely; plays on words are reduced to a minimum; the individual phrases are tied together with short and relevant transitions. Going from Birken to Hellwig's modest, soothing language is rather like reaching a refuge after a march through a landscape of linguistic excess. Montano (Hellwig) and his friends have no need to draw such attention to themselves. The familiar stations of both earlier works are revisited and sung anew, but in a reserved manner. On the other hand, Hellwig does not shy away from insinuating criticism of the poems of his predecessors or even rejecting them altogether. He composes, for example, a new poem on the Haller meadow, if somewhat stiffly and with less virtuosity than Klaj. Instead of emulating the bridge verse made 'famous' by Floridan, he offers his own praise of the landscape:

> Schöne Matten!
> Deren grünbebäumter Lust gibet Ruh' und kühlen
> Schatten;
> deines Platzes reiche Zier
> grune/ grüne stets allhier.
>
> Flutgerienne;
> Laß/ daß diese Pegnitzflur neubegrünte Krafft ge-
> wienne/
> und daß euer Liebesbund
> sey der hohen Stämme Grund!
>
> BlumenAue!
> Hier mit stoltzem Lindenblat dich in deinem Strom be-
> schaue:
> jährlich dich in dich verneu;
> uns die Schäferzunft erfreu![104]

---

[104] *Noris* 10.
> Lovely meadows!
> Leafy pleasure branching green offers peace and cooling
> Shadows;
> Beauty's riches ev'rywhere,
> Green and growing ever here.
>
> River streaming;
> Bring this Pegnitz valley now nutriment for life's re-
> greening;
> Let these trees be rooted fast
> In your bond of love to last!

In the hand of the spiritual didact, an artillery range in the vicinity is transformed into a gnomic exemplar of the transience and joylessness of earthly existence:

> So trägt man an nichtigen Dingen Belieben!
> Es rauchet und schmauchet das Leben dahin/
> die zeitliche Freude hat kurtzen Gewinn;
> oft Jammer und Leide die Freude betrüben.[105]

The figure poem that follows (13) has the form of a heart on a white marble grave stone in the St Johannis cemetery; its grim message is that transitoriness suppresses every note of joy. The depiction of the gloomy pomp of a cemetery is rare, though memorable, in eclogue literature.[106] In the present case, it is based on a real event, the death in 1645 of Hellwig's sister Helena.[107] A second figure poem in her memory, an intensely personal expression of grief, ends in a *memento mori* admonition:

> Stella schön und wolgeart / truge lust am Künstenspiel'
> in der besten Freudenzeit sie der schwartze Neid anfiel:
> Hirten und der Hirtinn Zunfft / wollet ihrer nicht vergessen
> in Betrachtung ihres Falls / auch der Jahre Freude messen![108]

In a moment remarkable in the history of pastoral, the grieving poet weeps and must be comforted by his companion, Periander.[109] His lament makes mention of

---

> Valley teeming!
> Mirrored proud in linden leaves, see reflected there your being;
> Year by year to life respring,
> Make the guild of shepherds sing!

[105] *Noris* 11.
> Thus wasting our efforts on nothing but toys!
> Puffing and smoking our lives pass away.
> Pleasure is fleeting and lasts but a day;
> Thus sorrow and pain often dampen our joys.

[106] Most notably in the classic study by Erwin Panofsky, '*Et in Arcadia ego:* Poussin and the Elegiac Tradition', in *Meaning in the Visual Arts*, 295–320 (Garden City, NY: Doubleday, 1955).

[107] Hellwig also had a daughter Helena Sabina, but she was not born until 1646; the 'young lady' in question here died, as the lemma indicates, in 1645. This must have been his sister Helena, born 1619, who died on 8 September 1645. See Max Reinhart, *Johann Hellwig: A Descriptive Bibliography*, 6 n. 37.

[108] *Noris* 14.
> Stella, lovely, courteous, skilled in ev'ry noble art,
> Taken in the midst of spring, overcome by Envy swart.
> Shepherdess and shepherd guild ne'er forget her living here,
> Stella's death commemorate, measure thus the joys of years.

[109] Friedrich Lochner (1602–73).

'those flowers, fruits, and herbs that show themselves in summer and early fall' (15). The knowledge of the natural scientist is obvious here as well as later in his description of the 'garlic land' near Kleinreuth and Grossreuth (22).

The Act of Reading

Repeated examples show that Hellwig must have been a driving force in the sociocritical movement of German Baroque pastoral. One occasion presents itself in Periander's critique of the social (especially courtly) foolishness of trying to improve on nature. But, Helianthus rejoins, will not 'God's wondrous omnipotence' thereby mean all the more to the 'ignorant and inexperienced?' (17)[110] It is Montano's task to mediate in this important issue.

> 'Yes,' Montano answered, 'as long as it does not lead to pride and pomp; and such activity is reserved as a special privilege to those who have been blessed with wealth, and to those of high estate. But to use one's property in an ill-suited manner, to attempt to rise above one's social level and thus to make a surplus of one's abundance, results, I say, in a poor reputation and dubious character. Thus it is more proper to praise the simplicity of our free shepherd's estate, which little desires such vanities and is satisfied, rather, with whatever God bestows and Nature and her surroundings provide.'[111]

The movement of this argument is more complicated than it at first seems. Shaping nature remained the privilege of the affluent, and it was not the goal of the pastoral in the seventeenth century to shake the established order. As in earlier humanism, criticism is aimed rather at certain newcomers, whose wealth presumably has not been attained by honest means or who flaunt it as 'pride and pomp'. The (middle-class) shepherds, insofar as they may express appreciation for material goods, prefer the kind that have lasting value. What the shepherds lack in social standing and wealth, they compensate with inner nobility, inner wealth. Pastoral does not treat this idealized form of upward mobility as a fixed social datum but promotes it in a playful, experimental fashion via modesty topoi. The implicit contrast between lowly shepherds and persons of high rank made the genre attractive and

---

[110] Johann Georg Volckamer (1616–93), a renowned zoologist and intimate colleague of Hellwig.

[111] *Noris* 17. 'Ja/ antwortet Montano/ wann es zu keinem Stoltz und Pracht geschihet/ und solcher Handel allein denen mit Reichthum Gesegneten/ und hohen Standes Personen/ zu einer zuläßlichen Ergetzligkeit heimgestellet verbleibet. Mit seines Nächsten bößlich an sich gebrachtem Gut aber/ auser dem Stand prachten/ und solchen Uberfluß treiben/ ist es/ traun/ ein schlechter Ruhm und ärgerliches Wesen. Darum noch billicher unser freyer Schäferstand in seiner Einfalt zu loben ist/ der sich solcher Eitelkeiten nicht achtet/ und sich an deme/ was Gott bescheret/ und die Natur und LandesArt gibet/ genügen lässet.'

valuable to the learned. In the early modern period it was doubtless the most important medium of self-reflection for the nobilitas literaria, which explains the sense of the many passages that are plainly critical of court and city. Here a counter-world is formed in which the learned shepherd's estate establishes its own identity, its social equality, in terms of a negative reference system. This equality is in the first place an inner one; but eventually it turns into an external equality as well with the evolution of the Third Estate in the Enlightenment.

The competition between the praise of courtly and pastoral life has a long tradition. Prose eclogue is an especially useful vehicle for this practice, given the great flexibility of its prose conversations in particular. In a lyrical contest with Helianthus, Montano claims for himself the role of praising the pastoral life:

> ES hat die HimmelsGnad die Schäfer so begabt/
> > daß auch der Adelsstand nicht ihnen zu vergleichen.
> Der fromme Schäfersmann sich sonder Müh' erlabt/
> > es ist ihm eine Lust die Trieften zu durchstreichen;
>
> . . .
>
> Bey der Zufriedenheit die Frommkeit hellt und quillt/
> > in solchem nidren Stand die Tugend gerne heget.
> Ihm ist die gröste Sorg/ wie er unschuldig leb'/
> > und seines Namens Ruhm bey seinem Nachvolk schweb'.[112]

Allegorical reading, as pastoral poetry demands, implies the ability to discover the proper relationships between the various levels of speaking. The learned conversation of the shepherds, as a pastoral form, may claim fictional status, but as prose it is more intensively controlled than verse, which enjoys comparatively greater poetic license. In verse, the opposition between country and meadow, city and court, is strictly dualistic, whereas prose conversation requires mediation. The art of reading prose eclogue takes a sophisticated approach that refuses to oversimplify, and the reader must be able to keep both lyrical and prose sections in mind.

---

[112] *Noris* 18–19.
> The grace from heav'n above has shepherds so endowed,
> > That none compare to them, not even noble blood.
> The shepherd with his flocks has all he'll ever need,
> > And wanders at his pleasure about the lovely mead.
>
> . . .
>
> For where contentment reigns, love and goodness stream,
> > And virtue richly thrives in shepherds' low estate.
> To live a life not pure, that were his greatest fear;
> > His wish: that his good name be honored year by year.

Helianthus feels compelled to justify his boldness in assuming the role of the courtier: 'What I did was for the sake of amusement and should not make me therefore guilty of disloyalty' (20). But in the same breath he defends the notion of a divinely preordained social hierarchy: 'For every estate, including court life, has its proper place, and God in his wisdom does not dissolve the differences in rank but has himself so ordained it.' In fact, Helianthus's opponent himself concurs, which suggests that the entire exchange is to be understood as an antiphone, in which both the shepherd's estate and that of the court have their various legitimate roles. From the courtier's love of hunting, his pleasure in 'plenteous food', his loathing of 'the coarse peasantry', there is no path leading to the pastoral ideals. However, the courtier accepts an obligation to the ethical norms of the pastoral world when 'love of language and arts' is attributed to him, or when he is challenged by his opponent to live virtuously: 'The courtier ever strives on this earth so to live, / So that beyond his death his own he'll honor give' (19). This obligation is further intensified when he is addressed as the ideal servant of the state, one who steadfastly and unswervingly maintains justice against the caprices of the prince:

> Sein Tugendhaffter Sinn mit nichten wird berukkt/
> wann über ihm ergrimmt der Fürst/ ihn unterdrukkt.[113]

This ethos, derivative of the medieval mirror of princes, has a genuine place in pastoral, the nature of which tends toward a constantly playful exchange between the social estates. In fact, the intentional blurring of class distinctions simply makes pastoral's adherence to the traditional order the more obvious.

As much as it underscores the poetic license that Hellwig allows himself, his application of shepherdly ideals owes essentially to the founder of modern German literature. What would be unthinkable in either Harsdörffer or Birken is possible in Hellwig, namely, the praise of Opitz from the mouth of his fellow Silesian, Friedrich Lochner of Oels. Opitz, so Lochner, embodied the true pastoral ideal, everything that shepherds wish to be:

> ES lacht/ veracht des Opitz hoher Geist
>   im runden Zirk/ was hier wird hoch geacht/
>   weil Lust und Last/ ja Frucht und Furcht vermenget:
> Dis alles er ein schnödes Tantwerk heisst/
>   ein Windsgesäuß/ und unbeschmukten Pracht/
>   da Freud mit Leid/ ja Schertz mit Schmertz besprenget.
>   zuletzt der Tod anhänget.
> Dorten die Freud auf ewig lässt sich schauen/
>   wann Opitz Seel

---

[113] *Noris* 19.
     His loyal service true, unwav'ring come what may,
     Let petty despot rage or over him hold sway.

> ohn allem Fehl
> des Höchsten Güt erwegt/
> Ihm allen Ruhm zulegt;
> und uns bezeugt den Nutzen des Vertrauen.[114]

Up to this point Hellwig has emphasized two things: the duality between the temptations of the world and the promises of transcendence, and the preservation of a successful pastoral life. His shepherds enjoy worldly pleasures without losing sight of their home in the hereafter. They are models for human beings in general, who through death enter eternity stripped of rank but not of name. But more yet, they are also qualified as no other individuals to praise the governing families of the city. Three givens are necessary to this praise: 1) Its panegyrical elements must not vary essentially from those already present in the opening section. 2) There exists a literary estate that has always been in possession of the traits ascribed to the great ones of this world. 3) Heroes and shepherds belong to incomparably different worlds yet are equal insofar as they are all exemplars of virtue. It is in discovering what they have in common, in seeing the identical in the non-identical, that pastoral marshals its arsenal of amplifying, critical, and, in the end, anticipatory powers.

In Praise of the Governing Families

It is in this middle panegyrical section that *Die Nymphe Noris* moves significantly beyond the *Pegnesisches Schäfergedicht* and the *Fortsetzung der Pegnitz-Schäferey*. As Hellwig explains in his preface (5–6), the panegyric is dedicated to the idea of the Nuremberg 'fatherland' and its 'form of government', as well as its noble families, memorable history, and renowned buildings. Nuremberg's patriciate, one of the most glorious of the old empire, enters pastoral here more forcefully than in any other Nuremberg work.[115]

---

[114] *Noris* 21.
> It laughs and taunts – transcendent Opitz-mind
> In nobler realm – what's held for worthy here,
> Which worth and waste, boon and bane inverts:
> These things he knows are of an idle kind,
> A puff of wind, conceit without its gear,
> Which hope to hurt, cheer to drear perverts,
> At last to death reverts.
> But far above is seen eternal bliss,
> When Opitz' eye,
> With perfect sight,
> The Highest Good surveys,
> Then sings his final praise –
> And testifies to faith's great usefulness.

[115] There is hardly room here to give a proper accounting of the history and mentality of the Nuremberg patriciate. For this, see Hofmann, 'Nobiles Norimbergenses'.

Whereas in the thirteenth and fourteenth centuries a certain latitude for vertical mobility still existed within the higher ranks in Nuremberg, by the seventeenth century the lines had hardened. From 1380 to the end of the fifteenth century twenty-eight families succeeded in gaining entry into the small council, the chief executive organ of the city council. One of these families, the Fütters, came from the merchant class. From 1521 on the council definitively transformed itself into a caste through the institution of a dance ordinance, whereby only certain families were invited to dance at the city hall. The ordinance was established according to anciency: twenty old families, seven new ones, and fifteen families that had risen to meet the qualifications of becoming council members since 1440. The Harsdörffers belonged to this last group. The Schlüsselfelders were accepted in 1536 and the Starcks in 1544; these two families represent the last ones to be recruited into the small council. This regimentation laid the groundwork for incessant conflicts, especially between the learned grouping (*doctores*) and high city officials on the one hand, and the prominent but non-governing merchant-patrician families on the other. Both of these consistently opposed granting any further privileges once the uprising of the guildsmen had been broken early in the fourteenth century. The effects of this conflict cannot be dealt with here, although it reaches directly into the history of early modern literature and is important for the understanding of learned mentality as related to pastoral. The process of the patriciate's separation was marked by a successive retreat from economic activities and the move into the countryside as landed gentry. The latter, however, remained after the fourteenth century somewhat apart from the non-feudal groupings, which for their part operated more in terms of the knightly code and the new worldly orders of knightly orders and societies, epitomized by the Heidelberg Order of Tournaments of 1485. This order rejected the merchant grouping of the urban patriciate as being of inferior birth.[116] Temporarily cut off from the landed nobility, the patriciate created its own elite class in civic circles through strict segregation from the merchant and other lower groupings. They documented this elitism with chivalric honors, orders, titles, codes of dress, and a proliferation of coats of arms.

These social distinctions, which were ordained by the city council, were clearly not in tune with 'a mobile society governed by the laws of capitalism'.[117] The economic and social developments of the sixteenth century would eventually

---

[116] Hofmann, 'Nobiles Norimbergenses' 135. The upper classes of Nuremberg, 'after being rejected by the nobility, created their own qualification in a tourney consisting of their own class instead of the chivalric tourney. They also granted to themselves alone the privilege of establishing priories and monasteries of the imperial city. When in the 1470s the quite normal practice of connubial alliance with the landed gentry suddenly stopped, the bourgeois classes married within their own circles.'

[117] Ibid., 138.

overtake them. Fewer and fewer patricians would be counted among the merchants, having turned instead towards land ownership. Some found acceptance in the noble ranks of imperial chivalric orders. With the Imperial Patent of 1696, the patriciate of the free cities was formally made equal to imperial knighthood. An imperial decree one year later expressly forbade mercantile activity. Accordingly, the entire eighteenth century was full of merchants and tradespeople turned retailers against the 'caste dictatorship' of the council.[118] Only late in the seventeenth century and then more regularly in the eighteenth did the merchants succeed in establishing their own professional organizations independent of the city council. It is interesting to see the merchants, now barred from the council, eagerly striving, in imitation of the patriciate, to own land – exactly as the city jurists, who had been elevated to the ranks of the nobility, had done.

Against this backdrop we may now take a more detailed look at the memorial panegyric of the Nuremberg patriciate. It remains intimately connected to the praise of the old imperial city itself. The two nymphs Alithea and Dorila, who lead the city's glorification, are introduced as beauties in whom nature 'did not wish to be seen as a stepmother' (26). Hellwig offers a portrait straight out of courtly description, suitable, he says, for a 'world famous city'. Alithea and Dorila have been charged by the 'great nymph NORIS, who is a powerful warden of the national character' (28), to lead these, and expressly these, excellent shepherds 'to the place where you may observe the greatest splendor of your beloved fatherland'. Unlike the playful lightness typical of the Pegnitz shepherds, this characterization of Nuremberg is a somber model of virtue, piety, and loyalty to the emperor. It has an unmistakably pre-Opitzian ring about it, audible in the language, which has more in common with Weckherlin or Hoeck or even Rompler than with Opitz and his followers:

> Alith. Neronsburg heisst und ist der Francken Cron;
> Pallas hat dieses Orts die stete Wohn'/
> und daselbst in dem Paner führt die Tugend.
> Dor. ziert die Jugend.
>
> Alith. Neronsburg/ du des Grossen Kaisers Aug/
> dein Verstand dessen Gnade Gunsten saug':
> ach! dir nichts sich an Teutschland recht vergleichet.
> Dor. Alls erbleichet.
>
> Alith. Neronsburg/ unter deines Gottes Schutz/
> du getrost/ biete deinen Feinden Trutz.

---

[118] Ibid., 143.

Nun dein Ruhm grunend im Nachvolk bekleibe;
Dor. Ewig bleibe.[119]

Once again it is a 'beautiful round temple' (28) that rises upon a 'beautiful green meadow covered with many little flowers', within which the jewels of Nuremberg families and history are set. It is splendidly appointed, like a magnificent courtly building, decorated all around with insignias and emblems, all expressive of how the patrician families see themselves. Most importantly, there is the allegory of Prudence with mirror and snake and the motto 'What wisely benefits', followed by the allegory of Bravery with a lion and the motto 'And steadfastly protects' (29). The portal has the shape of Europa, with the emperor's crown on her head, the scepter and imperial orb in her hands. She sits on an eagle, beneath whose outstretched wings both of Nuremberg's coats of arms are visible: On a blue shield stands the crowned, nude virgin with yellow wings, the back side of the lower body flowing into the feet and tail of a yellow eagle with the motto 'Virgin pure'. On the other shield, the eagle with three red bars and the motto 'Light of Grace'. Nearby is a fountain with lambs and the words 'Innocence and Patience', which can be seen opposite the nymph Noris.

> DEr Nymphen NORIS Macht und Herrligkeit zu sehen
> ist hier an diesem Ort/ kein Frefler dörf sich nähen:
> in Unschuld und Gedult erwart der rechten Zeit/
> wann dich der Nymphen Gnad an dieses Ort herleit.[120]

As in Birken's Pan episode, sacrificial cleansing is expected of Hellwig's shepherds as well. Only then may they enter the temple, where the names of those

---

[119] *Noris* 27.
> Alith. Neronsburg: thus we call the Frankish crown;
> (Forever more Athena's cultic home);
> Emblazoned, Virtue leads the way to truth.
> Dor. Honors youth.
>
> Alith. Neronsburg, our exalted emp'ror's eye,
> Your counsel he rewards with special right.
> Oh, what compares to you in German land?
> Dor. Nothing can.
>
> Alith. Neronsburg, safe within the Master's hand,
> With naught to fear, your enemies withstand.
> The future race will hold your glory high.
> Dor. Never die.

[120] *Noris* 29.
> The might of Noris nymph and splendor fill the air
> In this her sacred place; no scorner enters here.
> Await in patient prayer the moment set by fate,
> Until the nymph approach and guide you through the gate.

'who have proven themselves worthy in both word and deed' glitter starlike on sapphire tablets, and 'whose memory now shines forth as an example to later generations of the transformation of light into virtue' (30). But it is not solely about them. Next to the family columns with their coats of arms, the temple itself contains 'a notable history'. It is a 'famous and renowned building', the most notable in 'Neronsburg'. Thus Hellwig dovetails praise of the patricians and the city, a strategy that elevates his work beyond a pure panegyric of governing families. Instead of observing the principle of anciency, he elects for an alphabetical sequence of the twenty-eight families, 'with impartial preference of the one family or the other because of older descent or entrée to the council'. The quatrains on the impresas of the families contain moral and edifying interpretations, into which critical and hortative ideas can flow. The symbiosis of art and virtue is apostrophized as the essence of truly noble, patrician, and learned life:

> DEr Vogel und die Blum bezieren/ besingen hier dieses Geschlecht/
> der Vogel zeigt die Kunst/ wie gleicher Maß Lilien Treue mit Recht:
> O Gott/ der du versorgst/ und speissest die Vögel/ bekleidest die Blum/
> in deiner Hut erhalt' hier aller Geschlechten wol edelen Ruhm.[121]

This wish, prompted by the Baumgärtner coat of arms, reads like a general motto to the work, in which fear of God, trust in God, and thoughts of eternity are articulated in alternating concepts and images according to figures on the impresas. Usually the first two lines describe the physical aspects of the respective family's coat of arms, from which the maxim or didactic precept of the last two lines is formed. God is the granter of all gifts of life, of 'Glük' (happiness; no. 2) no less than 'Unglük' (unhappiness; no. 3), 'aiming' in both for the 'state of grace' (no. 5) The formulation is reminiscent of the message in the Sermon on the Mount:

> Fromkeit lebet sonder Schulde; Fromkeit träget Tugendhuld;
> Fromkeit ihren Feinden reichet ofters alles mit Gedult.[122]

As always in the seventeenth century, biblical precepts are supported by stoic virtues, such as loyalty, which causes 'the wheel of misfortune to break and crumble' before it gives in to 'grim envy' (34). The final quatrain draws its moral from what the lily signifies:

---

[121] *Noris* 30.
> The flower and the bird embellish and magnify this fam'ly name;
> The bird here stands for art; the lilies for fealty and justice the same.
> O Lord, thou great provider, who clothest the flower and feedest the bird,
> We pray thee, hold and keep the noble respect that the families earned.

[122] *Noris* 41.
> The pure in heart live godly lives; the pure in heart bear honor's prize;
> The pure in heart forebearance show to enemies as need arise.

> WAs soll der Lilie Weiß' und Röte hier vergleichen?
> das Tugendlieb nicht soll zur Krieg- und Friedzeit weichen:
> > der TugendRuhm erhallt hier noch in dieser Zeit/
> > verbleibt auch einverleibt der grauen Ewigkeit.[123]

Hellwig invents especially penetrating turns of expression in those instances where he is able to pick up the theme of a family's commitment to the fatherland. A 'crown of glory' (36) is gained by the Grundherr family in the temporal realm, which to the eye of the poet patriot appears to equate to the eternal crown:

> Zu Lieb dem Vatterland Ehr/ Gut/ und Leib wer wagt/
> dem ohn der Zeiten End die EhrenCron behagt.[124]

This is made specific by holding unshakably to justice. The sword of judgment, as the Kress coat of arms signifies, 'in fury punishes who masters and who serves' (40).

At the same time, public acts are unthinkable apart from the art of rhetoric, which is capable of controlling 'heat' and taming 'wildness' (39). As with Harsdörffer and Klaj, service to the fatherland appears in Hellwig as a triadic combination of council, church, and school:

> WIe der dreygesetzten Blum Ruch und schöne Farb erhellet/
> so des Rahts/ der Kirch'/ und Schul' Ehr und Nutz wird vorgestellet/
> > wann mit Treuen sie vereint in des grossen Adlers Schutz:
> > solche Lieb Gott wolgefällt/ biet den Neidern Hohn und Trutz.[125]

But common everyday wisdom is also worthy of inclusion in the Temple of Honor. Thus, with respect to the Holtzschuhers:

> WEr viel weiß/ viel Schue zureisst/
> > ist ein altes Wortt der Alten;

---

[123] *Noris* 54.
> Wherewith shall we the lily white and pink compare,
> Whose virtue never yields in times of peace or war?
> > For virtue's fame resounds throughout the present age,
> > And shall endure inscribed upon eternal page.

[124] *Noris* 36.
> Who wagers life and home for love of fatherland,
> His crown of glory shines beyond time's misty strand.

[125] *Noris* 44.
> As the lovely triple flower's scent and color signify,
> Thus the use and high esteem that council, church and school enjoy,
> > Bound in loyal faith as one in the mighty Eagle's care:
> > Love like this well pleases God, defies with boldness envy's snare.

> Doch mit Witz wer weit geraisst/
> kan Stadt/ Land und Leut verwalten.[126]

Hellwig's acumen comes through not only in the transference of the individual into the general, but also in the veiled consideration, bordering on the enigmatic, of the specific in the history and rhythm of individual families. The path followed by the Ebners delicately reminds us 'that one through sweat alone / can gain the highest name; a little toil oft profits' (34). The Harsdörffers are credited with the religious, moral, and erudite virtues that have been praised since early humanism:

> DEs HERREN Namen ist die starke Burg und Vest'/
> auf der sich der Gerecht in aller Noht verlässt:
> die hohe Wartt bezeugt/ wie Tugend/ Kunst/ und Recht
> in aller Wachsamkeit berühmt macht diß Geschlecht.[127]

Nobility loses its justification where it leaves the path of virtue:

> WIe das schöne Frauenbild als ein Wunderfisch sich endet/
> und die wolgestalte Lilie sich darob errot/ erbleicht:
> solcher Weiß der AdelsRuhm des/ der ihn zur Unbühr wendet/
> selzam scheint/ verleurt den Namen/ und sich aller Ehr' entzeucht.[128]

Let these illustrations suffice to show that the praise of families is less exhausted in a moralist like Hellwig than in others. And certainly Hellwig presents himself in his work as a loyal citizen of his hometown by fortifying the cornerstone of its political order, oligarchical government, through the explication of the city's coats of arms. At the same time, one recognizes that the panegyrical components, consistent with the social history of humanism, are accompanied by hortative and normative as well as critical components. Moreover, the exemplifications are so conceived that they rather overshoot their targets (the addressees) and assume a didactic character – a fact of great utility

---

[126] *Noris* 38.
> Worn-out shoe: wisdom due –
> A proverb often verified.
> Who to truth through travel grew,
> City, land, and folk can guide.

[127] *Noris* 37.
> A mighty fortress is the Lord Jehovah's name,
> In need the righteous man may trust salvation's claim;
> The ramparts testify how virtue, art and right
> – for service ever ready – this family glorified.

[128] *Noris* 46.
> Above all female loveliness, the mermaid has a fishlike end;
> Lilies, too, the eye's delight, pale at last in death and bend:
> Thus betimes a noble name, used for some improper gain,
> Curious seems, changes form, and bears henceforth a shameful stain.

for us in trying to understand the urban community in the mid-seventeenth century. Finally, although the panegyrical elements take their starting point with the urban upper estate, they are not applicable only to a single social grouping; they are formulated as binding and guiding principles for everyone, derived as they are from the axioms of Christian faith and ancient moral philosophy. It is therefore crucial to observe in these panegyrics how the poet interlaces the representation of historical stations and the monumental artifacts of his hometown. For analytical reasons, however, these two aspects must be dealt with separately.

Praise of City

Hellwig, of course, does not pass up the chance to mention the role played by the Romans in the 'famous origins' of the city, specifically, of 'Drusus Nero in the year 10 before the birth of Christ' (31). The earliest valid date mentioned by Hellwig for Nuremberg's origins, however, is 912: 'the first beginning of the city of Nuremberg during the reign of Emperor Conrad'.[129] The city's attitudes of 'Honesty and courage fresh' (33) are said to have contributed to its destruction in 1105. The 'entire body' of the empire was 'ravished as a mutilated member' (35). Reconstruction succeeded through the 'gracious good will' of a 'great hero', the Hohenstaufen Conrad III. The annexation of the fortress into the city under Heinrich VII in 1313 also took place under the stamp of imperial protection, to which the city entrusted itself, as a 'virgin', in keeping with the conventional *sponsa* allegory: 'weil meine JungfrauEhr des Kaisers hohe Macht / Gemeiner Stadt befohln/ die treulich mich bewacht' (34).

This close connection to the emperor is manifest in the construction, funded from his 'charitable treasury' (39), of the 'Imperial Chapel of our Dear Lady on the Market Square' (38). As a free imperial city Nuremberg remained a center of imperial patriotism, though not at the expense of ideas of peace and unity, some of which were directed against sovereign autocracy and the discord that often accompanies it. This is visible in the epigram on the signing of the Golden Bull of 1356. The motto 'German loyalty' and the emphasis on the 'bonds of true love' are strikingly reminiscent of the sentiment of the German intellectual societies:

> SO war die guldne Bull gantz löblich aufgerichtet/
> und so der Fürsten Fehd' im Teutschland auch geschlichtet.
>   Ach! laß durch deine Gnad'/ o höchster Gott/ bestehn
>   diß Band der treuen Lieb'/ im Unfried nicht zergehn![130]

---

[129] On the earliest history of Nuremberg, see Gerhart Pfeiffer (ed.), *Nürnberg – Geschichte einer europäischen Stadt* (Munich: Beck, 1971), 11–72.

[130] *Noris* 39.
>   Thus was the Golden Bull so fitly executed,
>   And thus the princely feuds in German lands concluded.
>   Almighty God of grace, we pray it never cease,
>   This bond of loyal love, this attitude of peace.

This loyalty relates to the empire, in which, as in the earlier grand Italian cities, it proved useful in the development away from particularism. The orientation toward the empire did not, however, as we have witnessed repeatedly in earlier chapters, exclude a 'national' humanist element.

The poet ignores Harsdörffer's advice to maintain political neutrality, when he is concerned with memorializing the two margravial wars. Not only does he refuse not to avoid the subject, he gives it three tableaux. Nuremberg's brave struggle against the marauding margraves illustrates two kinds of boldness:

> KUhnheit/ die aus Frevel kommt/ selten Nutz und Frommen bringet/
> Kühnheit/ die mit Füg' und Recht/ tringet durch/ und alls bezwinget.
> Nicht der Kützel dich geluste deinem Nächsten seyn zum Schad
> sonder Ursach/ leichtlich könte dich selbst treffen solches Bad.[131]

One kind of boldness is 'hubris'; the other springs from 'moral cause'. Thus the turn to the sphere of universal ethics, but now in order to detract from specific cases so that attention stay clearly fixed on the thematic thrust. The treatment of the feud between the margraves and the Nuremberg patriciate is handled similarly:

> FReyer Sinn und Adel liebet
>   Rennen/ Stechen/ Ritterspiel;
>   wol dem/ der mit gleichem Ziel
> auch in Kunst und Zucht sich übet.[132]

The image derives from the urban realm and is applied as a challenge to the territorial realm. Any doubt about Hellwig's position in the struggle for survival of the free imperial city is dispelled in the quatrain dealing with the second margrave war:

> EIn freyer Held wolt' hier mit unverschuldten Straffen
>   bestraffen mich/ wo nicht Gott sonders hielte Wacht/
> wer ich unschuldiglich erödet in den Waffen.
>   Gott hat ans Tageliecht mein' Unschuld auch gebracht.[133]

---

[131] *Noris* 44.
  Boldness that's of hubris born causes pride that leads to fall;
  Boldness sprung from moral cause gathers strength and conquers all.
    Let your neighbor's sad misfortune never bring delight to you
    Needlessly, for such a turn could easily befall you too.

[132] *Noris* 45.
  Nobles and free spirits relish
    Racing, fencing, knightly jest.
    Happy, who with equal zest
  Art and learning also cherish.

[133] *Noris* 50.
  A freeboot hero sought to punish me for harms
    I did not do. If God his vigil e'er should halt,
  I wrongfully should be destroyed by savage arms.
    But God at last revealed my innocence of fault.

Just what kind of 'hero' this is, is obvious in view of the 'innocence' of the city besieged 'for harms I did not do'.

Hellwig integrates into his pastoral a description and praise of the coats of arms of the towns and surrounding possessions (69–71), where the struggle with the margraves over jurisdiction was especially severe, and which represented a kind of first line of defense for Nuremberg.

The Reformation represents an important moment in the ecclesiopolitical history of Nuremberg, and Hellwig does not fail to include it in his memorial work. Two signals point to the particular theological content of the Protestant Reformation: the insistence on the 'Word of God' and on investigating the truth rather than subjugating oneself unquestioningly to authority and dogmatic tradition. All confessional allusions are purposefully omitted. Hellwig finds of particular importance the criticism, already articulated in the pre-Reformation church, of the modern penchant for 'earthly honor':

> SChnell die weltlich' Ehr verschwindet/ und hält ihre Wäre nicht;
> Gottes Wort auf ewig bleibet. Wol! wer wandlet in dem Liecht/
> und der Warheit forschet nach. Gott kan alles wieder geben;
> was man ihm zu Lieb verlässt/ hier und auch in jenem Leben.[134]

The last political date that Hellwig includes is 1632, 'Wallenstein's Camp' (53). What hidden message can he have meant to convey in this event? Wallenstein's siege is a proof-stone of the 'patience' of the city. It is the 'enemy' that failed to break God's defense, on which Protestant Nuremberg continues to rely completely, much as it formerly had relied on the (Catholic) emperor:

> SChikt uns Gott ein Leiden zu/ wil er seine Lieb erweissen/
> drum diß mit Gedult man trag'/ er kan auch mit Troste speissen:
> dieses Creutz ist wie die Wolkke/ die der Sonnen Glantz bedekkt/
> aller unsrer Feinde Sturme Gott zernicht/ und Heil erwekkt.[135]

Hellwig leads his citizen readers through many other stations of Nuremberg's history, pointing out along the way great cultural events of the past. There is the St Lorenz Church, which owes its existence to the sacrificial dedication of the

---

[134] *Noris* 48.
    Swift all earthly honor fades, hastens forth into the night.
    God's own Word forever lives. Blessed who wanders in the light,
        Searches, tireless, after truth. All we trust to him in love,
        God restores all this at last, here and in the life above.
[135] *Noris* 53.
    Trials sent from God betimes only prove his loving care.
    That we patiently endure, consolation too he'll share.
        Like a cloud this cross may be, hiding sun, our spirit quakes.
        Then a bolt of lightning strikes: the foe's destroyed, salvation wakes!

nobility: 'One thane's devotion here, and others' gen'rous tithes, / Has built me in all glory, raised me to the skies' (36). There is the Hospital of the Holy Spirit, endowed by Konrad Gross (*gross* 'great'): 'Great that these good works are done, / Great that poor are mercy shown' (37). There is the Sacramental Cabinet of St. Lorenz Church, an endowment of the Imhoffs: 'May their praise be ne'er destroyed' (42). There is the grave of St Sebald, which continues to be venerated in the Protestant city (43). There is the newly constructed city hall, in which 'Prudence and the law of justice / Here their home and altar keep' (49). And must Nuremberg not view its library with pride, even if its treasures owe more to the far-sightedness of the citizens than to the generosity of the magistrates? 'Naught but the Muses' grace all things immortal makes, / And thus their gifts we here with high respect do take' (45). Even the arsenal deserves a verse of acknowledgment (46); and the newly dedicated theater (52); and the newly constructed Fleischbrücke (47); and the Rossmülle (50). The pastoral is as much at home in the urban sphere as at the court. It is a worthy vehicle for the representation of civic culture and values:

> DEn Geitz/ den Eigennutz/ das Wuchervolk vertreiben/
> zur Aufnam einer Stad/ ist vieler Lobred werth/
> so kan des Nächsten Lieb/ so kan die Treue bleiben;
> da hat Gott seine Wohn'/ und alles Guts beschert.[136]

Hellwig also devotes commemorative verses in Part One to the eighteen Nuremberg patrician but non-governing families.[137] To these families he adds, in Part Two, an appreciation of twenty-seven council families that had died out.[138] This observance further differentiates the social picture but does not fundamentally change it. In Part Two there is yet another gallery (121–35) of more than fifty individual patricians, 'well deserving and praiseworthy persons of the highest rank' (121), who performed important service for their city between the fourteenth and seventeenth centuries. Hellwig gives them epithets (such as, the Generous, the Prudent, the Decorated, the Victorious) according to the practice of the sodalities, thereby integrating them across the centuries into a kind of imaginary Association of Virtuous Men.

---

[136] *Noris* 47.
> All greed and selfishness, all usury expel,
> To city's betterment: all this is meet and just,
> For thus can charity and loyalty be well:
> For this is God's own home, He does here what He must.

[137] *Noris* 62–9, under the heading 'Wappen der Adelichen, doch unrathsfehigen Geschlechten.'

[138] *Noris* 139–49, under the heading 'Wappen der abgestorbenen Rathsfähigen Geschlechten.'

The Realm of Noris

The proud city-state finds its allegorical representation in the nymph Noris and her realm. At the temple entrance, or exit, Apollo stands on one side, Hercules on the other (57), a duality of intelligence and courage, spirit and power, which is maintained throughout. Only now, after the shepherds have made the acquaintance with the 'heroes' of 'Neronsburg' does Hellwig make a first summary and hint at how all of this is to be read. The temple serves not only forebears but also posterity. These patricians once exemplified and affirmed what the worldly behavior of the urban community should be now and in the future. The task of the learned estate is to assist the formulation and establishment of a normative system that overlaps all classes, that is, to be historians, or, by analogy to the courtly dynasts, historiographers and educators of princes. Seen in this way the wondrous temple becomes an allegorical showcase of urban identity as reflected through its learned writers:

> WEr diesen Wunderbau beschaut/ bey sich betrachte/
> daß nächst des Höchsten Hülf' und unendlicher Machte
>   die kluge Vorsicht hier und unverdrossner Fleiß
>   erhalten dieses Werk in seinem Ehrenpreiß.
> Wie nun das Oberhaubt/ so seynd die Unterthanen:
> wann jene ihren Weg mit Tugendvorbild bahnen/
>   auch diese folgen nach. Der Wolstand blüet und grünt
>   mit Ruhm in solchem Land/ und Gott zu Ehren dient.[139]

Loyalty and love, devotion, honor and praise are the cardinal virtues, allegorically represented by three female figures in the interior. All are grounded in 'purity of heart', proclaimed in the vow that is taken 'Not with false hypocrisy' (58). Because the temple is apostrophized as 'a representative of the great glory of the divine nymph and governor of this place and land named Noris', the virtues visible within it have double signification: as an expression of ideal self-understanding and as a challenge to make it permanent through practice. The ethos of the constitutional reality of the city-state, allegorized in the temple, manifests itself in the seven elders of the government, the 'older privy council', the bearer of the 'highest power', the keeper of the 'arcana' (59). The arcana of

---

[139] *Noris* 57.
> Reflect here as you gaze upon this wondrous sight,
> How, helped by God on high and His unending might,
>   A prudent government, with never daunted will,
>   Maintains the work begun in all due honor still.
> What's good for rulers here applies to subjects too:
> The former walk the path of virtue tried and true,
>   Their lead the latter follow. Affluence thus is raised
>   In cities such as this, and God receives the praise.

the art of governing are accessible only to those who have distinguished themselves through 'modest patience and unimpeachable behavior', by their 'fairness' as well as their 'self-abasement', as symbolized by the lambs and little fountains.

But Hellwig is concerned with the canon of behavior and the morality of the civic community as a whole. Thus he rededicates the Pan altar, known to us from Birken's *Fortsetsetzung*, into an altar of Noris. It is a 'masterpiece wrought from nature', ordained by Noris herself. The constitution of the city-state, no less than the behavioral maxims of its citizens, is grounded in the law of nature. That is the deciding advantage of the city-state over royal absolutism as of about the mid-seventeenth century. It is articulated, as we shall see, more sharply in the figurative images and encoded conversations of pastoral than in explicit constitutional categories. The charitable acts of Noris are compared to the effects of the sun. All who serve her are granted 'comfort' and 'pleasure'. In this light, *Die Nymphe Noris* is a mirror of the gifts received from the city.

> Ihr Nam' hallt und schallt auf Auen/
> und durchklinget Berg' und Thal;
> herrlich ist ihr Thun zu schauen/
> prächtig ihrer Machten Stral.[140]

Only after the meaning of the Temple of Noris has been broadly explicated are the shepherds allowed to see Noris herself. Her appearance is ingeniously woven together with threads of Nuremberg's environment, for it is here that the gods of field and meadow are at home. A gilded triumphal wagon with the black-crowned eagle with outspread wings displays the coat of arms of 'the offices and towns under the jurisdiction of the worthy imperial city Nuremberg' (69). Springing about in front of the wagon are 'goat-footed forest-men crowned with ferns and furze and with small drums and reed flutes and chiming triangles' (71). Six snow-white oxen, decorated with floral wreaths, pull the wagon being driven by a nymph with a silver staff. It is a harvest wagon, and the fauns are garlanded with the fruits of the earth. Noris is enthroned in the midst of this procession, on her head a golden crown 'shaped like a wall or city battlement', in her hands a palm branch and scepter.[141] At her feet are the Pegnitz and the Regnitz as naked 'male

---

[140] *Noris* 61.
'Noris!' peals across the meads,
Echoing through hill and plains;
Splendid now behold her deeds,
Brilliant all that she attains.

[141] Hellwig created this figure – though he borrowed the name 'Noris' from Eobanus Hessus – in 1645, for a small pastoral called 'Lobgedicht an den Spielenden', which was published, as Reinhart has shown in *Johann Hellwig's 'Die Nymphe Noris* xxiv–xxv, in the fifth volume of Harsdörffer's *FzG* (46–52). There the nymph Noris is described as 'ein über alle massen schönes Weibsbild; derer Holdseligkeit jedoch mit

figures', their private parts hidden by the reeds. Following the wagon are nymphs, 'among whom one could distinguish Naiads, Napaeae, Dryades, Hamadryades, Oreades and Hymnids'. The shepherds seek in vain for the meaning of the scene. This concludes the role of the nymph Noris in Part One.

The scene is picked up later in Part Two. This time it is an old man in a costume decorated with stars and a winged hourglass (135). He is accompanied by a nude boy wearing silver silk, with grapes and sheaves of grain in his hand and poppy-crests on his head; various nymphs make music on harps, lutes, violas, and citharas. Again, a bacchanalian procession with a familiar message:

SO/ so/ so/ Nachsinnen üben/
   Tugend lieben
   macht bekant/
und bringt Nutz dem Vatterland.[142]

The boys sing while the nymphs place in the temple two honor-rolls made from cedar wood that show the likeness of Lucas Friedrich Böhaim, 'the Upstanding', who died in 1648. The pageantry witnessed by the shepherds, as one of the youths explains,

> is accessible to us at all times by way of the one or the other tablet, or picture, and serves not only to honor the one depicted but also to spur others to devote themselves to the same virtues and glorious deeds, from which not only one's own honor but also the honor of the fatherland may become evident through the well-being thus promoted.[143]

---

solchem Heroischen Ansehen vermenget/ welches ausser Zweiffel auch von dem ihrigen nicht gar jungen Alter her ursprünglich/ daß sie nicht allein ihre Begegnere mit Liebkosen/ sondern auch mit etwas Geboten gleichsam schiene/ zu ihren Willen zu bringen. Ihre Kleidung war oberhalb des Leibs/ und üm die Arme/ mit weissem Atlaß beleget/ der Unterrokk von rohten Daffet; der gantze Oberrokk gelb und mit schwartzen Adlern eingewirket: Sie hatte auf ihrem Haubt einen von eichenen Laub geflochten Krantz/ darunter ein guldenes Stirnblat mit diesen Buchstaben. N O R I S. Und in der einen Hand einen weissen Helfenbeinen Richterstab/ in der andern einen Palmenzweig haltend: Aus welchem der Schäfer leichtlich schliessen mögen/ daß sie etwas eine sonderliche Göttin oder Vorsteherinn dieser Landschaft seyn müste' (47–8).

[142] *Noris* 135.
   So, so, so, remembrance keeping,
     Virtue seeking,
     Teaching it,
   Thus our land to benefit.

[143] *Noris* 137. '[Das Gepräng aber/ wie ihr gesehen/] ist uns allzeit üblich bey Einholung einer und der andern neuen Tafel oder Bilde/ und dienet so wol zur Ehre des Abgebildeten/ als zur Anreitzung anderer/ sich auch in dergleichen Tugendhalt und rühmlichen Thaten zu befleissigen; woraus nicht allein eines ieden eigene Ehre/ als des Vatterlands durch ihn beförderter Wolstand erhellen möge.'

The old man represents Time and, as Noris's 'Grand Chancellor' (138), is responsible for the display of the monuments. The nymphs depict the virginal purity at various ages, to the joy of the 'little elemental beings', the 'faithful companions of such people'. Two of the nymphs, Consideratio and Judicium, are responsible for the election of those who are to be glorified; spreading their fame is the duty of Fama.

Thus the round dance of allegorical figures, handed down from medieval morality and love poetry to Boccaccio and other writers of early modern fiction, continues unbroken in the seventeenth century. That virtue is not a privilege of class is shown in an interpretive speech on the temple metaphysics. Helianthus asks, Is virtue only to be found among 'persons of high rank'? Can it not also 'be found among persons of lesser standing?' Yes, to be sure, the boy answers, for everyone 'is bound to his conscience to be an example to the glory of God the Highest and to serve his neighbor and fatherland'. Why, then, is preference shown for people of highest standing? Because the virtue observed in the ruler (or oligarchical body) is better suited for representation and education. That the virtue embodied by the nobility is not static or unmerited can be gathered from observing the scenes that fall outside of the central panegyrical section.

Not surprisingly, Hellwig's two-hundred-page prose eclogue contains numerous other themes. Whereas in Harsdörffer's multi-volume *Frauenzimmer Gesprächspiele* manifold topics are dealt with only briefly and from constantly changing perspectives, the shepherds of the prose eclogues must limit themselves to select topics and compensate for this limitation by deepening their inquiry. Hellwig's *Nymphe Noris* serves as a model for this.

Secrets of Nature – Regulation of the Emotions

After the completion of the panegyrical section in Part Two, Hellwig has a thunderstorm roll up (149), thereby providing the shepherds an opportunity to converse on the nature of thunder and lightning. Scientific questions abound in the work of Dr Hellwig, who was trained formally as a natural scientist. Hellwig's purpose in this instance is to offer a reasonable corrective to prevailing superstition. A thunderstorm, he explains, has 'natural causes'. His description is straightforward and avoids speculation on the supernatural:

> Such weather results from nothing other than the warmth and dryness that is caused by the sun, along with the combination of a rather heavy humidity that meets a steamy mass of air as it rises from the earth. When it arrives at a mid-level elevation in the sky, the humidity having been driven there by cool air and the warmth that increasingly gathers within itself as in a cloud, it becomes enwrapped in a skin, or bubble; then this rising steamy air mass, due to the coolness of the external humidity or enwrapped cloud, and owing to its natural movement, necessarily increases in heat and pressure, until at last it seeks to be released, which

cannot occur because of the higher atmosphere and because the cloud above is thicker and heavier; wherefore, to become free of being thus imprisoned, it explodes downwards, so that the cloud bursts, and then gradually dissipates through the rain.[144]

A factual explanation of the effects of lightning and thunder follows (151–6). Hellwig maintains that his intention is to instruct via generous communication of knowledge that is not commonly available to all learned shepherds. Thus he seeks to purge popular belief of deviant misconceptions. Even ancient myths and oriental symbolism become comprehensible in their factual core through this rational strategy. The belief in divine omnipotence vis-à-vis nature remains, of course, untouched.

Somewhat later, the poet scientist returns to the scientific discourse to deliver a homage to Altdorf University (171–7), one of Germany's most progressive centers for the study of the natural sciences, and the beloved alma mater of Hellwig and other of his Nuremberg colleagues. After describing the main features of the university, he proceeds to a discussion of bones, their preservation and medicinal qualities. People say that bones found in a cave in the vicinity, when ground to a powder, can be used as an antidote against poison. The task before Montano is to posit a modern, 'natural' theory for this phenomenon. And thus he proceeds: It is calcium marl, which, together with the water in the veins of the earth, has been formed into bone-like deposits. Out of a 'wonderful playfulness', nature uses 'the freedom mildly granted by the highest God and Creator' (175) to imitate divine forms. The healing properties come from the sulfur contained in the limestone. This kind of discussion is not out of place in pastoral. Hellwig simply is taking the quality of universal knowledge, classically ascribed to poets, and applying it as an instructive tool on behalf of the urban sodality.

Human social life beyond the political realm must also be considered and regulated. In this regard, Hellwig returns to the subject of proper love (157–64), a topic for which Opitz had reserved considerable space in *Hercinie*. Strefon states the conclusion for Hellwig: 'Accordingly, to love rationally and to strive for what is useful and praiseworthy is angelic; to love mere beauty and the gifts of the body is bestial; to observe both simultaneously is human' (158). In the wedding felicitations for Klajus the moral is expounded in verse:

---

[144] *Noris* 150. 'Massen solches Wetter nichts anders ist/ als eine durch der Sonnen Gewalt veranlasste Wärme und Trükne/ auch mit etwas zeher Feuchte vermengte Aufdämpfung aus der Erde/ welche/ wann sie an den mitlern Raum der Luft gelanget/ alda wegen Kälte des Orts die Feuchte zusammen getrieben/ und die Wärme sich ie mehrers in sich ziehend gleichsam in einer Wolke/ als in einer Haut oder Blase eingeschlossen wird; dahero dann nohtwendig folget/ daß solches aufgedämpftes Wesen/ wegen der Kälte der äussersten Feuchte/ oder umschlossner Wolke so wol/ als wegen seiner natürlicher Bewegniß/ desto mehrers sich erhitzt/ und einzwengt/ bis es endlichen seinen Ausgang suchet/ den es in die höhere Luft/ und weil die Wolke oberhalb dichter und fester/ nicht haben kan/ derowegen sich solches Gefängniß frey zu machen/ mit Gewalt herabwerts tringet/ und die Wolke zerreisset/ die Wolke aber algemächlich durch den Regen sich zerflösset.'

> DIe recht' und waare Lieb in nirgent etwas wanket;
> dann solche nicht nur sich im Freudenfall entdekkt/
> ja ihre Wirkung auch sich bis in Tod erstrekkt/
> im Glük' und Unglük sie hält standfest/ und nicht schwanket.[145]

In this manner the pastoral, quite apart from its panegyrical role, contributes to the improvement of morality, a responsibility that had always been expected of poetry and one that Hellwig eagerly assumes.

The second part of *Nymphe Noris* – an independent prose eclogue in its own right – also begins with a walk through nature, starting at the Wördt meadow and Kress pleasure garden and moving to the Imhoff Gleisshammer and then to Zabelshof. At every point of interest an excited discussion ensues. The shepherds come upon copious springs, the observation of whose healing properties arouses a complaint against gluttony and drunkenness, which destroy the beneficial effects of this divine gift. 'Such ill-bred types, with their small and slothful lives, do more to mock God than to be thankful for this blessing' (115). Behind this episode lies the problem of the regulation of the emotions. Independent thinker though he is, Hellwig does not question the sovereignty of reason over the senses:

> 'Oh, what vanity,' Helianthus replied, 'in such a person, whose reason tells him how swiftly life passes but who nevertheless refuses to discipline himself; nor is he able to control his passions, and consequently gives greater authority to the servant than to the master. Clearly, Almighty God ordained that authority be given to the rational soul, wherefore He created us in His own image, accordingly to which the body, as a servant, should be subject to and serve the soul. But, alas! man has inverted this, and the soul has become subject to the body, so that it must behave after the dictates of carnal lust and thus will be violently snatched away from the divine being in which it had its origin and, like a sinner, hurled into eternal damnation.'[146]

---

[145] *Noris* 160.
> A right and proper love in nothing ever falters,
> For such a love endures, no matter come what may;
> Even unto death its strength goes not away.
> In times both good and bad, love holds and never alters.

[146] *Noris* 111–12. 'O thorichter Wandel/ sprach anderseits Helianthus/ eines solchen Menschen/ der seinen Verstand nach wol weiß/ wie schnell es um ihn geschehen/ dannoch sich nicht regirn/ noch seine Begierde bezämen kan/ und also mehrers Herrschafft dem Knecht/ als dem Herrn einraumet. Sintemal Gott der allerhöchste der vernünftigen Seele die Herrschafft anbefohlen/ und dardurch uns Menschen ihme zum Ebenbild erschaffen/ derer nun zu Dienst der Leib/ als ein Knecht/ solle unterworffen seyn. Aber leider! man kehret es um/ und wird die Seele dem Leibe unterworffen/ daß sie ihre Wirkungen den fleischlichen Lüsten nach vollbringen muß/ und wird sie also dem Göttlichen Wesen/ aus welchem sie ihren Ursprung/ hat mit Gewalt entzogen/ und frefler Weise in das ewige Verderben gestürtzet.'

Anthropological dualism, with its pessimistic theological-philosophical and socio-psychological aspects, clearly informs this discussion. What has been less well understood by scholarship are the questions regarding early modern class distinction, which occupy a prominent place in the discursive type of pastoral poetry. *Die Nymphe Noris* is remarkable for the direct way in which it confronts the issue, as in the following episode.

On True Nobility

'As they walked along, these shepherds entered into a rather broad conversation, the main question of which was whether the sciences and moral philosophy are suitable subjects for their lowly shepherd's estate, and whether it had been so in years past' (117). In answer, two competing historical paradigms, that of Spartan and that of Athenian society, are juxtaposed. Helianthus points out that freeborn Spartan nobles demonstrated to their children the consequences of shameful conduct, such as drunkenness among their slaves, arguing that 'knowledge and moral conduct' were the preserve of 'the higher estate, including the nobility and the ruler', whereas the 'lower estate to which the shepherds belonged was excluded'. Montano rebuts this paradigm with that of the Athenians, 'among whom the lower as well as the upper estates, slave as well as freeman, servant as well as master, were held in high esteem with respect to learning. Servants were often given their freedom on this account. Without a doubt, the free nobility arose here and had its beginning' (117–18). Thus the historical argument for egalitarian access to education; apart from this basis the idea could not thrive nor poetry be practiced within humanism.

The discussion ultimately arrives at the conclusion that the shepherd's estate not only has a right to the sciences but is in fact uniquely qualified to study and teach them. It is a remarkable moment in the history of German pastoral:

> *Montano*: But given [as you say] that these sciences are comparatively more appropriate for the nobility and higher estate, since the art of governing well and wise counts among these sciences, does it necessarily follow that they are somehow inappropriate to the lower estates, including our shepherd's estate? No, not at all. Particularly since, unlike an aristocratic name or great wealth, which are inherited, they are a special divine gift, which can exist as well beneath a lowly shepherd's garment as under a purple royal vestment. Moreover, one of the areas of knowledge is not only that of ruling others, but rather what is in fact much higher, that of governing one's own sensual inclinations wisely, and this must be attached to the aforesaid art of governing as an edifying example. For just as the greatest victory consists in having overcome the enemy with patience, so does the highest art and science consist in being able to tame one's own self and one's senses; which, however, although a divine gift,

cannot always be acquired alone and apart from instruction at the hands of a dutiful teacher.

Helianthus: Why, then, in the times of our ancestors, were most schools and monasteries, in which instruction in the sciences and moral philosophy was given, thought to be most appropriately dedicated to the nobility?

Montano: Certainly, Helianthus, my good friend, you are correct to emphasize that it was for instruction in the sciences and the moral doctrines, particularly with respect to the nobility, since, if I may modestly suggest, our dear ancestors were already aware that the nobility, relying as it does on its wealth and boasting of its heredity, hold knowledge and virtue in little regard and would therefore otherwise have led a dissolute and wild life. Thus means were contrived to direct their better instincts and, by prescribing and measuring the daily sustenance needs of their bodies and avoiding the pampering of excess, to guide them in such a way that they might better grasp these doctrines and this instruction and, in the regular practice of them, come to a proper understanding both of themselves and their Creator, and moreover, through perceptive reflection, be able to see to what purpose they were created and what human path they should follow. By contrast, the more lowly, to wit, our simple shepherd's estate, behold! has this advantage: that, in its lowliness and simplicity it has overcome unnatural self-indulgence, harmful desires, the vain pride of ambition, sinful envy, and corrupting avarice; its faculties and thoughts are less repressed and more accountable in the conscientious practice, quite apart from one's vocation, of these sciences and mental exercises. These things, indeed, one can learn, without any other assistance, right out of the Book of Nature itself.[147]

---

[147] *Noris* 118–19. [NB: the original single-paragraph form in *Noris* has been modified in the English version in order better to visualize the dialogue]. 'Und gesetzt/ daß diese Wissenschafften dem Adel und höherem Stand etwas anständiger/ dieweil auch die Kunst wol und weißlich zu regirn darunter verhüllet ist/ solte es darum desto unthunlicher seyn/ solche imgleichen bey dem gemeinen/ wie auch unserm Schäferstand zu hegen? Nein/ keineswegs. Sintemal sie nicht/ wie der Adeliche Name oder stattliches Herkommen ererbet werden/ sondern eine sondere Himmelsgabe sind/ die so wol sich unter einem ringen Schäferskleid/ als einem Königlichen Purpurmantel erhalten können. So stekket über das unter solcher Wissenschafft nicht nur die Weise andere zu regirn/ sondern eine noch viel höhere/ sich und seine Sinnneigungen selbsten weißlich anzuführen/ die der vorbesagten Regirkunst/ als ein erbauliches Beyspiel/ an die Seiten gesetzet wird. Dann wie die Gedult als den stärksten Feind überwunden haben der grösseste Siegspracht ist/ also ist auch sich selbsten/ und seine Sinne zämen/ die höchste Kunst und Wissenschafft; welche/ obwol sie eine Himmelsgaab/ doch nicht iederzeit ohne Mittel und Anweisung getreuer Lehrmeister erlernet wird. Warum seyn dann/ fragte Helianthus weiters/ bey unserer vor Eltern Zeiten die meiste Stifftungen und Clöster nur dem Adel zum besten gewidmet worden/ in welchen man sie von allerhand Wissenschafften und Tugendlehren unterrichten solte? Freylich/ saget ihr recht/ ihr mein vertrauter Helianthus/ zur Unterrichtung in den Wissenschafften und Tugendlehren/ antworttete Montano/ und sonderlich

Knowledge and virtue, the decisive levers used by Hellwig, must be uncoupled from class hierarchies. They are uninheritable, not subject to laws of descent, and so cannot be a privilege of the upper classes, the principality, the nobility, or the wealthy bourgeoisie. They are called a 'gift of heaven' only in the sense of the granting of a power. The utilization of this power is within the freedom of the human being and is available to everyone. Even the privilege of the nobility and upper estate to rule is weakened by the 'art of governing' *oneself*, as we know from ancient moral philosophy. Every individual is capable of this by virtue of the gifts of heaven. This inner, moral art of governance is cultivated through knowledge. To that extent knowledge and morality form the basis of the life of the individual no less than of society. Not only are the emotions regulated by them, but the building of social consensus as well. Pastoral poetry is incessantly concerned with this matter, for it provides the mechanism by which the social structure can be influenced. In a Socratic gesture, Montano argues that the highest level of the nobility in fact endangers its position whenever it attempts to establish inherited rights and prestige. These rights are never first nature but always second nature. In other words, they are in need of being supplemented. They receive their full worth only through the acquisition of knowledge and the virtue upon which it is based. The shepherds, on the other hand, although of a lower class, live from first nature and receive their wisdom, knowledge, and virtue, not from society but directly from the 'Book of Nature'. This is the seal of origin; it indicates that pastoral values represent something primordial and non-derivative. These values as embodied in the Pegnesischer Blumenorden specifically and in the nobilitas literaria in general transcend time and place and conform to divine order and human reason.

Thus Hellwig's *Nymphe Noris* proves its greatness as a pastoral work. It manages to praise the ruling class while at the same time confronting it with those norms that have always existed in the lowly shepherd's estate. This is the sense of pastoral speech: that the divine gifts of science, art, and virtue 'can exist as

dem Adelstand/ dieweil meinem einfältigen Bedunken nach/ die liebe Vorfahren mit scharffrn Augen albereit gesehen/ daß der Adel auf seinen Reichthum sich verlassend/ und auf sein Herkommend pochend/ der Wissenschaft und Tugend sich wenig achten/ und demnach ein wüstes und wildes Leben führen würde/ also haben sie dieses Mittel erfunden/ die tauglichen Gemüther in solchen Schranken zu behalten/ und bey vorgesetzter und abgemessener Leibesunterhalt und täglicher Nohtdurft dieselbe/ mit Vermeidung des verzärtleten Uberflusses/ dahin zu leiten/ darmit sie desto bequemlicher würden besagte Lehren und Unterricht zu fassen/ und bey steter Ausübung derselben sich und ihren Schöpfer recht zu erkennen/ und im klugen Nachsinnen ersehen/ zu was Ende sie erschaffen/ und des Menschen Wandel anzustellen sey. Im Gegentheil hat der mindere/ wie auch unser ringer Schäferstand/ schauet! diesen Vortheil/ daß er in seiner Nidrigkeit und Einfalt/ des unnatürlichen Schwelgens/ schandlicher Wollust/ eitler Standshoffahrt/ frefler Mißgunst/ und Gewissenschädlicher Geldsucht überhoben/ seine Sinne und Gedanken was freyers hat/ und tüchtiger ist/ nebenst seinem Beruf solchen Wissenschafften und Unterrichten abzuwarten/ und zu rechtmässiger Ausübung zu bringen; ja wol solches alles/ ohne anderer Beyhülfe aus dem Naturbuch selber erlernen kan.'

well beneath a lowly shepherd's garment as under a purple royal vestment'. The universal quality that binds people across class boundaries lies under the protection of the shepherds, of people, that is, who do not stand at the top of the community. The ethical content of the Sermon on the Mount is in good hands with the shepherds, who, according to the poetic evidence, constitute the estate closest to creation. This realization is decisive in explaining the attraction of the genre between Dante and Fontenelle. It carried within itself the seeds of the Enlightenment.

The Pastoral Language of Patriotism

Typically among the Pegnitz poets, philosophy is dissolved in the musicality of the verse. With Hellwig, even this musicality is heavy with meaning:

> SChäfer und Schäferinn nidrigen Stande
>   Wissenschaft zieret/ belobet ihn macht.
> Tugend ist derer getreuestes Bande/
>   welches die Schäfer in Rufe gebracht.
>   Drum Tugend stets lieben
>   die Schäfer/ sich üben
>   in solcher mit Fleiß;
>   klugs wissen sie lernen
>   sich niemals entfernen
> so süssem beheglichen Nectar und Speiß.[148]

As such, the shepherds are the group appointed to pay homage to the nobles of the city-state. The precious gift of the German language is transferred to them. They are called upon to bring a poetic offering of thanksgiving for what they have witnessed around Noris.

The first topic to which they devote themselves upon leaving the Temple of Noris is the 'honor of our German mother tongue' (72), thereby returning to their own sphere, for the propagation of the language represents their 'heroic' work:

---

[148] *Noris* 120.
> Shepherd and shepherdess, knowledge commands,
>   Highly adorns, your lowly estate.
> Virtue's the bond on which all this depends,
>   Giving to shepherds a name that is great.
>   So, virtue admiring,
>   Daily aspiring,
>   In meadows they meet,
>   Pursuing their learning,
>   And constantly yearning
> For heavenly nourishment useful and sweet.

> Str. Der Teutschen Teutscher Sprach sich nirgend andre gleichet/
> wie hoch sie immer ist.
> Kl. Der Teutschen Zungen Lob der Sternen Bahn durchstreichet/
> ihr Ruhm sich nicht vermisst.
> Str. Was Ehr' und welche Gnad' hat oftermals erhoben
> ihr groß Vermögen hie?
> Kl. Daher die Reinligkeit derselben hoch zu loben;
> ihr Preiß ermanglet nie.[149]

The purity of the language and the old native German uprightness praised by Tacitus are related, interdependently, as the shepherds point out. That they have received protection from the highest offices of the empire, from Charlemagne to Rudolf I to Ludwig of Anhalt-Köthen, confirms their dignity even in the political realm. Their onomatopoeic practice hearkens back to their original Adamic state. Without 'foreign help', the German language 'reigns over others', because it partakes equally of nature and history. 'She clashes swords with Mars, she whispers with the flutes: / holds sway in ev'rything.'

Die Nymphe Noris is an abundant source of rhyming metaphors, riddles, and symbols. A particularly unique feature of prose eclogue consists in the shepherds' exchange of letters. This practice was initiated during Birken's residency at the Wolfenbüttel court, followed by his years of travel in northern Germany. Floridan is not only the subject of poetry, he himself contributes verse and prose to Hellwig's book from afar. *Die Nymphe Noris* offers, through these letters, a biographical source for the young poet struggling for self-expression. Floridan is frank in saying that his 'exile' far from the Pegnitz shepherds is not his own desiring:

> . . .
> Höret/ was mich wil vertreiben.
> Mir gebricht an Vieh' und Haab;
> meine Nahrung nimmet ab.
>
> Darum muß ich mich umschauen/
> wo ich weiter neme Brod;

---

[149] *Noris* 73.
> Str. To German people's tongue none else compares by far,
> Though lofty it may be.
> Kl. The praise of Germans' tongue floats there among the stars
> In striking dignity.
> Str. What honor and what grace did ever manifest
> Such power among men?
> Kl. And German's purity stands high above the rest;
> We praise it without end.

und zu Wendung meiner Noht
anderwerts mein Glükk erbauen.[150]

The Saale and the Oker may offer ever so many pleasures, but in comparison with those of the Pegnitz they seem insignificant. The repeatedly interwoven autobiographical song of the absent shepherd takes on, unconcealed, the character of a petition to the members of the Nuremberg order to do everything in their power to make possible the return home of this destitute wanderer:

> Having wandered around the rivers of Lower Saxony for three years, strolled across many a pasture and meadow, and fluted his flocks to the evening manger, playing on pipes carved from foreign reeds: now among his sheep he is visited by a fervent longing for the well-tuned flutes of the Pegnitz shepherds, a craving hunger for the clover-rich fields along the Pegnitz, a feverish thirst for the Pegnitz's golden-streaming, crystal-clear arms, and a passionate memory of the delightful shadows falling from the trees all about.[151]

Birken is not timid about taking advantage of the opportunity that Hellwig has provided to recapitulate the stations of his life, and there is no reason to doubt that his sufferings are real. Prose eclogue allows this personal tone.

The Celebration of Peace

For his own part, however, Hellwig is relatively unconcerned with biographical questions and remains focused on broader ethical and political issues. This raises his pastoral far above works that are dedicated solely to specific occasions. Let us look, for example, in Part Two, at his lengthy praise of the Kresses, with whom Hellwig felt particularly close and in whom he finds all the aristocratic virtues, culminating in their devotion to the fatherland (177–85). The Kress estate,

---

[150] *Noris* 81.
. . .
> Here's the reason I must leave:
>   Herds and goods – all these are gone,
>   Naught remains to live upon.
>
> Thus I hither look and yon,
>   Where some greener pastures wait;
>   There perhaps a kinder fate
>   Offers more to build upon.

[151] *Noris* 168. 'Nachdem selbiger nunmehr in die drey Jahr lang an den NiederSächsischen Flüssen herumgewandert/ mancherlei Haiden und Weiden betrieben/ und auf ausländischen Rohren geschnittenen Pfeiffen seinen Heerden bißhero zur Tafel gespielet und geflötet: befindet er bey seinen Schäfelein ein sehnendes Verlangen nach denen wolgestimmten Flöten der Pegnitzhirten/ einen lechtzenden Hunger nach den Kleereichen Pegnitzfeldern/ einen heisen Durst nach den goldrinnenden und krystallenklaren Pegnitz-Armen/ und eine verlangende Wiedergedächtniß der ergetzlichen Baumschatten in der Nähe daselbst.'

unfortunately, has been severely damaged in these recent 'heart-wrenching and blood-flowing times' (181). Happily, however, terrible times now belong to the past. The work ends in a praise of peace, occasioned by the Peace of Westphalia, which had been concluded in the meantime (1648), intertwined with praise of the emperor [see Plate 6].[152] Hellwig takes up this centenary theme and gives it his own special tone within the shouts of celebration around Nuremberg.

Now the shepherds are no longer being led. Peace is, after all, uniquely their metier. They set about establishing an 'artistic peace memorial' in the form of an allegorical palace. The reader can easily follow its construction to completion. Its gleaming white marble declares that 'precious peace is an upright, immaculate, and virginally pure being'. Peace can be approached only via the 'middle path of virtue'. Over the gate we see the portrait of Ferdinand III, to whom thanks are due that 'the shedding of native blood ceases henceforth in our fatherland' (183). Like Vergil, Hellwig invites the highest representative of secular power into his pastoral world, situating him on the peace memorial between the two greatest rulers in history, Alexander and Augustus (185). His work of peace is the gift of a 'charitable' deed (183). Through the 'wise sweat of concern' and 'devoted love', he has brought peace to 'the beloved fatherland'. Only after Ferdinand has been thus elevated and the bond between the imperial city and the sovereign asserted as immutable, are the other two 'potentates', the French and the Swedish, commemorated (184). The nymphs 'Upright Loyalty' and 'Precious Unity', along with the standard with the two-headed crowned eagle, stand on a platform; on the right waves the banner of the lily (France) and on the left the banner of the lion (Sweden). On the reverse side of these symbols of power their pastoral symbols are added. Victory and Peace embrace on the imperial dais, the former with a laurel wreath on her head and a palm branch in her hand, the latter with an olive branch on her head and a burst pomegranate in her hand. On the right is Humility with shepherd's staff and purse, and to the side a bouquet of flowers; on the left is Patience with reins and halter and a lamb. Raging war can be definitively quelled only through patience on the part of the victor and humility on the part of the vanquished. The ultimate penetration of peace into this world of war is expressed by a naked sword wound about with an olive branch and by a sword beat into a plowshare.[153] Destructive power withers in face of its opposite, pastoral non-violence. Is it any wonder that the symbols of the Golden Age arise again now, familiar to the western literary vision of a pacified history since the eclogues of Vergil? Strefon takes the elephant and lion as symbols from Egyptian political iconography and weds them with the Temple of Honor; Montano attends to the crowning conclusion by returning to pastoral symbolism. 'I would,' Montano says

---

[152] It has been established that *Die Nymphe Noris* was begun in 1646 and finished in the spring of 1650, which suggests a fascinating synchronicity between compositional and real time, both of which cover and conclude with the final events of the war leading up to the Peace. See Max Reinhart, 'Historical, Poetic and Ideal Representation in Hellwig's Prose Eclogue *Die Nymphe Noris*', *Daphnis* 19, no. 1 (1990): 41–66.

[153] In reference to Isa. 2:4.

Plate 6 'Peace Banquet' of 25 September 1649 in the Nuremburg *Rathaus*. Copper engraving by G.D. Heumann after a portrait by J. von Sandrart (right front). From ACTA PACIS WESTPHALICAE PUBLICA. *Oder Westphälische Friedens-Handlungen und Geschichte*. Part I (following p. 364), by Johann Gottfried von Meiern. Hannover: Joh. Chr. Ludolph Schultz, 1734.

fill the inner part of the archway at the top with many little angels and nature spirits, who appear to be strewing all kinds of pretty flowers onto those who pass through. Then on one side beneath an alder let a shepherd repose while playing on his flute. Next to him a large sheep dog lies sleeping, while sheep and wolves drink peacefully together from the nearby stream. Across from this in a smithy, the apprentice forges scythes, sickles, plowshares, and other useful tools from swords, lances, and other weapons. One notes the agreeable bliss of these lovers of peace and harmony.[154]

This represents the marriage of the pagan Vergilian world with the biblical world, which reaches its culmination in the combined images of the divine child from the prophecy of Isaiah (ch. 11) and that of Vergil's *Eclogue* 4. Thus Hellwig ends his celebration of peace:

> DU schönes Götterkind! Ach komm'/ ach komme bald/
> laß völlig schauen dich in deiner schön Gestalt.
> >   Du Wolstandsstiffterin! Friedseelig ist/ der find
> >   dich/ und umarmet hält/ du schönes Götterkind![155]

Transmundane Wisdom

The pastoral itself, however, has a different ending. As the sun sets, Montano remains behind in the field, 'reflecting further on the rumors of peace' (189).

> ANfangs aus blossem Nichts ward dieses Rund gestaltet
> >   durch Gottes Mund und Geist/
> >   die Schrifft es klärlich weisst/
> des Höchsten höchste Macht ob solchen heut noch schaltet.
>
> Des Menschen Ankunft ist hinwidrum aus dem Runde/
> >   das anfangs nicht gewesst;
> >   wann Gott die Hand ablesst/
> der Mensch und dieses Rund schnell senken hin zu Grunde.

---

[154] *Noris* 186. 'Und ich/ sagte anderseits Montano/ staffirte den inneren Raum der Pforten/ am Bogen oben mit vielen Engelein oder Naturgeisterlein aus/ die gleichsam begehrten allerley schöne Blumen auf die Durchgehende zu streuen. Dann an einer Seiten herab müste ein Schäfer unter den Erlen/ auf seiner Flöte dudlend/ ruhen/ nebenst dem ihm die grosse Schaafrüden schlaffend liegen/ die Wölffe und Schaafe aber untereinander sich friedlich aus dem nahligenden Bächlein tränken; hergegenüber sollen in einer Schmidten die Schmidtsknechte/ aus Schwertern/ Spiesen und Waffen Sensen/ Sichel/ Pflugschaar/ und andern zum Feldbau dienlichen Gezeug schmieden/ zu bemerken hiermit die behegliche Glükseeligkeit der Friedliebenden und Ruhgenossen.'

[155] *Noris* 187.
> Thou darling godly child, oh, hasten, go not slow!
> Come, let us thee behold, let all thy beauty show.
> >   Thou Lord Prosperity! hast surely on him smiled,
> >   Who finds and holds thee fast, thou darling godly child!

So unbeständig ist des Menschen eigenes Wessen/
    der steht/ und doch vergeht/
    fällt/ eh' er recht anfäht/
wie kan begründtes Stands sein Wandel sich vermessen?

Ein eingehauchter Luft dem Menschen gibt das Leben/
    ein aufgeglimter Dampf
    mit Luftbeseeltem Kampf
des Menschen Will' und Werk' ans helle Tagliecht geben.

Wie unstet diese Luft in ihrem Ort verbleibet/
    sich wandlet fort und fort/
    bald Sudwerts/ bald nach Nord/
der Luftbenöhtet Mensch so seinen Handel treibet.

Demnach was Menschenwitz erklüglet und ersinnet
    in Freundschafft oder Streit/
    sich richtet nach der Zeit/
gantz unverhofft es offt ein wiedrigs End gewinnet.

Der beste Fried auf Erd' ist die Gewissensraste
    die sonder Lasterschuld
    erwirbet Gunst und Huld;
dem Menschen ist die Sünd ein unberuhter Gaste.

Wer das Gewissen nun in solcher Ruhe findet/
    des Geist sich aufwerts schwingt/
    ein Lobgesang erklingt
zu Ehren dem/ der sich mit ihm in Lieb verbindet.

Ist nun der höchste Gott in Lieb mit uns verbunden/
    wer solt uns schaden dann?
    so haben wir die Bahn
in rechtbelobter Weiß zum waaren Fried gefunden.

Der Fried bey Gott erhebt/ und unsrem eignen Gwissen
    ernähret und erhelt/
    uns an die Stelle stellt/
wo sonder Zeit der Zeit wir Friedens Freud geniessen.[156]

---

[156] *Noris* 189–91.
    From utter nothingness the earth came into being,
        Inspired by God's command;
        God's Word we understand:
    The sovereign might of God creation still is leading.

    Then later man appeared, in turn from earth created,
        Which God himself did make.

To my knowledge, no other German poet spoke such a language in the seventeenth century. It is the language of an independent-thinking individual who shapes his own words. At the end of the pastoral the shepherd's pleasure in language games is over. And yet, what Hellwig gives us is not a simple Protestant hymn like that with which he opened Parts One and Two and closed Part One. Rather, once again like a Vergilian shepherd, the poet raises his voice to sing of

---

Should God the world forsake,
Both earth and man would fall, from God's grace separated.

The character of man, how wavering and passing:
    We live, but on the sand;
    We fall before we stand.
What arrogance to think this earth were everlasting.

For human life began with simple inhalation,
    An animated glow,
    A stirring wind to sow
The seed of warring wills of human aspiration.

So anxiously this breath away from home is tending,
    It wafts both here and there,
    North, south, and everywhere.
Thus breath-dependent man will ply his days in wand'ring.

Whatever human wit devises or supposes,
    Amity or crime,
    All is turned by time,
Which often unforeseen a grievous end composes.

No better peace on earth than conscience clear and smiling,
    Which, free of guilt and shame,
    Attains a worthy name;
For sin's a restless guest in human heart residing.

If honestly we find our conscience rests so sweetly,
    Our spirits upward wind,
    And hymns of praise we send
To honor him whose love joins him with us completely.

If God Almighty then with us in love's united,
    What evil shall we dread?
    For now the path we tread
Leads on in righteousness to peace that's undivided.

The peace of God uplifts; our conscience fat with sadness
    It lightens and sustains.
    It bears us to a plane,
Where, timeless, time will be to rest in peace and gladness.

the beginning of the world, although, contrary to the Hesiodic-Lucretian conception of his great classical predecessor, his view is entirely Judeo-Christian.

With this radical modification, Hellwig's *Nymphe Noris* adumbrates the demise of classical pastoral after more than a century of religious and civil wars in Europe. The greatness of man, 'which often unforeseen a grievous end composes', withers over the course of events between the St. Bartholomew's Day Massacre and the execution of Charles I. After the established denominations have exhausted themselves, only the searching soul is left and becomes, in the end – for want of a better expression – the lyrical 'I'. He is forced back upon himself, left only with his own conscience, which alone justifies his singing a hymn of praise to the Creator and his hope, nay, his certainty, of an answer. To such a person is granted a peace that is the foreshadowing of eternal peace. Thus pastoral language turns into the language of man; it does not, however, in the process of this translation, fail to uphold the sober content of truth in the pastoral sphere.

V. Thirteen Points Towards a Theory of Nuremberg Pastoral[157]

No city in the German-speaking lands of the seventeenth century had as lively a pastoral output in combination with the same high degree of theoretical reflection as Nuremberg. The production of pastoral writing in Nuremberg continued for about half a century at a degree of linguistic and intellectual experimentation that other centers of pastoral masquerade, such as Leipzig, could not even begin to approximate. On the basis of the preceding explication of the three major prose eclogues from the founding years of the Pegnesischer Blumenorden, the following points are offered towards a theory of the Nuremberg adaptation of the European pastoral tradition.

1. Pastoral enjoyed a fluorescence in Nuremberg, first of all, because, as a genre, it requires a high degree of non-literal speech, that is, indirect, enciphered, multi-layered language, which is eminently suited to *scharfsinnig* 'perspicacious' speech. Pastoral also thrived in Nuremberg because its first great German theoretician, Harsdörffer, stressed the imaginative and transformative powers of poetry in general and, specifically, of pastoral poetry.
2. These powers were well suited to a genre that was traditionally understood to be natural and simple and sprung directly from nature and the Creator. Within the hierarchy of genres it was precisely the modest, lowly genre that became

---

[157] [Editor's note: In translating these points, which in the original German are articulated at a rather high degree of specialist abstraction (they were also first published separately, for which see 'Bibliographical Note on the Essays'), the translators have taken a certain liberty in modulating them to the level of the first four sections of the essay, though of course with due regard for the content.]

the leading experimental vehicle for assertive and critical speech. This paradox is sharpened inasmuch as the perspicacious quality of pastoral speech results from the integration of what is natural and originary with what is highly intellectual and artificial. Such *coincidentiae oppositorum* were prized in Nuremberg, for they radicalized pastoral's traditional features and allowed practitioners to carry the inherently oxymoronic character of the genre to extreme levels.

3. Nuremberg pastoral in the second half of the seventeenth century in Germany thus represented a conspicuous and delicate variant within the history of concettism. This owed in large part to Harsdörffer's sensitive receptivity to Italian and Spanish cultural forms, which helped to make it possible for Nuremberg to develop into a leading center of modernist concettism. Nuremberg pastoral poetry is a version of that dominant figuration.[158] The creative differences evident in the three models are therefore only relative with respect to the concettic deep structure of Nuremberg pastoral.

4. The complexity of pastoral poetry as the 'most ancient genre' (J.C. Scaliger: *vetustissimum genus*) expanded into an extreme figuration in Nuremberg. Any theory of Nuremberg pastoral must account for this radical complication, which is constituted of linguistic, rhetorical, moral-philosophical, sociological, theological, and other factors.

5. The qualification of pastoral poetry as the most ancient genre, the oldest art form after music, places it in a special relationship to music. Scaliger observes that the shepherd, who lives a life of *otium*, is more inclined than the farmer to singing, for singing does not conflict with his only occupation, tending sheep. The shepherd's singing is in itself an imitative act of nature, whose sounds – the singing of birds, the rustling of trees – lend themselves to mimicry. Singing is a natural act, and the first poetic response of the shepherd gives expression to the most elemental and natural quality of the human being: love.

6. From this follows pastoral's unique capacity for developing the musical powers of language. We may say that pastoral is music become language. In music as well as pastoral, expression is preserved in pristine form; even the most elaborate and advanced language games reflect the light of creation. The unprecedented acoustic experiments in Nuremberg are inspired by the belief in the originality of the German language, and they press, as in no other genre, towards musical fulfillment. The language of pastoral sets in motion a return, through its dissolution into naive music, to an undifferentiated Adamic language.

---

[158] [Editor's note: Garber uses the term *Figuration* consistent with the 'figuration theory' of Norbert Elias (*The Civilizing Process* [1939], trans. Edmund Jephcott [New York: Pantheon, 1982], which implies the complex 'bundling' of structures and influences that together constitute the field of activity and identification, whether at the individual or macro-level. A given figuration can come to dominate a place or time, as in the present instance, as Garber argues, concettism did in mid-seventeenth-century Nuremberg.]

7. Thus Nuremberg pastoral has a profound language-philosophical component. The degree to which Buchner influenced verse theory in Nuremberg was matched in the area of language philosophy by J.G. Schottel, particularly with respect to pastoral. The 'deutsche Haupt- und Heldensprache' (German primary and heroic language) is the closest to the (Hebrew) primal language, and the most ancient literary genre serves as its genuine vessel.
8. What has been observed with respect to the relationship between music and pastoral language applies *mutatis mutandis* to all linguistic and stylistic forms of pastoral poetry. Even the cleverest figure poem, the most artful plays and riddles on letters, words, and sentences, or the most daring metaphors, are justified by their proximity to the primal language and they in turn underscore this relationship. The primal musical quality of pastoral language tends towards the suspension of 'meaning' in the individual work.
9. On the other hand, German's ethical gravity, which is strongly emphasized by Schottel, acts as a counterweight to the disengagement of the non-semantic quality of poetic language. We note such expressions as 'fromme tapffere teutsche Worte' (pious, brave German words), or 'uhralte Teutsche Redlichkeit, fleissiges und strenges Tapfer-seyn' (ancient German honesty, diligent and stern bravery), which now have semantic substance. The copious moral qualities of the German language came into circulation with the humanist reception of Tacitus and gained in importance as the theory of German's anciency was hypothesized. Pastoral, as the most ancient genre, could then be regarded as the ideal representation of this ethical privilege, for the speaker of this language is none other than the shepherd, who is ennobled by the primal language that he speaks. In turn, through its practice, he contributes to the further enhancement of its moral qualities.
10. Such a language can be spoken only by virtuous speakers – an indispensable condition for every speech act. Sociologically, there may be any number of different speakers. One thing, however, is a priori true: No speaker surpasses the poet shepherd in mastery of the primal language, for only he belongs to the most ancient estate. As such he is automatically the representative speaker of the true German language, not only because of his anciency, but also because he is the custodian and promoter of its ethical content.
11. The shepherd's social and other non-linguistic qualifications also derive from pastoral's closeness to the Adamic state, where it is infused with the elemental virtues. In the word games of the Pegnitz shepherds, the conceptual field exists between the border categories of humility (genre) and critical assertiveness (speech practice); on the moral field, similarly, the boundaries are also mainly binary. While the shepherds preserve the primal values, thereby creating the purest and most radical of norms, the other estates live comparatively removed from the norm-generating original state. This distance signifies a deficiency, and it is mitigated only to the extent that the norms of the shepherd's estate are accepted.

12. However, the social area must be distinguished from the linguistic, where the internal and external oppositions take place rather differently. Pastoral does not attain fulfillment by transforming everyone into a shepherd but in arriving at a conclusion where everyone, regardless of rank, accepts its norms. These norms belong to the sphere of leisure, the *vita contemplativa*, a prerequisite for poetic activity. Secondary to these are the norms of the *vita activa*, which belong to the historical realm and are realized in the moral perfection, courage, and invincibility of heroes. Peace is the highest good in pastoral; its attainment depends on a total symbiosis of shepherdly and heroic virtues. The power in this symbiosis is realized to the degree that the historical world yields to pastoral values. In Hegelian terms, it progresses from existence as spirit to existing in and of itself; that is, it at last intuits itself in a completed, objective sense as an absolute.
13. Within this signification system theological elements are articulated at varying levels of intensity. Given its theoretical proximity to creation, pastoral is an ideally predisposed medium for theological reflection on religious topics and forms that are universal in scope. Confessional particulars are rejected in favor of unifying principles. Thus the shepherd's ethos partakes of the age's interconfessional, ecumenical, and irenic spirit. Specifically, early modern pastoral manifests a natural affinity to Reformed theology, the goal of which was to promote basic and widely acceptable truths of the Christian faith, indeed, in principle, of all monotheistic religions. An interdisciplinary methodology could be developed along these lines that would explore the larger significance of theological, musical, and poetic reforms in Nuremberg.

In conclusion, it is clear that the Pegnesischer Blumenorden viewed itself as a society of poets, in and through which pastoral norms were symbolically represented. This coincidence of shepherd's estate and sodality was unique to the Nuremberg poets.[159] Furthermore, pastoral ideals put their stamp on other forms of composition, including epistolary correspondence, from which cultural, political, and social implications arise. We must look deeper than the pastoral habit itself pursuant to reconstructing the unique cultural and literary-historical group mentality, since it can only have derived from a complex variety of historical and aesthetic factors.

With respect to investigating the functionality of the *Sprachgesellschaften*, scholarship, candidly speaking, is still in its infancy. Scholars must at last begin to recognize that, with the emergence of the Nuremberg school, German intellectual societies achieved a connection with avant-garde European humanism in what was arguably the last great stylistic movement of European literature before the onset of the Enlightenment. In the final chapter of this book

---

[159] All German *Sprachgesellschaften* cultivated pastoral poetry, of course, though often in an unserious way that appreciated it mainly as a ubiquitous minor form of occasional poetry.

we shall look at three major tendencies of humanism that reached their culmination in the work, respectively, of Gottfried Arnold, Gottfried Wilhelm Leibniz, and Christian Thomasius. The irony is that these deeply rooted traditions prepared the way for the Enlightenment, only to be treated by new cultic personalities like Goethe (or so the reception of his work has been appropriated!) as though they had hardly existed. An 'imperiled heritage' indeed.*

---

  * Translated by Karl F. Otto, Jr and Michael Swisher; translation of the poems by the editor.

Chapter 7

Begin with Goethe? Forgotten Traditions at the Threshold of the Modern Age*

> 'I am glad,' Goethe then said with a laugh, 'that I am not eighteen now. When I was eighteen, Germany was in its teens also, and something could be done; but now an incredible deal is demanded, and every avenue is barred.'[1]

Such was the seventy-four-year-old Goethe's comment on 15 February 1824 to his biographer Johann Peter Eckermann, who had met the poet for Sunday breakfast and found him to be in 'excellent spirits'. One would do well, however, not to dismiss the comment simply as a passing witticism or self-indulgent remark. The older Goethe is known for often having made comments of this sort. In a conversation recorded by his friend Chancellor Friedrich von Müller six years later on 24 April 1830, he returned to the topic in a roundabout but emphatic way. As so often, the subject was Germany's uniquely precarious literary situation in comparison with that of its western neighbor:

> 'The French,' he began, 'will not have another eighteenth century, no matter what they do. What do they have to offer that might compare with Diderot? His tales, how clearly thought out, how deeply felt, how pithy, how powerful, how charmingly uttered! . . . It would be something indeed for the new writers in France if they could part from such traditions and examples, from such a developed, finished, excellent state and break new paths.'[2]

---

* This essay is dedicated to George Schoolfield.
[1] *Gespräche mit Goethe in den letzten Jahren seines Lebens* (Berlin: Deutsche Buchgemeinschaft, 1984): 'Ich freue mich,' sagte Goethe darauf lachend, 'daß ich jetzt nicht achtzehn Jahre alt bin. Als ich achtzehn war, war Deutschland auch erst achtzehn, da ließ sich noch etwas machen; aber jetzt wird unglaublich viel gefordert, und es sind alle Wege verrannt.' Translation: *Conversations with Eckermann (1823–1832)*, trans. John Oxenford (San Francisco: North Point Press, 1984), 31.
[2] Müller, *Unterhaltungen mit Goethe*, 2nd edn, ed. Renate Grumach (Munich: Beck, 1982), 190–91: 'Die Franzosen bekommen doch kein 18. Jahrhundert wieder, sie mögen machen, was sie wollen. Wo haben sie etwas aufzuweisen, das mit Diderot zu vergleichen wäre? Seine Erzählungen, wie klar gedacht, wie tief empfunden, wie körnig, wie kräftig, wie anmutig ausgesprochen! . . . Es will was heißen für die neuern Schriftsteller in Frankreich, sich von so großen Traditionen und Mustern, von einem so ausgebildeten, abgeschlossenen großartigen Zustand loszureißen und neue Bahnen zu betreten.'

Then, reflecting on the literary past of his own generation, Goethe remarked,

> The rest of us simple youths back in 1772 had an easier time of it. We had nothing behind us and could simply write away, being certain of applause if we were to come up with something that was even half-way decent.[3]

The Storm and Stress generation did, of course, have that one great name to whom Goethe pays homage in Book 10 of *Poetry and Truth*: the hero of the young, who had ennobled poet and poetry alike, Friedrich Gottlieb Klopstock:

> Now, however, the time was at hand when poetic genius would discover self-awareness, create its own circumstances, and understand how to lay the foundations for independent respectability. Klopstock had all the qualities required for instituting such an epoch.[4]

It remained the task of the author of *Poetry and Truth* to complete that epoch.

The history of German literature is a history of new beginnings and is characterized, down to the nineteenth century, by belatedness and forgetfulness.[5] There is, of course, more involved in this repeated beginning than simply the negation of old literary modes and the creation of new ones; such a pattern is familiar enough in other countries as well. The literary consciousness, however, the cultural memory, the very idea of tradition itself, are understood differently in Germany than elsewhere, a fact that robs Goethe's utterance, with which we began, of its uniqueness and suggests that it is but one in a long line of similar pronouncements. This may be demonstrated by a brief look at early modern German literary history prior to Goethe.

It was the ambition of the German 'arch-humanist' Conrad Celtis to secure a place for Latin studies, including neo-Latin poetry, at the courts among the nobility and at the universities and schools in Germany. This was the theme of his inaugural lecture at the University of Ingolstadt in 1492, which opens with an

---

[3] Ibid., 191: 'Wir andern dummen Jungen von 1772 hatten leichteres Spiel, wir hatten nichts hinter uns, konnten frisch drauf los gehen und waren des Beifalls gewiß, wenn wir nur einigermaßen etwas Tüchtiges lieferten.'

[4] Goethe, *From My Life: Poetry and Truth*, trans. Thomas Saine and Robert R. Heitner, vol. 4 of *Goethe's Collected Works* (New York: Suhrkamp, 1987), 295. 'Nun sollte aber die Zeit kommen, wo das Dichtergenie sich selbst gewahr würde, sich seine eignen Verhältnisse selbst schüfe und den Grund zu einer unabhängigen Würde zu legen verstünde. Alles traf in Klopstock zusammen, um eine solche Epoche zu begründen.'

[5] Wilfried Barner, 'Über das Negieren von Tradition: Zur Typologie literaturprogrammatischer Epochenwenden in Deutschland', in *Epochenschwelle und Epochenbewußtsein*, ed. Reinhart Herzog and Reinhart Koselleck, 3–51 (Munich: Fink, 1987), makes this point vividly in his discussion of how an epoch is defined in part through negating, or forgetting, what preceded it.

impassioned lament over the barbarian conditions in Germania.[6] In ancient times, Celtis says, when both Latin and Greek flourished among the Germans, no speaker needed to hesitate before addressing his listeners in Latin. That is no longer the case, as both the language and the content of learned speech have become equally unfamiliar. Neither at the courts nor among clerics nor scholars does one find a solid knowledge of antiquity; nowhere a willingness to dedicate one's life to the spirit and to study; nowhere inspired lives like Dante in exile, Petrarch in solitude, Coloccio Salutati at the head of the Republic invoking the republican idealism of ancient Rome. Consequently, Germany is despised by its neighbors, its authority jeopardized by arrogant princes and self-serving bureaucracies, its historical mission as successor to the *imperium romanum* nothing but an empty boast. Much of Celtis's speech is pure rhetoric, of course, increasing in pitch as the orator separates himself from his nation's intellectual decline. But even at that, what an audacious handling of tradition, this invocation of an idealized Germanic antiquity, or this vague reference to a golden age of arts and sciences under Charlemagne! All of these, apparently, are prefigurations of a hoped-for restitution under Maximilian I and a *creatio ex nihilo* of a revolutionary humanism.

> Emulate, noble men, the ancient nobility of Rome, which, after taking over the empire of the Greeks, assimilated all their wisdom and eloquence, so much so that it is hard to decide whether it has equaled all the Greek discoveries and equipment of learning or surpassed them. In the same way you who have taken over the empire of the Italians should cast off repulsive barbarism and seek to acquire Roman culture.[7]

But how, Celtis asks, and where shall all of this begin? And who are its patrons?

Latin poetry in Germany existed before Celtis, of course, and it continued to flourish throughout the sixteenth century, despite being hindered by the Reformation.[8] Literary quality in sixteenth-century Germany compared well, in fact, thanks to the neo-Latin writers, with that of other European countries. And

---

[6] Celtis, 'Inaugural Address, Ingolstadt', in *Selections from Conrad Celtis, 1459–1508*, trans. Leonard Forster, 36–65 (Cambridge: Cambridge University Press, 1948); pertinent bibliography in Garber, 'Zur Konstitution der europäischen Nationalliteraturen', in *Nation und Literatur im Europa der Frühen Neuzeit*, ed. Garber, notes 79–87 (Tübingen: Niemeyer, 1989).

[7] Celtis, 'Inaugural Address' 43. 'Aemulamini, nobiles viri, priscam nobilitatem Romanam, quae accepto Graecorum imperio ita omnem sapientiam et eloquentiam eorum iunxerunt, ut dubium sit, an aequasse aut superasse omnem Graecam inventionem et doctrinae supellectilem videantur. Ita et vos accepto Italorum imperio exuta foeda barbarie Romanarum artium affectatores esse debebitis.'

[8] Wilhelm Kühlmann, 'Nationalliteratur und Latinität: Zum Problem der Zweisprachigkeit in der frühneuzeitlichen Literatursprache Deutschlands', in Garber, *Nation und Literatur* 164–206, esp. 174–86 and 199–206, discusses the often conflicting demands of Latin and German writing during the sixteenth century.

yet when a new reformer, Martin Opitz, appeared a little over a century later, barbarian darkness still lay over Germany.[9] In his treatise *Aristarchus* (1617) Opitz writes that a state of pure language, a national literature, and a genuine passion for the arts and sciences once prevailed in Germania among an inspired group of learned German descendants of Tacitus, and that these proud humanists resolutely opposed the Roman cult with a Germanic cult of their own. Thanks to the philological efforts of the constitutional lawyer Melchior Goldast, the memory of the most important German medieval poets had also been kept alive.[10] That, however, was all Opitz, as a twenty-year-old student in Beuthen (Upper Silesia), was able to adduce in support of his call for German literary reform. The roster of enthusiastic and ambitious reformers would grow in the coming years. As it had for Celtis, the Carolingian Renaissance would become an important reference point for the seventeenth-century reformers. In the meantime, Prince Ludwig of Anhalt-Köthen and his Fruchtbringende Gesellschaft would assume the court-inspired cultural leadership that cities and states had long enjoyed elsewhere in Europe. The medieval poets and their noble patrons provided a useful model in the early modern period of how ties between the privileged classes and the learned poetic elite should be cultivated.

But here again, what an eccentric picture Opitz presents of the German literary heritage! He completely ignores the whole of urban bourgeois poetry, including that of the upper-German free imperial cities of the fifteenth and sixteenth centuries. One looks in vain through Opitz's annals for the names of Sebastian Brant, Jörg Wickram, or Johann Fischart, not to mention Hans Sachs and the Meistersinger. Martin Luther and the Protestant hymn are also absent; not one word about the popular literature that agitated the masses in the Reformation and its aftermath – a literature without precedent in all of Europe. Opitz does credit the Renaissance with progressive achievements, but only insofar as it serves his own purpose. In true humanistic fashion he stylizes himself as the new founding father, arrogantly suppressing illustrious names like Paul Melissus-Schede and Georg Rudolph Weckherlin, or even that of his loyal Heidelberg friend and promoter, Julius Wilhelm Zincgref. Opitz found the fifteenth and sixteenth centuries valuable only for their neo-Latin writings and their renewal of foreign national literatures; he rejected German writings of the period as raw and formless. Literary historiography after the late-eighteenth century would answer

---

[9] Garber, 'Zur Konstitution' n. 90, reviews the scholarship on Opitz's appeal for reform in his *Aristarchus*; on this still under-appreciated work, see Garber, 'Martin Opitz', in *Deutsche Literatur des 17. Jahrhunderts*, ed. H. Steinhagen and B. von Wiese, 133–45 (Berlin: Erich Schmidt, 1984).

[10] On Goldast's philological and conservationist activities, see Rudolf von Raumer, *Geschichte der germanischen Philologie vorzugsweise in Deutschland* (New York: Johnson, 1965), 48; and Wolfgang Harms, 'Das Interesse an mittelalterlicher deutscher Literatur zwischen Reformationszeit und der Frühromantik', in *Akten des VI. Internationalen Germanisten-Kongresses Basel 1980*, pt 1, 60–84 (Bern: Francke, 1981).

this capricious act with the equally arbitrary one of valorizing the vernacular literary tradition of the fifteenth and sixteenth centuries and disparaging the learned poetry favored by Opitz. This development disrupted the precarious theoretical balance of traditions and, in its popularization, lent itself to dangerous political exploitation.

Surprising as it may seem, the style with which Opitz had orchestrated literary reform changed very little with the onset of the Enlightenment.[11] Johann Christoph Gottsched was every bit Opitz's equal as a strategist and organizer, running his operation from his secure position as professor of rhetoric and philosophy in Leipzig, already a stronghold of rationalism. Like Opitz, he had the uncanny ability to sense and then reconstruct the traditions behind German literary culture. Gottsched had a lively hand in expanding the eighteenth century's knowledge of writers and texts, particularly of the German Middle Ages. His untiring efforts as a collector, editor, and bibliographer cannot obscure the fact, however, that his standards of evaluation, rooted in the rigorous classicizing spirit, were absolutist in nature. Gottsched's own *Versuch einer Critischen Dichtkunst* (1730; Towards a Critical Poetics) is one such example.[12] In the first section, 'On the Origins and Growth of Poetry in General', we come upon the surprising assertion that although alternating rhymed verse originated in the Middle Ages, it was in truth a creation of sixteenth-century Germany. At the top of Gottsched's list are the hymns of Luther, for which Opitz, operating out of a Calvinistic spirit, had so little empathy. But Gottsched likewise finds that secular authors too 'at the time of the Reformation were busy making iambic and trochaic verses of every conceivable length' (80). For Gottsched, however, these remained isolated achievements by individuals of extraordinary aesthetic sensibility; furthermore, these achievements, as laudable as they may have been, were sucked into the whirlpool of popular writing and never meshed into a genuinely literary tradition. Gottsched goes on to commend Opitz and his followers for having put a stop to it:

> If others had continued in the tracks of the great [Reformation] writers, we would have had acceptable verse in German long before Opitz. However, because Hans Sachs, Ringwaldt, Rollenhagen, and others after him had a less sensitive ear and kept to the old styles, the father of our reformed

---

[11] Wilhelm Kühlmann, 'Frühaufklärung und Barock: Traditionsbruch – Rückgriff – Kontinuität', in *Europäische Barock-Rezeption*, ed. Klaus Garber, 2:187–214 (Wiesbaden: Harrassowitz, 1991), compares continuity and change in seventeenth-century reforms.

[12] Gottsched, *Versuch einer Critischen Dichtkunst*, 4th edn (Darmstadt: Wissenschaftliche Buchgesellschaft, 1962). On the changing literary principles in the early Enlightenment, esp. Gottsched's role in this development, see Gunter E. Grimm, 'Gottscheds "Critische Dichtkunst" und die Vernunft-Poesie der Frühaufklärung', in *Literatur und Gelehrtentum in Deutschland*, 620 ff. (Tübingen: Niemeyer, 1983).

poetry obviously had to start all over. He built upon Dutch models much as Heinsius and Cats had done for their own country.[13]

Once again, therefore, a break and a fresh start, this time under the foreign star of the Netherlands, which, at the time of Opitz's birth in 1597 had recently won independence from Spain. In his *Gedächtnisrede auf Martin Opitzen von Boberfeld* (1739; Commemorative Oration for Martin Opitz of Boberfeld) Gottsched praises his great predecessor without reserve, in some of the most flattering words ever used to describe the father of German poetry.[14] Still, he is filled with horror to think of what is threatened with oblivion in Germany as a result of Opitz's obsession with foreign models: the linguistic and cultural terrain conquered by the Brants, Wickrams, Fischarts, and Sachses – as though Opitz's nationalist reticence somehow conflicted with Gottsched's own preference for an enlightened European model!

> Rest assured, we will carefully conserve the scraps from previous carvings, which allowed virtue its right in stone and bronze. We admire and honor them even now in an almost superstitious manner. Yes, we often loathe the fury of our barbarian ancestors, the Goths, the Normans, and the Lombards, who in their invasions of Italy cast down, crushed, and destroyed countless marble, iron, and other magnificent works of art by the wisest, most courageous and virtuous people in history. But in [conserving them] we follow to a certain degree in their very footsteps. So great is our injustice! We praise Athens and Rome for accomplishing what we ourselves do not. By carefully conserving and interpreting antiquity, we help foreign virtue to its reward, and yet we fail to acknowledge our own native accomplishments.[15]

---

[13] *Versuch* 81. 'Wären nun ihre Nachfolger in der Poesie auch den Spuren dieser großen Vorgänger gefolget, so würden wir lange vor Opitzen taugliche Verse im Deutschen bekommen haben. Da aber Hans Sachs, Ringwald, Rollenhagen und andere nach ihm, kein so zartes Gehör hatten, und bey der alten Art blieben; so mußte freylich der itzt gedachte Vater unsrer gereinigten Poesie von neuem die Bahn darinn brechen. Er nahm sich die Holländer zum Muster, als unter welchen schon Heins und Cats ihrem Vaterlande eben den Dienst geleistet hatten.'

[14] In *Gottsched: Schriften zur Literatur*, ed. Horst Steinmetz, 212–38 (Stuttgart: Reclam, 1972). Klaus Garber, *Martin Opitz* (Stuttgart: Metzler, 1976), 44–54, discusses at some length Gottsched's praise of Opitz.

[15] *Gedächtnisrede* 213–14. 'Zwar die Überreste der vormaligen Schnitzkunst, die durch Stein und Erzt der Tugend ihr Recht haben widerfahren lassen, werden von uns noch sorgfältig aufgehoben. Wir bewundern und verehren dieselben noch jetzo auf eine fast abergläubische Weise. Ja wir verabscheuen oftmals die Wut unsrer barbarischen Vorfahren, derjenigen gotischen, normannischen und longobardischen Völker, die bei ihren Einfällen in Welschland eine unzählbare Menge von marmornen, ehernen und andern noch wohl prächtigern Gedächtnisbildern der tapfersten, weisesten und tugendhaftesten Leute zu Boden geworfen, zermalmet und vernichtet haben. Allein, indem wir dieses tun, so treten wir selbst gleichwohl gewissermaßen in ihre Fußtapfen. So groß ist unsre Ungerechtigkeit! Wir loben an Athen und Rom dasjenige, was wir doch selbst

Not only the ancient Greeks and Romans, but also the modern Dutch and English publicly honor their great personalities with statues. Why not the Germans? Who can understand

> why Leipzig has not similarly honored its Johann von Münsterberg, Augsburg its Celtis, Franconia its Ulrich von Hutten, Wittenberg its Melanchthon, Nuremberg its Pirckheimer, Thorn its Copernicus, Königsberg its Sabinus, Magdeburg its Guericke, Danzig its Hevelius, Lusatia its Tschirnhaus, Berlin its Leibniz, and Halle its Thomasius, not to mention many others living today.[16]

Gottsched is at pains to restore the honor due all of Germany's earlier poets and thinkers. But why this emphatic show of a rescue just now, when in fact the entire seventeenth century had brimmed with exuberant praise for Opitz as the hero of the modern age? Quite simply because Gottsched, at once enlightened reformer and traditionalist, desperately wishes to build a new wall – a threshold of reception, as it were – against the recent literary tradition that stemmed from Opitz: the hated Baroque. This same conflict continues in our own day to divide literary scholars of seventeenth-century German literature.

Daniel Casper von Lohenstein, Christian Hofmann von Hofmannswaldau, Johann Christian Hallmann, and Christian Gryphius, among other Silesians of the second half of the seventeenth century were subjected to the ruthless aesthetic, moral, and social judgment of the early Enlightenment in Leipzig and Halle.[17] The purpose was to apply the norms respectively of French Classicism and the English Enlightenment and Sentimentalism to German literature. For the new reform of German literature Gottsched considered reason, virtue, and the middle-class standard of taste essential, especially in view of the existing cultural monopoly of the courts and educated upper classes, whose support he was eager to gain. Consequently, the formal refinement, magical charm, and erotic delicacy of the late-Baroque lyric were stigmatized in literary history for the following two centuries. A quick end was made of the playfully disinterested, pure art of language – an important but hardly appreciated feature of Baroque poetry – in

---

nicht tun. Wir helfen, durch die sorgfältige Bewahrung und Erklärung der Altertümer, einer ausländischen Tugend ihren Lohn erteilen; sind aber zu gleicher Zeit gegen einheimische Verdienste unerkenntlich.'

[16] *Gedächtnisrede* 214–15. 'warum nicht Leipzig seinem Johann von Münsterberg, Augspurg seinem Celtes, das Frankenland einem Ulrich von Hutten, Wittenberg seinem Melanchthon, Nürnberg seinem Pirkheimer, Thorn seinem Kopernikus, Königsberg seinem Sabinus, Magdeburg seinem Guericke, Danzig seinem Hevelius, die Lausnitz ihrem Tschirnhaus, Berlin seinem Leibniz und Halle seinem Thomasius, vieler andern voritzo zu geschweigen, eine gleiche Ehre haben widerfahren lassen?'

[17] The seminal study, originally written in Italian, on the early-Enlightenment treatment of the Silesian Baroque movement of the later seventeenth century is Alberto Martino, *Daniel Casper von Lohenstein: Geschichte seiner Rezeption*, vol. 1: 1661–1800, trans. Heribert Streicher (Tübingen: Niemeyer, 1978).

order to enable one innovator to install himself as the new arbiter of taste and form. And with only questionable success. He soon enough clashed with the younger lyric talents of his day, was mocked by the Zurich art critics Bodmer and Breitinger, saw his star eclipsed by the intellectually far more agile Gotthold Ephraim Lessing, and was despised and ignored by young Goethe's generation.[18] The game had to start again. A new beginning was proclaimed – and a tradition of some five hundred years was, if not totally annulled, relativized to the point of indifference.[19]

And thus we return to Goethe. Would his witty statement to Eckermann have been meaningful, or even possible, at the time of the Enlightenment in any other country of the new literary Europe?[20] In Italy, where almost all European literary innovations down to the Enlightenment had their origin, the appeal to the Florentine triumvirate of Dante, Petrarch, and Boccaccio had been, with slight modification here and there, a ritualistic gesture ever since the Quattrocento; it was expected that one would consciously attempt to write in the literary language created by these three poets. This practice originated with the biographies of Dante and Petrarch, written respectively by Boccaccio and Leonardo Bruni. In Spain, the influence of the Golden Age drama and novel remained strong, and Spanish moral literature from Antonio de Guevara to Francisco de Quevedo to Antonio Gracian enjoyed an unprecedented afterlife throughout Europe. In France, the influential reforms instituted by the Pléiade were integrated in the rise of the newer monarchy under Francis I and his successors with far greater success than the reforms of Celtis and his contemporaries in their frantic wooing of the Renaissance patron Maximilian I. This is to say nothing of the enlighteners Michel de Montaigne, Jacques Auguste de Thou, and Etienne Pasquier. England had already produced Lord Shaftesbury and John Locke, not to mention Shakespeare and Milton, Spenser and Sidney. And finally, in Holland, the heroic formation of a national literature in the years 1570 to 1640 between Jan van der Noot, Constantijn Huygens, Dirck Volckerszoon Coornhert, and Joost van den Vondel substantially contributed to the creation of the young republic.

---

[18] The 'rediscovery' of Gottsched in the late-twentieth century came about as a result of new thinking about the Enlightenment, begun in the 1970s in the former GDR by Werner Krauss and Eduard Winter. See esp. Werner Rieck, *Johann Christoph Gottsched: eine kritische Würdigung seines Werkes* (Berlin: Akademie, 1972). The groundbreaking studies by Krauss and Winter are, respectively, *Studien zur deutschen und französischen Aufklärung* (Berlin: Rütten & Loening, 1963), and *Frühaufklärung: Der Kampf gegen den Konfessionalismus in Mittel- und Osteuropa und die deutsch-slavische Begegnung* (Berlin: Akademie, 1966).

[19] For the corresponding literary historical premises and consequences in the nineteenth and twentieth centuries, see ch. 2 of my reception study *Martin Opitz*.

[20] [Editor's note: Garber gives to the period term Enlightenment the broadest possible range, embracing approximately the final two-thirds of the eighteenth century and extending into the nineteenth until about the time of Goethe's death.]

Nowhere but in Germany could the heretical comment be made in the Enlightenment that a nation and its literature had begun with one's own birth. Instinctually opposed as he was to nationalism and its accompanying social discontent from below, Goethe in 1824 was looking back on the time of the wars of independence and the development of a national spirit from above, ignited by the Francophile Prussian king, Frederick the Great. He knew only too well that for literature to break through the veneer of esoteric learning it could not dispense with the element of nationalism. Classicism and national identity – Thomas Mann emphasized the point in 1929 in his famous Lessing speech before the Prussian Academy of the Arts[21] – are more dependent on each other than the ahistorical, abstract aesthetic of classicism would suggest. But that Frederick of all people should be championed as the inspiring force behind national literature was too much for literary realists at midcentury. The idea could not be credibly espoused by Klopstock or Wieland or even Lessing; if at all, then only by lesser lights such as Ludwig Gleim or Karl Wilhelm Ramler.[22] Goethe himself could only resort to citing Kant's view of discord as the elixir of progress – not in the political and moral, but in the literary and cultural-philosophical realm – in order to be believable. In truth, of course, it was something else. The real nation of culture did not grow up with Lessing or Wieland or Klopstock but with the writer of *Poetry and Truth*. Goethe represented, as Thomas Mann said, not only the bourgeois age, but the entire educated German nation.

It would be worthwhile to collect and interpret Goethe's comments on German literature written during the century in which he was born.[23] His most important literary observations are contained in the seventh and tenth books of *Poetry and Truth*, though there are still many more in his conversations, notes, and letters. However one understands the finer points, one thing comes through with absolute clarity: there is no writer of the German Enlightenment, understood in the broadest sense of the word and including Herder, whose talent or writing did not fall short, in one aspect or another, of Goethe's discriminating standard. Even Klopstock, the celebrated poet of the *Messias* (1751), would have to agree that the first cantos of his monumental spiritual epic are 'not without prolixity'. Lessing, author of *Minna von Barnhelm* (1767), a work valued so highly by Goethe for its 'definitely contemporary content' and fine balance between Prussia and Saxony (permanently divided by Frederick), is faulted for having returned only in *Nathan der Weise* (1779; Nathan the Wise) to the 'cheerful naiveté that

---

[21] In Mann, *Adel des Geistes: Sechszehn Versuche zum Problem der Humanität* (Stockholm: Bermann-Fischer, 1945).

[22] It continued to be a subject of scorn and derision as late as the 1960s. See Franz Mehring, *Die Lessing-Legende*, vol. 9 of *Gesammelte Schriften* (Berlin: Dietz, 1963); and Werner Krauss, *Studien zur deutschen und französischen Aufklärung* (Berlin: Rütten & Loening, 1963).

[23] Barner, 'Über das Negieren von Tradition', has laid the groundwork for such an investigation.

becomes him so well'. Wieland, the writer of *Agathon* (1767), while praised by Goethe as the most endowed talent of the eighteenth century, is still, both in his famous novel as well as in *Don Sylvio* (1764) and the *Komische Erzählungen* (1765; Comic Tales), 'occasionally prolix'; only in *Musarion* (1768) and *Isdris und Zenide* (1768) does he become 'miraculously compact and precise'.[24] Then there is the charming but reserved portrait of Herder. Even when Goethe occasionally issues an impulsive word of praise, as when he calls Gleim and Ramler poets of national stature, he is quick to dash it with cold water. Gleim, he says, truly earned undeniable merit in his fostering of young talent. Indeed, Goethe adds sarcastically, his 'friends, debtors, and dependents' readily accepted his wordy verse, since they had nothing to give him in return for his 'abundant benevolences except toleration of his poems'.[25]

Goethe made similar use of his *Propyläen* (1798–1800), a journal that, as he said, 'would involve not so much my estimation of the specific nature of this literature as my own personal reactions to it'.[26] Its purpose was to provide a forum for commentary on his own creative experience and understanding of art. This standard was far higher than what he believed his contemporaries capable of achieving. It represented his own artistic entelechy as it arose directly from his inner nature, by which he would be able to attest the uniqueness of his own poetic life:

> And so began that tendency which throughout my life I have never overcome, namely to transform whatever gladdened or tormented me, or otherwise occupied my mind, into an image, a poem, and to come to terms with myself by doing this, so that I could both refine my conceptions of external things and calm myself inwardly in regard to them. It is likely that no one needed this talent more than I, since my nature kept propelling me from one extreme to the other. Therefore all my published works are but fragments of one great confession, which this little book is a bold attempt to complete.[27]

These sentences prompted gullible critics, as Goethe anticipated, to make a simplistic connection between the poet's life and work and to turn him into their primary model. I know of no investigation in literary history and aesthetics of the reception of Goethe's dictum to Eckermann. Nevertheless, enough information

---

[24] Goethe, *Poetry and Truth* 4.205, 213.
[25] Ibid., 4.297.
[26] Ibid., 4.197.
[27] Ibid., 4.214. 'Und so begann diejenige Richtung, von der ich mein ganzes Leben über nicht abweichen konnte, nämlich dasjenige, was mich erfreute oder quälte, oder sonst beschäftigte, in ein Bild, ein Gedicht zu verwandeln und darüber mit mir selbst abzuschließen, um sowohl meine Begriffe von den äusseren Dingen zu berichtigen, als mich im Innern deshalb zu beruhigen. Die Gabe hierzu war wohl niemand nötiger als mir, den seine Natur immerfort aus einem Extreme in das andere warf. Alles, was daher von mir bekannt geworden, sind nur Bruchstücke einer großen Konfession, welche vollständig zu machen dieses Büchlein ein gewagter Versuch ist.'

does exist to justify our assertion that no utterance represented a more troublesome hurdle to evaluating the place and quality of German literature of the early modern period and the German Enlightenment than this.[28] It suggests the presence of an aesthetic or literary theory that Goethe was able to exploit rather handily. On the basis of his authority, certain eternal 'truths' about the nature of poetry and its tradition gained currency, including the one about the very hour of its birth in the third quarter of the eighteenth century. Long before literary historians in the following century turned it into a commonplace, the view was accepted, starting with Goethe, that the literature and thought of humanism lacked organic truth: it had no basis in experience; it could only mimic the authentic world of feeling; it lacked the natural connection between life and work that could have elevated it to a classical norm.[29]

Let us now turn back to the time around 1700, to the late, consolidating phase of German territorial absolutism, and look at three figures: Gottfried Arnold, Gottfried Wilhelm Leibniz, and Christian Thomasius, whom we may take, respectively, as representative of the traditions of church history, national education and culture, and political theory. Is it true that they shared no common cultural heritage? nothing of cultural substance upon which Goethe could have built, short of making a new beginning? Did the traditions as they existed around 1700 in fact belong to a world *in extremis*? Or were they not still vital and full of promise?

---

[28] Barner, 'Über das Negieren von Tradition' 4, supports this view in his discussion of Herbert Jaumann's revisionist assessment of the Baroque, *Die deutsche Barockliteratur: Wertung-Umwertung. Eine wertungsgeschichtliche Studie in systematischer Absicht* (Bonn: Grundmann, 1975). Jan-Dirk Müller, *Ideologie und Methode: Ein Kapitel deutscher Wissenschaftsgeschichte 1870–1930* (Darmstadt: Thesen, 1973), a study of ideology as a component of the German intellectual scene between 1870 and 1930, is also relevant here.

[29] This aesthetics of empathy dominated literary history through the late-nineteenth century; in positivistic biography it was *the* paradigm, in fact, as witnessed in Wilhelm Scherer's formulation, in *Geschichte der deutschen Literatur* (Berlin: Knauer, 1883), of the Experienced, the Learned, and the Inherited. *Geistesgeschichte* did no more than transform this psychological formulation into the more prestigious history of ideas. Even in the supposedly unbiased, so-called work-immanent interpretations, it plied a scarcely concealed trade. Walter Benjamin, the most knowledgeable opponent of this experience-and-empathy epidemic in aesthetic theory, which raged in Germany as nowhere else, aptly stated, first on the eve of fascism and then in its very face, that the literary science of his day had failed to rid itself of the 'hydra of school aesthetics with its seven heads: creativity, empathy, timelessness, re-creation, experience, illusion, and artistic enjoyment.' Because these concepts were exploitable by fascism, they appeared in 1935 on his 'index' for elimination. They were to be replaced by others that would be 'totally useless for fascist purposes' – an operation that was possible only because the deciding action, the destruction of the symbolic theory of art, had already been accomplished in his reconstruction of allegory in the medium of Baroque tragedy. See Benjamin, *Gesammelte Schriften*, ed. R. Tiedemann and H. Schweppenhauser (Frankfurt a.M.: Suhrkamp), I-2, 435 and I-3, 286. I have discussed this at length in *Rezeption und Rettung: Drei Studien zu Walter Benjamin* (Tübingen: Niemeyer, 1987).

The Imperiled Heritage

1. Arnold and the Church of the Spirit [30]

Arnold's two-volume *Unpartheyische Kirchen- und Ketzer-Historie, Vom Anfang des Neuen Testaments biß auf das Jahr Christi 1688* (Impartial History of the Church and Heretics, from the Beginning of the New Testament up to the Year 1688),[31] each volume containing more than 1,000 pages in folio, appeared in 1699

---

[30] Erich Seeberg remains the standard authority on Arnold: 'Christian Thomasius und Gottfried Arnold', *Neue kirchliche Zeitschrift* 31 (1920): 337–58, and *Gottfried Arnold: Die Wissenschaft und die Mystik seiner Zeit: Studien zur Historiographie und zur Mystik* (1923; reprint, Darmstadt: Wissenschaftliche Buchgesellschaft, 1964), 1–65; ch. 5, its major section, deals with the roots of the heresy issue in church history. Bibliography: Dietrich Blaufuss and Friedrich Niewöhner (eds), *Bibliographie der Arnold-Literatur ab 1714* (Wiesbaden: Harrassowitz, 1995). Earlier important biographical studies: Franz Diebelius, *Gottfried Arnold: Sein Leben und seine Bedeutung für Kirche und Theologie* (Berlin: Hertz, 1873), and William Freiherr von Schröder, *Gottfried Arnold*, pt 1 of *Studien zu den deutschen Mystikern des siebzehnten Jahrhunderts* (Heidelberg: Winter, 1917), 22–36. A leftist Hegelian assessment of Arnold's writing was made in the nineteenth century by F. Ch. Baur, *Die Epochen der kirchlichen Geschichtsschreibung* (reprint, Darmstadt: Wissenschaftliche Buchgesellschaft, 1962), esp. 84–107; this ideological tradition is also reflected in the studies by Walter Nigg, *Die Kirchengeschichtsschreibung: Grundzüge ihrer historischen Entwicklung* (Munich: Beck, 1934), 76 ff., and *Das Buch der Ketzer* (Zurich: Artemis, 1949); cf. Martin Schmidt, 'Die Interpretationen der neuzeitlichen Kirchengeschichte', *Zeitschrift für Theologie und Kirche* 54 (1957): 174–212, esp. 180 ff., and Peter Meinhold, 'Die radikale Verfallsidee: Gottfried Arnold', in *Geschichte der Kirchlichen Historiographie*, 1:430–42 (Freiburg: Alber, 1967). The return to Arnold studies began in 1963 with Hermann Dörries, 'Arnolds Stellungnahme zu seinen Lebensentscheidungen', in *Geist und Geschichte bei Gottfried Arnold* (Göttingen: Vandenhoeck & Ruprecht). Jürgen Büchsel, *Gottfried Arnold: Sein Verständnis von Kirche und Wiedergeburt* (Wittenberg: Luther, 1970), reviews scholarship to 1970, esp. on the history of heretics. The status of Arnold for modern evangelical theology was assessed at mid-twentieth century by Emanuel Hirsch, *Geschichte der neueren evangelischen Theologie* (Gütersloh: Bertelsmann, 1951), 2:225 ff. Introduction: Friedrich Wilhelm Kantzenbach, 'Gottfried Arnold', in *Orthodoxie und Pietismus*, ed. Martin Greschat, 261–75 (Stuttgart: Kohlhammer, 1982). Other important studies include Kantzenbach, 'Gottfried Arnolds Weg zur Kirchen- und Ketzerhistorie 1699', *Jahrbuch der Hessischen Kirchengeschichte Vereinigung* 26 (1975): 207–41; Johann F. G. Goeters, 'Gottfried Arnolds Anschauung von der Kirchengeschichte in ihrem Werdegang', in *Traditio, Krisis, Renovatio aus theologischer Sicht*, ed. Bernd Jaspert and Rudolf Mohr, 241–57 (Marburg: Elwert, 1976); and esp. the innovative analysis by Hanspeter Marti, 'Die Rhetorik des Heiligen Geistes: Gelehrsamkeit, poesis sacra und sermo mysticus bei Gottfried Arnold', in *Pietismus-Forschungen: Zu Philipp Jacob Spener und zum spiritualistisch-radikalpietistischen Umfeld*, ed. Dietrich Blaufuß (Frankfurt a.M.: P. Lang, 1986), of Arnold's rhetorical language concerning the Holy Spirit.

[31] There are three editions: 1) Frankfurt a.M.: Thomas Fritsch, 1703 (with 'Supplementa, Illustrationes und Emendationes zur Verbesserung der Kirchen-Historie'); Dutch trans. 1701. 2) Frankfurt a.M.: Fritschens Erben, 1729 ('Additamenta' in pt 2, 1180 ff.; references in the present essay are to the 1967 reprint of this edition [Hildesheim:

and 1700 at Frankfurt am Main in the publishing house of Thomas Fritsch. Arnold had already written the foreword in March 1697 while in Giessen, where he had been called by Landgrave Ernst Ludwig of Hessen-Darmstadt as professor of universal history one year after having published his first long work, *The First Love of the Communities of Jesus Christ, that is, A True Picture of the First Christians Based on Their Lively Faith and Holy Life* (1696).[32] Even though he had almost immediately lost his position as tutor in Dresden – the job had been facilitated by Philipp Jakob Spener – for refusing to abandon the primitive Christian radicalism in his pedagogical work, he did not hesitate, when he found that the academic formalities there were incompatible with his religious beliefs, to give up his university position in Giessen after just one year. He then returned to Quedlinburg, a center of mystical spiritualism and early pietism and home to a respectable community of followers of the seventeenth-century mystic Jacob Böhme. It was also in Quedlinburg where Spener's friend Christian Scriver wrote his physico-theological *Zufällige Andachten* (1667; Chance Religious Reflections), which would influence the composition of Brockes' *Irdisches Vergnügen in Gott* (1721–48; Earthly Pleasures in God).[33] Klopstock too, residing here in his home town at this time, was deeply affected by the inner piety that radiated from Scriver's book. Arnold, who was much given to prayer and meditation, found in Quedlinburg the leisure to write the church history that was to make him renowned. He claims in the foreword that he assembled the work, on an anonymous request, from notes collected over many years; and indeed, especially in the later parts, it contains a veritable archive of portraits, events, news items, and spiritual ephemera. This eclecticism obviously satisfied the hunger of his readers for both devotional and sensationalist readings.

Olms]). 3) Schaffhausen: Emanuel and Benedikt Hurter, 1740–42, 3 vols (vol. 3 includes criticisms and defenses of the work). Martin Schmidt's 1973 Heidelberg dissertation, 'Der Kampf um Gottfried Arnolds Unpartheyische Kirchen- und Ketzerhistorie', is based on this third edition. The context of the *Unpartheyische Historie*, esp. as related to Cyprian, is investigated by F.W. Kantzenbach, 'Theologisch-soziologische Motive im Widerstand gegen Gottfried Arnold', *Jahrbuch der Hessischen Kirchengeschichte Vereinigung* 24 (1973): 33–51, though its broadest study is still Seeberg, *Arnold*. Reinhard Breymayer, 'Die Bibliothek Gottfried Arnolds', *Linguistica Biblica* 39 (1976): 86–131, examines Arnold's scholarly library, which is still extant.

[32] *Die Erste Liebe der Gemeinen Jesu Christi/ das ist Wahre Abbildung der Ersten Christen nach ihren lebendigen Glauben und heiligen Leben.*

[33] This interesting connection is discussed in Hermann Beck, *Die religiöse Volksliteratur der evangelischen Kirche Deutschlands in einem Abriß ihrer Geschichte* (Gotha: Perthes, 1891), 141 ff.; Else Eichler, 'Christian Scrivers "Zufällige Andachten": Ein Beitrag zur Geistes- und Formgeschichte des 17. Jahrhunderts' (PhD diss., University of Halle, 1926); and Martin Schmidt, 'Christian Scrivers "Seelenschatz", ein Beispiel vorpietistischer Predigtweise', in *Wiedergeburt und neuer Mensch: Gesammelte Studien zur Geschichte des Pietismus*, 112–28 (Wittenberg: Luther, 1969). On Arnold in Quedlinburg, see Schmidt, 'Gottfried Arnold: Seine Eigenart, seine Bedeutung, seine Beziehung zu Quedlinburg', in *Wiedergeburt* 331–41.

Arnold's stated intention is to present 'a study of historical reality that avoids factional and other interests' (a1[r]). Truth and factionalism are contradictions, because to take sides means to write only from the point of view of one religious group or particular philosophy. The premise of Arnold's *Impartial History* is that truth cannot be represented adequately by any one religion, a position that places Arnold within the early modern traditions of mystical spiritualism and humanist Erasmianism. He confidently reiterates the argument put forth by Erasmus, Sebastian Franck, and other free thinkers in the midst of the religious turmoil accompanying the Reformation, that when theology and history are beholden to confessional interests they lead only to useless bickering, which turns people away from righteousness. Unity, not divisiveness, creates the pre-condition for correct Christian practice, and unity is possible only when denominational factionalism has been overcome. Theological controversy is inconsistent with the true religious life. This opposition vanishes to the extent that the causes of strife are removed, which implies that we must advance beyond the need for denominations. The apparent anti-intellectualism in Arnold's warning against 'the struggle over the crumbs of mere science and history instead of true obedience to God and his eternal truths' is only polemical; history in fact fits seamlessly into the divine scheme of things. Interestingly, Arnold sought to control the work's reception by taking pains to guarantee that it would be read in a manner consistent with his intentions. The 'main goal' of his work, he says, is 'to hold on to faith and a good conscience'. Thus the author, the work, and the reader all share a form of communication based on inner faith and conscience. Strictly speaking, then, history can be written only by a true Christian like Arnold's great model, the mystic Johann Arndt.[34] However, Arnold's authority rests firmly upon his own claim to an authentic life, thus justifying the work's truth and placing it above any criticism of his sources and beyond factional rancor. The incontestable experience of the pure godly life, accessible only to true believers, allows history to be written on the basis of personal experience alone. The congruence of historiography and spirituality leads to 'the rejection of all preconceived opinions, human concerns and illusions, patriarchal habits, and anything else that darkens or extinguishes this bright light and therefore blocks the message of salvation'.

The method of the *Impartial History* is formally that of the humanists: a return to the sources in order to gain a true picture of church history.[35] The internal experience of faith, essentially unaffected by the external church, and a faith-

---

[34] On Arndt as 'Arnold's saint', see Seeberg, *Arnold* 342–3. More recently, F.E. Stoffler, 'Johann Arndt', in *Gestalten der Kirchengeschichte*, ed. Martin Greschat, 7:37–49 (Stuttgart: Kohlhammer, 1982); Christian Braw, *Bücher im Staube: Die Theologie Johann Arndts in ihrem Verhältnis zur Mystik* (Leiden: Brill, 1986).

[35] Seeberg, 'Die Historisierung der Theologie durch den Humanismus', in *Arnold* 280–312; also Helmar Junghans's classic study of the relationship between Luther and the humanists, *Der junge Luther und die Humanisten* (Weimar: Böhlau, 1984).

driven exploration of the revisited sources are complementary. The 'innocence and truth' that speak to us out of the 'documents' of the 'very first Christians' are re-experienced by born-again individuals as the primary basis of their existence. Church history, properly understood, is nothing other than an account of the invisible church, the 'church of the spirit'. History is not limited to 'those sundry conditions, ceremonies, regulations, and customs common to natural men', for that would mean failure to portray 'the image of true Christians'; the 'counter-image' of 'false, depraved Christians' is of only secondary importance. Nevertheless, 'the origin, growth, high point, and other conditions or accidents of the mystery of evil, as well as of divine bliss', can be read in the counter-image 'as clear as day' (a1^V). The *Impartial History* is a kind of magna carta of Christian history, sorting out phenomena into the true and the false, and passing on what is left, critically purified, to following generations.

Historiography for Arnold is, as for the humanists, the great *magistra vitae* 'preceptor of life'; its purpose is to provide 'the true character as well as the proper interpretation of what has occurred', thereby helping the reader to distinguish judiciously between *imago* 'theory' and *imitatio* 'practice'. Precisely because historical fact has the status of kerygma – the salvific truth divinely given to mankind through Jesus's preaching – precise knowledge of things is essential. Thus Arnold's concern with how his sources have been transmitted across time. His loyalty to the sources and his willingness to start over from the beginning are striking features of his voluminous work. The further proliferation of legends, so Arnold, must be stopped, once and for all. Only after history has been treated with this critical aqua fortis can it make the claim of being definitive. Arnold's narration continues into the year 1688. It refuses to be sucked back into the whirlpool of controversy. Only what can be shown to be exemplary in the life and teachings of the so-called 'heretics' can have kerygmatic value. Truth quietly consigns controversy to oblivion. The right of criticism is allowed only those who have been granted God's inspiration and have turned it to a sanctified life. Untested by actual life, criticism is ineffective; understanding of the heretics is possible only to those who have experienced inner revelation. Arnold's pietistic method is therefore a hermeneutics of the heart and will be adopted as such in the secularized ethics and aesthetics of Sentimentalism.[36]

Like all great moral philosophers Arnold was a rigorist, but his authority rested on his claim to having returned to the principles of original Christianity. He insists that the utopia of primitive Christian life can be fully restored in the

---

[36] Wolfgang Schmitt, 'Die pietistische Kritik der 'Künste': Untersuchungen über die Entstehung einer neuen Kunstauffassung im 18. Jahrhundert' (PhD diss., University of Cologne, 1958); Schmitt's work derives from Richard Alewyn, the great master of German Sentimentalism. See his pithy resumé, 'Die Empfindsamkeit und die Entstehung der modernen Dichtung', *Zeitschrift für Ästhetik und allgemeine Kunstwissenschaft* 26 (1932): 394–5.

present.[37] His point of reference is the first congregation, and his definition of 'heretic' follows logically: one who has distanced himself from the established, institutional church and all its accouterments in favor of a pure life of the spirit, in which past and present become one and time loses its secular-temporal structure. In Arnold's view, Jesus and his apostles shared one essential feature: a negation (the young Hegel expounds on it at length in his religio-philosophical writings) that put them at odds with the spirit of their time. They resolutely followed only their own inner voice and thereby restored the original religion of prelapsarian Adam. It is this religion that God plants again and again in the hearts of all who are true to him; it miraculously sustains itself in the face of historical, institutional, and rational resistance:

> It is 'wisdom,' which through the centuries enlightened all witnesses of truth in all religions; which constituted the sanctity of the patriarchs and heroes of the old covenant; which was present even before 'scripture'; and which is the heart of the New Testament . . . The individual who bears witness to the truth sets himself apart from the self-love of the priests, the contentiousness of science, the illusions of the church, and the immorality of the masses. Consequently, he is persecuted by the majority and those in power. Being persecuted is therefore a sign of truth.[38]

Only through suffering and struggle can religious purity be preserved, even while it is being disseminated. Rapprochement with temporal powers has always been a sign of religion's sinfulness. Seeberg again observes:

> What arises from this, despite all Lutheran capitulation, is something almost revolutionary. Worldly powers, princes, and dignitaries have never worked to the advantage of Christianity, which is, after all, inherently different from the world; they have always muddied its purity. This spiritualist element introduces a social aspect into the whole idea: the poor and needy have always been the carriers of the Christian religion. Arnold, as mystics and spiritualists in general, always appreciated that the apostles were 'simple and disreputable' and that the adherents of the new religion were 'usually insignificant people.'[39]

Arnold recognizes that, as communal life evolved in the first century, religion devised its forms ad hoc, adjusting them to the needs of the moment to avoid coercion, when in fact true spirituality needs no external forms, much less canonized doctrines with their binding regulations, councils, and excommunications.

---

[37] Seeberg, ch. 2, on the history of the church and heretics, in *Arnold* 65 ff.; also Martin Schmidt, 'Das Frühchristentum in der evangelisch-lutherischen Überlieferung vom 18.–20. Jahrhundert', *Oecumenia* (1971–2): 88–110.

[38] Ibid., 67–8.

[39] Ibid., 68–9. In n. 1, p. 69 Seeberg remarks, 'That Arnold gives value to social good works is obvious from bk. 3, ch. 10 of his "Erste Liebe" entitled "On Care for the Poor Among the First Christians", as well as in chap. 12.'

This error arose as early as the second century: 'At that time the affairs of the church were already beginning to be formulated in accordance with those of the secular state.'[40] The most harmful and drastic turn in the church's development was the consolidation of the church into bishoprics.[41] It affected the teachings, symbols, and sacraments, the discourse with heretics, and the morality of church leaders, reaching its ultimate crisis under Constantine, and continued down to the Reformation. True believers fled into the desert, and thus the true church has always operated at the political, social, and ecclesiastical margins.

The *Impartial History* reaches a natural high point in its portrayal of the age of the Reformation. The central chapter is entitled 'On the Condition of the Papacy before Luther and on the Instruments and Advocates of the Reformation, most notably Luther.'[42] Luther is portrayed in his younger years as a receptacle of the divine spirit and steadfast in his opposition to both temporal and spiritual authorities, a significant force in the restoration of mystical theology after scholasticism. Arnold repeatedly makes an observation that for him has the weight of a historical truism: that earthly success weakens faith and encourages discord among believers:

> Now it is true that in the early years of the Reformation a great movement and change of heart occurred in countless people in Saxony and elsewhere, such as Switzerland, where Zwingli taught. For many this was like first love, strong and hot, and was fanned on by the fires of tribulation. What came to pass after a certain peace and stability had set in was very much like the condition that prevailed in the first church. At that time Luther, Zwingli, and all the others stood together as one man against the pope; their purpose was the noblest possible one, and quarreling and other evils were absent. There existed a state of unsurpassed blessedness.[43]

---

[40] *Impartial History* I:2,2,10.

[41] Seeberg, *Arnold* 73.

[42] 'Vom zustand des Papstthums vor Luthero und denen werckzeugen und beförderern der reformation, insonderheit von Luthero.' Seeberg, *Arnold* 108 comments: 'The sixteenth-century chapter is vast, encompassing pages 619–959 in the Schaffhausen edition. But the seventeenth century is given still more space. It becomes obvious to what extent the present determines the image of the past, to what extent, in other words, our understanding of the past lies rooted in the present. The power of the dominant ideas and the intent of the work, "that the reader should gain wisdom from unfamiliar and previous errors", as Arnold puts it in the foreword to pt. 2, are obvious here.'

[43] *Kirchen- und Ketzer-Historie* 1:509. 'Nun ist wahr, daß gleich in den ersten jahren der reformation, eine grosse bewegung und veränderung der hertzen in unzehlichen menschen, so wohl in Sachsen und andern orten, als in der Schweitz, da Zwinglius gelehret hat, vorgegangen, indem freylich bey vielen noch die erste liebe war, die nicht nur von ihr selbst kräfftig und hitzig, sondern auch durch der feuer der trübsal trefflich gefeget und unterhalten wurde. Womit sichs aber bald nach ereigneter ruhe und sicherheit änderte, nicht anders als es in der ersten kirchen etwa zugegangen ist. Denn dazumal stunden sie noch alle, Lutherus, Zwinglius und die übrigen vor einen mann gegen den Papst, haten auch reinere absichten, und blieben noch die ärgernisse des gezäncks und auch anderer bösen affecten zurücke, daher ungleich mehr segen gespühret wurde.'

However, he continues, the Reformation declined, not least because of Luther's personal weaknesses, into orthodoxy and in the direction of a state church. This in turn prepared the ground for the massive entrance of the true heirs of the Reformation: the mystics and spiritualists, imbued with the Holy Spirit, in whose tradition Arnold sees himself and to whom he appeals in his *Impartial History*.[44]

True Christians exist everywhere; their spirit is ubiquitous, unlimited by time or place, institutions or traditions. Arnold's express desire is to find 'the invisible, universal church', one not 'tied to a particular visible society, but scattered about the world, hidden within all peoples and communities' (b2r). Seeing through the eyes of only one religious group leads to factionalism. Not societal loyalty – he doubtless has in mind here the religious orders, especially the Jesuits – but rather 'sweet harmony and tranquillity are the true hallmarks of the historian who seeks, through writing, to attract readers to the virtue of reconciliation'. On the other hand, Arnold does not agree that criticism harms the church or strengthens its detractors. If there were only 'peacemakers' in the world, the church would be superfluous. There is but one undivided Truth, and as long as a difference obtains between the original church and its later manifestations, 'non-factional' criticism, that is, legitimate criticism based on early Christianity, will be essential. It is a given for Arnold at the outset of the eighteenth century that this criticism can reach people for whom the truth is primarily intended through only one medium, the mother tongue.[45]

Let us pause briefly at this point to consider the consequences of these observations. Arnold locates the fountainhead of the indestructible, 'true, eternal religion' in the very place where the Erasmians and spiritualists found it, original Christianity. As Arnold reads religious history, the pure ethos of original Christianity lasted for three centuries, until the 'Babylonian exile' under Constantine, at which time the church entered into an unholy alliance with the state. What is new about Arnold's work is this kind of panoramic view, proceeding century by century, under the guiding question of whether the church has contributed to the betterment or corruption of Christianity. Arnold employs a triadic scheme in his overview of European religious development:[46] 1) The original Christian spiritualism and its institutions, still intact even after the long period of papal deformation of the church, were answered, by 2) the Reformation's attempt to align itself with the precepts and practices of original

---

[44] Seeberg, *Arnold* 327–431, in his chapter on modern mysticism and the new sects and their influence on ideas and historiography. Related observations in Joachim Rogge, 'Gottfried Arnolds Müntzerverständnis', in *Der Pietismus in Gestalten und Wirkungen*, ed. Heinrich Bornkamm, 395–403 (Bielefeld: Luther, 1975), and, in the same volume, Alfred Schindler, 'Dogmengeschichte als Dogmenkritik bei Gottfried Arnold und seinen Zeitgenossen', 404–19.

[45] This insight owes esp. to Marti, 'Die Rhetorik des Heiligen Geistes.'

[46] For Arnold, the high point of religious evolution is represented by Joachim of Fiore and the Franciscan Spiritualists. See Ernst Benz, *Ecclesia Spiritualis* (Stuttgart: Kohlhammer, 1964), on the Franciscan reformation.

Christianity. However, in creating the orthodox state church, 3) the Reformation committed the old sins of institutionalizing religion, canonizing dogma, and isolating individual confessions. Arnold tries to replay this third moment by reconstructing the history of true Christianity, hoping somehow to turn back the tide of orthodoxy. It is important to see his return to the origins for the radical critique that it is. Throughout the *Impartial History* the same uncompromising will to demonstrate the one Truth is present.[47] Both the secular and ecclesiastical traditions are corrupt and in need of an 'ordeal by fire': first, before the court of reason, which is incorruptible, unconditional, and obedient only to its own standards; and second, before the court of the pure spirit-religion, unspoiled by external power and possessing the unimpeachable norms of original Christianity. The various paths should not obscure the one thing they have in common, however: an originary model as the basis of criticism. A look at natural law, for example, or at poetics, with its designations of original, early, and natural forms of poetry, illustrates that this critical principle would continue to function as the chief hermeneutic of the Enlightenment.[48]

Arnold, however, did more than this. His historical method offered the new century an unprecedented inheritance, drawn not only from original Christianity but from post-Reformation early modernity as well. For him, this heritage was the gift of the finest ecumenical minds, from the humanist theoreticians of irenicism and tolerance to the quietists, passivists, and spiritualists of every stripe. Arnold's methodological achievement was to combine past with future. His is a history of the church under the aspect of original Christianity as original history, whereby he is able to justify the lives of all descendants of the apostolic spirit. His valorization of the 'Early' as originary and normative, together with his interpretation of its hidden afterlife in European spirituality as a binding inheritance in the present, remains his lasting contribution to the history of conscience in the early modern age. As the narrative voice suggests in the introduction to his *Impartial History*, Arnold is conscious of having recovered a vast train of forgotten, unrecognized, or lost figures. Arnold was the greatest heir and spokesman for the host of non-conformist believers down to his day, the pathbreaking writer of unauthorized church history, which he bequeaths, in incomplete form, to the Enlightenment. His history can claim, quite beyond Goethe, unmatched success until well into Romanticism.[49]

---

[47] Similar in its daring and provocation to Pierre Bayle's *Dictionaire philosophique*; see Paul Hazard, *The European Mind: The Critical Years 1680–1715*, trans. J. Lewis May (New York: Fordham University Press, 1990), 99–115.

[48] Reinhart Koselleck, *Critique and Crisis* (Cambridge, Mass.: MIT Press, 1988), 98–123.

[49] For this, see ch. 6, 'Die Nachwirkungen Gottfried Arnolds', in Seeberg, *Arnold* 535–611; further, Richard Brinkmann's comparison of the heretical thought in Arnold with that in Goethe: 'Goethes *Werther* und Gottfried Arnolds *Kirchen- und Ketzerhistorie*', in *Versuche zu Goethe*, ed. Volker Dürr and Geza von Molnar, 167–89 (Heidelberg: Stiehm, 1976). On the theology of heretics, see Nigg, *Das Buch der Ketzer*, and Eduard Winter,

2. Leibniz and the 'German-Minded Society'

In the year in which Arnold completed his *Impartial History of the Church and Heretics* the Prussian Academy of Sciences was founded in Berlin,[50] a coincidence that was not entirely accidental. With familiar belatedness, Germany still lagged behind its culturally advanced western neighbors France and England. By this time, however, the gap had been narrowed to the extent that German culture could have, for example, a determining influence on the formation of the Slavic scientific academies.[51] A year before the Brandenburg Elector Frederick III had himself crowned Frederick I, King of Prussia,[52] Electoral Prussia announced its intellectual and political leadership of divided Germany. This claim had credibility because one man, Gottfried Wilhelm Leibniz, for decades had been in intimate contact with European developments, directing his inexhaustible imagination to the founding of a scientific academy in Germany. Now, after all previous efforts to establish an academy under imperial patronage had failed (they would fail again later in the eighteenth century), Leibniz invested his hopes

---

Ketzerschicksale: Christliche Denker aus neun Jahrhunderten (Zurich: Benziger, 1980). Winter begins his study with Joachim of Fiore and deals with Arnold in the chapter on heretics in Brandenburg.

[50] The standard work on the Berlin Academy of Sciences is Adolf von Harnack, *Geschichte der Königlich Preussischen Akademie der Wissenschaften zu Berlin*, 3 vols (1900; reprint, Hildesheim: Olms, 1970). Vol. 1: history of the Academy; vol. 2: source materials, including Leibniz's drafts; vol. 3: index of Academy papers 1700–1899. Also Gerhard Dunken, *Die Deutsche Akademie der Wissenschaften zu Berlin in Vergangenheit und Gegenwart* (Berlin: Akademie, 1958); Werner Hartkopf and Gerhard Dunken, *Von der Brandenburgischen Sozietät der Wissenschaften zur Deutschen Akademie der Wissenschaften* (Berlin: Akademie, 1967); and Conrad Grau, 'Anfänge der neuzeitlichen Berliner Wissenschaft 1650–1790', in *Wissenschaft in Berlin: Von den Anfängen bis zum Neubeginn nach 1945*, 14–95 (Berlin: Dietz, 1987).

[51] See Eduard Winter, esp. his *Frühaufklärung* (1966), a pioneering work on the confessional conflicts between East and West in the early Enlightenment; but also his edited volume *Die deutsch-russische Begegnung und Leonard Euler: Beiträge zu den Beziehungen zwischen der deutschen und russischen Wissenschaft und Kultur im 18. Jahrhundert* (Berlin: Akademie, 1958), as well as the two monographs: *E.W. von Tschirnhaus (1651–1708): Ein Leben im Dienste des Akademiegedankens* (Berlin: Akademie, 1959), and *Lomonosov, Schlözer, Palas: Deutsch-russische Wissenschaftsbeziehungen im 18. Jahrhundert* (Berlin: Akademie, 1962). Specific to Leibniz's role in the Russian academies, see Mechthild Keller, 'Wegbereiter der Aufklärung: Gottfried Wilhelm Leibniz' Wirken für Peter den Großen und sein Reich', in *Russen und Rußland aus deutscher Sicht, 9.–17. Jahrhundert*, ed. Keller, 391–413 (Munich: Fink, 1985).

[52] Technically, Elector Frederick III remained only a prince of the Holy Roman Empire, since monarchy lay outside of imperial boundaries.

in Prussia.[53] His plans for an academy reached back to the 1660s, when in his youth he lived with the Schönborn family in Electoral Mainz.[54] It would require a separate study to follow the long sequence of projects that led ultimately to the Berlin Academy of Sciences. We will concentrate instead on a work that Leibniz published three years before its founding: *Ermahnung an die Teutschen, ihren Verstand und Sprache besser zu üben, samt beigefügten Vorschlag einer teutschgesinnten Gesellschaft* (Exhortation to the Germans to Make Improved Use of Their Reason and Language, along with the Added Suggestion of a German-Minded Society).[55]

Leibniz's *Exhortation* was not conceived specifically for Berlin and thus has no princely or electoral addressee, as the formal prefaces to works by seventeenth-century writers commonly did. Accordingly, its territorial horizon is not limited to a given state. In standard humanist fashion, Leibniz presents the educational task of the Academy as a benefit to the 'welfare' of the 'fatherland'. Whenever humanists, since Salutati and Bruni in Florence, had pondered the

[53] The secondary literature on Leibniz as organizer of sciences and philosopher of the Academy idea encompasses approx. 100 titles in the bibliography by Kurt Müller and Albert Heinekamp, *Leibniz-Bibliographie: Die Literatur über Leibniz bis 1980* (Frankfurt a.M.: Klostermann, 1973), 91–9; supplemented by Werner Schneiders, 'Sozietätspläne und Sozialutopie bei Leibniz', *Studia Leibnitiana* 7 (1975): 55–80, and 'Gottesreich und gelehrte Gesellschaft: Zwei politische Modelle bei G.W. Leibniz', in Hartmann and Vierhaus, *Der Akademiegedanke im 17. und 18. Jahrhundert* 47–61, and Wilhelm Totok, 'Leibniz als Wissenschaftsorganisator', in *Leibniz: sein Leben, sein Wirken, seine Welt*, ed. Totok and Carl Haase, 293–320 (Hannover: Literatur und Zeit, 1966). Harnack's opening chapter, 'Leibniz und der Gedanke der Akademien: Die Vorgeschichte der Brandenburgischen Societät der Wissenschaften 1697–1700', evolves into a sketch of the European idea of the academy between Renaissance and early Enlightenment and is one of the richest studies ever undertaken on the early modern societal movement. It begins by considering the plans of the Great Elector in 1667 to found a Brandenburg university (I:3) and goes on to discuss how these plans anticipated the Academy project (I:4–5). Wilhelm Dilthey, 'Die Berliner Akademie der Wissenschaften: Ihre Vergangenheit und ihre gegenwärtigen Aufgaben', *Deutsche Rundschau* 103 (1900): 416–44, discusses Harnack's work; Dilthey's work on the age of Leibniz may be found in the 1961 edition of his writings, *Studien zur Geschichte des deutschen Geistes*, 4th edn, vol. 3 of *Gesammelte Schriften* (Stuttgart: Teubner; Göttingen: Vandenhoeck & Ruprecht).

[54] Paul Wiedeburg, *Der junge Leibniz: Das Reich und Europa*, pt 1 (Wiesbaden: Steiner, 1962–70), on the younger Leibniz's thinking about the Reich and Europa.

[55] In the collection *Politische Schriften*, ed. Hans Heinz Holz, 2:60–80 (Frankfurt a.M.: EVA, 1966), which also contains most of Leibniz's other writings on the subject of the Academy and cultural-political concerns. Also Paul Joachimsen, *Der deutsche Staatsgedanke von seinen Anfängen bis auf Leibniz und Friedrich den Großen: Dokumente zur Entwicklung* (Munich: Drei Masken, 1921), 243–60. When one observes that the *Exhortation* was published in the Philosophische Bibliothek (vol. 116) by Meiner in 1916 as part of Leibniz's *Deutsche Schriften*, the absurd chauvinistic conclusions forced from it during the age of Imperialism are immediately transparent. In this regard, see Walter Schmied-Kowarzik (ed.), *Der europäische Freiheitskampf gegen die Hegemonie Frankreichs auf geistigem und politischem Gebiet* (Mainz: Kirchheim, 1913).

question of cultural politics, territorial boundaries were exploded in favor of some larger national group embraced by a single language that was by no means limited to city or territorial boundaries. To Celtis, for example, the emperor still represented the nation prior to the great religious schism. That was true also for Opitz, who continued to place his political hopes in the far-reaching policies of the Palatine House. Nor would it be any different for Gottsched in the early Enlightenment. In the comprehensive scheme of the young Leibniz, a century and a half after the Reformation, the emperor still represents the ideal of unity. However, Leibniz adds an element that reaches beyond the scope of humanism:

> Our pleasure is in our nation's prosperity. For in prosperity we have a surplus of all things that make life enjoyable. We live among our grape vines and fig trees; foreigners recognize and praise our good fortune; and because each of us is a citizen of this body, we receive strength from its good health and are affected, by special ordinance of God, by everything that touches it. How else can it be explained that we know of so few good people who do not rejoice from the bottom of their hearts over the good fortune of their land and nation, and especially of their leaders, or who, in a foreign country, do not readily share their hearts' concerns with a fellow countryman? The ties of language, of customs, of a common name – these unify people in a powerful if invisible way and create a kind of kinship.[56]

We immediately discern an echo of the humanist topos of *laus patriae* here as *laus Germaniae*, in Leibniz's paeon to his 'beloved Germany', beginning as it does with a description of the pleasant climate and rich mineral deposits and ending in praise of the Germanic virtues of courage and honesty. Yet it is not only the warmth of tone that gives special meaning to this praise of country, set here against the background of Louis XIV's policy of blatant annexation.[57] Rather, it

---

[56] *Ermahnung* 60. 'Des Vaterlandes Wohlstand [ist] unsre Vergnügung. Denn dadurch haben wir Überfluß von allen Dingen, so das Leben angenehm machen, wir wohnen unter unserm Weinstock und Feigenbaum; die Fremden erkennen und rühmen unser Glück, und weil jeder ein Glied dieses bürgerlichen Körpers ist, so empfinden wir Kräfte von dessen Gesundheit und fühlen alles, was ihn angehet, durch eine sonderbare Verordnung Gottes. Denn wo sollte es sonsten herkommen, daß wenig gutartige Menschen zu finden, die sich nicht über ihres Landes und Nation und sonderlich ihrer Obrigkeit Glück von ganzem Herzen freuen, oder in der Fremde nicht gleichsam ihr Herz mit einem Landsmann teilen sollten? Das Band der Sprachen, der Sitten, auch sogar des gemeinen Namens vereinigt die Menschen auf eine so kräftige, wiewohl unsichtbare Weise und machet gleichsam eine Art der Verwandtschaft.'

[57] Wiedeburg, *Der junge Leibniz*, pt 2. Among the studies – many now nearly a century old and lacking systematization of sources – regarding events in the wake of the annexation policy of Louis XIV, see esp. Hubert Gillot, *Le règne de Louis XIV et l'opinion publique en Allemagne* (Paris: Champion, 1914). On the influence of Leibniz's writings on public law, see Edmund Pfleiderer, *Leibniz als Verfasser von zwölf anonymen, meist deutschen politischen Flugschriften* (Leipzig: Fues, 1870), but esp. with respect to the related subject of the evolution of public law, the numerous studies by Michael Stolleis,

is the nation as a whole, unified in custom and language, that Leibniz addresses as the protagonist of the political and cultural reform now crystallizing in the Berlin Academy, the symbolic model of social unity.

For the impassioned politician, the beauty of a country is perfected in a well-wrought constitution, Leibniz's life-long ambition.[58] Given his aversion to change, his fear, like Goethe's, of disruption, and his search, like Hegel's, for the rational in reality, Leibniz welcomed the idea of a written constitution for the Holy Roman Empire of the German Nation. *Libertas Germaniae*, the vital core of which Leibniz found in his country's principalities, nobility, free imperial cities, and industrious peasants, was not a dead slogan in 1700 but still a living reality.[59] It was not Leibniz's intention to disturb the traditional system of schools and universities, with its corporate rights of the professoriate. Like the humanist sodality, his Academy would add an educational enzyme to the body of the German nation, the goal being as revolutionary as it had ever been in the European sodality movement. At the same time, it was so current and relevant that it may be taken as an important historical indicator of the changes taking place in the system of principalities and class hierarchies, as well as in the attitudes of the most forward-thinking intellectuals. Leibniz believed that the educational needs, not only of intellectuals but of 'courtiers and worldly individuals' as well, even of young ladies, could be met by the Academy. Boundaries of class, gender, and denomination were to melt away, just as Arnold envisioned would occur in the invisible Church of the Spirit. 'For it is neither wealth nor power nor gender, but one's gifts that make the difference' (66–7). To belong to the 'common herd' was not principally a social matter, as far as the humanists were concerned; it connoted, rather, exclusion from formal participation in reason, knowledge, and the vita contemplativa, which is to say, from the privileged initiation into those special areas that guaranteed freedom from animal-like bondage to material reproduction:

---

e.g., *Reichspublizistik und Policeywissenschaft 1600–1800*, vol. 1 of *Geschichte des öffentlichen Rechts in Deutschland* (Munich: Beck, 1987), and *Staat und Staatsräson in der frühen Neuzeit: Studien zur Geschichte des öffentlichen Rechts* (Frankfurt a.M.: Suhrkamp, 1990), specific to Leibniz: 190–95; cf. Horst Denzer, 'Spätaristotelismus, Naturrecht und Reichsreform: Politische Ideen in Deutschland 1600–1750', in *Pipers Handbuch der politischen Ideen*, 3:233–73 (Munich: Piper, 1985).

[58] The literature on the political activities of Leibniz cannot be summarized, but the starting place is Müller and Heinekamp, *Leibniz-Bibliographie* 69–90. As these activities relate to the empire, see Notker Hammerstein, 'Leibniz und das Heilige Römische Reich deutscher Nation', *Nassauische Annalen* 85 (1974): 87–102.

[59] Michael Stolleis, 'Public Law and Patriotism', in *Infinite Boundaries: Order, Disorder, and Reorder in Early Modern German Culture*, ed. Max Reinhart, 11–33, Sixteenth Century Essays & Studies, 40; Early Modern German Studies, 1 (Kirksville, Mo.: Sixteenth Century Journal Publishers, 1998).

> If someone were to ask me what is meant by the term 'common man', I could only define it as people whose minds are concerned with nothing other than thoughts of food; people who seek nothing higher and can no more imagine what the desire for knowledge or mental pleasure is than a person deaf from birth can appreciate a lovely concert. Such people lack passion and fire. They seem to be made from the adamite earth, but the spirit of life was somehow never breathed into them. They live only for the day and move like animals; history is for them but a tale; journeys and descriptions of the world do not affect them (thus they seldom consider the wisdom and governance of God); they think only as far as they can see. You will even find that they are enemies of those who seek higher things and separation from the common herd.[60]

If the common herd may be identified by its scorn for the gift of education (and thus its blasphemy of religion as well), then all who belong to the aristocracy of the mind are naturally set apart. 'The more of these people in a country,' Leibniz writes, 'the more the nation is refined and civilized, and the happier and braver are the inhabitants' (67–8). Parallel but counter to the social hierarchy, a hierarchy of the mind begins to form. Bound by other laws, maxims, and perspectives, it does not ignore the laws of reality, but it does relativize them as contingent historical constructs. To serve the fatherland means to contribute to the expansion of this educated elite. 'Teutschgesinnte Genossenschaft' (German-Minded Society – the name resonates with the spirit of the seventeenth-century reform sodalities) is the exalted name for an assembly of the nobilitas literaria; it lays the groundwork for the renowned eighteenth-century intellectual societies.

Like all reformers of culture, Leibniz had to come to terms with the belatedness of Germany's cultural mission. The great centuries of humanism had produced eminent intellectualism in Italy, France, and England, and the transition from Latin to the vernacular had emanated secondarily from this intellectual renewal. 'There are many reasons why it has not advanced as far among us Germans,' Leibniz remarks. Among them are the war, including the defensive struggle against the French at the end of the century; the lack of a metropolitan center ('hence, minds have neither found a common path nor consolidated their

---

[60] *Ermahnung* 67. 'Wann man mich fragen will, was eigentlich der gemeine Mann sei, so weiß ich ihn nicht anders zu beschreiben, als daß er diejenigen begreife, deren Gemüt mit nichts anders als Gedanken ihrer Nahrung eingenommen, die sich niemals höher schwingen und so wenig sich einbilden können, was die Begierde zu wissen oder die Gemütslust vor ein Ding sei, als ein Taubgeborener von einem herrlichen Konzert zu urteilen vermag. Diese Leute sind ohne Erregung und Feuer; es scheint, sie seien zwar aus der adamitischen Erde gemacht, allein der Geist des Lebens sei ihnen nicht eingeblasen worden. Sie leben in der Welt in den Tag hinein, und gehen ihren Schritt fort wie das Vieh; Historien sind ihnen gut als Mährlein, die Reisen und Weltbeschreibung fechten sie nichts an, daher sie auch die Weisheit und Regierung Gottes wenig betrachten; sie denken nicht weiter als sie sehen; man wird auch sogar finden, daß sie denen Feind seien, so etwas weiter gehn und sich von diesem Haufen absondern wollen.'

opinions, so that many good ideas wither and die, as it were, like strewn and broken flowers'); the disinterest of the upper classes; the 'fault line' running through Germany in the wake of the 'religious division'; and the educational and social divisions (69). On the other hand, Leibniz observes, Italy too has no real capital city. The difference, obviously, has to do with how the reigning elites participate in the nation's cultural life:

> The attitudes of the nobility . . . can either awaken or destroy the spirit. We know that Leo X and Francis I actually poured new life into education, and France owes it to Cardinal Richelieu for elevating not only its power but its eloquence as well to the present level. Still, we have nothing to complain about here in Germany in this regard; it appears that our problems are more the fault of a few of our learned men than of our rulers.[61]

Why? Because the educated class is failing to make the transition from the learned idiom to the vernacular and consequently is not fulfilling its enlightened ideals. The emptiness of learned knowledge may be concealed in this way, but only to the detriment of the non-elite of the nation who remain excluded from higher education. As the example of France shows, it is primarily through popular education in the vernacular that a true nation is born. Germany's finest are turning to other countries, having lost all hope, apparently, for a happy reversal in their own land.

That is the unvarnished state of things in the Holy Roman Empire of the German Nation at the turn of the eighteenth century, two centuries after Luther, one century after Opitz. The real scandal for Leibniz and his enlightened admirers, whether Thomasius or Gottsched or Gellert, is that the language of the sciences, of the so-called 'Hauptmaterien' (primary corpora of knowledge), remains Latin. Literary reform alone avails nothing – a jab at the venerable Fruchtbringende Gesellschaft and the sodalities spawned by it:

> One ought not to be surprised that so many persons of social stature, as well as other excellent people, never brought their work to fruition; for despite having the name 'fruit-bearing', they applied themselves only to plants that produce flowers, not fruit. The flowers of delicate ideas lose their pleasantness as soon as they are picked and quickly become a

---

[61] *Ermahnung* 69–70. 'Hoher Personen Neigung ist . . . dasjenige, so die Gemüter erwecken und niederschlagen kann. Man weiß, daß Leo der Zehnte und Franz der Erste den Studien gleichsam ein neues Leben eingegossen, und Frankreich hat dem Kardinal von Richelieu zu danken, daß nicht nur seine Macht, sondern auch seine Beredsamkeit auf diese gegenwärtige Staffel kommen. Allein wir haben auch diesfalls in Teutschland nicht zu klagen, und scheinet, daß bei uns mehr einigen Gelehrten als hohen Potentaten die Schuld zu geben.'

nuisance if they do not contain the nourishing juice of the immortal sciences.[62]

Leibniz fully intended, through Germanizing and refining the literary culture, to arrive at a vernacular base for all verbal disciplines and cultural intercourse. Service to the nation, the obvious purpose of his impassioned and relentlessly realistic diagnosis, must begin, no matter how desolate the situation may at first appear, as a war on the shameless flirtation with foreign culture and the obsessive reliance on Latin.

Admiration for what already has been accomplished – where else but in the sodalities? – and admission of failure are two sides of the same coin, as Leibniz sees it. Germany in 1700 remains unprepared for a culture of enlightenment. The cosmopolitan German intellectual in communication with the international scientific community can only be embittered by the picture that Germany offers his foreign peers:

> I know distinguished Frenchmen whose business and travels provide them the opportunity and interest in learning our language, but who, as I am aware, have spoken disparagingly about all the nonsense they witness . . . [They] could clearly see that Germany was on the decline, that unity, courage, and reason were all lost, whereas in their own country the sun was in its bright ascendant. How that made me feel I do not care to say. Instead, I ask all of you to examine whether there be German blood in your veins if you are able to hear or read this without being aroused.[63]

---

[62] *Ermahnung* 72. 'Hat man sich also nicht zu verwundern, warum so viel hohe Standespersonen und andere vortreffliche Leute das Werk, so sie angegriffen, nicht gnugsam gehoben, dieweil man ungeacht des Namens der fruchtbringenden sich gemeiniglich nur mit solchen Gewächsen beholfen, welche zwar Blumen bringen, aber keine Früchte tragen. Maßen die Blumen der zierlichen Einfälle ihre Annehmlichkeit gleichsam unter den Händen verlieren und bald Überdruß machen, wenn sie nicht einen nährenden Saft der unvergänglichen Wissenschaften in sich haben.' Cf. Harnack, *Geschichte der Königlich Preussischen Akademie* 1:22, on the Fruchtbringende Gesellschaft; Ludwig Keller, 'Gottfried Wilhelm Leibniz', *Monatsheft der Comenius-Gesellschaft* 12 (1903): 141–55, although controversial, offers useful comments on the history of German sodalities.

[63] *Ermahnung* 73. 'Ich kenne vornehme Franzosen, denen ihre Geschäfte und Reisen Gelegenheit und Lust gemacht, unsre Sprache zu verstehen, und denen ich nachsagen kann, daß sie weder aus Bewegung, noch aus Ekel, sondern aus bloßer Verwunderung über ungereimtes Wesen mit verächtlichen Worten herfürgebrochen. Sie sähen wohl, daß es mit Teutschland auf die Neige komme, und Einigkeit, Tapferkeit und Verstand miteinander sich verlieren, dahingegen bei ihnen die helle Sonne aufgehe. Wie mir dabei zumute gewesen, mag ich nicht wohl sagen, und laß ich einen jeden bei sich selbst prüfen, ob er teutsch Blut in seinen Adern habe, wenn er dieses ohne Empfindung hören oder lesen kann.'

It is the same feeling of shame that Celtis experienced in the company of the more advanced Italians, or that Opitz felt in comparison with larger Romania, now made even more painful in view of small but flourishing Holland.

On the other hand, Germany has the wonder of the Luther Bible, the simple but precise speech of the common people, and the German language of the imperial laws. Leibniz asks, 'How did our forefathers of a hundred or more years ago manage to fill whole folios with pure German? Whoever says that they wrote nothing worth reading has never read them' (75). Germany in the sixteenth century was on its way to a single German language, both written and oral. This significant insight experienced by the bourgeoisie in its heroic phase between 1770 and 1848, between Herder and Hoffmann von Fallersleben, had already occurred to Leibniz with respect to his own age, as it had in fact to the late humanists around 1600, and then to their followers. That would seem to suggest that a neo-classicist restoration, based primarily on poetics, rhetoric, and grammar, was an impossibility. According to Leibniz, the very ground of the nation had to be replowed. 'From that time on,' he observes, speaking of the last third of the sixteenth century,

> German armies served under foreign commanders against their own fatherland, and German blood was sacrificed for foreigners under false pretexts in order to whitewash foreign greed for land. From that time on, our language also had to bear the stigmata of our early servitude. May God in His mercy avert this punishment, lest the same thing happen to German freedom as to the German language, which has been nearly destroyed.[64]

Of course, Leibniz overlooks the fact that the constant pressure on German cities and the brutal suppression of the peasants' revolts also had a hand in quashing the spontaneous expression of a lively and 'körnige' (pithy) German language, as Herder describes it. Scholars now are obliged to enter into an esoteric pact with their princes, but this pact is only a poor imitation of foreign models and is oblivious to its former national-humanist impulse for linguistic reform. For Leibniz, liberty must be predicated on two things: the protection of a genuinely imperial constitution, and the restoration of the linguistic culture of the entire nation. Leibniz knows only too well, as did Opitz and the earlier humanists,

> that a nation and a language typically flourish at the same time; that the power of the Greeks and the Romans was at its height when Demosthenes lived among the Greeks and Cicero among the Romans; that the accepted

---

[64] *Ermahnung* 73. 'Von der Zeit an haben teutsche Kriegsheere fremden Befehlighabern gegen ihr Vaterland zu Gebote gestanden, und das teutsche Blut ist der Ausländer mit falschen Anerbieten übertünchter Landgierigkeit aufgeopfert worden. Von der Zeit an hat auch unsre Sprache die Zeichen unsrer angehenden Dienstbarkeit tragen müssen. Gott wende diese Ahndung in Gnaden ab, damit ja nicht, nachdem es nun fast an dem, daß die Sprache zugrundegerichtet, es mit der teutschen Freiheit geschehen sein möge.'

writing style in France today is almost Ciceronian, and precisely at a time when that country, so unexpectedly, is at the forefront in matters of war and peace. That this could simply happen on its own I do not believe; rather, I maintain that, like the moon and the sea, the ebb and flow of nations and languages are somehow related.[65]

What is new in this argument is the reference to France. The late humanist co-operation between the Pléiade and the French royal house had provided the most compelling paradigm for the relationship between intellect and politics in modern times. Leibniz was looking at a France in which the confessional wars had ended a hundred years earlier and the *Fronde* (1648–53) had been overcome. Of course, the Edict of Nantes had been revoked (1685) and the Huguenots expelled; but Leibniz is taking the nation as a whole, internally secure, externally alert, equally sovereign in war as in peace. Its classical literature of the sixteenth century Leibniz calls 'Older Humanism' and apostrophizes as 'almost Ciceronian' a literature in which national and cultural elements combine in a great high point. Compared with French, the best spoken German around 1700 occupies the lowest rung of the linguistic ladder. Even French women, he offers, who form an essential component in the salon culture, would disapprove of a French spoken at the same mean level as contemporary German. One point is central in Leibniz's decisive parting-of-the-ways with Opitzian humanism and in his anticipation of the early Enlightenment: language must not be a scholarly monopoly but become a true people's language, with the power to transcend class distinctions. It must be rooted in the very culture of the nation. In short, it must create a moral force. Women in France can chat about their domestic chores more earnestly, accurately, and cogently than imperial advisers in Germany can expound on matters of national import. It may be true that reading and conversation play an essentially different role in the culture of France than in Germany. However, old German virtue – a Tacitean idea that Leibniz borrows from the earlier movement of intellectual societies – implies a cultivation of nature through eloquence that is able to thrive only in the maternal soil of native customs.[66]

---

[65] *Ermahnung* 75–6. 'daß gemeiniglich die Nation und die Sprache zugleich geblühet, daß der Griechen und Römer Macht aufs höchste gestiegen gewesen, als bei jenen Demosthenes, bei diesen Cicero gelebet, daß die jetzige Schreibart, so in Frankreich gilt, fast ciceronianisch, da eben auch die Nation in Krieg und Friedenssachen sich so ohnverhofft und fast unglaublich hervorthut. Daß nun solches ohngefähr geschehn, glaub ich nicht, sondern halte vielmehr dafür, gleich wie der Mond und das Meer, also habe auch der Völker und der Sprachen Ab- und Aufnehmen ein Verwandtnis.'

[66] Sigrid von der Schulenburg, 'Leibniz' Verhältnis zur deutschsprachlichen Bewegung und zur Dichtung seiner Zeit', in *Leibniz als Sprachforscher*, 115–72 (Frankfurt a.M.: Klostermann, 1973). On the relationship between Leibniz and Schottel, the chief authority on German of the later seventeenth century, two older studies remain essential: August Schmarsow, *Leibniz und Schottelius* (Strasbourg: Trübner, 1877), and Hoffmann von Fallersleben, 'Leibnitz im Verhältniß zur deutschen Sprache und Litteratur', *Weimarer Jahrbuch für die deutsche Sprache, Litteratur und Kunst* 3 (1855): 80–118.

With this observation, Leibniz moves beyond the older integrated model of the scholar-ruler-nobleman, or urban patrician, thoroughly rooted as it was in the theory of imitation of ancient and foreign models. For Leibniz, the Romance cultural model of mimesis has outlived its usefulness; a true national language can now be institutionalized in the mother country of Germany. 'It is better to be an original of a German than a copy of a Frenchman' (78). Success on a national scale is measured by the degree to which all citizens participate in the nation's educational and linguistic culture. For, 'among peoples thriving on success and hope, there are everywhere in evidence love of fatherland, honor of country, reward of virtue, and an inspired kind of judgment from which linguistic accuracy flows and reaches even to the commoner' (79). The familiar egalitarian societal model is now to be based less on privileged participation and more on an appeal to classless boundaries, ultimately aimed at including the commoner. The name 'German-Minded Society' remains, but its educational goal transcends that of the older sodalities. What was best is conserved, but the mission is now radicalized, its humanist horizons broadened. 'Fame and the welfare of the German nation': that is the primary goal of the Leibnizian Academy.

3. Thomasius and the Christian Egalitarian State

There appeared in Halle in 1696, one year before Leibniz's *Exhortation* and four years before Arnold's *Impartial History*, a broadsheet from the pen of Christian Thomasius and his student Enno Rudolf Brenneysen: *Das Recht Evangelischer Fürsten In Theologischen Streitigkeiten/ gründlich ausgeführet/ und wider die Papistischen Lehrsätze eines Theologi zu Leipzig vertheydiget* (The Right of Evangelical Princes in Theological Disputes, Analyzed in Detail and Defended against the Papist Teachings of a Leipzig Theologian).[67] Thomasius, a 'German scholar without misery', in Ernst Bloch's famous formulation,[68] often found occasion in his life to fire off heated replies to ideas that he found offensive. Just the year before, he and Brenneysen had openly challenged the 'Lutheran Papacy', as he was wont to call the orthodox establishment.[69] Not only had they argued for a broad definition of latitudinarian indifferences, they had also refused to put

---

[67] The secondary literature on Thomasius up to 1955 is collected in Rolf Lieberwirth, *Christian Thomasius: Sein wissenschaftliches Lebenswerk* (Weimar: Böhlau, 1955). The most complete bibliography before the late 1990s of Thomasius's works was Walter Becker, 'Thomasius-Bibliographie', in *Christian Thomasius: Leben und Lebenswerk*, ed. Max Fleischmann, 511–53 (Aalen: Scientia, 1979). See now Friedrich Vollhardt (ed.), *Christian Thomasius (1655-1728): Neue Forschungen im Kontext der Frühaufklärung* (Tübingen: Niemeyer, 1997).

[68] Bloch, *Christian Thomasius: Ein deutscher Gelehrter ohne Misere* (Berlin: Aufbau, 1953).

[69] Lieberwirth, *Christian Thomasius* 53–4 n. 107, discusses the origins of the polemic at length; cf. Ernst Landsberg, *Geschichte der deutschen Rechtswissenschaft* (Munich: Oldenbourg, 1898), 83 ff.

these 'adiaphora' at the discretion of either the individual or the church, leaving them instead to state jurisdiction. Orthodox Lutherans, firmly entrenched in Thomasius's home town of Leipzig (from which he had to flee in 1690), were furious.[70] A professor of theology in Leipzig and pastor of St Thomas Church, Samuel Benedict Carpzov, brother of the senior court preacher in Dresden, railed from the pulpit against the pamphlet; his former teacher, Valentin Alberti, twice had it confiscated, and Carpzov followed up with a polemic of his own: *De jure decidendi controversias theologias* (On the Authority to Decide Theological Controversies), thereby occasioning Thomasius and Brenneysen's *The Right of Evangelical Princes*, one of the most frequently reprinted broadsheets of the early Enlightenment.[71] The broadsheet is dedicated to the Brandenburg director of church affairs Paul von Fuchs, who had sometimes advised Thomasius and his students. Thomasius declares that, with the help of his student Brenneysen (mainly responsible for refining and explicating Thomasius's principles), he hopes to deliver 'a short but hopefully emphatic defense' in face of his continuing persecution. Properly read, Thomasius's polemic is unprecedented in its radical message, and eventually it proved equally hard for both church and state to digest.

---

[70] Fleischmann, *Christian Thomasius*, gives the fullest account of Thomasius's life. Cf. Walther Bienert, *Der Anbruch der christlichen deutschen Neuzeit dargestellt an Wissenschaft und Glauben des Christian Thomasius* (Halle: Akademischer Verlag, 1934); Gertrud Schubart-Fikentscher, *Unbekannter Thomasius* (Weimar: Böhlau, 1954), summarizes the research; Erik Wolf, *Große Rechtsdenker der deutschen Geistesgeschichte*, 4th edn (Tübingen: Mohr, 1963), 371–423, includes portraits; and Klaus Luig, 'Christian Thomasius', in *Staatsdenker im 17. und 18. Jahrhundert: Reichspublizistik, Politik, Naturrecht*, 2nd edn, ed. Michael Stolleis, 228–47 (Frankurt a.M.: Metzner, 1987). On Thomasius in Leipzig, see Rolf Lieberwirth, 'Christian Thomasius' Leipziger Streitigkeiten', *Wissenschaftliche Zeitschrift der Martin-Luther-Universität Halle-Wittenberg* 3 (1953–4): 155–9, and 'Christian Thomasius' Verhältnis zur Universität Leipzig', in *Karl Marx Universität Leipzig 1409–1959: Beiträge zur Universitätsgeschichte*, 1:71–92 (Leipzig: Enzyklopädie, 1959). His tenure in Halle is addressed in Wilhelm Schrader, *Geschichte der Friedrichs-Universität zu Halle* (Berlin: Dümmler, 1894); Georg Mende, 'Die Universität Halle als Zentrum der deutschen Aufklärung', in *450 Jahre Martin-Luther-Universität Halle-Wittenberg*, 2:1–11 (Halle: Selbstverlag, 1952); and, in the same volume, Hans Freydank, 'Christian Thomasius: Ein Erzieher der deutschen Jugend', 13–25. The lengthy funerary composition 'Zeichen eines geneigten Andenckens womit einige Gönner/ Freunde und nahe Anverwandte das Grab des Seeligen beehret' contains, besides the sermon by Johann Georg Francke, many epicedia by friends and colleagues (copies in Staats- und Universitätsbibliothek, Göttingen).

[71] Cited edition in Staats- und Universitätsbibliothek, Göttingen (8° Jus. feud. 37/106). For other editions, see Lieberwirth, *Christian Thomasius* 59 n. 120, and Becker, 'Thomasius-Bibliographie' 526 n. 68. Thomasius's principles were reprinted, without Brenneysen's commentary, as late as 1794; see *Christian Thomasius: Person und Werk in Schrift, Buch und Bild: Katalog der Thomasius-Ausstellung zur 200. Wiederkehr seines Todestages* (Halle, 1928), 29 n. 167. Other writings of Thomasius relevant here: 'Dreyfache Rettung des Rechts Evangelischer Fürsten in Kirchen Sachen', ed. Johann Gottfried Zeidler, and 'Rechtmäßige Erörterung der Ehe- und Gewissens-Frage', published in Halle by Christoph Salfeld in 1689.

The Right of Evangelical Princes consists of nineteen theses with detailed commentary. It eschews the typical lengthy preliminary discussion about the essence of religion. The first thesis begins, 'Under the term religion I understand opinions about God and divine things, as well as the performance of public worship in accordance with those opinions' (7). The second thesis addresses the relationship between church and state in a manner consistent with the tradition of Michel de L'Hôpital and Jacques de Thou in Paris, with which the finest minds of late humanism were in sympathy (though it was still far from dominating opinions in Thomasius's day): 'Both reason and experience teach that different religions by and of themselves do not threaten the state.' Friends need not agree in order to be friends. Furthermore, Thomasius says, what is valid in 'Societäten' (sodalities) is equally valid in large groups, including the republic, since large groups simply consist of many small groups. The state need not fear the disagreements among the various denominations, for they all agree on one basic law, namely, that the teaching of Christ is love (8).

Thomasius, much as Arnold and Leibniz, reduces Christianity to simple, indispensable, universally valid essentials. The duty of the state to settle religious disputes derives from Christianity itself, not primarily from a doctrine of state's rights. The state's task of pacification correlates in fact with the essence of religion. Going one step further, Thomasius postulates the affinity of religion with natural law, basing both on the one law of charity, which binds all Christian religions to one other.[72] The example of Holland shows that there is 'no reason why, for public peace, only a single religion is necessary in the republic'. The welfare and reputation of the young republic rely on 'trading and merchant companies', and all that is needed for these to function, besides suitable economic conditions, is that 'people be honorable individuals who keep their word'. Religious affiliation is completely irrelevant, and it follows that no one is 'persecuted for religious reasons'. Even the Anabaptists, hounded in Germany, 'live [in Holland] entirely in peace'. Accordingly, public disunity is inconsistent with both religion and state and should be encouraged by the state under no circumstances:

---

[72] Werner Schneiders, *Naturrecht und Liebesethik: Zur Geschichte der praktischen Philosophie im Hinblick auf Christian Thomasius* (Hildesheim: Olms, 1971), and 'Vernunft und Freiheit: Christian Thomasius als Aufklärer', *Studia Leibnitiana* 11 (1979): 3–21; also Hinrich Rüping, *Die Naturrechtslehre des Christian Thomasius und ihre Fortbildung in der Thomasius-Schule* (Bonn: Röhrscheid, 1968), and Notker Hammerstein, 'Thomasius und die Rechtsgelehrsamkeit', *Studia Leibnitiana* 1 (1979): 22–44. Hans-Peter Schneider on Christian natural law in Leibniz, *Justitia Universalis: Quellenstudien zur Geschichte des 'Christlichen Naturrechts' bei Gottfried Wilhelm Leibniz* (Frankfurt a.M.: Klostermann, 1967), relates closely to Thomasius, as does the chapter 'Naturrecht und ius publicum universale' in Stolleis, *Reichspublizistik und Policeywissenschaft* 268–97.

> It is unnecessary for the sake of public peace to encourage all subjects to be of one religion. It neither hurts nor helps the republic if someone is, for example, Lutheran or Calvinist, just as it is of no concern to a master whether a servant is Lutheran or Calvinist, as long as the servant is otherwise loyal, for loyalty has nothing to do with religion in the sense that it were the property of only one religion or that only one religion made use of it.[73]

If the church or the state persecutes unorthodox believers, it is 'always as a cover-up' for some end and not in order to ensure the purity of religion or the inviolability of state's sovereignty. From this it follows that tolerance should be practiced – a principle about which Thomasius is fervent. Thomasius's work thus undermines the leading doctrinal tradition even as it reaffirms the clandestine and suppressed efforts of heterodoxy to cleanse and reevaluate the reformist tradition.[74]

At first glance the state does not appear to lose any authority in Thomasius's work.[75] The prince is to 'maintain public peace and tranquillity among his subjects through appropriate means of force' (27). The anthropological pessimism extending from Luther to Hobbes is momentarily audible in Thomasius's explanation of contract theory. 'For the sake of peace and tranquillity,' he explains,

> human beings have built republics at the expense of their natural freedom, subjecting themselves to rulers when deemed necessary to the common good. For after the evil of the expanding human race increased to the point where neighbors could no longer enjoy peace and tranquillity among one another, reason, having taken leave of its own senses, could contrive no

---

[73] *Das Recht Evangelischer Fürsten* 9. 'Dannenhero es denn zum äußerlichen Frieden unnöthig ist/ dahin zu arbeiten/ daß die Unterthanen einerley Confession haben. Es schadet und nützet der Republique nichts/ ob einer z. e. Lutherisch oder Reformiert sey/ gleich wie einen Herrn nichts daran gelegen ist/ ob er einen Reformirten oder Lutherischen Diener habe/ wenn sonsten der Diener nur treu ist/ welche qualität mit der Religion/ so ferne sie für eine Confession oder Kirchen Gebrauch genommen wird/ nichts zu thun hat.'

[74] See Seeberg, 'Christian Thomasius und Gottfried Arnold', on the relationship between Thomasius and Arnold. The subject of pietism common to both is investigated in Harald Herrmann, 'Das Verhältnis von Recht und pietistischer Theologie bei Christian Thomasius' (JD diss., University of Kiel, 1971), and Hans Leube, 'Die Geschichte der pietistischen Bewegung in Leipzig: Ein Beitrag zur Geschichte und Charakteristik des deutschen Pietismus', in *Orthodoxie und Pietismus: Gesammelte Studien*, 153–267 (Bielefeld: Luther, 1975).

[75] Günther Biber, 'Staat und Gesellschaft bei Christian Thomasius: Ein Beitrag zur Ideengeschichte des preußischen Staates' (PhD diss., University of Giessen, 1931); Rudolf Hoke, 'Die Staatslehre des jungen Thomasius: Seine Erstlingsschrift aus dem Jahre 1672', in *Festschrift Heinrich Demelius zum 80. Geburtstag: Erlebtes Recht in Geschichte und Gegenwart*, ed. Gerhard Frotz and Werner Ogris, 111–25 (Vienna: Manz, 1973); and Mario A. Cattaneo, *Delitto e pena nel pensiero di Christian Thomasius* (Milan: Giuffrè, 1976).

better way to escape this dreadful fate than that a certain group of people should band together and promise mutual succor and assistance; and in order to implement this the more effectively, they empowered one or more individuals with the governance of this society.[76]

Then, however, as a counter-measure, Thomasius provides an enlightened caveat: 'If people had lived together only according to the laws of nature, it would have been unnecessary to establish such large societies.' Sociability is not a natural trait of human beings, wherefore the institution of the state does not necessarily derive from the nature of humankind. Those who maintain otherwise are interested only in legalizing force and violence. Thomasius categorically agrees with the natural law historian Samuel Pufendorf that 'man in a state of innocence' would not require a state. He is also emphatic about the price of founding a nation: in acquiescing to a social pact, man 'must give up his natural freedom in many areas'.[77] Opinion to the contrary seems 'to arise from ambition and the desire to dominate in people who would like to rule others' (28). Natural law and the theology of creation, inextricably linked in the early Enlightenment, keep their critical function in political theory as a means of defying the rampant Lutheran sanctioning of the state. It is not 'nature itself' that demands 'the order of rulers and subjects', as the Leipzig disputants claim, but postlapsarian humanity. If, through the enactment of an authentic *imitatio Christi*, life were to be restored to its condition at creation, then an ideal Christian community bound solely by the spirit of love would be plausible without the state. 'True virtue' and the 'peace of mind that ensues from it' may be practiced everywhere and under every condition, independent of the state, whose raison d'être is 'to keep the public order'. It is not a princely duty to assist his subjects in becoming virtuous, for virtue is available to the reason of every individual. Even less ought a prince to be concerned with the eternal salvation of his subjects, for that is a matter solely of religion and its institutions. The exclusive field of princely action is to maintain public order.

---

[76] *Das Recht Evangelischer Fürsten* 27. '[Um] Ruhe und Friedens willen [haben] die Menschen mit Hindansetzung ihrer natürlichen Freyheit die Republiquen aufgerichtet/ und sich einem Oberhaupte unterworffen in solchen Sachen/ die zur Erhaltung des gemeinen Wesens für nöthig befunden werden. Denn nachdem die Boßheit des Menschlichen Geschlechts bey dessen Vermehrung so hoch gestiegen/ daß kein Nachbar für den andern keine Ruhe und Friede haben können/ hat die sich selbst gelassene Vernunfft kein besser Mittel gewust/ dem daraus zu befürchtenden Unheil zu entgehen/ als daß eine gewisse Menge Menschen sich vereinigten/ und einander Hülffe und Beystand versprächen/ und solches desto besser ins Werck zu stellen/ einem oder mehrern die Regierung dieser Gesellschaft auftrügen.'

[77] Erik Wolf, *Grotius, Pufendorf, Thomasius: Drei Kapitel zur Gestaltgeschichte der Rechtswissenschaft* (Tübingen: Mohr, 1927), and Mario A. Cattaneo, 'Staatsraisonlehre und Naturrecht im strafrechtlichen Denken des Samuel Pufendorf und des Christian Thomasius', in *Staatsraison: Studien zur Geschichte eines politischen Begriffs*, ed. Roman Schnur, 427–39 (Berlin: Duncker & Humblot, 1975).

The revolutionary consequences of this self-evident statement are best observed in what is at once the cardinal problem and the touchstone of every philosophy of state in the early modern period: how to deal with the problem of religion. The first response concerns the maintenance of public order. In return for the voluntary self-restriction by its citizens, the state commits itself to leave religious affairs untouched, as long as they do not adversely affect public order. The prince has prohibitive rights. He does not carry the power of the state over into the religious sphere but rather prohibits the religious agenda from compromising the ability of state organs to operate. The ruler's 'watchful eye', the emblem of his circumspection and protection, must be especially attentive to the habit of theologians to couple special religious interests with political powers and to conceal their real agenda behind them.[78] An intelligent prince is careful,

> that when theological quarrels arise he forces no one to accept this or that opinion. However, if the parties attempt to prevail by force, he summons the authority of his office to prevent the public order from being disturbed, and under these circumstances truth will of itself have enough power to prevail and bring disgrace upon the lies.[79]

The entire explanation is subject to one law, namely, that 'the Christian church must not be mixed with the secular state', in order that each be guaranteed its respective sphere of freedom. With that, a great accomplishment of the late-humanist *nobilitas literaria* is ratified in the early Enlightenment.

By the same token, the state's sphere remains sacrosanct. The autonomous sphere of religion, as of any other weltanschauung, ends at the point where the state's authority is endangered, that is, where the state could be hindered internally or externally from its basic task of keeping the peace. To this extent as well, Thomasius completes the Berlin initiative, abetted most notably and grandly by certain members of the French Parlement, to free state and church from their mutual entanglements and thereby to heighten their legitimate spheres of activity: here the right to practice religion freely, there the duty to act neutrally in philosophical and religious matters. The privatization of the religious sphere corresponds to a legalization of the state's sphere. Thomasius, as in late humanism, anticipates in nuce the strict division of legality and morality in Kant's moral philosophy.

---

[78] Gotthardt Frühsorge, *Der politische Körper: Zum Begriff des Politischen im 17. Jahrhundert und in den Romanen Christian Weises* (Stuttgart: Metzler, 1974), 54 ff.

[79] *Das Recht Evangelischer Fürsten* 147. 'daß er nemlich bey Entstehung Theologischer Streitigkeiten niemand zwinget/ diese oder jene Meinung anzunehmen; Wenn aber die Partheyen mit Gewalt durchdringen wollen/ nimt er sein Amt in acht/ und verhütet/ daß der äusserliche Friede nicht gestöret werde/ in welchem Fall die Wahrheit schon vor sich selbsten so viel Macht haben wird/ daß sie durchdringe/ und die Lügen zu schanden mache.'

Thus, in Thomasius we have a noble summary of early modern philosophy of state and religion. A country's people are 'never subject to the prince in matters of faith', and it would be blasphemous for anyone to swear as follows:

> I [Name] vow and promise to subject my will to the will of the prince even in this, that I shall love, honor, and trust in my God according to the prince's desire, and that I shall form no ideas in divine matters other than what he prescribes for me.[80]

For indeed, Thomasius continues,

> God gave each of us an intelligence of our own, that we might employ it to recognize useful truths, and not only to understand natural things but the revelation of supernatural things as well; He will in fact demand an accounting from every one of us at the Last Judgment, when no one will be able to put the responsibility on someone else.[81]

In matters of faith no one can be represented and no one, not even our rulers, can call on a third party – and thus the concordat formula *cuius regio eius religio* 'whose territory, his religion' is rendered obsolete.[82] The same holds true for preachers, spiritual ministers, consistories, synods, university professors, and related officials. Luther did not wage his uncompromising battle against pope and clergy and tradition so that 'popishness' and 'precious clerics' could rise again as spiritual authorities with sanctioning power in orthodox Lutheranism. Each person, whether theologian or shoemaker, is called to speak in matters of theology. As the word itself denotes, a *theo-logian* is anyone who speaks before and with God, and every created being is duty-bound to do just that. Social hierarchies collapse within the spiritual community. As in the humanist sodality, social criteria are in principle irrelevant in the assembly of believers. For instance, 'someone who is a superior officer in the military of the republic has no more rights in the church or the congregation than a common soldier' (44).

---

[80] *Das Recht Evangelischer Fürsten* 82. 'Ich N. N. gelobe und verspreche/ daß ich meinen Willen des Fürsten Willen auch darin unterwerffe/ daß ich nach seiner Willkühr meinen Gott lieben/ ehren/ und auff ihn vertrauen/ auch mir keine andere Concepten von göttlichen Sachen machen wolle/ als mir mein Fürst vorschreiben wird.'

[81] *Das Recht Evangelischer Fürsten* 82–3. 'Es hat ja Gott deswegen einen jeden seinen eigenen Verstand gegeben/ daß er denselben zur Erkäniß [*sic*] nützlicher Warheiten anwenden solle/ und solches nicht allein in natürlichen/ sondern auch in Begriff geoffenbahrter übernatürlichen Sachen; ja er wird auch am Tage des Gerichts von einem jeden insonderheit Rechenschafft fordern/ da sich keiner auff den andern wird beruffen können.'

[82] This phrase represents the policy adopted in the Peace of Augsburg (1555), by which the choice of confessions was determined by the respective territory. The phrase itself was coined only in 1582. See Lewis W. Spitz, 'Imperialism, Particularism and Toleration in the Holy Roman Empire', in *The Massacre of St. Bartholomew: Reappraisals and Documents*, ed. Alfred Soman (The Hague: Nijhoff, 1974), 72.

Thomasius and Brenneysen are in agreement here with Pufendorf. Egalitarian speech in spiritual matters applies as well to a secular egalitarian community: every reasonable and informed person is to be granted a voice. Thomasius is especially clear on this point, because the power of dogma has now been broken; whether in humanism, spiritualism, or pietism, Christianity justifies itself to the extent that it encourages participation in a spirit of love, and it ultimately survives only through such practice. Living in the spirit, imitating Christ under the motto 'Do penance!' is for Thomasius, as for Arnold, the crux of faith. Only one precondition is attached to this construct of logic and ethics, theology and law: that a person prove worthy of the ability to think. In other words, reason must be allowed to operate freely in all areas, beholden to no individual, institution, or doctrine. Examining, reflecting, deciding: that is everything; tradition, authority, dogma: nothing. What for Arnold amounts to a return to original Christianity means for Thomasius a return to natural law. Both seek liberation from tradition, a return to fundamental principles, and an egalitarian obligation on all rational beings. Thomasius is familiar with the objection that, if all people practiced only private religion, the articles of faith would lose validity. Far from denying it, he agrees in order to sharpen his objection:

> The religions publicly introduced and accepted in a given place are the confessions of particular individuals who are considered holy and learned for the way in which they conceived of the mysteries of the religion, and one does well, therefore, to encourage young people to read these individuals diligently; but if one tried to force their writings on someone who thinks differently, they would no longer be religions but laws, which would contradict the intent of the writer, because law and religion differ totally from each other. The right to make laws is given only to princes; religions, however, to one and all.[83]

The fact that many individuals have different faiths means nothing at all; truth obeys no numerical principle. That having been said, need it again be emphasized that the primary obligation of a prince is the unrestricted observance of the law of tolerance, namely, 'that no one be persecuted because of his religion' (167)? This is a law of religion as it is of nature and, over and above that, one of reason of state.

Arnold's work is dedicated to the alleged heretics. Their spiritual justification in Arnold is matched in Thomasius by their worldly justification as a guarantee of unrestricted activity. Religious quarrels had put the state to a crucial test.

---

[83] *Das Recht Evangelischer Fürsten* 139. 'Die öffentlich an einem Orte eingeführte und recipirte Confessiones sind Bekänissen [*sic*] gewisser Personen/ die man für fromm und gelährt gehalten/ wie sie sich die Mysteria darin concipireten/ und also thut man wohl/ daß man dieselbe jungen Leuten vorleget/ dieselbe fleißig zu lesen; aber wenn man einem/ der andere conceptus hat/ dieselbe mit Gewalt auffdringen wolte/ würden sie keine Confessiones bleiben/ sondern Leges werden/ welches selbst wider die intention der Bekenner wäre/ weil ein Gesetze und Confession gantz von einander entschieden. Das Recht Gesetze zu machen kömt allein den Fürsten zu/ Confessiones aber einen jeden.'

Jurists, especially in France and the Netherlands, pointed to a way out. At the turn of the eighteenth century, Germany was preparing to bequeath the religious and national legacy of the confessions and humanists of the early modern period to a new class of educated citizens in a period of enlightened absolutism.

Conclusions

Like all early modern intellectuals, Arnold, Leibniz, and Thomasius operated within fixed traditions. We have discussed some of these traditions and discerned in them three major discourses: 1) the Reformation and the radical religious renewal; 2) humanism and the movement of intellectual societies; 3) early modern political theory as it developed in context of the French-Spanish wars for hegemony in Italy, the religious wars of the sixteenth century, and the Thirty Years' War.

1. The Reformation and the radical religious renewal. The inner experience of faith, proclaimed by Luther to be the single necessary condition of spiritual life, was a revolutionary insight. Although Luther continued throughout his life to modify it, and however exploitable by self-interested territorial princes it often was, the new doctrine proved to be an inextinguishable force in Europe. Even if we question the reasoning of the radical spiritualists between Franck and Breckling, it is clear that they saw themselves as the benefactors of Luther's legacy.[84] They continued to cling to inner inspiration, which could be neither replaced by nor transferred to temporal or ecclesiastical powers. Inner inspiration molded life in its entirety, shaping it into a receptacle for the unlimited influence of the Holy Spirit. The testimony of divine revelation manifested itself everywhere in nature and history in hidden signs of the Divine.[85] Prayerful individuals immersed

---

[84] Siegfried Wollgast, *Philosophie in Deutschland zwischen Reformation und Aufklärung 1550–1650* (Berlin: Akademie, 1988). Reinold Fast (ed.), *Der linke Flügel der Reformation: Glaubenserzeugnisse der Täufer, Spiritualisten, Schwärmer und Antitrinitarier* (Bremen: Schünemann, 1962), compiles writings by heterodox groups in the Reformation. Also Richard van Dülmen, *Reformation als Revolution: Soziale Bewegung und religiöser Radikalismus in der deutschen Reformation* (Munich: dtv, 1977), and 'Die Lehrentwicklung im Rahmen der Konfessionalität', in *Handbuch der Dogmengeschichte*, ed. Carl Andresen (Göttingen: Vandenhoeck & Ruprecht, 1980). Of course, no serious historical study of spiritualism in the sixteenth century can overlook Ernst Troeltsch, *The Social Teaching of the Christian Churches*, trans. Olive Wyan (Chicago: University of Chicago Press, 1981).

[85] Horst Weigelt, *Sebastian Franck und die lutherische Reformation* (Gütersloh: Mohn, 1972); Christopf Dejung, *Wahrheit und Häresie: Eine Untersuchung zur Geschichtsphilosophie bei Sebastian Franck* (Zurich: Samisdat, 1980); and Wilhelm Kühlmann, 'Staatsgefährdende Allegorese: Die Vorrede zum Adler in Sebastian Francks "Geschichtsbibel" (1531)', *Literaturwissenschaftliches Jahrbuch* N.F. 24 (1983): 51–76, and Patrick Haydn-Roy, *The Inner Word and the Outer World: A Biography of Sebastian Franck* (New York: P. Lang, 1994). Bibliographies: Klaus Kaczerowski, *Franck-Bibliographie* (Wiesbaden: Pressler, 1976), and Christoph Dejung, 'Sebastian Franck', in *Bibliotheca Dissidentium*, ed. André Séguenny, 7:39–119 (Baden-Baden: Koerner, 1986).

themselves in these signs and unearthed there great troves of knowledge, the most notable feature of which was not that knowledge was based on ecclesiastical authority, nor that it conformed to a doctrinal system of belief and grace, but rather that it arose from personal religious experience. Social groupings were therefore merely secondary manifestations; they could be freely formed, but they could not be turned into fixed institutions with compulsory regulations.

2. Humanism and the intellectual societies. The sodalities too took shape in opposition to established educational institutions, especially the medieval universities within which the Aristotelian scholastic traditions continued to hold sway. Among the topoi to be found in the mass of institutional documents pertaining specifically to their incorporation is that of 'social access'. Access is available to all who have distinguished themselves by a virtuous life, through knowledge, accomplishment, and independent use of reason. To apply the sociological terms of Max Weber, these are not 'traditional' but 'functional' arguments for the establishment of an elite class. They represent the arguments of those classes that emancipated themselves from the clerical estate and carved out for themselves a certain niche in the northern Italian city-states between the emerging factions of guildsmen and the high bourgeoisie. The arguments of this topos demonstrate that these new groupings made every effort to justify and safeguard their positions ideologically. The writings on true nobility are especially prominent in this regard. They show that the meritocracy of the mind not only took issue with the older feudal privileges of inheritance and corporate identity but also criticized high-bourgeois materialism as incompatible with the eternal values of the mind.

In ignoring the bourgeois identity of the educated estate, scholarship has failed to appreciate this humanist criticism, as well as the degree to which bourgeois thinking (which first became possible in Italy as urban power increased) contributed to the undermining of the social and intellectual base of feudalism.[86] The liaison between the humanists and the seigneurs from the high-

---

[86] This thesis is, admittedly, controversial. Conrad Wiedemann, 'Barocksprache, Systemdenken, Staatsmentalität: Perspektiven der Forschung nach Barners *Barockrhetorik'*, in *Internationaler Arbeitskreis für deutsche Barockliteratur*, ed. Paul Raabe, 21–51, here 41 (Hamburg; Hauswedell, 1976), remarks, 'I consider it of little use to investigate Baroque formal culture in terms of the genesis of a bourgeois mentality, in hopes, thereby, of polishing up an old chestnut.' But see my polemic, 'Gibt es eine bürgerliche Literatur' in answer to Dieter Breuer's 'Gibt es eine bürgerliche Literatur im Deutschland des 17. Jahrhunderts? Über die Grenzen eines sozialgeschichtlichen Interpretationsschemas', *Germanisch-romanische Monatsschrift* 30 (1980): 211–26; cf. Gunther Grimm, *Literatur und Gelehrtentum in Deutschland: Untersuchungen zum Wandel ihres Verhältnisses vom Humanismus bis zur Frühaufklärung* (Tübingen: Niemeyer, 1983), 123 ff.; Notker Hammerstein, 'Res publica litteraria – oder Asinus in aula? Anmerkungen zur "bürgerlichen Kultur" und zur "Adelswelt"', in *Respublica Guelpherbytana: Festschrift für Paul Raabe*, ed. August Buck and Martin Bircher, 35–68 (Amsterdam: Rodopi, 1987); and Wilhelm Kühlmann, 'Nationalliteratur und Latinität'.

bourgeois families makes sense. Elevated upon the rising wave of early bourgeois formation, the humanist elite did not itself belong to the traditional trade, finance, and manufacturing sector, and thus its sphere of activity developed typically under the auspices of princely institutions.[87] These activities and positions ranged from poetic commissions to chancellery and university posts, from chroniclers of dynastic deeds to trusted diplomats. An extensive category of humanist literature developed around matters related to the structure and goals of the new polity, its officialdom, and magistracy; the theme of pure competence pervades this literature.[88] This explains why learned circles gathered regularly under the patronage of the court, and why these 'middle-class' writers actively promoted courtly-affirmative ideas without fear of being personally or corporately corrupted, as though they were some sorts of agents of modernization, as it were.[89] It is thus understandable that Leibniz himself, in seeking sponsorship for his unprecedented program, looked to Frederick III, Elector of Brandenburg.

3. Early modern political theory. As we observed in Thomasius, a covert egalitarianism was at work in early modern political theory. More clearly even than in Thomasius, however, we see in the work of French and Dutch theoreticians of the modern state, most notably Jean Bodin and Hugo Grotius, how the systematic impedance of confessionalism should eventually bring about a non-confessional identity among the state's citizens, notwithstanding all religious diversity and private convictions. This new unity would be predicated on a shared national identity.[90] Whatever their religious differences, the inhabitants of a national territory under one crown, one government, belonged to a single nation. The nation placed demands on its citizens distinct from their other obligations, because they derived from a different value system, at the top of which stood the undivided and unrestricted exercise of national sovereignty. This sovereignty was formulated and enacted by learned jurists in close cooperation with the monarch, largely on the basis of Roman law, whereby feudal prerogatives were subverted.

---

[87] August Buck (ed.), *Höfischer Humanismus* (Weinheim: VCH Acta humaniora, 1989).

[88] Garber, 'Zur Statuskonkurrenz von Adel und gelehrtem Bürgertum', in *Hof, Staat und Gesellschaft in der Literatur des 17. Jahrhunderts*, ed. Elger Blühm, et al., 115–43 (Amsterdam: Rodopi, 1982), details the ethical and behavioral ideals of the emerging officialdom as articulated in *Teutscher Fürstenstaat* (1656) of Veit Ludwig von Seckendorff, minister of the Elector of Brandenburg at Halle.

[89] Jan-Dirk Müller, *Gedechtnus* (Darmstadt: Thesen, 1982).

[90] Pertinent entries and chapters in Roman Schnur (ed.), *Staatsraison: Studien zur Geschichte eines politischen Begriffs* (Berlin: Duncker & Humblot, 1975), and Herfried Münkler, *Im Namen des Staates: Die Begründung der Staatsraison in der frühen Neuzeit* (Frankfurt a.M.: Fischer, 1987).

Without knowledge of these traditions, it is easy to overlook whatever is unique in a given historical situation. We must also ask, however, how these traditions were interrelated around 1700. I see at least three ways:

First, in their formal consolidation. The three traditions are clearly assignable to three carriers, or institutions: church (Arnold), national education and culture (Leibniz), and political theory (Thomasius). Arnold's work aligned itself with the apocryphal, but still rational, reformist wing of the Lutheran tradition. Its hallmark of social isolation was the exact opposite of the institutional university, consistory, city, or territory. The tradition of the persecuted, exiled, expelled, and martyred Christians, all of whom had refused to yield to pressures to join an institutional church, extended from Franck and Böhme to Kuhlmann, Breckling, the Frankfurt Pietists Johann Wilhelm Peterson and his wife Johanna Eleonora, all the way down to Arnold.

A second and more important way in which these traditions related was in the new forms of community that had begun to take shape among enlightened citizens. The direct social antecedents were the sectarian movements and mystical conventicles, whose most important successors became the sentimental poetic and friendship circles of the eighteenth century. Formally, the Leibnizian Academy stood in the humanist societal tradition, but it could also count among its paradigms the national institutions in England and France, aligned as they were with the natural sciences and having the utilitarian mission, radicalized by Leibniz, to serve society and the nation. Both Leibniz and Thomasius appealed to the territorial state, and it is doubtful that their work would have been effective if Brandenburg, given its Calvinist connections, had failed to promote the close connection with the West, which Lutheranism had largely abandoned.

Third, these traditions around 1700 were integrated and consolidated by a complicated bureaucratic system. The evolution of the territorial state after 1648, as the German equivalent of the western nation-state, was accompanied by massive growth in bureaucracy. This apparatus was the most important beneficiary and agent of early enlightened thought; over the course of the eighteenth century it would assist the establishment and stabilization of enlightened absolutism.[91] The high bourgeoisie had far less power than the bureaucracy and exerted significant political influence in only a few centers. In those few cities where it was prominent, however, such as Hamburg, Leipzig, and Zurich, it offered effective channels of communication for the ideas emanating from the English and French Enlightenments. The early 'public' media, including the newspaper (from Thomasius to Johann Mencke), the moral weekly, the learned gazette, the lexicon, and the encyclopedia, achieved a comparatively

---

[91] Alberto Martino, 'Barockpoesie, Publikum und Verbürgerlichung der literarischen Intelligenz', *Internationales Archiv für Sozialgeschichte der deutschen Literatur* 1 (1976): 107–45; cf. Gunther E. Grimm, *Literatur und Gelehrtentum* 15 ff. See also Rudolf Vierhaus, *Deutschland im 18. Jahrhundert: Politische Verfassung, soziales Gefüge, geistige Bewegungen* (Göttingen: Vandenhoeck & Ruprecht, 1987).

supra-regional scope of communication, reaching a much broader readership than that which the decentralized forms of production in the seventeenth century had been capable of.[92] This addressing of the educated by the educated ensured an ever-widening national base for a reading and writing public and constituted the most important precondition for the public dissemination of enlightened ideas.

It may have appeared at times, in following these broad traditions, that we moved rather too far away from the literature of the early modern period. In fact, quite the opposite is true. The repertoire of discourses and traditions during this time was thicker and more interdisciplinary than at perhaps any time before or after, inasmuch as early modern texts typically embody the intersection of multiple institutional speech forms. Learning to see them in this intertextual way is the purpose of what may be called 'configuration analysis', through which the presence of elements not specific to a given genre are viewed simultaneously and appear either to constitute new textual forms or to reveal, in such moments, the compound influence of multiple traditions. All three traditions that we have been following affected the fictional structure of early modern literary texts; indeed, only through the persistence of these and other old traditions can we appreciate the meaning, still deep in the eighteenth century, of certain ancient genres, such as pastoral.

Literature in the early modern period was extraordinarily genre-bound to its classical roots. Genre historians are skeptical of theorists who assert the superiority of totalizing structures over individual authorial intention, subjective expression, or unique forms. To follow the demands of a method that requires us to account simultaneously for totalizing structures and individual forms is part of the daily regimen of early modern genre historians. However, this two-millennia-old system of genres is not simply to be accepted as absolute; indeed, it is our responsibility to continue to probe it aggressively in search of what its functional differences were at specific times. Genres are not institutions; genres are literary conventions.[93] While these two statements appear to be expressing the same truth, in fact they are exclusive. Functional analysis proceeds only from institutional analysis, not from genre or the fictional text. The nature of the fictional text is to appropriate widely different functions in spite of largely identical motivic, thematic, and formal structures. These functions are determined by the institutional givens within which the text operates.

---

[92] Felix Rooke, 'Die Stellung der Zeitschriften des Thomasius zur Philosophie ihrer Zeit' (PhD diss., University of Haale, 1923), and Monika Ammerman-Estermann, 'Literarische Öffentlichkeit', in *Zwischen Gegenreformation und Frühaufklärung: Späthumanismus, Barock, 1572–1740*, ed. Harald Steinhagen, 107–16 (Reinbek: Rowohlt, 1985).

[93] Wilhelm Voßkamp opened this discussion with his study 'Gattungen als literarische-soziale Institutionen: Zu Problemen sozial- und funktionsgeschichtlich orientierter Gattungstheorie und -historie', in *Textsortenlehre – Gattungsgeschichte*, ed. Walter Hinck, 27–42 (Heidelberg: Quelle & Meyer, 1977).

This can be readily demonstrated. In 1630 Opitz, the preeminent master of genres in German literature, invented a prosimetric form of pastoral that we have learned to call prose eclogue (as we recall from Chapter 5). His *Schäfferey von der Nimfen Hercinie* is a panegyric to the princely house of Schaffgotsch in Silesia; but it is also, on another level, as it were, a highly effective medium of learned communication for the late humanist nobilitas literaria. Two years later an anonymous author introduced into this model elements of pastoral novel, turning it into a vehicle for a private love story from the Silesian landed gentry.[94] By the 1640s the genre had become a versatile enough instrument to provide the emerging urban sodalities with a literary organ of self-portrayal. As we saw in Chapter 6, it offered Nuremberg's Pegnesischer Blumenorden both a convenient format for experimental poetry and a forum for aesthetic and social commentary. Even the picaresque novel toyed with the form, using it to convey a satirical point of view on contemporary culture. In this way the Opitzian pastoral penetrated into the non-learned sphere of readers, enriching itself with farcical and anecdotal as well as anti-courtly elements. Later still, it functioned as a vehicle of personal devotion and early enlightened deistic or creationist thought.

To understand the functional use of a given genre requires two things: knowledge of the intellectual traditions from which the motifs and content derive, and recognition of the specific historical milieu in which they are employed. In this way a space of literary communication is opened up, revealing the mechanics both of the work's production and of its reception.[95] Both steps are indispensable, since it is the universalizing nature of genre to resist fictional specifics. Changes arise only in a subsidiary – one is tempted to say, subversive – way and surface only within an extra-literary context, namely, in intellectual, social, or institutional contexts, which allow structural, semantic, and other kinds of differences in functionality to become visible. Ultimately, the method is one of synthetic interpretation. To dwell exclusively on the micrological differences between individual genres or works is to attend to only half of the task. It is necessary, in ever broader analytical steps, to integrate everything historically.[96]

---

[94] *Schäferei von Amoena und Amandus* (1632).

[95] Norbert Elias, 'Thomas Morus' Staatskritik: Mit Überlegungen zur Bestimmung des Begriffs Utopie', in *Utopieforschung*, ed. W. Voßkamp (Frankfurt a.M.: Suhrkamp, 1985), 2:101, speaks of a 'sociogenetic' locus of pastoral: 'The originators (*Urheber*) speak out of a social situation, or a social situation that they have experienced; they speak into a social situation, or one based on experience, which is characteristic of a very specific ... society ... and for a specific public, a specific grouping of people.'

[96] No methodology is better suited for this task than that of *longue durée*. The early modern period, with its fast genre categories, is particularly suited to the approach. One must be cautious not to be misled, however, as certain followers of E.R. Curtius have been, into hypostatizing identities where they are historically untenable. Judgments about identity and difference cannot be made on the basis of texts and generic categories alone, but only through holistic analysis.

In conclusion, let us recall the words of the elderly Goethe: 'I am glad that I am not eighteen now. When I was eighteen, Germany was in its teens also, and something could be done; but now an incredible deal is demanded, and every avenue is barred.' Like Gottsched and Lessing and Herder and the rest, Goethe realized that, without the five-hundred-year-long humanist and early-bourgeois heritage, there would have been no Enlightenment. Since Goethe, however – in part because of the misconstruing of such remarks as these in the post-Goethe era – scholars have largely been content to ignore and eventually to forget precisely that tradition. Accordingly, we may close with a remark by Paul Hazard – one of the great literary historians, like Dilthey and Harnack, whose work has been unjustifiably ignored by German literary historians in recent years – which corroborates the main argument of the present study:

> All of the ideas that were called revolutionary around 1760, or, for that matter, 1789, were already current as early as 1680. Then it was that a sort of moral clash took place in Europe. The interval between the Renaissance, of which it is the lineal descendant, and the French Revolution, for which it was forging the weapons, constitutes an epoch that yields to none in historical importance. For a civilization founded on Duty – duty towards God, duty towards the sovereign – the new school of philosophers wanted to substitute a civilization founded on the idea of rights – rights of the individual, freedom of speech and opinion, the prerogatives of man as man and citizen.[97]

Goethe simply was Germany's greatest recipient of this heritage.*

---

[97] Hazard, *The European Mind* xviii (trans. slightly adapted).
* Translated by Karl F. Otto, Jr.

Bibliographical Note on the Essays

Preface, never before published.

Chapter 1, 'Prophecy, Love, and Law: Visions of Peace from Isaiah to Kant (and beyond)', was presented as a lecture in German at the Universität Osnabrück and printed under the title 'Die Utopie des Friedens im friedlosen Europa: Versuch einer aktuellen Vergegenwärtigung – Von Jesaja bis Benjamin', *Europäische Perspektive – Perspektiven für Europa: Ringvorlesung an der Universität Osnabrück*, 137–51 (Osnabrück: Universitäts-Verlag, 1995).

Chapter 2, 'Your arts shall be: to impose the ways of peace' – Tolerance, Liberty, and the Nation in the Literature and Deeds of Humanism', was originally titled 'Krieg und Frieden: Dogmatismus und Toleranz in der Literatur des europäischen Humanismus' for Münster's 1998 exhibition *350 Jahre Westfälischer Friede*. The exhibition text included only parts I and III of the essay, and it is to be published in this form in volume 2 of the exhibition catalogue *1648 – Krieg und Frieden in Europa*, under the editorship of the Westfälisches Landesmuseum für Kunst und Kulturgeschichte, Münster. An English translation of the abbreviated essay was commissioned, and it accompanied the original German text in the exhibition. This earlier translation provided the basis for the present translation of parts I and III, though it has been significantly modified; translation of the middle part, 'Peace and the Nation: The Experiment of Cola di Rienzi', is new here.

Chapter 3, 'The Republic of Letters and the Absolutist State: Nine Theses', originally included an additional, opening, thesis on the state of research as of the early 1980s, and was published as 'Gelehrtenadel und feudalabsolutistischer Staat: Zehn Thesen zur Sozial- und Mentalitätsgeschichte der "Intelligenz" in der Frühen Neuzeit', in *Kultur zwischen Bürgertum und Volk*, ed. Jutta Held, 31–43 (Berlin: Argument-Verlag, 1983).

Chapter 4, 'Paris, Capital of European Late Humanism: Jacques Auguste de Thou and the Cabinet Dupuy', was first published in a preliminary form in French in *Le juste et l'injuste à la Renaissance et à l'âge classique: Actes du colloque international Saint-Etienne*, ed. C. Lauvergnat-Gagnière and B. Yon, 157–77 (Saint-Etienne: Université de Saint-Etienne, 1986). It was revised and republished in German as 'Paris, die Hauptstadt des europäischen Späthumanismus: Jacques Auguste de Thou und das Cabinet Dupuy', in *Res publica litteraria: Die Institutionen der Gelehrsamkeit in der Frühen Neuzeit*, ed. Sebastian Neumeister and Conrad Wiedemann, 2:71–92 (Wiesbaden: Harrassowitz, 1987). The English translation is based on the German version.

Chapter 5, 'Utopia and the Green World: Critique and Anticipation in Pastoral Poetry', was originally published as 'Arkadien und Gesellschaft: Skizze zur Sozialgeschichte der Schäferdichtung als utopischer Literaturform Europas', in *Utopieforschung: Interdisziplinäre Studien zur neuzeitlichen Utopie*, ed. Wilhelm Voßkamp, 2:37–81 (Stuttgart: Metzler, 1982; reprint as suhrkamp taschenbuch, 1159, Suhrkamp Taschenbuch Verlag, 1985).

Chapter 6, 'Nuremberg, Arcadia on the Pegnitz: The Self-Stylization of an Urban Sodality', was previously unpublished, except for the final pages ('Thirteen Theses'), which were published separately as 'Pastorales Dichten des Pegnesischen Blumenordens in der Sozietätsbewegung des 17. Jahrhunderts: Ein Konspekt in 13 Thesen', in *der Franken Rom: Nürnbergs Blütezeit in der zweiten Hälfte des 17. Jahrhunderts*, ed. John Roger Paas, 146–54 (Wiesbaden: Harrassowitz Verlag, 1995). The full German title of the complete essay is as follows: 'Pegnesischer Blumenorden und Freie Reichsstadt: Zur geschichtlichen Physiognomie einer kommunalen Sozietät und ihres arkadischen Selbstentwurfs im Spiegel von Harsdörffers und Klajs "Pegnesischem Schäfergedicht," Birkens "Fortsetzung" und Hellwigs "Nymphe Noris."'

Chapter 7, 'Begin with Goethe? Forgotten Traditions at the Threshold of the Modern Age,' was originally published as 'Gefährdete Tradition: Frühbürgerliches Erbe und Aufklärung (Arnold – Leibniz – Thomasius)', in *Kulturelles Erbe zwischen Tradition und Avantgarde*, ed. Thomas Metscher and Christian Marzahn, 3–64 (Cologne, Weimar, and Vienna: Böhlau Verlag, 1991).

About the Translators

Joe G. Delap is Associate Dean of Liberal Arts at the University of Central Arkansas in Conway. His specialization is German literature of the Reformation, with particular focus on the dramatists Hans Folz, Burkhardt Waldis, and Paul Rebhun. He also publishes on electronic media and is co-author, with Els Stronks, of *Beginning Dutch Workbook*.

James F. Ehrman is Assistant Professor of German at the University of Kentucky in Lexington. His research specialization is the literature of the German Baroque, particularly that of mysticism and spiritualism. He has published on Böhme, Knorr von Rosenroth, and alchemical images in pietist hymns.

Michael T. Jones is Professor of German at the University of Kentucky in Lexington. He has published widely in the areas of aesthetics and the philosophy of literature, with particular focus on Schiller, Hölderlin, Lukacs, Hannah Arendt, Benjamin, and especially Adorno. With Theodore Fiedler he is co-editor of *Literarische Antworten auf die deutsche Einigung und den Untergang der DDR*.

Karl F. Otto, Jr is Professor of German at the University of Pennsylvania in Philadelphia with a research specialty in German literature of the seventeenth century. He is the author of many books and studies on writers and topics of the German Baroque, including *Die Sprachgesellschaften des 17. Jahrhunderts*, *Philipp von Zesen: A Bibliographical Catalogue*, and, with Jonathan Clark, *Bibliographia Kleschiana: The Writings of a Baroque Family*. Most recently he has published an edition of the *Sinn-Tafeln of Friedrich Scherertz*.

Max Reinhart is Professor of German at the University of Georgia in Athens and specializes in early modern German literature. His publications include *Johann Hellwig's "Die Nymphe Noris" (1650): A Critical Edition* and *Georg Philipp Harsdörffer: "Lamentation for France" and Other Polemics on War and Peace (The Latin Pamphlets of 1641–1642)*; he has edited *Infinite Boundaries: Order, Disorder, and Reorder in Early Modern German Culture* and, with James Hardin, *German Writers of the Renaissance and Reformation 1280–1580*.

Peter Rosenbaum is a doctoral candidate in the Department of German at New York University. His dissertation on memorials deals with concepts of space and place as they relate to memory and identity. He has published on topics in contemporary German literature and, most recently, on the Buchenwald memorial.

ABOUT THE TRANSLATORS

Michael Swisher is Associate Professor of German and Chair of the Departments of Art and Literature, and of Humanities, at Truman College in Chicago. His research specialty is early German language and literature. He has published on Wolfram's *Parzival* and the *Heliand*, as well as on the language of nature in Old High German literature.

Index

Accademia Aldina (Venice) 45
Accademia degli Orti Oricellari (Florence) 45–6
Accademia della Crusca (Florence) 46–7
Accademia Fiorentina (Florence) 45
Accademia Platonica (Florence) 45–6, 48
Accademia Pomponia (Rome) 45
Accademia Pontaniana (Naples) 45–6
Académie Française (Paris) 57
Académie Putéane (s. Cabinet Dupuy)
Adorno, Theodor W. (1908–69) xvi, xxii, xxvii, 117
Africa 32, 76, 84
Aix 69
Alais, Peace of 71n
Alba, Fernando Alvarez de Toledo (1507–82) 31
Alberti, Valentin (1635–97) 238
Alcalá, University of 32–3
Alençon, Duke of (s. Anjou, Francis)
Alewyn, Richard (1902–79) 223n
Alexander the Great (356–23 B.C.) 199
Alexander III, Pope (r. 1159–81) 9n
Alkinoos, Gardens of 139n
Alsace xv
Altdorf, University of 118, 159, 169, 191
Althusser, Louis xii
America 39, 115
Amsterdam xiv
Anabaptists 35, 239
Andreae, Johann Valentin (1586–1654) 48
Anglican Church 32, 37–8
Anhalt (Anhalt-Köthen) 47, 95, 153, 197, 212
Anjou 21
Anjou, Francis, Duke of Alençon (d. 1584) 88
Ansbach 119
Anti-Trinitarians 39, 50
Antony, Marc (83–30 B.C.) 4
Antwerp 33
Apennine Peninsula 21
Arabs 32–3
Aragon (Aragonese) 21, 32, 85, 87
Arians 50
Aristotle (384–22 B.C.) 6, 11
Arminian (Arminianism) 35, 37
Arminius, Jacob (1550–1609) 35

Arndt, Johann (1555–1621) 222
Arnold, Christoph (1627–85) 159–60
Arnold, Gottfried (1666–1714) 32, 40, 208, 219–28, 231, 237, 239, 244–5, 248
 Die Erste Liebe der Gemeinen Jesu Christi 221–2
 Unpartheyische Kirchen- und Ketzer-Historie 32n, 40, 220–28
Athens 214
Athenians 193
Auditorium publicum (s. Nuremberg)
Augsburg 46, 215
 Peace of (1555) 15n, 31, 144n, 243n
St Augustine (354–430) xxiii, 6–9, 24
 Confessiones 6
 De civitate Dei 6–9
Augustus, Caesar (Octavian; r. 29 B.C. – A.D. 14) 4, 6, 11, 24–5
Austria xi, 98, 124
Avignon 25, 84

Bacchylides (fl. 5th c. B.C.) 139
Bacon, Francis (1561–1626) 157
Baïf, Jean-Antoine de (1532–89) 59
Balzac, Jean-Louis Guez de (1597–1654) 69
Baptists 37, 50
Barbarossa, Frederick (r. 1155–90) 9
Baron, Hans xi(n), 44n
Basel xiv, 19n, 39
Bavaria (Bavarian) 47, 124, 153
Bayle, Pierre (1647–1706) 14, 36
 Dictionnaire historique et critique 36
 Dictionnaire philosophique 227n
Bayonne, Bishop of 34
Bayreuth 119, 144n
Belgium 31
Benjamin, Walter (1892–1940) xii–iii, xvii–xxviii, 17–18, 40, 219n
 Ursprung des Deutschen Trauerspiels xxv
Bergara, Francisco de (Spanish humanist, fl. 1530) 33
Berlin 215, 228–9, 242
Bernegger, Matthias (1582–1640) 69, 118
Bernhard of Saxe-Weimar (1604–39) 153
Bertrando del Poggetto, Cardinal (fl. 1329) 10n

INDEX

Betulius
   Christian (s. Birken, Christian)
   Daniel and Veronica (parents of Sigmund) 144n
   Sigmund (s. Birken, Sigmund)
Beuthen xiv, 212
Bèze, Théodore de (1519–1605) 68
Bibliothèque Nationale (Paris) 62n, 66
Bibliothèque Royale (Royal Library) 65–6, 68, 72
Birken, Christian (brother of Sigmund) 142n
Birken, Sigmund von (Betulius; 1626–81) 95, 98–101, 121n, 125, 142–65, 169, 175, 179, 197–8
   Fortsetzung der Pegnitz-Schäferey 142–65, 171, 188
   Fürtrefflichkeit des Lieblöblichen Frauenzimmers 98–101
Bloch, Ernst (1885–1977) xvi, xix, xxiii–v, 40, 237
   Ein deutscher Gelehrter ohne Misere 237
Boccaccio, Giovanni (1313–75) 130, 164, 167n, 190, 216
   Ninfale fiesolano 167n
Bodin, Jean (1530–96) 34, 247
   Six livres de la République 34
Bodmer, Johann Jakob (1698–1783) 111, 216
Boecler, Johann Heinrich (1611–72) 69
Böhaim, Lucas Friedrich (1587–1648) 189
Bohemia 30–1, 47, 52, 144, 147, 159n
Bohemian Brothers 25, 39
Böhme, Jakob (1575–1624) 36, 40, 221, 248
Boileau-Despréaux, Nicolas (1636–1711) x
Böllinger Collection (Copenhagen) 67
Bologna 45
Book of Nature 194–5
Bordeaux, Parlement of 60
Bossuet, Jacques Bénigne (1627–1704) 69
Bracciolini, Poggio (1380–1459) 28, 43–4
   De nobilitate 43n
Brandenburg 228, 229n, 238, 247–8
Brandenburg-Ansbach 119
Brandenburg-Kulmbach (Bayreuth) 119
Brant, Sebastian (1457–1521) 212, 214
Breckling, Christian (17th-century irenicist) 40, 245, 248
Breitinger, Johann Jakob (1701–76) 216
Brenneysen, Enno Rudolf (student of Ch. Thomasius, fl. 1700) 237–8, 244

Breslau 118
Briçonnet, Bishop Guillaume (1470–1534) 34
Brockes, Barthold Heinrich (1680–1747) 104, 221
   Irdisches Vergnügen in Gott 221
Brockmann, Rainer (Reval friend of Paul Fleming) 152
Brown, Harcourt (b. 1900) 70
Bruni, Leonardo (1370–1444) 28, 216, 229
Buchner, August (1591–1661) 136–7, 206
Bucquoy, Charles Bonaventure de Longueval, Count of (1571–1621) 153
Budé, Guillaume (1468–1540) 34
Burdach, Konrad (1859–1936) xvii, 10n, 28, 134
   Rienzo und die geistige Wandlung seiner Zeit 28–9
   Vom Mittelalter zur Reformation 10n
Bürger, Peter xxiv
Burgos 33
Burgundy (Burgundian) 19, 141

Cabinet Dupuy (Paris; Académie Putéane) 53–72
Calpurnius (fl. A.D. 50–60) 80–2
   Bucolica 80–2
   Buc. 1 (81)
   Buc. 4 (82)
   Buc. 7 (82)
Calvin, John (1509–64) 38, 68
Calvinist (Calvinism) 12, 31, 35–40, 47, 50–2, 68, 95n, 213, 240, 248
Cambrai 19
Cambridge 36
Cardano, Girolamo (1501–76) 60
Carpzov, Samuel Benedict (1595–1666) 238
   De jure decidendi controversias theologias 238
Casaubon, Isaac (1559–1614) 68
Castile 32
Castellio, Sebastian (1515–63) 38
Cateau-Cambrésis, Peace of (1559) 21
Catherine of Aragon, Queen of England (1485–1536) 36
Catholic (Catholicism) xiv, 8, 12, 31–2, 34–5, 38–40, 46, 50–1, 59–60, 67, 70, 72, 88, 98, 124–5, 144n, 153, 185
Cats, Jakob (1577–1660) 214
Celtis, Conrad (1459–1508) x, 137, 210–2, 215–6, 230, 235

Cervantes, Miguel de (1547–1616) 89–90, 93
   Don Quixote 93
   Galatea 93
Chambre de Guyenne (Paris) 60
Chapelain, Jean (1595–1674) 69
   Dictionnaire 69
Charlemagne (724–814) 8, 25n, 197, 211
Charles I, Stuart king (r. 1625–49) 32, 37, 204
Charles V, Emperor (r. 1519–58) 19, 21, 32–3, 50, 141
Charles VIII, King of France (r. 1483–98) 21, 46, 85–6
Charles IX, King of France (r. 1560–74) 31
Cherasco, Treaty of 71n
Chartres 60, 69
Christian I of Anhalt (1568–1630) 153
Chytraeus, Nathan (1543–98) 169
Cicero (106–43 B.C.) 6, 235
Cisneros, Cardinal Jiménez de (1437–1517) 32
Clement VI, Pope (r. 1342–52) 27n
Colbert, Jean-Baptiste (1619–83) 66
Coler, Christoph (1602–58) 70–1
   Umständliche Nachricht von des weltberühmten Schlesiers Martin Opitz 70–1
Colet, John (1467–1519) 36
Collection Dupuy (Paris) 66–8
Comes, Natales (s. Conti, Natale)
Condé family (cadet branch of Bourbons) 68
Conrad I, Emperor (d. 918) 183
Conrad III, Emperor (d. 1152) 183
Constance, Council of (1414–17) 31
Constantine I, Emperor (r. 310–37) 38, 225–6
Conti, Natale (Natales Comes; 1520–80) 151, 157
   Mythologia 151n, 157, 159
Coornhert, Dirck Volckerszoon (1522–90) 35, 216
   Proces van 't Ketter-wooden 35n
Copenhagen 67
Copernicus, Nicolaus (1473–1543) 215
Cromwell, Oliver (1599–1658) 37
Crypto-Judaism 32
Cujas, Jacques (1520–90) 59
Curione, Celio Secundo (1538–67) 39
Curtius, Ernst Robert (1886–1956) xix, 250n

Cusa, Nicholas of (1401–64) 34

Dante Alighieri (1265–1321) x, xiii, xxiii, xxvii, 9–13, 25–6, 28, 36, 38, 43, 52, 74, 82–3, 89, 134, 196, 211, 216
   Convivio 43
   De Monarchia 9–12, 26
   Divina Commedia xiii, 82
   Epistolary eclogues 45, 82–3
Danzig xiv–xv, 215
Darmstadt 221
David, King 24, 84
Day of the Barricades 60
Demosthenes (384–22 B.C.) 235
Denmark 153
Descartes, René (1596–1662) 69
de vera nobilitate (*vera nobilitas*) 43, 48
Diderot, Denis (1713–84) xi, 209
Dilherr, Michael (1604–69) 118, 123
Dilthey, Wilhelm (1833–1911) 35, 229n, 251
Dobeneck, Catharina Margaretha (d. 1683) 98
Dohna, Castle of 72
Dohna, Karl Hannibal von 70, 72
Dordrecht, Synod of (1619) 35
Dresden 221, 238
Dresserus, Matthaeus (1536–1607) 169
Drusus Nero 183
Du Bellay
   Guillaume de (brother of Jean) 34
   Jean de (Bishop of Bayonne) 34
   Joachim de (1522–60) 59
Du Cange, Charles Du Fresne (1610–88) 69
   Glossarium mediae et infimae latinitatis 69
Duchesne, André (1584–1640) 69
Duplessis-Mornay, Philippe (1549–1623) 34, 68
Dupuy
   Brothers (Puteani; s. Jacques Dupuy and Pierre Dupuy)
   Claude (father of Jacques and Pierre) 60, 68
   Collection (s. Collection Dupuy)
   Jacques (1591–1656) 60–71
   Pierre (1582–1651) 60–71
Dutch War of Independence 12
Du Vair, Guillaume (1556–1621) 68

Ebner family (s. Nuremberg)
Eckermann, Johann Peter (1792–1854) 209, 216, 218
  Gespräche mit Goethe in den letzten Jahren seines Lebens 209n
Eden, Garden of 2–3
Edict of Nantes (1598) xiv, 15, 34–5, 60, 236
  Retraction of (1685) 15, 35, 236
Edict of Restitution (1629) 119, 144n
Eger River 145–6
Egidien Church (s. Nuremberg)
Egidien School (s. Nuremberg)
Eguia, Miguel de (publisher in Alcalá of Erasmian writings) 33
Eichendorff, Joseph von (1788–1857) 40
Elbe River 131
Elias, Norbert (1897–1990) xi, xxiv(n), xxv, 94, 205n
  The Court Society 94
Elizabeth I, Queen of England (r. 1558–1603) 38, 88
Endelechius, Severus (fl. 395) 82
Engels, Friedrich (1820–95) 17
  Die Lage der arbeitenden Klasse in England 17
England 17, 30–2, 36–9, 95, 159n, 216, 232, 248
Eobanus Hessus (1488–1540) 139, 167n, 188n
Erasmian (Erasmianism) 19n, 32–4, 39–40, 222, 226
Erasmus, Desiderius (1466–1536) xviii, xxiii, 12–15, 18–24, 31–3, 35–7, 39–40, 222
  Querela Pacis 12–15, 18–24
Ernst Ludwig, Landgrave of Hessen-Darmstadt (1667–1739) 221
Estaples, Lefèvre de (member of School of Meaux) 34

Falkenberg, Dietrich (d. 1631) 153
Federigo, King of Naples (capitulated 1501) 85–6
Ferdinand II, Emperor (r. 1619–37) 119n, 144n
Ferdinand II, King of Aragon (r. 1479–1516) 32
Ferdinand III, Emperor (r. 1637–57) 199
Ferdinand, Infant (Spain) 153
Ferrante I, King of Naples (r. 1458–94) 85

Ferrara 38
Fetzer, Dr. (Nuremberg councilman) 121
Ficino, Marcilio (1433–99) x, 20, 38
Finckelthaus, Gottfried (1614–48) 152
Fischart, Johann (1546–91) 163, 167, 212, 214
Fisher, John (Bishop of Rochester) 36
Fleming, Paul (1609–40) 128, 133–4, 142, 152
Florence (Florentine) xi, 10n, 12, 19n, 20–1, 26, 28, 44–6, 229
Foix, Paul de (French jurist) 60
Fontenelle, Bernard de (1657–1757) 74, 196
Foucault, Michel (1926–84) xii
Fourier, Charles (1772–1837) 17
France xiv–xv, 11, 21, 25, 31, 33–4, 36, 49–50, 54–72, 85–8, 106, 113–6, 122, 124, 153, 199, 209, 216, 228, 232–3, 236, 245, 248
Francis I, King of France (r. 1515–47) 21, 67, 216, 233
Franciscans, or Franciscan Spiritualists x, 9–10, 25, 30, 226n
St Francis of Assisi (1182–1226) 9
Franck, Sebastian (1499–1542) 35, 40, 222, 245, 248
Franckenberg, Abraham von (1593–1652) 36
Franconia 119n, 120, 215
Frankfurt am Main 220n, 221, 248
Frederick Barbarossa (s. Barbarossa)
Frederick I, King of Prussia (r. 1713–40) (formerly Frederick III, Elector of Brandenburg) 228, 247
Frederick II, Emperor (r. 1220–50) 25
Frederick II ('the Great'), King of Prussia (r. 1740–86) 217
Frederick III, Elector of Brandenburg (s. Frederick I, King of Prussia)
Frederick V, Elector Palatine (1596–1632) 51n
French Revolution xvii, 45, 73n, 113, 115–6, 251
Fritsch, Thomas (Frankfurt a.M. publisher, fl. 1700) 221
Froben, Johann (Basel publisher, fl. 1515) 19n
Fromm, Eric (1900–80) xi
Fruchtbringende Gesellschaft (Anhalt-Köthen) 47, 95, 125, 131, 148, 212, 233

Frundsberg, Georg von (leader of German mercenaries in sack of Rome, 1527) 21
Fuchs, Paul von (Director of Church Affairs in Brandenburg, fl. 1696) 238
Fürer, Christoph (1634–90) 119
Fütter family (s. Nuremberg)

Gabor, Bethlen (r. 1613–29) 153
Gallican (Gallicanism) 59, 64, 67
Garcilaso de la Vega (1503–36) 88, 92
Gassendi, Pierre (1592–1655) 69
Gattinara, Chancellor Mercurino (1465–1530) 33
Gellert, Christian Fürchtegott (1715–69) 233
Geneva 31, 68
George Circle 6n
Gessner, Solomon (1730–88) 79, 106–14
   Der Wunsch 107–14
   Idyllen 107, 112–3
Giessen 221
Giovanni del Virgilio (d. after 1327) 45, 82–3
Gleim, Ludwig (1719–1803) 111, 217–8
Godefroy, Théodore (1580–1649) 63–4, 69
Goethe, Johann Wolfgang von (1749–1832) x, xxvii, 40, 106, 112, 115–6, 208–51
   Dichtung und Wahrheit 210, 217–8
   Die Leiden des jungen Werthers 112
   Hermann und Dorothea 115–6
   Propyläen 218
Göhring, Martin 59
   Weg und Sieg der modernen Staatsidee in Frankreich (1947) 59
Goldast, Melchior (1578–1635) 212
Golden Bull of 1356 (s. Nuremberg)
Golgotha 150
Goodwin, John (1594–1665) 37
Goths 214
Gottsched, Johann Christoph (1700–56) x, 48, 53, 213–6, 230, 233, 251
   Gedächtnisrede auf Martin Opitzen von Boberfeld 214–5
   Versuch einer Critischen Dichtkunst 213–4
Gracian, Antonio (private secretary to Philip II of Spain) 216
Granada xiv, 32
Greece (Greeks) 6, 215, 235

Greenblatt, Stephen Jay xiii(n), xxi, xxii(n), xxiv(n), xxviii
Gregory of Nazianus (d. 381; Nazianus) 82
Gregory IX, Pope (r. 1227–41) 25
Greiffenberg, Catharina von (1633–94) 98
Grimmelshausen, Hans Jakob Christoffel von (1622–76) 95
Grisons (in Switzerland) 39
Groethuysen, Bernhard (1880–1946) xi
Gronovius, Joannes Fredericus (1611–71) 69
Gross family (s. Nuremberg)
   Konrad 186
Grotius, Hugo (1583–1645) 35–6, 68–9, 71, 247
   De jure belli et pacis 36
Grünau 115
Gruter, Janus (1560–1627) 68–9
Gryphius
   Andreas (1616–64) 95
   Christian (1649–1706) 215
Guarini, Battista (1583–1612) 89–92, 95
   Il Pastor fido 90–2
Guericke, Otto von (1602–86) 215
Guevara, Antonio de (1480–1545) 91, 216
   Menosprecio de corte y alabanza de aldea 91
Guise family (Lorraine) 60
   Henri, 3d Duc de Guise (1550–88) 60n
Gustav II Adolf (1594–1632) 71n, 119, 130n, 153
Guyot, François (French linguist) 69

Habermas, Jürgen xii, xxiv, 46n
Habsburgs 51, 70, 119, 124
Hagedorn, Friedrich von (1708–54) 104, 110
   Fabeln und Erzählungen 110
Halle 215, 237, 238n, 247n
Haller, Albrecht von (1708–77) 104–6
   Die Alpen 104–6
Haller family (s. Nuremberg)
   Hans 141
   Hans Jacob 141
   Wilhelm 141
   Wilhelm the Younger 141
Haller meadow (s. Nuremberg)
Hallmann, Johann Christian (1640/45–1704) 215
Hamann, Johann Georg (1730–88) 40
Hamburg 67, 104, 118, 248

INDEX

Hankamer, Paul xxviii, 54
Harnack, Adolf von (1851–1930) 229n, 251
Harsdörffer family (s. Nuremberg)
    Georg Philipp (1607–58) 119, 122–44, 147, 151–2, 157–9, 162, 168, 175, 181, 184, 190, 204–5
    Frauenzimmer Gesprächspiele 123–5, 190
    Pegnesisches Schäfergedicht 125–44, 148, 165, 176
Hazard, Paul (1878-1944) 251
Heer, Friedrich xvii, 30n
    Die dritte Kraft 30n, 57n
Hegel, Georg Wilhelm Friedrich (1770–1831) (Hegelian) 9, 17, 40, 106, 207, 224, 231
    Jena lectures 17
Heidelberg xiv, 46, 51n, 212
Heidelberg Order of Tournaments 177
Heilbronn League 119
Heinrich VII, Emperor (d. 1313) 183
Heinsius, Daniel (1580–1655) 68–9, 214
Hellwig
    Helena (1619–45) 172n
    Johann (1609–74) 121n, 125, 143, 159, 162–204
    Die Nymphe Noris 165–204
Henry III, King of France (r. 1574–89) 59–60
Henry IV, King of France (r. 1589–1610) 15n, 34, 60–2, 67
Henry VIII, King of England (r. 1509–47) 36
Henry of Navarre (r. 1572–89; later Henry IV) 60
Herdegen, Johann (1692–1750) 146n
Herder, Johann Gottfried (1744–1803) 40, 106–7, 217–8, 235, 251
Herrera, Francisco Manuel de (1684–1752) 92
Hesiod (fl. ca. 7th c. B.C.) 20, 24, 163, 204
    Theogeny 20
Hessen 221
Hevelius, Johannes (1611–87) 215
Hirsch, Arnold (1901–54) xi, 101–2
Hobbes, Thomas (1588–1679) 240
Hoeck, Theobald (1573–1658) 178
Hoffmann von Fallersleben, August Heinrich (1798–1874) 235

Hofmannswaldau, Christian Hofmann (1617–79) 215
Hohenberg 144n
Hölderlin, Friedrich (1770–1843) 9
Holland 216, 235, 239
Holstenius, Lucas (1596–1661) 69
Holtzschuher family (s. Nuremberg)
Homburg, Ernst Christoph (1605–81) 142
Homer (fl. 700 B.C.) 84
    Illiad 139
Horace (65–8 B.C.) 6, 96, 104n, 167
Horkheimer, Max (1895–1973) xi
Hôtel de Thou (Paris) 65, 68, 72
Hotman, Jean (1552–1636) 69, 72
Huguenots 31, 34, 60, 62, 71, 236
Hüls, Dr. Heinrich (Nuremberg councilman) 121
Hund, Samuel (fl. 1650) 159
Hungary (Hungarian) 39, 141
Huss, Jan (1369–1415) 30–1
Hussites 25, 31
Hutten, Ulrich von (1488–1523) 215
Huygens, Constantijn (1596–1687) 216

Iberian Peninsula 32
Ignatius of Loyola (1491–1556) 38
Imhoff family (s. Nuremberg)
Imperial Patent of 1696 (178) 48–9n
Index of Forbidden Books 24, 61
Ingolstadt, University of 210
Inquisition, Spanish 32
Isabella, Queen of Castile (r. 1474–1504) 32
Isaiah (fl. 740–701 B.C.) 2–4, 13, 17, 24, 201
Iser, Wolfgang 88
Istanbul 64
Italy xv, 10n, 12, 20–1, 25–8, 30, 38, 44–6, 67, 71, 84n, 85–8, 89n, 92, 123–4, 134, 137, 141, 214, 216, 232–3, 245–6

Jacobins 112
Jean Paul (J. P. F. Richter; 1763–1825) 40
Jena 145–7, 150
    Luther Fountain 146
    Philosophers' Plaza 146
    Johannis Tower 146
    University of 145–7
St Jerome (331–420) 82

Jerusalem 2
Jesuits (Society of Jesus) 38, 65n, 167, 226
Jesus (Christ, or Jesus Christ) 5–6, 8, 10–15, 23–4, 33, 35, 37–9, 128, 221–4, 239, 244
Jews 32, 37
Joachimites 25
Joachim of Fiore (1132–1202) x, 8–10, 226n, 228n
Johnson, Dr. Samuel (1709–84) x
Joyeuse, François Cardinal de (1562–1615) 61
Judas 37
Judea 2
Jungius, Joachim (1587–1657) 48

Kant, Immanuel (1724–1804) 11, 15–17, 217, 242
 Zum ewigen Frieden 15–16
Klaj, Johann (1616–56) 121n, 123–63, 171, 181, 191
 'Hellgläntzendes Silber' 136
 Pegnesisches Schäfergedicht 125–44, 148, 165, 176
 Redeoratorien 123
Kleist, Christian Ewald von (1715–59) 107–8, 111
 Der Frühling 108
Klopstock, Friedrich Gottlieb (1724–1803) 111, 210, 217, 221
 Der Messias 217
Kofler, Leo (Austrian émigré) xi
Königsberg 118, 215
Kos (Greek island) 75
Krakow 19n
Kress family (s. Nuremberg)
 Jobst Christoph (1597–1663) 119
Kuhlmann, Quirinus (1651–89) 36, 248

Lambeck, Peter (1628–80) 69
La Mothe Le Vayer, François de (1588–1672) 69
Landino, Cristoforo (1424–98) 43
 De vera nobilitate 43n
La Rochelle xiv, 68, 71
League (Catholic) 50n, 59, 60n
Leibniz, Gottfried Wilhelm (1646–1716) x, xviii, 36, 47–8, 208, 215, 219, 228–39, 245, 247–8
 Ermahnung an die Teutschen (Exhortation) 229–37

Leiden xiv, 19n
Leipzig 19n, 118, 152, 204, 213, 215, 237–8, 241, 248
Leo X, Pope (r. 1513–21) 233
Lessing, Gotthold Ephraim (1729–81) xi, 216–7, 251
 Minne von Barnhelm 217
 Nathan der Weise 217
L'Hôpital, Michel de (1503–73) 34, 59, 68, 239
Limburger, Martin (1637–92) 146n
Lingelsheim, Georg Michael (fl. 1620) 65, 68
Lipsius, Justus (1547–1606) 35
Lochner, Friedrich (1602–73) 172n, 175
Locke, John (1632–1704) 38, 216
 Letters on Tolerance 38
Lodi, Peace of (1454) 20
Lohenstein, Daniel Casper (1635–83) 215
Loisel, Antoine (jurist colleague of Jacques Auguste de Thou) 60
Lombards 214
London 36, 65n
longue durée x, xx, 250n
Longus (A.D. 3d c.?) 89
 Daphnis and Chloë 89
Lope de Vega Carpio, Félix (1562–1635) 89–90, 93–4, 128, 136, 139
 Arcadia 92–3, 136
Lothringen, Karl von (field general) 70n
Louis XIII, King of France (r. 1610–43) 50, 153
Louis XIV, King of France (r. 1643–1715) (Sun King) xv, 15, 35, 230
Louvain 19n
Lower Saxony 198
Ludwig, Prince of Anhalt-Köthen (1579–1650) 95n, 197, 212
Lullians 25
Lusatia 215
Luther, Martin (1483–1546) 12–14, 31–2, 35, 39, 130n, 146, 212–3, 222n, 225–6, 233, 235, 240, 243, 245
Lutherans (Lutheranism) 31, 35, 39–40, 53, 144, 146, 169, 224, 237–8, 240–1, 243, 248
Lyons 65n

Machiavelli, Niccolò (1469–1527) 28, 44
Madrid 64
Magdeburg 150, 153, 215

Mainz 46, 229
Malherbe, François de (1555–1628) 69
Manetti, Giannozzo (1396–1459) 43n
    De dignitate et excellentia hominis 43n
Mann, Thomas (1875–1955) 217
Mansfeld, Ernest, Count of (1580–1626) 153
Mantua 71
Manutius, Aldus (1547–97) 20, 60
Margarete of Navarre 34
Margrave Wars (s. Nuremberg)
Marseille 69
Marsilius of Padua (1290–1343) 10n
    Defensor Pacis 10n
Marx, Karl (1818–83) xxv(n), 17
    Kritik des Hegelschen Staatsrechts 17
    Das Kapital 17
Maximilian I, Emperor (r. 1493–1519) 47, 141, 211, 216
Meaux, School of 34
Medici family 20–1
    Catherine de (1519–89) 31
    Cosimo de' (1389–1464) 46
    Lorenzo de' (1449–92) 38, 46
Meissen 130, 147, 159n
Meistersinger 118, 212
Melanchthon, Philipp (1497–1560) 33, 39–40, 68, 215
Melissus-Schede, Paul (1539–1602) 63n, 139, 212
Ménage, Gilles (1613–92) 69
    Les Origines de la Langue Françoise 69
Mencke, Johann Burkhard (1674–1732) 248
Mercury (god) 33, 147, 157–8
Mercy, Franz (1590–1645) 153
Mersenne, Marin (1588–1648) 69
Metellus of Tegernsee (fl. 1165) 82
Milan 12, 20, 85
Milton, John (1608–74) 38, 159n, 216
Mincio River 130
Mirandola, Pico della (1463–94) 38
    Oratio de hominis dignitate 43n
Montaigne, Michel de (1533–92) 216
Montemagno, Buonaccorso da (1391–1429) 43
    De nobilitate 43n
Montemayor, Jorge de (1519–61) 89, 92–3, 95, 130, 139
    Diana 92–3

Moors 32
More, Thomas (1478–1535) xxiv, 36, 78
    Utopia 36, 78
Morel, Jean (1539–1633) 59
Moritz of Orange (1567–1625) 153
Moscherosch, Johann Michael (1601–69) 70n
Müller, Chancellor Friedrich von (1779–1849) 209
Munich 46
Münsterberg, Johann von (d. 1416) 215
Muret, Marc-Antoine (1526–85) 60
Muses 158
Muslims 32
Mussato, Albertino (1261–1309) x

Naples (Neapolitan) 12, 20–1, 45–6, 84–7, 159n
Naudé, Gabriel (1600–53) 69
Nazianus (s. Gregory of Nazianus)
Nazi regime xi
Neo-Stoicism (Neo-Stoic) 50, 68, 94, 163
Nero, Emperor (r. A.D. 54–68) 80–2
Netherlands 31–2, 35–6, 39, 214, 245
Neumark, Georg (1621–81) 95
New Historicism xii, xvi, xx, xxii
New Testament 5, 9, 13–14, 23, 158, 220, 224
    Matthew 5
    Acts 158
nobilitas literaria (*respublica literaria*) ix, xxvii, 42, 45, 52, 73, 85, 141, 147, 174, 195, 232, 242, 250
noblesse de robe 57
Nördlingen, Battle of (1634) 119
Normandy 60
Normans 214
Novalis (Friedrich von Hardenberg; 1772–1801) 40
Nuremberg 46, 48, 75n, 95, 98, 102, 153–208, 215, 250
    Arsenal 186
    Auditorium publicum 118
    City council 119, 141, 144, 177–8
    City hall 177, 186
    Dance ordinance 177
    Destruction in 1105 (183)
    Ebner family 182
    Egidien Church 123
    Egidien School 118
    Fleischbrücke 144, 186

Nuremberg (cont'd)
  Frauenkirche (Dear Lady Chapel) 183
  Fütter family 177
  Gleisshammer 192
  Golden Bull of 1356 (183)
  Grave of Sebald 186
  Gross family 186
  Grossreuth 173
  Grundherr family 181
  Guild rebellion 177
  Haller family 140–1
  Haller meadow 126, 137, 144, 171
  Harsdörffer family 177, 182
  Holtzschuher family 181
  Hospital of the Holy Spirit 186
  Imhoff family 186, 192
  Kleinreuth 173
  Kress family 181, 192, 198–9
  Library 186
  Margrave Wars 119–20
  Origins 138, 183
  Paper mills 132, 144
  Pegnesischer Blumenorden 95, 98, 117–208, 250
  Pegnitz River 130–4, 144–8, 154–6, 158, 171, 188, 198
  Ratsfähige (governing families) 120–1, 139, 141, 176–7, 180, 186
  Reconstruction under Conrad III 183
  Reformation 120, 185
  Regnitz River 188
  Rossmülle 186
  St Johannis Cemetery 137, 172
  St Johannis Church 137
  St Lorenz Church 185–6
  Schlüsselfelder family 140–1, 177
  Small council 120–1, 177
  Societas Christiana 48
  Starck family 177
  Tetzel family 140, 141n
  Theater 186
  Wallenstein's siege 185
  Wire mills 132, 144
  Wördt meadow 192
  Zabelshof 192
Nützel, Carl (patrician scholar) 169

Ochino, Bernardino (1487–1564) 39
Octavian (Octavianus; s. Augustus)
Oels (in Silesia) 175
Oker River 198
Oldenbarnevelt, Johan van (1547–1619) 35
Old Testament 4, 9, 13, 24
  Isaiah (2, 201) 199
  Song of Songs 158, 160
Opitz, Martin (1597–1639) xv, xviii, 51n, 54, 70–2, 95–6, 108, 117, 124–5, 128–9, 133, 135–6, 139–40, 142, 150–2, 168–9, 175, 178, 191, 212–5, 230, 233, 235–6, 250
  Arcadia 95
  Aristarchus 51n, 135, 212
  Buch von der Deutschen Poeterey 54
  Dafne 95
  Oratio ad Fridericem 51n
  Schäfferey von der Nimfen Hercinie 97, 129, 135–6, 146, 156, 191, 250
  Teutsche Poemata 51n, 96
  Trostgedicht in Widerwärtigkeit des Krieges 150
  Zlatna 96–7, 108
Orléans xiv
Orsini family (Rome) 60
d'Ossat, Arnald Cardinal (1536–1604) 61

Padua xiv
Palatinate (Palatine) 47, 52, 70n, 230
Pan (god) 157–60
Panner, Johann (d. 1641) 153
Pappenheim, Gottfried Heinrich (d. 1632) 153
Paracelsus, Theophrastus Bombastus von Hohenheim (1493–1541) 40
Paris 19n, 54–72, 122, 239
Parlement (Paris) 57, 59–60, 64, 67, 71–2, 242
Pasquier, Etienne (1529–1615) 216
Patin, Guy (French natural scientist) 69
St Paul (Pauline) 5, 8, 27, 158
Peasants' War (1524–5) 31
Pegnesischer Blumenorden (s. Nuremberg)
Pegnitz River (s. Nuremberg)
Peiresc, Nicolas-Claude Fabri de (1580–1637) 69
Persons, Robert (1546–1610) 36–7
St Peter 27, 128
Peterson
  Johann Wilhelm (Pietist) 248
  Johanna Eleonora (wife of Johann) 248

INDEX

Petrarch, Francesco (1304–74) 11, 27n, 28–9, 52, 83–4, 89, 134, 160, 164, 211, 216
  Africa 84
  De vita solitaria 83
  Parthenias 83
Peucerus, Caspar (1525–1602) 169
Pfeiffer, Gerhard 119
Philip II, Emperor (r. 1556–98) 31
Philip IV, Emperor (r. 1621–65) 153
Philipism 68
Physiocrats 112
Piccart, Michael (1574–1620) 169
Pico della Mirandola (1463–94) 38, 43n
Pietists 223, 248
Pinerolo 71n
Pirckheimer, Wilibald (1470–1530) 215
Pithou, François (colleague of Jacques Auguste de Thou) 60, 63–4
Platina, Bartolomeo Sacchi (1421–81) 43
  De vera nobilitate 43n
Plato (427–347 B.C.) 6
Pléiade 59, 88, 216, 236
Poggio (s. Bracciolini)
Poland (Poles) xiii–xv, 36, 39, 71
Polish Brotherhood 39
Politiques 34–5, 37, 50, 60
Pompey ('the Great'; 106–48 B.C.) 4
Pontano, Giovanni (1429–1503) 85–6
  Wife of 86
Pope, Alexander (1688–1744) xi
Postel, Guillaume (ca. 1510–81) 34
Potentes 46
Prague 30–2, 119
  Defenistration (1618) 31
  Treaty of (1635) 119
  University of 30
Protestant Union (s. Union, Protestant)
Prussia 217, 228–9
Prussian Academy of Sciences 217, 228
Pufendorf, Samuel (1632–94) 241, 244
Puritans (Puritanism) 32, 37
Puteani (s. Dupuy brothers)

Quedlinburg 221
Quesnay, François (1694–1774) 112n
Quevedo Villegas, Francisco de (1580–1645) 216

Rambouillet, Madame Catherine de (1588–1665) 69

Ramler, Karl Wilhelm (1725–98) 217–8
Regensburg 124
Regnitz River (s. Nuremberg)
Renato, Camillo (16th-century Italian spiritual reformist) 39
Republicanism (Republican) xiv, 16, 26, 28, 44–5, 51–2, 77, 105, 211
respublica literaria (s. *nobilitas literaria*)
Reval 152
Rhediger Collection (Wroclaw) 67
Rhine River 70n, 123
Rhode Island 37
Richelieu, Cardinal Armand Jean du Plessis (1585–1642) 47n, 50, 57, 62–4, 70–2, 122, 233
Richter, Dr. Georg (1592–1651) 121
Rienzi, Cola di (1313–54) 11, 24–9, 84
Rigault, Nicolas (1577–1654) 62n, 65–6, 69, 72
Ringwald, Bartholomeus (1530–99) 213
Rinuccini
  Alamanno (1426–99) 46
  Ottavio (1562–1621) 95
  Dafne 95
Rist, Johann (1607–67) 134, 142
Robespierre, Maximilian Marie Isidore (1758–94) 112
Rochester 36
Rollenhagen, Georg (1542–1609) 213
Rome 3–4, 6, 8, 11–12, 20–1, 25, 27n, 28–9, 33, 45, 51–2, 60–1, 64, 76, 84, 115, 134, 138, 211, 214
Rompler von Löwenhalt, Jesaias (1605–76) 134, 178
Ronsard, Pierre de (1524–85) x, 59, 88, 128
Rosicrucians (Rosicrucianism) 50, 52
Rostock 48
  Societas Ereunetica 48
Rotterdam 36
Roussel, Gérard (member of School of Meaux) 34
Royal Library of France (s. Bibliothèque Royale)
Rucellai, Bernardo (fl. 1494) 46
Rudolf I, Emperor (d. 1291) 197
Russia 39
Rutherford, Samuel (1600–61) 37
  A Free Disputation against Pretended Liberty of Conscience 37

Saale River 198
Sabinus, Georg (1508–60) 215
Sachs, Hans (1494–1576) 212–4
Sack of Rome (*sacco di Roma*) 21, 33
Saint-Amant, Marc Antoine Girard de (1594–1661) 69
St Bartholomew's Day Massacre (1572) 12, 31, 204
St Giorgio 26
St Johannis Cemetery (s. Nuremberg)
St Johannis Church (s. Nuremberg)
St Paul's School, London 36
St Sabina, Church of 26
St Sebald (s. Nuremberg: Grave of)
St Thomas Church, Leipzig 238
Salin, Edgar (1892–1974) 6n
Salmasius (s. Saumaise)
Salutati, Coluccio (1331–1406) 28, 44, 211, 229
Sannazaro, Jacopo (1456–1530) 85–7, 89, 128, 130, 139, 151
   Arcadia 85–7, 135, 159n
Sarazin, Jacques (1588–1660) 69
Sarpi, Paolo (1552–1623) 67
Saumaise, Claude de (Salmasius; 1588–1653) 68–9, 72
Sauvage, Jean Le (Burgundian chancellor, fl. 1515) 19
Savoy 71n
Saxony 119, 217, 225
Scaliger
   Joseph (1540–1609) 59, 68
   Julius Caesar (1484–1558) 205
Schaffgotsch family (Silesia) 250
   Hans Ulrich von (patron of Martin Opitz) 152
Scheffler, Johann (Angelus Silesius; 1624–77) 40
Schelling, Friedrich Wilhelm (1775–1854) 40
Scherer, Wilhelm (1841–86) 219n
Schiller, Friedrich (1759–1805) 16, 116
Schlang, Colonel (d. 1642) 153
Schlegel
   August Wilhelm (1767–1845) 106
   Friedrich (1772–1829) 106
Schlüsselfelder family (s. Nuremberg)
   Carl the Elder 141
   Carl the Younger (religious figure) 141
   Wilhelm, family sire (d. 1549) 141
   Wilibald (d. 1589) 141

Schmalkaldic War (1546–7) 12, 21, 31
Schöffler, Herbert (1888–1946) xiv
Schönborn family (Mainz) 229
Schottel, Justus Georg (1612–76) 134, 142, 143n, 148, 157, 206, 236n
Schwenkfeld, Caspar (1489–1561) 40
Schwenkfelder family (patron of Gottfried Finckelthaus) 152
Scriver, Christian (1629–93) 221
   Zufällige Andachten 221
Sechst, Johann (Nuremberg poet, fl. 1645) 159
Seckendorff, Veit Ludwig von (1626–92) 247n
Sédan 68
Seeberg, Erich 224
Sermon on the Mount 5–6, 24, 180, 196
Servetus, Michael (1511–53) 38
Sforza (Milan) 85
Shaftesbury, Anthony Ashley Cooper, Earl of (1621–83) 216
Shakespeare, William (1564–1616) 216
Siculo, Giorgio of Ferrara (d. 1551) 38
Sidney, Philip (1554–86) 88, 95, 128, 133–4, 139, 216
   Arcadia 95, 128n
Sigismund III, King of Poland (r. 1587–1632) 71n
Silesia (Silesian) xiv–xv, 39, 70, 72, 124, 175, 212, 215, 250
Sleidanus, Johannes (1506–56) 169
Societas Christiana (s. Nuremberg)
Societas Ereunetica (s. Rostock)
Socinianism (s. Unitarianism)
Socinians 38–9, 50
Solomon, King 24
Sophists 20
Sorel, Charles (1602–74) 164
   Berger Extravagant 164
Sozzini (Socinus)
   Fausto (1539–1604) 39
   Lelio (uncle of Fausto) 39
Spain xiii–v, 12, 21, 32–5, 50–1, 70–1, 85, 88, 92–4, 124, 153, 214, 216
Sparta (Spartan) 193
Spee, Friedrich von (1591–1635) 40
Spener, Philipp Jakob (1635–1705) 221
Spenser, Edmund (1552–99) 88–9, 216
   The Shepheardes Calendar 88
Spinola, Ambrogio (1569–1630) 153
Spinozism xi

INDEX

Spiritualists x, 9, 50, 226n
Starck family (s. Nuremberg)
Stesichorus (fl. 485 B.C.) 139
Stockfleth, Heinrich Arnold (1643–1708) 100–2
  Die Kunst- und Tugendgezierte Macarie 102
Stockfleth, Maria Catharina (1633–92) 98, 100–2
  Die Kunst- und Tugendgezierte Macarie 102
Stockholm 64
Stolleis, Michael xxiv
Strasbourg xiv–xv, 19n, 70, 118
Sudetenland 144
Sun King (s. Louis XIV)
Sweden 71–2, 153, 199
Switzerland 225

Taborites 31
Tacitus (A.D. ca. 55–ca. 117) (Tacitean) 134, 212, 236
  Germania 138
Tasso, Torquato (1544–95) 89–91, 95, 105, 128, 136
  Aminta 89–90
Tertullian (ca. 160–ca. 240) 82
Tetzel family (s. Nuremberg)
  Carl (humanist) 141
  Friedrich (grandson of Jobst) 141
  Jobst (d. 1575) 141
  Johann Jacob (d. 1646) 119
Theocritus (fl. ca. 270 B.C.) 74–5, 77, 92, 107–8, 114, 128, 139
  Idylls 74–5
    Id. 1 (139)
    Id. 3 (148)
    Id. 5 (148)
    Id. 7 (*Thalysia*) 74–5, 148
    Id. 8 (148)
Theodulus (10th c.) 82
Thilenus, Daniel (Silesian in Paris) 72
Thirty Years' War 31, 84, 102, 124, 135, 152, 245
Thomas, Johann (1624–80) 102–3
  Damon und Lisille 102–3
Thomasius, Christian (1655–1728) 208, 215, 219, 233, 237–45, 247–8
  Das Recht Evangelischer Fürsten in Theologischen Streitigkeiten 237–44

Thomson, James (1700–48) 111
Thorn xiv, 215
de Thou
  Christofle (father of Jacques Auguste) 59, 68
  François Auguste de (1607–42) 65
  Jacques Auguste de (1553–1617) 34, 57–61, 64–7, 72, 216, 239
    Historia sui temporis 61–2, 65, 67
  Jacques Auguste de, the younger (frondeur) 59, 66
Tilly, Jean Tserclaes (1559–1632) 153
Toulouse 69
Tours 60
Transylvania xiv, 39
Treaty of Prague (s. Prague)
Trent, Council of 38
Tristan l'Hermite, François de (1601–55) 69
Troyes 63
Tscherning, Andreas (1611–59) 142
Tschirnhaus, Ehrenfried Walter Graf von (1651–1708) 215
Turgot, Anne Robert Jacques (1727–81) 112
Turks 37

Uffenbach-Wolf Collection (Hamburg) 67
Ulrich, Prince of Denmark (ally of Gustav Adolf of Sweden) 153
Union, Protestant 47, 118
Unitarianism (Socinianism) 39
uomini nuovi 46
Upper Rhine 70n
Urfé, Honoré de (1568–1625) 61, 74, 89, 94–5, 130
  L'Astrée 61, 94–5
Utrecht, Union of (1579) 31

Valdés
  Alfonso de (1490–1532) 33
    Diálogo de Mercurio y Carón 33
    Diálogo de las cosas ocurridas en Roma 33n
  Juan de (1500–41) 33
    Diálogo de doctrina cristiana 33
Valerius, Marcus (fl. 1175) 82
Van der Noot, Jan (1538–96) 216
Vaucluse 83
Vega (s. Lope)
Venice xiv, 12, 19n, 20, 45, 60

Vergil (70–19 B.C.) 3–4, 24–5, 73–84, 85n, 86, 89, 95–7, 104n, 107, 114–15, 117, 126–8, 139, 142, 149, 159n, 199–201
   Aeneid 4, 139
   Eclogues (*Bucolica*) 4, 74–81, 104n, 199n
      Ecl. 1 (76–9, 89, 114) 83
      Ecl. 4 (3, 79–80, 126, 201) 143n
      Ecl. 9 (77)
   Georgics 4, 104n, 139, 156n
Vienna 46, 64
Virues, Fra Alonso de (Spanish Erasmian) 33
Vives, Juan Luis (1492–1540) 33
Volckamer
   Georg Christoph (1560–1633) 119
   Johann Georg (1616–93) 173n
Vondel, Joost van den (1587–1679) 216
Voss, Johann Heinrich (1751–1826) 114–15
   Ährenkranz 114
   Die Erleichterten 115
   Die Pferdeknechte 114
   Idyllen 114n
   Luise 115
Vossius, Gerard (Dutch humanist) 35
Vossius, Isaac (1618–89) 69

Wallenstsein, Albrecht Wenzel Eusebius von (1583–1634) 153
   Siege of Nuremberg (s. Nuremberg)
Wars of Religion (1562–98) 31
Weber, Max (1864–1920) 246
Weckherlin, Georg Rudolf (1584–1653) 178, 212
Weigel, Valentin (1533–88) 40
Weissenburg (Transylvania) xiv
Weizsäcker, Carl Friedrich von (b. 1912) 5–6
   Die Geschichte der Natur 5–6
Westphalia, Peace of (1648) 102, 199
Wickram, Jörg (1505–61) 212, 214
Wicquefort, Abraham (1606–82) 70
   Mémoires touchant les Ambassadeurs 70
Wieland, Christoph Martin (1733–1813) 111, 217–8
   Agathon 218
   Don Sylvio 218
   Isdris und Zenide 218
   Komische Erzählungen 218
   Musarion 218
William II of Orange (1626–50) 153
Williams, Roger (1603–83) 37–8
Wittenberg 12, 136, 137n, 215
Wolffenbüttel 197
Wroclaw 67, 70
Wyclif, John (1328–84) 30

Zamosc xiv
Zesen, Philipp von (1619–81) 96, 128, 133, 142
   Adriatischer Rosemund 96
Zincgref, Julius Wilhelm (1591–1635) 212
Zurich 216, 248
Zwingli, Huldrych (1484–1531) 225
Zwinglian (Zwinglianism) 31, 39–40, 68